LORD MELBOURNE
1779–1848

Lord Melbourne
1779–1848

L. G. MITCHELL

OXFORD UNIVERSITY PRESS

1997

Oxford University Press, Great Clarendon Street, Oxford OX2 6DP

Oxford New York
Athens Auckland Bangkok Bogota Bombay
Buenos Aires Calcutta Cape Town Dar es Salaam
Delhi Florence Hong Kong Istanbul Karachi
Kuala Lumpur Madras Madrid Melbourne
Mexico City Nairobi Paris Singapore
Taipei Tokyo Toronto
and associated companies in
Berlin Ibadan

Oxford is a trade mark of Oxford University Press

Published in the United States
by Oxford University Press Inc., New York

British Library Cataloguing in Publication Data
Data available

Library of Congress Cataloging in Publication Data
Data applied for
ISBN 0–19–820592–9

1 3 5 7 9 10 8 6 4 2

Typeset by Hope Services (Abingdon) Ltd.
Printed in Great Britain
on acid-free paper by
Biddles Ltd.,
Guildford & King's Lynn

A la mémoire de Nieuil

Preface

MY debts are many. I acknowledge with gratitude the kindness of the following owners of manuscript collections in allowing me access to their materials: Her Majesty the Queen for access to the Royal Archives and the Melbourne papers held at Windsor; the Controller of HMSO and the Trustees of the Broadlands Archive for the Wellington, Palmerston, and Melbourne papers held in Southampton; the Duke of Devonshire and the Chatsworth Settlement Trustees for the Chatsworth manuscripts; the Earl of Derby for the Derby manuscripts; the Earl of Harewood for the Canning papers; the Earl of Clarendon for the Clarendon papers; the kind permission of the Howard family in allowing access to the Castle Howard papers; Lord Cobbold for the Lytton manuscripts; Lord Lytton for the Lovelace papers; the Keeper of the Bodleian Library for the Bruce manuscripts. The papers of the Dukes of Richmond are reproduced by the courtesy of the Trustees of the Goodwood Collections and the good offices of the County Archivist and staff of the West Sussex Record Office. The Petworth archive was made available by the courtesy of the Rt. Hon. Lord Egremont and the assistance of Dr A. McCann. The Bessborough collection was consulted by the courtesy of the Rt. Hon. the Earl of Bessborough and the good offices of Dr T. McCann. I was able to make use of the archive at Woburn Abbey by kind permission of the Marquess of Tavistock and the Trustees of the Bedford Estate. The Provost and Fellows of Oriel College, Oxford, generously allowed me access to the Hampden papers, and Dr H. Cecil to the Palmerston papers at Hatfield House. I am grateful to the Marquess of Anglesey and the Deputy Keeper of the Records of Northern Ireland for permission to use the Anglesey papers.

As usual, the archivists and staff of county record offices have been unfailingly helpful. I would particularly like to make mention of those at Hertfordshire, who gave me invaluable assistance with the Panshanger collection; and, those in Devon, Staffordshire, Norfolk, and the Centre for Kentish Studies. The Keeper of Manuscripts at the University of Nottingham gave invaluable assistance with the Newcastle and Denison manuscripts, and University College London Library helped materially with the Parkes and Brougham collections. Copies of records in the Nottinghamshire Archives Office are reproduced by permission of the Principal Archivist.

I would like to recognize the generosity of the British Academy in funding certain sections of the research for this book, which would otherwise have been impossible.

Above all, I would like to thank certain individuals for their encouragement and support; Lord Ralph Kerr, for not only allowing me access to the Melbourne Hall archive, but also for providing hospitality and a chance to share enthusiasms; my Oxford colleagues, James McConica, John Walsh, William Thomas, and Christopher Pelling, for help of a technical nature; Dr J. Fewster of Durham and Dr C. Woolgar of Southampton, for assistance with manuscript collections that were of vital importance to this study; my friends, Penny Hatfield, Arlene Shy, and Douglas McNeill, for sending material from Eton, America, and Edinburgh; Diane Burton for secretarial patience and cunning; and Dr A. I. M. Duncan, whose toleration and expertise has never been found wanting. I hope they will all be entertained by what they read.

L.G.M.

University College, Oxford
1996

Contents

List of Plates

List of Genealogical Tables

List of Short Titles

In referring to sources, the following short titles have been used:

Cecil   Lord David Cecil, *Melbourne* (London 1955).

Custance   'The Political Career of William Lamb, Second Viscount Melbourne, to 1841', Oxford D.Phil., Bodleian Library.

Greville   H. Reeve, *A Journal of the Reigns of King George IV, King William IV and Queen Victoria by the late Charles Greville* (London 1888).

Melbourne MSS   Papers of the Second Viscount Melbourne held at Windsor Castle. Bodleian Library microfilm.

Parl. Hist.   *The Parliamentary History.*

QVJ   Queen Victoria's Journals. Royal Archives, Windsor Castle.

Ziegler   P. Ziegler, *Melbourne* (London 1976).

Author's Note: In using quotations, all original spellings and styles of punctuation have been retained.

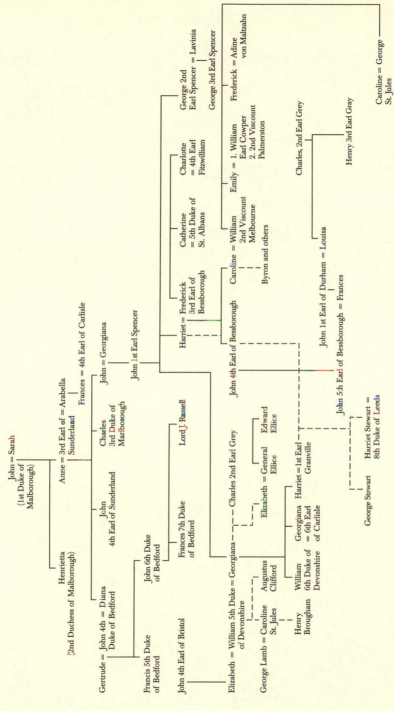

Key: Marriages and legitimate descent are represented by unbroken lines. Illegitimacy is represented by dotted lines.

Fig. 1. Whig kinship

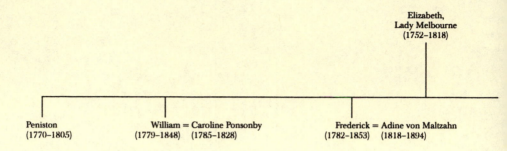

FIG. 2. The children of Lady Melbourne

```
┌──────────────────┬──────────────────────────────────────┬──────────────────┐
```

George = Caroline St. Jules   Emily = 1. 5th Earl Cowper   Harriet
(1784–1834)   (1785–1862)   (1787–1869)   (1778–1837)   (1789–1803)
                                            2. 2nd Viscount Palmerston
                                               (1784–1865)

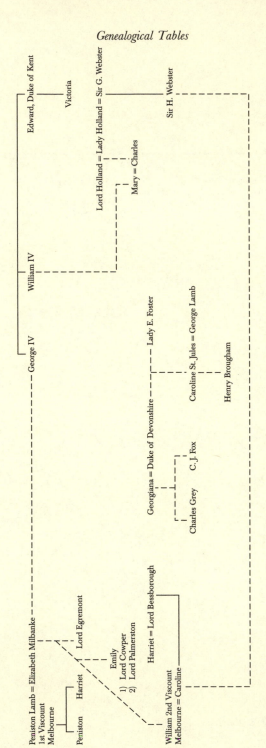

Key: Marriages and legitimate descent are represented by unbroken lines. Illegitimacy is represented by dotted lines.

Fig. 3. The extended family of William Lamb

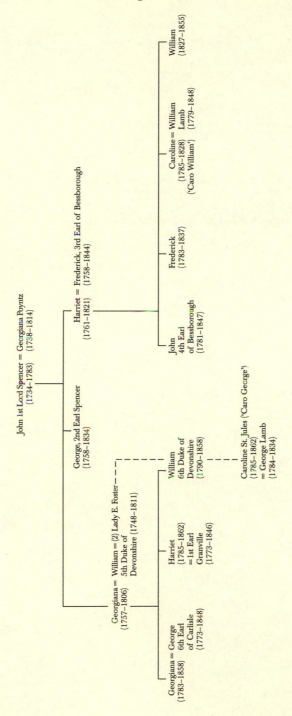

Fig. 4. The Cavendish and Ponsonby families

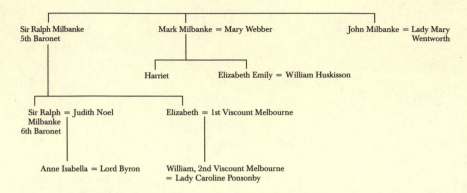

F<small>IG</small>. 5. The Melbourne, Byron, and Huskisson families

PART I

1

A Whig Inheritance

WILLIAM LAMB, second Viscount Melbourne, disliked the idea of biography. He particularly disliked any notion that his own life should be examined. Late in life, he looked back 'with astonishment at the things I've done; they seem to me so absurd, and so wrong; it seems quite impossible, quite incredible'.[1] He liked to claim that he had once been the assiduous keeper of a journal, but that 'looking back to it some time afterwards he was so alarmed at what he saw that he made up his mind to destroy everything'.[2] This was probably untrue. The gap between Melbourne's public statements and behaviour and his private emotions was huge. No man hid his feelings more effectively. In this case, he kept a journal intermittently for the first thirty-four years of his life, and began an autobiography at roughly the same age. All these volumes survive. So far from destroying his past, Melbourne was intensely interested in it.

Contemporaries were clear that any account of William Lamb should concentrate as much on family background as on politics. This might be thought a strange remark to make about a future prime minister, but Lamb was 48 years old before he held any government office, and 51 before he entered a Cabinet. He came to high politics late. His character and views had already been formed by experiences that were not political. Rather, he had been fashioned by membership of a distinctive family within the distinctive world of early nineteenth-century Whiggery. As contemporaries noted, the Whig world was as much a social organism as it was a political party. It had prominence in public life and was proudly dynastic. For Melbourne, politics was only an extension of a particular notion of social living. As a result, 'he interests less as a statesman than as a person',[3] or, as the *Morning Chronicle* observed in its obituary notice on Lamb, 'in this particular instance, the statesman is indissolubly mingled, blended, and associated with the man'.[4]

Melbourne himself once famously described the Whigs as 'all cousins'.[5] As the family tree of Whiggery suggests (Fig. 1), this was hardly an overstatement. Even so, the Lambs were relative newcomers to this charmed circle.

Melbourne's grandfather, Matthew Lamb, had been a successful lawyer, who had acted for both the Cecils of Hatfield and the Fitzwilliams of Wentworth Woodhouse.[6] With the latter family, there was 'a great connection'.[7] William Lamb took his Christian name from one of the Earls Fitzwilliam,[8] who 'used to be a good deal at Brocket',[9] the Lamb family home. In 1740 Matthew Lamb married a great heiress, Charlotte Coke of Melbourne Hall in Derbyshire. On this marriage was the family fortune built, and William was so conscious of this, that he piously transcribed the correspondence of his famous ancestor Sir John Coke, who had been secretary of state to James I.[10] Matthew Lamb became a baronet, sat for the Fitzwilliam borough of Peterborough for twenty-one years, and, when he died in 1768, left an estate in excess of one hundred thousand pounds.[11]

Title and property duly passed to Matthew's son, Peniston. He would be the presumed father of the future prime minister, but was otherwise of a quite remarkable dullness and insignificance. He sat in Parliament for over forty years, and only tested the patience of the House by speaking once. Had he not chosen two lively women as mistresses, Sophia Baddeley and Harriette Wilson, little would have been known about him. Their journals give him a historical character. Looking for qualities to commend, one of them significantly emphasized the fact that he was 'not one of your stiff-necked, moralizing fathers, who preach chastity and forbearance to their children'.[12] The Lamb brothers and sisters were not reared in any conventional morality. As a reward for long years of service in undemanding jobs around the Court, Peniston Lamb was created first Viscount Melbourne in 1781.

By great good fortune, this unprepossessing man married a very remarkable woman. Elizabeth Milbanke, the daughter of a substantial Yorkshire squire, came, with her wit, charm, and beauty, to preside over one of London's most popular salons. She, with her friends Georgiana, Duchess of Devonshire and Elizabeth, Lady Holland, made their homes the centres of Whig life, where politics was facilitated and society modulated. Predictably, the union of such a woman with such a man led to irregularities. Lady Melbourne once advised a young bride that the only thing she owed her husband was one male heir, and this was advice that she took seriously herself. In a very public manner, she became the mistress of a series of men incuding the Earl of Egremont and the future George IV. Her husband, who also found affection outside marriage, was largely complaisant.[13] Indeed, it was alleged that Egremont had 'bought' Lady Melbourne from Lord Coleraine for £13,000, with the lady's husband taking a commission on the deal. This was more believable than another contemporary story that Lady Melbourne always wore a choker of pearls in portraits, in order to cover marks left on her neck by her husband's attempt to strangle her. Whatever the truth of these stories, William Lamb accurately described his mother as 'a remarkable woman, a devoted mother, an excellent wife—but not chaste, not chaste'.[14]

The eccentricities of the Lamb marriage intrigued cartoonists and pamphleteers of a moralistic disposition, but it was hardly remarkable according to Whig values. Following these, marriage was undertaken to join two properties, not two people. The purpose of the union was to produce a male heir to the joint venture. That done, the marriage could be considered a success. Chastity was not prized, and it was perfectly legitimate to seek affection outside marriage. As Melbourne himself informed Victoria: 'People when they married in those days, never changed their lives; they were very fond of their wives, but did not take care of them, and left them to themselves.'[15] There was 'great licence'.[16] If marriage was nothing but a way of regulating the transmission of property from one generation to the next, the moral code governing the practice need not be too severe, and could indeed be the subject of satire. When William Lamb was invited to provide an epilogue for a play in 1801, *The Fashionable Friends*, he penned these words for a character called Lady Selina Vapour;

> Does not our play with pow'rful int'rest tend
> To teach our Being's greatest aim, and end?
> To form the infant mind, and to explode
> The old morality's mistaken code—
> To teach what friendship means, in modish life,
> A passion for *her* husband, or *his* wife;
> And to set forth, in love's important trade
> The whole advantage of a masquerade.[17]

Inevitably, the Whig world was much censured. Throughout Melbourne's life, his friends, relations, and he himself were regularly held up to public scrutiny and found wanting. Most of England could not accept that marriage was merely a business contract, or that adultery was a necessary adjunct to fashionable life. Yet the Whig world was largely insensitive to such criticism. Its wealth was social armour. With an assured position in politics and society, it could ignore comments from outside its own ranks. Melbourne himself was unusual in this respect, being sensitive to what others said and thought, but he fully shared the sense of exclusiveness that membership of the Whig world allowed. When Melbourne's nephew reflected on his uncle's career, he was first clear that 'the circumstances of a man's early life have such an influence in moulding his character', that close scrutiny had to be given to 'that society, in which dissipation and intellectual refinement were so singularly combined'. Its presiding characteristics he identified as 'a spirit of justice and generosity', 'a cultivated taste', and 'an enthusiastic worship of liberty'. All of these were in some measure Melbourne's inheritance.[18]

Lady Melbourne had six children; Peniston, born in 1770, William in 1779, Frederick in 1782, George in 1784, Emily in 1787, and Harriet in 1789 (see Fig. 2). Of these, her husband was the father only of the first and, possibly, of the last. When Harriet died in 1803, he was certainly much moved.[19] William Lamb, however, took the death of his young sister philosophically: 'youth in the midst of its career of ambition and pleasure pauses but for a short time to weep even over the grave of those whom it loved the best and regrets the most.'[20] George's father was the future George IV, after whom he was named. William, Emily, and sometimes Frederick, were attributed to the third Earl of Egremont. Emily resembled her brother strikingly. Victoria observed that 'she has got his blue eyes or rather greyish blue eyes, and dark eye lashes, and a great deal of his manner'.[21] Just as strikingly, the brothers and sisters were otherwise very different in appearance and temperament. William's and Emily's hair was black, George's auburn, and Frederick's fair.[22]

Contemporaries took it for granted that Egremont was indeed the prime minister's real father. Greville, the diarist, baldly stated that Melbourne looked remarkably 'like his father, the late Lord Egremont'.[23] Lord Holland, who knew the Lambs better than anyone was equally confident.[24] Egremont himself observed that when William IV reported William's progress as a politician, 'there was something in his manner, which without anything of the tacenda locutus seemed to imply that I had more than a common interest in the subject'.[25] There was very little attempt at secrecy. The liaison between Lady Melbourne and Egremont was so well known that it was an established channel for patronage proposals.[26] Both Emily and William were frequent visitors to Egremont's houses at Petworth and Brighton, and had open access to his box at the opera. Portraits of the children hung at Petworth.[27] In addition, Egremont followed William's political career closely and with evident pride.[28] When Caroline Ponsonby married William Lamb, she too accepted the Egremont connection. Visiting Petworth, she found the house 'magnificent and Lord Egremont more amiable among his children than in any other point of view—only it is a pity to think how they came to be his'.[29]

Emily Lamb was always very comfortable with her Egremont relations. When one of them sent her a miniature of her mother, which had once graced the drawing room of the Egremonts' London home, she accepted it thankfully, 'having passed so many days of my Youth' at Petworth.[30] William was more equivocal about his parentage. He described his father as an 'excellent man', but also 'a very odd man'.[31] There were visits to Petworth 'when all sentiment gave way to fear', and when William prudently took refuge in extended silences.[32] So great was this ambivalence towards Petworth and its owner that Melbourne was sometimes moved to deny the rumours about his paternity. To Landseer, he insisted that the whole idea of Egremont being his father was 'all a lie'.[33] The world thought otherwise. No one was surprised that, when Egremont lay dying in 1837, the prime minister should be hurriedly summoned to his bedside.[34] Nor did it cause much comment when the same prime minister repeatedly used the power of his office to help Egremont's legitimate offspring.[35] Any other course of action would have been unnatural.

With or without ambiguity, William Lamb felt more for Egremont than he did for the first Viscount Melbourne. Relations between the two men were never cordial, and there is little evidence to suggest that the older man had any real influence on the younger. Their lives intersected ceremonially, without warmth. The first Viscount tolerated this situation, because it fell within the rules of the game. He found affection with his mistresses, not with his wife and putative children. Above all, he was sure that he was the father of Lady Melbourne' eldest son, Peniston. As a result, he could be confident that his title and property would pass to someone of his own blood. Little else mattered. There was no reason why he and William Lamb should have undue regard for each other. As for William himself, any deficiencies in paternal influences were more than supplied by his extraordinary mother.

Contemporaries were well aware that Lady Melbourne was the focal point in Lamb family life, giving it dynamism and éclat. Married at 17 to a man 'who did not care for her in the least',[36] or, as the Duke of Sutherland put it, 'to a short fat man' who did not look 'like any of his children',[37] she overcame these disadvantages to become a major figure in London society. By sheer force of personality, she transformed Melbourne House[38] in London and Brocket in Hertfordshire into two of the most 'recherché' houses 'in all the fashionable world, and the most difficult of access'.[39] The famous and the infamous were drawn to Lamb family entertainments by the attraction of a woman who allied intelligence with discretion. Lady Melbourne lived within the rules that Whig society set itself, if not those preferred by the country as a whole. She was always aware that 'Anyone who braves the opinion of the world sooner or later feels the consequences of it.'[40] It was a quality much appreciated by Byron and her other admirers. It was a quality that would be noticeably lacking in Lady Caroline Lamb, William's wife and Lady Melbourne's daughter-in-law.

William Lamb therefore grew up in a world that was fashioned by his mother, free-thinking and rich in character. By birth, he was at the centre of everything of interest in literature, politics, or the intellect. Much later, the young Victoria cross-questioned Melbourne mercilessly about his mother, recognizing the dominant role she had played in his upbringing. By way of reply, Melbourne offered two thoughts. First, he observed that his mother had, in temperament, been 'very like my sister, only of a stronger character; more masculine'.[41] Masculine is a word that recurs frequently in Melbourne's description of women to whom he felt strongly attached. Much of his life was directed by such women and he was happy to accept such direction. Secondly, he acknowledged the influence of his mother in his own life. Victoria recorded a dinner conversation at Windsor in 1837, during which Melbourne 'said, he thought almost every body's character was formed by their mother, and that if children did not turn out well, the mothers should be punished for it. I daresay *his* noble fine and excellent character was formed by his mother, for she was a remarkably clever and sensible woman.'[42] On another occasion, Melbourne bluntly admitted that 'My mother was the most sagacious woman I ever knew . . . as long as she lived, she kept me straight.'[43]

Not surprisingly, therefore, Lady Melbourne's death in 1818 was described by her son as 'the heaviest misfortune which could befall us'.[44] His sister Emily kept the day of her mother's death, 6 April, sacred for the rest of her life. In 1840 her diary entry for that day reads: 'A day which even now at the end of 22 years I can never think of without pain.' In 1842 the comparable entry was 'day of deep affliction which I never can fight . . . the best of mothers'.[45] After 1818, Emily herself, to some extent, took on her mother's role. She tried to oversee the careers of her brothers, and would endlessly try to bring a little order into William's life, but her efforts were not always successful. Lady Melbourne's loss was, in this sense, irreparable. She had moulded the Lamb children into what Melbourne's first modern biographer called 'a compact family group'.[46] After her death, the cohesiveness of the family was weakened significantly, though one important element remained. The Lamb brothers and sisters were unusually affectionate towards each other. In a crisis, they closed ranks with the precision of a guards regiment. The love and concern shown by his siblings was to be one of William Lamb's greatest personal resources. This was his mother's most valuable legacy to him.

Strangely, in a draft autobiography written in 1812–13, Melbourne, with the exception of one reference to his brother Frederick, makes no mention of his family at all. Given his dependence on them at crucial moments in his life, this reticence should be seen as an indication that the document was intended as a political vindication rather than a total account of his early life. He had just lost his seat in Parliament, and, as a result, felt estranged from his erstwhile friends. Melbourne felt that points of a strictly political nature should be made. At this moment of professional crisis, brothers, sisters, and mother were, as usual, totally supportive. Their sense of common purpose was still formidable.

Only one family member stood aside. Peniston Lamb, the eldest boy, had little in common with his brothers and sisters. They were intelligent, bookish and quick. He was slow-thinking and dull. His great interest in life was horse-racing to which he was addicted. Nearly a decade older than his siblings, he was always a remote figure to them. In every way, he was his father's son. The younger children chose to follow their vivacious mother. When Melbourne commented on his relationship with Peniston, he spoke with more than a hint of resentment. He described his brother to Victoria as 'very dis-passionate, but letting everything go to rack and ruin,—idle and indolent'.[47] Melbourne disliked the Turf, and as 'a younger brother', he had 'to make my own fortune'.[48] He significantly reminded Victoria that younger brothers always have to 'submit'.[49] It was galling that the dullard of the family should be promised an easy passage through life, when more gifted children were offered no such security. Peniston, who was 'no companion to him',[50] would have title and property in due course. William Lamb could expect nothing.

Peniston's sudden death in 1805 changed everything. William Lamb's prospects were transformed. He would now become the second Viscount Melbourne in due course, and be assured of a significant disposable income. This was not, however, an outcome that was universally welcomed. The first Viscount was indignant. By the death of his eldest child, his title and estates would now pass to someone who was recognized to be not of his own blood. Egremont's bastard son would inherit everything. The smooth transmission of property from one generation of Lambs to another had broken down. Predictably, it was at moments like these that the distinctive, Whig rules governing marriage and affection no longer met the case. William Lamb could not be denied the title, but his control of family property could be circum-scribed. After 1805 he was allowed only £2,000 a year by the first Viscount. Peniston had enjoyed £5,000.[51] Further, by his will, the first Viscount entailed as much property as he could. William would enjoy the income of these estates during his lifetime, but Emily and her children would be the residual heirs.[52] This behaviour was hostile and gave proof, if any were needed, that William Lamb was not his father's Benjamin.

Whatever difficulties existed between William Lamb and his father and elder brother, they were more than compensated for by his close and endur-ing affection for his other relations. Foremost among these was his sister, Emily. Intelligent, gregarious, and determined, Emily, first as the wife of Lord Cowper and then of Lord Palmerston, took on her mother's role as keeper of one of the major Whig salons. Panshanger, Palmerston's home, became, in the early nineteenth century, what Melbourne House had been in the late eighteenth. The phenomenon of the salon demanded the organizational gifts of a dynamic woman as its presiding presence. Lamb women fitted this role perfectly. It was a form of social life that was free-thinking and hard on the

shy or reticent. Such people found it demanding. Emily Eden described
Panshanger as 'full to the brim of vice and agreeableness, foreigners and
roués. It sounded awful, and I declined paying a morning visit, which is at
best an awkward business, to twenty people all accustomed to each other's
jokes.'[53] By contrast, William Lamb had been reared in the clamour of social
bustle. It was comforting that his sister should have inherited their mother's
gift for orchestrating social life. Panshanger, situated only a few miles from
Brocket, was a point of stability in Melbourne's later life.

Emily resembled her mother in one other crucial respect. Both women
took the view that William Lamb needed to be managed. It was clear that he
had little will of his own, and that therefore he was a likely victim of the
unscrupulous. He needed to be protected. Further, both women believed that
he was incapable of taking a decision, and that therefore decisions had to be
taken for him. Both points had particular reference to William Lamb's dealings with women. First the mother and then the sister would try to mitigate
the consequences of his lapses of judgement in this respect. Ironically,
William jokingly described his sister on one occasion as full of 'indecision and
irresolution', because 'all women are irresolute, and never can decide'.[54]
Emily herself was sure that these attributes were more properly her brother's.
In a crisis, William was hopeless. When a decision had to be taken, William
would procrastinate. As their mother lay dying, Emily noted that William was
being 'attentive and kind', but that 'he has no observation and no judgement
and not likely to suggest anything that might be of use'.[55] Brother and sister
remained on close terms throughout their lives. The one enjoyed directing,
and the other was usually happy to be directed.

With his brother Frederick there was a more uneven relationship. There
was never any serious disagreement between the two men, but accident and
differences in temperament occasionally separated them. Close in age, they
had grown up together and were companions in education. Frederick, like his
brother, easily absorbed his mother's values. He was described as 'agreeable
and clever', but as seeing 'life in the most degrading light, and he simplifies
the thing by thinking all men rogues and all women ———'.[56] Until well into
middle age, 'he was always addicted to gallantry, and had endless liaisons
with women, most of whom continued to be his friends long after they had
ceased to be his mistresses, much to the credit of all parties'.[57] He and
William Lamb entered into the full glare of Whig society at the same time
and with equal success. As young men, they were predictably on 'very intimate terms'.[58]

In middle age, the two brothers became more distant. Frederick, as a
career diplomat, was out of England for long periods of time. Until
Melbourne was offered a post in government in 1827, Frederick was the more

notable and successful of the brothers. He was created Baron Beauvale in 1839, in recognition of his diplomatic efforts. He was 'a good man of business', altogether 'less peculiar and eccentric' than Melbourne.[59] Further, his European experiences led Frederick to be considerably more sceptical about liberalism and its proponents than his less travelled brother. While many contemporaries saw European liberals as martyrs and figures of romance, Frederick Lamb, the friend of Metternichs and Lievens, saw them as down-at-heel visionaries. He was 'no particular friend of Liberalism'.[60] Melbourne himself was too armoured in cynicism to be unduly hopeful about the claims of nationalists and liberals, but, even so, a clear difference of emphasis was perceptible between the two brothers on this point, and it was sufficiently marked to produce political difficulties.

During Melbourne's prime ministership, the Foreign Office was the fief of his future brother-in-law, Palmerston, for whose character and policies Frederick Lamb had little liking. To avoid what a contemporary diarist described as 'a rupture between his brother and his brother-in-law',[61] Melbourne sent Frederick as ambassador to Vienna, when he might reasonably have expected Paris. In Austria, he could indulge his more conservative views on European politics without unduly clashing with Palmerston. In Paris, such clashes would have been unavoidable. Even so, these points of friction within the Melbourne family complicated William Lamb's tenure of office, and put pressure on his friendship with Frederick. In 1839 the latter told Emily that, for everyone's sake, it would be better if he stayed out of England.

I don't believe that my presence in England would be of the least use to William, perhaps the contrary for there is so much jealousy and suspicion of me in many quarters that I believe myself to be better out of the way, as indeed most mere lookers on usually are, and I am much mistaken if He does not often feel this himself. The best use I can be to him is by managing well what I have the charge of.[62]

Frederick Lamb retired from diplomacy in 1841 and returned to England. Almost immediately the old warmth between the two brothers was rekindled. With Melbourne now also in retirement, differences over nuances in policy no longer had any force. In addition, Frederick had finally married in 1841, and Melbourne was much taken by the new Lady Beauvale. Adine von Maltzahn, though much younger than her husband, was happy to spend her life in the English countryside with his family. She never seemed to resent the exclusiveness of the Lamb siblings, a phenomenon that repelled so many others. In the years between his retirement and death, the Beauvales were Melbourne's most constant companions and the most solicitous of friends. Living with him at Brocket almost continuously, they nursed him when ill, providing that intelligent and diverting company of which Melbourne was always in need, and shielding him from anything that could disturb or incon-venience. Like Emily, Frederick always felt protective about his brother William.

It was, however, with George Lamb that William felt most comfortable. It was of this younger brother that he talked most often to the young Victoria. Entries in her journal repeatedly recorded his preference. George was Melbourne's 'great favourite . . . he became very much affected in speaking of his brother and his eyes filled with tears. He used to live a great deal with Lord Melbourne.' Although 'he drank a great deal, much more than we did', he was in every way 'a most agreeable man'.[63] Capable and a good speaker, George Lamb had initially established himself in politics before his brother became prominent. More radical than William or his other siblings, George was liked by all of them. When Home Secretary from 1830 to 1834, Melbourne relied heavily on the advice and support of this brother, who was given the post of under secretary in that department.

George Lamb was distinguished by the possession of animal high spirits. He was red-faced and noisy. His company could be tiring:

he really has not half an hour's good behaviour in him . . . he is like a schoolboy, when he has been good and quiet for a long time for him he begins making a noise, teizing (sic) the dogs, spoiling the furniture and then we say, 'Don't, George, pray be quiet, dear George. Oh, leave that alone,' just as I do to your children when they question.[64]

His interest in politics was almost overwhelmed by his passion for the theatre, 'upon which he . . . raves', speaking of it with his 'usual courseness'.[65] Associated with the management of Drury Lane for a number of years, he was himself the author of two plays, *Who's the Dupe* and *Whistle For It*. The lat-ter, a Gothic tale of banditti, daggers, and gloomy forests, enjoyed some suc-cess when it was presented in 1807. This was a point of common interest with William, who could also turn his hand to an epilogue or prologue. Both brothers also put a real value on the Classics. George published a more than competent edition of the poems of Catullus. Surprisingly for a Lamb, he took the poet to task for envincing 'a gratification of the passions, none of the heart',[66] which was not a constraint that much informed his own conduct.

He married Caroline St Jules, the illegitimate daughter of the fifth Duke of Devonshire, thereby tying the Lambs even more firmly to the Devonshire House set. Henceforth, his wife was known as 'Caro George'. She was less intelligent than most of her adopted family, gossipy and good-natured, if inclined to give herself airs. Among her relations, she was known as 'Cleopatra', while George was affectionately called 'Curly Pate'. A mis-match of temperament produced a stormy marriage. In 1817, Lord Auckland 'narrowly escaped an elopement with Cleopatra Lamb'. Almost immediately afterwards, Brougham did elope with the same lady. A formal separation was talked of. In the event, matters were smoothed over, but it is important that, throughout the crisis, the Lamb family had closed ranks in support of George, and the memory of this incident almost certainly coloured the political relationship between Melbourne and Brougham in the 1830s.[67]

George Lamb died suddenly in January 1834. Always unhappy about showing emotion, Melbourne affected to accept this loss with philosophical detachment, but Egremont and others were aware that this was merely 'his careless manner'.[68] Caro George knew well that 'William suffered severely'. She acknowledged that, even though he had been much pressed by political duties, he had 'staid with me night and day'. The two brothers had shared an office for four years, and she reflected on 'what a pang it must give him to go into that room, where they were so happy together'.[69] Unlike Emily and Frederick, George had never taken the view that William Lamb needed to be watched and protected. Rather, in his own marital difficulties, he was himself the grateful recipient of family backing. As a result, Melbourne felt freest in his company, enjoying his extrovert animation.

Contemporaries were very aware that the Lamb family was a distinct subset of the genus Whig, or at least that Lady Melbourne, William, Emily, Frederick, and George were. Melbourne, throughout his life, prized the clannishness that was based on 'the affection subsisting between members of a large family'.[70] It was a totally self-contained world that largely kept out critical draughts from outside. To emphasize their exclusiveness, Whig families like the Lambs operated an elaborate system of nicknames that were unintelligible to outsiders. They even pronounced English with a distinct accent. When Queen Victoria was asked if Melbourne had been a real Whig, she answered in the affirmative because he had pronounced English Whiggishly. Rome was pronounced 'room' and gold 'goold', for example.[71] It was a world of mannerisms and eccentricities. Melbourne prefaced nearly every remark with 'eh, eh', never kept a watch, had no fixed sleeping patterns and increasingly conducted conversations with himself.[72]

More publicly, the world of the Lambs ran on rules peculiar to itself. As has been noted, marital arrangements were distinctive, and Melbourne saw little wrong with them. When discussing the journals of a political friend, his only point of criticism was as follows: 'as to his Amours a terrible set of battered old Harridans—not a decently creditable affair amongst them.'[73] In addition, it was a society of heavy drinking and feverish levels of gambling. Melbourne himself was not a gambler[74] and never drank to excess, but he had some sympathy with those who did. When the House of Lords discussed the regulation of the opium trade, Melbourne assured his audience that he considered 'temperance as a greater heresy than excess'.[75] A figure like William Wilberforce, who tortured himself because 'he amused himself too well', was something of a puzzle to the Lamb imagination. Such people seemed to provide confirmation of the maxim that 'Nobody ever did anything very foolish except from some strong principle.'[76] If such openly professed hedonism shocked the world at large, Whig society, by virtue of its wealth and ancestry, could simply ignore criticism. Significantly, when Lady Bessborough, Melbourne's mother-in-law, used the word 'world', she only described 'that set of people they usually live with'.[77] No one else much mattered. If Melbourne himself was a little more careful of what others thought, he was unusual.

Above all, Whig society was one in which real belief, commitment, or feeling was always so overlaid by a carapace of irony, that the biographer is presented with a grave problem of distinguishing the true from the affected. Melbourne was famous for a torrent of off-the-cuff remarks, which, if taken literally, would suggest an almost nihilistic indifference to life. Sarcasm he claimed to value because it was impossible to have 'a witty saying, which is not sarcastic'.[78] William Lamb gave the impression of being a lounging kind of fellow, psychologically horizontal rather than vertical. It was rumoured that the Lamb family, finding Ten Commandments rather taxing, subsumed all life into one, namely 'Thou shalt not bother'.[79] So marked was this quality that even other Whigs were sometimes moved to protest. The sixth Duke of Devonshire was irritated by 'these indifferent damn your eyes people', and thought that Caroline Lamb might have been saved from despair and scandal, 'had she not got into the hands of these blackguards'.[80] In fact, she shared Lamb values to the extent that she defined truth as 'what one thinks at the moment'.[81]

Beneath this persiflage, there were genuine Whig beliefs to be excavated, but so considerable was the covering that many contemporaries either refused to credit their existence or refused to put in the effort to discover them. In failing to do so, they could not come to terms with Whiggery. It was a state of mind, a way of living, a particular way of expressing views, as much as it was a political creed. Whether Melbourne was or was not a Whig in politics was often a matter of debate. No clear answer could be given, for the very good reason that there were very few issues on which all the people claiming the title would be found on the same side. They all broke ranks from time to time. What kept them together was cousinhood, the knowledge that they were not as other people, and the view that history and wealth gave them responsibilities in politics. In these fundamental senses, the Lambs were profoundly Whig. As they knew only too well, Whiggery was more than politics.

To outsiders, all of this could look smug and dangerously complacent. Spending time with the Lambs was a demanding business. They were enthusiastic advocates of amateur theatricals. The pieces performed were not infrequently written by George Lamb, and William acted 'both in tragedy and comedy' as a young man.[82] Pencil-and-paper games, which involved the coining of epigrams or the describing of a friend in a single verse, were hugely popular. In the Melbourne archive, scraps of paper record some of the family's better efforts. One, in William's handwriting, accounted for the success of 'Poodle' Byng as a salon wit as follows:

> If he's famous for telling the secrets he knows
> Why do ladies unto him their secrets disclose?
> To publish their secrets they either think nice
> Or they think that his friendship is worthy the price.[83]

Lamb humour was boisterous. One guest declared herself 'stunned' by 'les rires des Messieurs Lambs'.[84] Another feared that 'they will knock out my tooth. It is like getting among savages, there is no knowing how far their vivacity may carry them.'[85] Friends had to be prepared for practical jokes more usually associated with a sporting club dinner. Lord John Townshend was directed to a bedroom as his own, which in fact contained a sleeping, female guest.[86] Most disconcerting of all was the tendency of the Lamb family, when in their cups, lispingly to invite guests to join them in their defiance of convention. As Harriet Cavendish recorded: 'On Sunday we went to a sort of Assembly at Lady Melbourne's: it was not pleasant. The two Lambs, William and Frederick, had dined out and were very *drunk*, and the former talked to me in a loud voice the whole time of the danger of a *young womans* believing in *weligion* and *pwactising mowality*.'[87] There was an arrogance and disdain among the Lambs, that was a function of their own family self-sufficiency.

This sense of caste had no clearer expression than in its off-hand treatment of kings and queens. Whigs had always invested themselves with the historical mission of defending parliamentary government against monarchs. Many such families had martyrs in the family, who had died at the hands of Charles I and his sons in the seventeenth century. It was simply in the nature of all rulers to be potential tyrants. The executive had therefore to be endlessly watched and checked. This standard Whig theme, which had dominated party thinking in the eighteenth century, would resonate throughout Melbourne's career in the nineteenth. The Lambs were too young a family to claim seventeenth-century martyrs, but they had other reasons for holding kings in little esteem. By birth they were so close to them, that their imperfections were all too obvious (see Fig. 3). If illegitimacy is not thought a bar to relationship, then George IV was the father of William's half-brother, George. The illegitimate daughter of William's natural father, the Earl of Egremont, married an illegitimate son of William IV. That king's younger brother, Edward, Duke of Kent, was the father of Queen Victoria. As prime minister to two monarchs in the 1830s, Melbourne was, in an oblique way, serving his cousins.

The connection began in the spring of 1783, when the future George IV began a very public *affaire* with Lady Melbourne. As one Whig lady reported to another: 'I have no *gossip* to tell you, but that the Prince of Wales is *desperately* in love with Lady Melbourne, and when she don't sit next to him at supper he is not commonly civil to his neighbours: she *dances* with him, something in the cow stile (sic), but he is *en extase* with admiration for it.'[88] Melbourne later recalled that he had met the Prince often at this time, because he had visited the Lambs 'morning, noon and night'.[89] The complaisant husband of Lady Melbourne was rewarded with office. From 1783 to 1796, and again from 1812 to 1828, he was a Lord of the Bedchamber to George IV. The gap in years of service was accounted for by the Lambs refusing to give up Mrs Fitzherbert when George did. When the lady was once again taken into favour, so was the Lamb family, vacillating behaviour which Melbourne described as 'treacherous'. The best that could be said for it was that it was the action of 'a very strange man'.[90]

In old age, George IV was much given to fantasizing. He told stories about leading a cavalry charge at the battle of Salamanca; he insisted that he had recently ridden the winner of the Cheltenham Gold Cup; and he dramatized the memory of Lady Melbourne. He said,

he used, during her last illness to walk across the parade to her house every day, see her constantly and said that at last she died in his arms!! Lady Cowper knowing all the time that for the last ten days of her mother's life she never was out of her room, and that, so far from the King calling to see her or having her die in his arms, he never even sent to enquire after her.[91]

Melbourne himself dismissed George IV as 'so great a liar', that no weight could be given to anything he said, though he charitably added that illness played a part in determining the king's behaviour.[92]

If the Lamb family were sometimes snubbed by George IV, at other times he was their greatest patron. Indeed, Melbourne himself admitted that his family had 'quite belonged' to the Prince's circle at Carlton House.[93] There were innumerable small kindnesses, from boxes at the opera to the loan of Brighton Pavilion as a place of refuge after the death of Peniston Lamb in 1805.[94] More significantly, the future king was happy to promote the careers of Lady Melbourne's family. Not only was her husband snugly provided for, but so were her sons. Frederick's career in diplomacy was launched partly because the Prince was 'interested about him'.[95] George apologized to Lady Melbourne for not being immediately able to help William in 1803,[96] but, nine years later, he not only offered him a seat in Parliament, but also bullied Spencer Perceval into thinking of him for minor, government office. Lamb's hostility to Perceval's politics led him to decline the Prince's offer, at the same time acknowledging 'the understanding kindness which I have experienced during the whole course of my life'.[97]

For a young man to dismiss the patronage of a future king was high-handed behaviour. William Lamb quite simply believed that he had not been offered enough:

If I considered a similar, indeed a higher offer made me two years before by my own political friends as a degradation, it may easily be conceived that the proposition was a death blow to my vanity and the destruction of all my notions of my own self-importance.[98]

An irritated father had to apologize to the Prince for his son's ingratitude, assuring George that his friendship had been 'the pride of my life'.[99] In spite of this jolting episode, George IV never lost interest in William Lamb's career. When he finally took office, the King expressed real pleasure. As Victoria noted in her journal: 'Lord Melbourne said he hardly ever saw anything of George IV after he became King; Lord Melbourne being so much engaged in politics. "He was very kind to me in '27," said Lord Melbourne, "when I took office; he was very glad of that; he said there was nobody he liked to have better than me," added Lord Melbourne with tears in his eyes.'[100] When the Lambs dealt with kings, it inevitably became something of a family affair.

Late in life, Lord Melbourne was endlessly cross-questioned by the young Victoria about her uncles, George IV and William IV, who she had barely known. What strongly emerges from these conversations is just how ambivalent Melbourne was about his personal closeness to royalty. On the one hand, he was always ready to admit that George IV in particular had been 'very kind'.[101] In recognition of this, Melbourne chose George as one of the names for his own son.[102] He never met Princess Charlotte, George's daughter, because, in his view, she had treated her father unjustly.[103] By the same token, when George's wife, Caroline of Brunswick, became the source of so much trouble, the Lambs were happy to dismiss her as 'a very worthless woman!', even though 'she *was* accused of things she never had done, *having* done many other wrong things'.[104] There was much sympathy for the King, as he struggled with a rebellious daughter and a maddening wife.

On the other hand, Melbourne had no qualms about opposing any king in politics, whatever the degree of personal indebtedness involved. No quarter was given, even though George was profoundly hurt by Lamb's behaviour. The memory of it was later to haunt Melbourne himself. He confessed to Victoria that, 'we didn't behave well to the King, we treated him very roughly, we needn't have done so; I would not do so now. I was so anxious not to be thought to be influenced.'[105] Even more poignant was the fact that Melbourne's brother, George, should have attacked a king, who was in fact his natural father. This was 'very wrong'.[106] However, such difficulties were bound to arise. The Lambs could not escape the consequences of their anomalous position. In politics, they were the friends and associates of Whigs, who took a distrust of kings to be the basis of their creed. By birth and connection, they were honorary members of the royal family. These factors set up pressures that were difficult to reconcile, in a period when members of the royal family were so often at the centre of political crises.

The first such crisis occurred in 1810, when Frederick, Duke of York, George IV's younger brother, was hounded by the allegation that he had been in the habit of awarding commissions in the army on the recommendation of his mistress, who in turn was paid a fee for her efforts by grateful clients. In retrospect, Melbourne was sorry that the whole issue had ever come to light. Queen Victoria's journal is once again the source for his views:

Lord Melbourne said, 'I remember the time very well; and I remember thinking with him.' He said the Country knew very well that there was a great deal of profligacy going on, but still they weren't aware of the nature of it, and to have the fact known that the Duke, being a married man, was living with a woman who was also married, to have that *constaté* was a very bad thing.[107]

At the time, however, Melbourne suggested no hint of reticence or qualification in his belief that an investigation of the Duke's conduct was 'necessary', and that he should be removed from office if charges were proved. He admitted that it gave him 'great pain' to vote in the way he did, and that the Duke had been 'very hardly dealt with', but neither of these factors influenced his voting. At County meetings in Hertfordshire and in Parliament, Lamb denounced the Duke.[108] Yet the ambiguity of the Lamb family's relationship with monarchy remained. At the same time that Lamb upbraided the Duke, he also privately offered what a critic called 'paltry, paling penitences'.[109] It was a half-hearted attempt to square a circle.

The same problem was presented in magnified form by the political debate provoked by the marital difficulties of George IV and Caroline of Brunswick. The King's decision to deny the Queen any place in the Coronation Service or in the Anglican Liturgy, together with her sensational trial for adultery before the House of Lords, forced everyone to take sides. William Lamb found it hard to do so. On the one hand, he disliked the King's evident desire to persecute his wife. It was unnecessary and unseemly.[110] On the other hand, Caroline's reputation was so besmirched that it was impossible to cast her in the role of heroine. Indeed, her past was such, that even a free-thinker like Melbourne baulked at putting her name in the Liturgy. As a result, Melbourne made speeches of such a nuanced kind, that his audience was left in a fog. His own sister dismissed them as 'twaddling and foolish', and thought that William had simply 'run aground' on the issue.[111] He added nothing to the debate, and merely irritated his political friends.[112] The King himself was so offended that he gave up speaking to Lamb for a considerable time.[113]

Significantly, Melbourne, throughout the affair, was less interested in the principal actors than in wider implications. As in 1810, he thought that this royal embarrassment had been 'wretchedly mismanaged'. As in 1810, he thought that 'it ought to have been kept quiet'.[114] Nothing should ever be done to weaken the respect of the lower orders for established institutions. Melbourne distrusted those whom he designated 'the people'. On no account should opportunities be presented for agitation and lobbying. Safety lay in restricting debate to the world of élite politics. When the injured Queen was taken up by Radicals, and used to justify frightening disturbances, Melbourne could only conclude that those in authority 'had actually lost their understanding'.[115]

His priorities were clearly set out in a letter to Wilberforce, who had sought to engage him in the gathering of petitions. Melbourne was against all such action; 'I lean too much to the side of doing nothing and awaiting the course of events.'[116] He went on to explain that he wanted the trial of the Queen to be terminated in a way that would not give any status to popular violence. It must not appear that the political élite had retreated in the face of threat. If people attempted to argue that 'the higher orders etc. were sensible that this trial if persisted in would have brought about a revolution',[117] such arguments must be proved baseless. For the royal family to invite Parliament to regulate its behaviour was always a grave mistake. That kings should behave unwisely came as no surprise to Whigs. For Melbourne, difficulties arose because these same kings were his patrons and family associates.

These incidents are revealing about the general politics of the Lamb family. The foibles of princes, even corruption, were to be deplored in private, but never held up to public scrutiny. The mystique of institutions had to be upheld at all costs. Melbourne exclusiveness made him unresponsive to pressure from outside a propertied élite. A mob had no worthwhile contribution to make. If, however, issues came into open debate, it was incumbent on men like Melbourne to vote against corruption or the misuse of executive power.

Near majesty, they were never in awe of it and were always suspicious about its intentions. In the last resort, government was for the people, if not by them. Whigs were trustees for popular government in this sense. The salon world of the Melbournes was immensely restrictive in terms of entry. Yet they always claimed to be acting in the interests of groups of people who they never met.

William Lamb was happy to live with most of these assumptions. He passed the whole of his life following the rituals of a very few families, absorbing their sense of caste. His social and geographical range was narrow. In his political career, he would have more than enough opportunity to witness both the deviousness and ingratitude of monarchs and the destructive capacity of mobs. His response to both was quietist. He liked to bend before the prevailing wind, until commonsense reasserted itself, and once more committed government to the hands of educated men of civilization like himself. In the meanwhile, in adversity, the *esprit de corps* of the Lamb family was always there as his most vital resource.

2

The Whig Context

IN addition to the questions of blood and heredity, a Whig inheritance involved the absorption of certain prejudices that created a psychological mood, a context for thinking. Some contemporaries saw Melbourne's personality struggling against this family bequest. The diarist Greville, for example, explained the ambiguities in Melbourne's career by opposing his personality to his intellectual inheritance. 'A thorough Conservative at heart', he was 'from education and turn of mind, and from the society in which he was bred and always lived, . . . a Whig.' As a result of this tension, 'he was only half-identified in opinion and sympathy with the party to which he belonged in office', and was 'secretly the enemy of the measures which his own Government originated'.[1] In other words, Melbourne was a conservative who, by sad chance, had been wrapped in Whig swaddling clothes. It was a popular line of argument with those of Melbourne's critics, who felt that he could have done more to retard the speed of reform in his lifetime.

This idea has some force. Conservatively-minded men sometimes wander into progressive parties. Melbourne himself loved to play up to this image, teasing radicals with outrageous remarks. He shocked reformers by saying 'that the authors of the Reform Bill ought to be hanged'. Lord John Russell was informed that education was a complete waste of time, because everyone knew that the Paget family was illiterate, and yet they had done well in life. But all of this was, as his nephew pointed out, nothing but 'mischief'. Melbourne was a moderate man, but was ultimately, and with his back to the wall, 'on the Liberal side of the line'.[2] Major themes in Melbourne's intellectual inheritance made it impossible for him to be a Tory. Of these, the most important were a conviction that politics should be the preserve of a propertied élite, led by London-living, cosmopolitan grandees; a belief that the countryside was an unfortunate mistake, only to be thought about as an ideal; and the wistful acceptance that the claims of religion, while intellectually of consuming interest, were probably untrue. At times, he could sympathize with the Tory and the man of religion, but, in the last resort, he was not of their number.

Politics was for the few. Melbourne had a horror of involving a wider constituency. He deplored the new fashion in politicians of either taking their
injuries to the editors of newspapers[3] or, worse, of writing justificatory memoirs. Such behaviour was to have politics 'proclaimed at Charing Cross'. It
was 'the vice of the present day'.[4] He disliked receiving petitions from elec-
tors, even when they were sympathetic to his views.[5] As for public meetings,
he did 'not much like' them. 'My opinion is the fewer of them the better.
They call them safety valves, and so they may be, but . . . it is always a hazard to hold them.'[6] Worst of all, was the new phenomenon of lobbies and
lobbyists putting pressure on elected Parliaments to move in a particular
direction. Lords and Commons should deliberate calmly, but these men
made politics a hustling business. They also encouraged expectations that
could not be met. Blaming the lobbyist, Thomas Attwood, for the
Birmingham riots of 1839, Melbourne described his activities as a 'danger to
those whom you encouraged, danger to the state and their own future'.[7]
There was no reason to overreact to expressions of popular politics, however.[8] The correct, Whiggish response was simply to ignore them. As
Melbourne observed: 'I have long thought that Petitions and Public Meetings
are but poor signs of the real feeling even of those who sign them or attend
them.'[9]

Such views ill-prepared Melbourne to confront a society in the throes of
industrialization. He never visited industrial England, he had no friends
among its leading figures and, above all, he distrusted its values. Steadily, he
championed the hierarchical structures of agricultural England against the
industrial intruder. Inevitably, this fact led some contemporaries to see him
as a Tory manqué, but the truth is more complicated. Melbourne loathed the
countryside. London had 'a strong tendency to make useless profligates of
men, and almost an irresistible one to make whores of women',[10] but it was
the only place for a man of discernment to live. The countryside was inhabited by country gentlemen, Tony Lumpkins to a man, who were dismissed
by John Russell as the 'most ignorant, prejudiced, and narrow-minded of any.
The uneducated labourers beat them hollow in intelligence.'[11] Melbourne
agreed. For him, 'There is no bore so great to a Prime Minister, as a Country
Gentleman.'[12] His own county, Derbyshire, was 'the stupidest county', inhabited by 'the stupidest gentry'.[13] People who lived in the country too long were
inclined to become odd and to 'pick up strange ideas'.[14] When Melbourne
himself lived there, usually as a refugee from London scandal, he was a keen
shot, even though it was 'dangerous' and 'cruel', but he never hunted for fear
of taking a tumble.[15] He was prepared to exercise the local yeomanry, but
not if it rained.[16]

What he liked about agricultural society, as opposed to the industrial alternative, was an idea of living that was firmly distinct from the people who actually lived it. Melbourne was deeply attached to the notion that land ownership carried with it large, social responsibilities and privileges. The landowner took care of his inferiors. They, in turn, deferred to his social and political leadership. The result was social harmony and stability. By contrast, the industrialist saw only personal profit, leaving the working man to fend for himself. As a result, in industrial England, all was antagonism. Contrasting models of society in this way, Melbourne was always solicitous for 'the Squire and the Landed Gentleman who are loaded with fixed Charges, Mortgages, younger Childrens' fortunes, Jointures'.[17] In particular, his marked opposition to any relaxation of the Corn Laws, which so complicated his later career, was determined by such beliefs. Yet, Disraeli was wrong to see Melbourne as 'a thorough Tory and agriculturist'.[18] He admired the model of social living, which the countryside in theory represented. Whiggishly though, he had no wish to live there or much to be thrown into the company of its bucolic inhabitants.

Whiggery lived in the squares of West London and in great houses. Every one of Melbourne's contemporaries had to confront the consequences of change. Indeed, no generation had perhaps been more challenged in this respect. Yet Whigs were insulated from direct contact with industrial society, and Melbourne discussed it in abstraction. He thought that an economy based heavily on manufacturing was vulnerable:

A country subsisting to a great extent by manufacturing industry, with vast masses of population dependent upon the demand of foreign countries and our own demand for manufactured goods, always stood upon the brink of a precipice, was exposed to the risk of a mighty danger when those vast masses were thrown out of employment.[19]

Unlike landed society, the industrial world was open to terrible dislocations, and, when these occurred, there was no social consensus that could prevent the savage conflict of interests. Financiers and industrialists had no sense of social responsibility. He told Lady Holland never to 'mind the Clamour of the moneyed interest. They grunt and wail like Pigs unless every thing is done to meet their convenience.'[20] The labour force in industrial cities was no better. Selfishly, 'they endeavoured to regulate that which could not be regulated; they wished to settle the rate of wages upon one particular footing, when every person who thought on the subject must see, that the rate of wages must be regulated by the quantity of labour in the market, and by the demand which existed for it.'[21] Between tenant and landlord was respect and responsibility. Between employer and workman was envy and self-interest.

So profound were Melbourne's feelings that he refused to accept industrial wealth as a qualification for office or honour. It should not make a man a JP:

It is certainly true that I always admitted a man's being in trade to be an objection to his becoming a magistrate, and I believe it is upon this principle, that . . . manufacturers would not be considered impartial judges in cases between the workmen and their employers—you may certainly say the same with respect to country gentlemen in disputes between farmers and their men and also upon the Game Laws, but after all country gentlemen have held and still hold a higher character than Master Manufacturers.[22]

Equally, bankers were not to be candidates for baronetcies, because such fortunes 'are not the firmest of things'.[23] For Melbourne, the quality of a gentleman rested totally on the ownership of land and the fulfilment of the duties that went with it. Whig and Tory could agree about this, but, whereas the Tory lived out this idea, Melbourne, cocooned in South Street and in Holland House, favoured it as an ideal.

Melbourne's Whiggish ambivalence towards industrial society is best caught by his response to railway building, one of the pivotal and symbolic industries. As he remarked to Victoria: 'when people talk of bridges and rail roads, they are generally liberal.'[24] On the one hand, Melbourne was a major investor in a Nottinghamshire railway. On the other, all his remarks about this form of enterprise are disparaging. They were built by Irishmen, 'who mind neither Lord nor laws'. He absolutely refused to have any line running closer than fifteen miles to his house at Brocket. In short, to Victoria's questioning on the importance of railways, Melbourne simply asserted, 'I don't care about them.'[25] It was a deep antipathy. 'None of these modern inventions', he solemnly informed the young queen, 'consider human life.'[26] Repetitive work, the substitution of contract for responsibility and duty, and the preference for machinery over inter-reactive human agencies, were all features of the industrialized world that Melbourne and the Whigs feared. It was not, perhaps, an ideal set of prejudices for a man who was to become prime minister in the 1830s.

In particular, industrialization brought with it other features that began to put intolerable pressure on the Whig idea that politics was for the few. Newspapers, demands for mass education, protest movements such as Chartism, and calls for huge extensions of governmental activity in areas such as poor relief, all threatened élite politics. Melbourne disliked them all. He was only too aware that the conversation in salon and drawing-room was being drowned by a noise in the streets, but psychologically, he made little adjustment. By family upbringing and education, he totally shared the Whig sense of caste. It would be asking a great deal of anyone to suggest that such an inheritance should be completely overthrown. Even so, his reluctance to modify his attitudes brought difficulties into his political life over and over again.

Newspapers, for example, were things, according to Melbourne, that 'cannot be helped . . . and therefore they must be endured'.[27] Throughout his married life, he had to suffer the public scrutiny of his wife's behaviour. Almost without exception, the Lamb family had an appalling press. When prime minister, he endlessly complained of mistreatment:

I hate subscribing to the Press, for this reason, that it is really subscribing against myself. These fellows write, as they say, for the Government, but they never write for me; they never take the same views of a subject that I do nor defend it, as I would have defended, and in general they abuse one and all most cordially.[28]

His sister protectively agreed with William's protest. Although 'one ought not to care so much for such things', it was 'very painful to have those one loves misrepresented'.[29] When a newspaper said something complimentary about Melbourne, he was genuinely touched. It was something of a 'novelty and surprise'.[30] Most of the time, however, a newspaper was merely a method of spying through a keyhole at the closed world of Whiggery. Inevitably, perceptions so gained were misfocused.

There was no remedy for this irritant. There was no point in denying newspaper reports, because: 'Denials have great disadvantages—they act as compleat (sic) admissions in all cases in which you do not deny.'[31] There was even less in initiating prosecutions:

The real fact is that prosecutions are subject to so many objections, liable to so many difficulties, followed by so many consequences, which entirely counteract their effect, that they are no check whatever upon the violence and malignity of the press, which however, if they be not checked, must ultimately destroy all the institutions of the country.[32]

Instead, he favoured reducing duties on newspapers, in the hope that an unburdened, legitimate press would defeat unstamped illegal publications which the government could not control.[33] But, basically, there was nothing to be done. As in his response to so many other issues, Melbourne was fatalistic. The prying and harassing of the press, like bad weather, had to be suffered and lived through.[34] It was a symptom of public pressure upon élite politics. For the moment, it could be ignored, but Melbourne was not sure how long this would continue.

A comparable pressure from below was represented by demands for popular education. In this area, as in so many others, Melbourne's public statements diverged from his private beliefs. Whigs approved of mass education but understandably feared its consequences for their closed world. In the Lords, Melbourne supported reformers like Brougham, assuring the House that 'his Majesty's Government are deeply impressed with a desire of promoting the Education of the People; and I am perfectly convinced that the repression of crime, and the propagation of virtue, peace, general tranquillity, and order, are objects inseparably connected with a well-considered and well-directed system of education.'[35] Such remarks are specifically clear, but when Melbourne talked of virtue and general tranquillity, it was reasonable to suspect irony. From time to time, Melbourne could attribute to the progress of education the surprising patience of both manufacturer and workman in the face of distress. When people were informed, it seemed to be 'upon the whole favourable to tranquillity and order'.[36] More often, however, scepticism kept breaking in. When evaluating schemes for mass education, Melbourne had a simple yardstick: 'If knowledge does not make them more patient and better, it is useless. If it makes them bitter and refractory, it is prejudicial.'[37]

In fact, nearly every comment on the subject in private correspondence or conversation is dismissive. Brougham's crusading for the cause of education was 'tiresome'. It was also 'tiresome to educate and tiresome to be educated'.[38] In marked contradiction to his public statements, he had no real belief that education improved behaviour. Crime, for example, 'has existed in all ages, all attempts at eradication have hitherto proved useless. Education will not help, for education is knowledge . . . which can be good or bad.'[39] Delegations of well-intentioned people hoping to engage Melbourne's support for educational causes were unimpressed by their reception. An obviously bored prime minister pulled feathers from cushions and blew them into the air.[40] He was unromantic on the subject of children. Although he publicly supported measures which regulated child labour, he privately thought that since education would never 'do any good', parents should be entirely free 'to send their children who are under a certain age, to work'.[41] It was better that children 'should work than be idle and starve'.[42]

Above all, the provision of education was not a matter for government. Cabinet colleagues were left in no doubt about this. In 1839, one recorded in his diary that, 'Lord Melbourne said some fierce things about the demand for education, and confessed as he had often done before that he wished we had not meddled in the matter.'[43] The whole business was better left to voluntary organizations and enthusiasts like Joseph Lancaster or Henry Brougham. As he explained to Victoria, any idea of government creating a national system of schooling was out of the question;

'I daren't say in these times, that I'm against it,—but I *am* against it;' He says it may do pretty well in Germany, but that the English would not submit to that thraldom; he thinks it much better be left to Voluntary Education, and that people of any great genius were educated by circumstances, and that 'the education of circumstances' was the best.[44]

To raise an army of schoolmasters was to call up a mass of 'blockheads'.[45] In 1838, when Lord John Russell argued for a new initiative on education, Melbourne declined to veto the idea, but insisted that the country already had as much education as was either feasible or desirable.[46]

Melbourne was a tease, and no subject offered more opportunities to shock and tease than education. He particularly enjoyed provoking the young Victoria with unsentimental remarks about children. Yet, his badinage had substance. By educating, 'you may fill a person's head with nonsense which may be impossible ever to get out again'.[47] It was a mistake to 'bother' the ignorance of the poor.[48] They would be better off with 'the elementary doctrines of Christianity and the simple rules of society'.[49] Whiggery believed passionately in government for the people, but not in government by the people. That formula might be less and less acceptable if minds were opened. Education was a Pandora's Box, full of bothersome consequences. Better it remained closed.

Whigs rarely confronted the poor directly. Social conditions in industrial towns were much talked of and little known. Through no fault of their own, the poor were uninteresting. Nothing that they would say or do could be subtle, nuanced, or intriguing. Worse, to a fastidious man like Melbourne, the poor were distressing to behold. Victoria recorded his reaction to the success of *Oliver Twist*; 'It's all among Workhouses, and Coffin Makers, and Pickpockets,' he said, '. . . it's all slang; it's just like the Beggars' Opera; I shouldn't think it would tend to raise morals; I don't like that low debasing view of mankind . . . I don't like those things; I wish to avoid them; I don't like them in *reality* and therefore I don't wish to see them represented.'[50] Throughout his life, Melbourne never confronted unpleasantness, but always fled before it. Poverty was horrible. He frankly admitted that he did 'not like any of the Poor, but those who are poor through their own fault, I quite detest'.[51] Philanthropists seeking assistance were told that he was not 'a subscribing sort of fellow'.[52]

When forced to deal with the problems of the poor, Melbourne was predictably more prudent than compassionate. Poor Laws and the provision of relief were matters 'upon which public feeling is very sensible and misrepresentation and exaggeration may produce great and pernicious effect'.[53] Like it or not, care had to be taken. After all, 'no human nerves can bear to see people dying in the streets'.[54] Poor relief was 'in itself a great evil, and never should be resorted to except to avert a greater evil, the extremity of want or destitution',[55] but minimum guarantees had to be offered. Even those among the poor who made a nuisance of themselves by joining trade unions and other associations had to be allowed access to assistance.[56] To try to punish them by withholding relief was simply to invite disturbances. Common sense demanded that Whiggery had no choice but to confront poverty and attempt to relieve it.

Relief, however, had a cost. Over much of his political career, Melbourne expressed concern about the sums expended under the Poor Law. In 1817, he told Parliament that:

the sums raised for the support of the poor, in the shape of rates, now amounted to a tax almost as great, and on certain classes of the community certainly more oppressive than the property tax. It was impossible that . . . this tax was collected and administered, without the greatest oppression to the landed interest, and the ultimate diminution of the industry and resources of the country.[57]

In 1834, his views were unchanged.[58] A growing population, many of whom were subject to the economic dislocations of an industrial world, was putting intolerable strain on the provision of relief. Its cost was positively threatening. As he told Althorp: 'It is melancholy to consider what enormous funds are devoted in this country to the production of Evil, for I cannot consider the Poor Laws as having any other tendency whilst we are squeezed so close with respect to measures of undoubted advantage and utility.'[59]

As a result of these concerns, Melbourne expressed genuine pleasure at the enactment of a new Poor Law in 1834. Concentrating relief in the workhouse would deter all but the genuinely indigent from seeking assistance. It would make it easier to distinguish between the deserving and undeserving poor. After seeing the new system in operation for three or four years, Melbourne was sure that 'it has been attended with a success beyond any expectations, which could fairly or reasonably be anticipated from it'.[60] He regarded it as one of the great achievements of Whig government, even though he recognized that the measure had lost the party votes in subsequent elections. The Poor Law of 1834 had so completely struck the right balance between the under- and over-provision for poverty, that no amendment was necessary. It was simply a question of maintaining 'the ground, which we have already taken', and of not occupying 'fresh ground in advance without much consideration'.[61]

Demands that government should take responsibility for poverty, a critical press, mass literacy, and the education of the people at large were all manifestations of that industrial world that Melbourne suspected. He knew that its development could not be checked. He admitted that responses had to be made to it. But it could only be done by holding the nose. Like so many of the generation which had witnessed the French Revolution, Melbourne admitted to 'not having quite the confidence in the stability of popular and constitutional forms of government which others have'.[62] The Chartism of the 1830s and 1840s seemed to realize his worst fears. As a man who regularly instructed his own tenants on how to vote in elections Melbourne predictably found the Chartists' claims absurd.[63] Universal male suffrage was no more possible than a flight to the moon. As Home Secretary and Prime Minister between 1830 and 1841, everything he said and did was enacted against a backdrop of 'growing discontent and some fearful seditions',[64] but Melbourne remained unmoved. The French press, fascinated by Chartism and anxious to demonstrate that England had a more repressive system of government than France, expected Melbourne to have 'quelques paroles d'intérêt ou de pitié pour les populations ouvrières', but saw instead 'l'action exclusive des charges de cavalerie et des coups de canon'.[65]

In fact, Melbourne had no objection to the advocacy of change in itself. On one famous occasion, he raised a whirlwind by introducing the utopian socialist, Robert Owen, to Queen Victoria at Court. He did so, in spite of telling Owen to his face that 'his doctrines appeared to me the most absurd and he himself one of the most foolish men I ever conversed with'. Quite simply, he would do wrong 'in refusing to present a Gentleman at Court on account of his opinions either political or religious'.[66] New, or even outlandish, ideas in themselves were unexceptional. As a good Whig, Melbourne was also acutely aware that political agitation was often the result of imprudent and obstinate Tory resistance.[67] Whig historiography was clear that revolution was more often provoked by stupid rulers than instigated by malevolence in the lower orders. Melbourne would look quizzically at the visionary who pointed to far horizons, but knew him to be a legitimate and constant feature of the political landscape.

The Chartism of 1839 went beyond the mere advocacy of change, however. It importantly predicated all its demands on the real or implied threat of violence, and with that Melbourne would have no truck. Chartism was based, in his view, upon 'open professions of an intention to plunder, violence, and bloodshed'.[68] When involved in either Irish or English politics, Melbourne always refused to countenance any lobby or protest group that saw the threat of coercion as a proper means of promoting its end. Too much of popular politics in the 1830s and 1840s seemed to fall into this category. Secrecy and oath-taking confirmed suspicions that there was a conspiracy against government itself.[69] Melbourne and his colleagues were fond of contrasting the constitutional behaviour of someone like Owen with the implied violence of Chartism.

When violence became explicit, as in the Newport rising of 1839, Melbourne was implacable. This was a 'serious' business.[70] Its suppression was to be vigorous, and, breaking with normal, Whig practice, the troops involved were to be congratulated.[71] Above all, the execution of John Frost, the uprising's leader, was essential. Hobhouse recorded in his diary a conversation with Melbourne on this point. The Prime Minister thought that 'some decided manner would be indispensable to prevent anarchy . . . I replied that as the object of the Chartists was to knock us on the head and rob us of our property we might as well arrive at that catastrophe after a struggle as without it—we could only fail and we might succeed. Exactly so, said Lord Melbourne.'[72] Again, in 1843, Melbourne criticized Peel for allowing the Rebecca Riots in South Wales to go on with impunity for far too long.[73] Popular pressure on Westminster politics was wearing yet had to be endured. But it had also to be contained within constitutional channels. The moment that it took other courses, there was no alternative to blows.

If Whigs hesitantly responded to the approach of industrial society, they overwhelmingly, in Melbourne's generation, turned away from gods in general, and the Christian god in particular. Exceptions could be found, but Lady Holland, claiming to hear the Lord's Prayer for the first time at the age of 60, was more typical of the Whiggery of her lifetime. Quite how far Melbourne himself shared these secular prejudices was a matter of keen debate among his family and friends, and has remained so ever since. Unlike the Hollands, he never entirely shunned religion as an intellectual exercise, and he liked his clergyman to be sincere. Significantly, he never cared for Sydney Smith, whose collar never inhibited him at Holland House gatherings. Melbourne's religion was Whiggish in the essential fact that he could not ultimately believe. Yet, his response to religion was more nuanced than that bald statement would imply. He found it an absorbing study and held it in respect, while at the same time avoiding all personal involvement.

First and foremost, most of his opinions were informed by a fatalism of so profound a depth that it could be called religious. Man was the plaything of the gods and there was no remedy for it. He believed that, 'With respect to the Prophecies of the Holy Scripture, Divine Providence either has fulfilled or will fulfill them by its own means and at its own Season. Man has neither the knowledge nor the Power, which can enable him either to hasten or to hinder their completion, and it appears to me to be almost as presumptuous to attempt the one as the other.'[74] As a result, the only way was to 'try to do your best and leave the rest to fate'.[75] There was a mystical element in his views. He believed, for example, that something called 'Divine Providence' had smiled on the English, scattering French and Spanish invasion fleets with celestial winds.[76] Life was a flux. If purpose was inherent in it, it could not be discerned by man. He could only bow his head before the chaos. As he advised his nephew, 'Human affairs never stand still, particularly not religious affairs. They are always moving, forward, backward, laterally, up, down, straight, crooked, in some direction or another.'[77] Melbourne's response to terrible problems in personal and political life was a soulful passivity.

Secondly, Melbourne was clear that it was possible to have too much religion. Its precepts had nothing to do with the regulation of personal morals, a point that was made epigrammatically on a number of occasions. He disliked the religious enthusiast and any suggestion of mortifying the flesh. To the young Victoria, he specifically contrasted religion with fun:

'Nobody is gay now; they are so religious . . . I think you will live to see this country become very religious; too much so; I always thought it would be so for some time!' How did he think it would be too much so? 'I think there'll be a good deal of persecution in the country before long,' he replied, 'and that people would be interfering with one another, about going to church, and such things.'[78]

In the 1830s, he was depressed to see even young Whigs, or 'Whiglings', growing 'mad about religion'.[79] By contrast, he was pleased to describe his nephew as a rake, 'which is quite refreshing to see'.[80]

Lastly, Melbourne never went to church if he could possibly avoid it. He adopted a wide range of tactics to deflect Victoria's bullying on this point. He tried humour, telling the Queen that he was 'afraid to go to church for fear of hearing something very extraordinary'.[81] He teased her by claiming to be a quietist, and therefore 'so perfect that you are exempted from all external ordinances, and are always living with God'. Victoria thought this 'all stuff'.[82] He blamed his parents, saying that they never went to church because 'it wasn't the fashion'.[83] As a last resort, he simply told lies.[84] When he was coaxed into a church, he behaved badly. Victoria had to upbraid him for fidgeting, sleeping through the sermon, and excessive snoring. Disraeli caught Melbourne's embarrassment when finding himself in religious surroundings. At Victoria's coronation, he described him as looking 'very awkward and uncouth, with his coronet cocked over his nose, his robes under his feet, and holding the great sword of state like a butcher'.[85]

In these responses to religion, Melbourne was once again simply following Lamb family practice. As has been noted, his parents had not been churchgoers. His sister, Emily, was, but her appearances were controversial:

Lady Cowper and her family go to church, but scandalize the congregation by always arriving half an hour late. The hour matters not; if it began at nine, or ten, or twelve, or one o'clock, it would be the same thing; they are never ready, and always late, but they go. Lord Cowper never goes at all.[86]

Blasphemous expletives were a standard feature of the Lamb vocabulary. So much so in fact, that Sydney Smith thought that much time could be saved in a conversation with Melbourne, if they simply assumed that 'everybody and everything to be d——d'.[87] Evidence such as this, together with Melbourne's ability to evaluate Christian claims in the original Greek texts, proved to some contemporaries that he had been led to 'a perfect *conviction* of unbelief'.[88]

In a sense, this judgement was correct, but it fails to say everything about Melbourne's religion. Certainly, he was not a believer in any orthodox sense. He had no creed, no particular liturgy. He saw little point in the standard expressions of religious observance. No priest should comment on private life. There would be no mention of a clergyman in attendance when he was dying. Family background and Whiggish philosophy made such things unlikely. Yet, unlike the Hollands, Melbourne was never an enemy of religion. He retained a profound respect for it throughout his life. It was intriguing as an intellectual pastime, and was invaluable as one of the factors holding society together. Christianity, in particular, had a beauty in many of its claims. Melbourne wished it could have been true. The point is captured in a conversation he had with a contemporary scientist:

'I wish,' said Lord Melbourne, 'to put a question to you not in a religious, but a purely scientific, light. Do you believe in the possibility of a future life?'

'Answering you strictly as a man of Science, and guarding myself, as you properly have done, from any religious opinion, I have no hesitation in saying, that I think it utterly impossible.'

Upon which Melbourne gave a shrug and a groan, ordered his horse and galloped home.[89]

Scepticism about the ultimate truth of Christianity in no way precluded an intense interest in religious systems. One of his secretaries described him as 'a great theologian'.[90] It was a passion that was established early. Among his personal papers is a commonplace book, whose contents are largely theological. Quotations from the Greek Gospels are intermingled with such questions as, 'What is the apology of the Church of England referred to in Canon 30—Bishop Jewel's apology.'[91] Holding high political office was no distraction from this interest, but rather allowed him to indulge it fully by making bishops. Contemporaries marvelled at how much he continued to read, even as Prime Minister, and noted, with a sense of awe, that favoured friends would be presented with commentaries on Revelations, 'stuffed with marginal notes of his own'.[92] He valued corresponding with bishops whom he admired, like the Bishop of Salisbury, and he equally enjoyed taunting those he disliked, like the Bishop of Exeter.[93] He preferred robust churchmen to saints. A 'simple hearted man', like a certain contemporary archbishop was 'the damnedest fool alive'.[94] Too many bishops were theological simpletons and were afraid of their clergy'.[95]

Melbourne's standing in this area was of the first importance, since so much of his prime ministership was taken up with regulating the affairs of the churches in England and Ireland. In 1835, Lady Holland complained that 'the Lords are half made with theology and topicks of ecclesiastical policy more like the polemics of other ages than of this'. She went on, however, to note that 'the Bishops were surprized at finding Lord Melbourne such an able and learned adversary upon the subjects they chose to make prominent'.[96] As far as he enjoyed debate at all, he relished argument about religion. It was probably the ground on which he felt most secure. To be able to correct the Bishop of Exeter on the history of the word 'Protestant' gave him enormous pleasure.[97] It was unusual in a Whig to consort with churchmen, but it was entirely Whiggish to have them as sparring partners rather than friends.

Beyond the intellectual games of theology, Melbourne always proclaimed himself to be a friend of the Church of England. Newspaper proprietors who suggested otherwise were reprimanded.[98] He was happy to reassure an anxious Victoria of his 'firm determination to maintain the Church of England as settled at the reformation', together with a 'firm belief in her articles and creeds, as hitherto understood and interpreted by her . . . Divines'.[99] Nothing in his behaviour gave credence to the second part of this statement, but his first protestation is quite plausible. Quite simply, the religious instinct was common to all societies at all times. An established religion regulated that instinct, checked its wilder manifestations, and stopped it from becoming silly. For this purpose, as he explained to Howick, any religion would do:

I am for an established Church—I do not know and cannot foresee by what means divine Providence may intend hereafter to disseminate its own truths. But using my own understanding I cannot take upon myself the responsibility of recommending a reliance on the voluntary system. An established Church appears to me to be necessary for the instruction of the People and for the maintenance of the rational purity of religious doctrine. I think there is so much of the truth of Gospel, mixed I dare say with error, in the Church of England form, in the Roman Catholic form, and in the Presbyterian form of Christianity, as to justify a Christian in acquiescing in the establishment of any of them.[100]

This being so, it was better not to meddle with or change Church establishments too often. Ironically, much of the Melbourne administration was taken up with precisely this activity. The Prime Minister went along with it, because he accepted that there was widespread dissatisfaction with the status quo. At the same time, he frankly told Parliament that he was 'not dissatisfied with the Church as it stood at present'.[101] The Established Church had nothing to fear from Melbourne himself.

If a religious establishment was useful, the Anglican variant of Christianity was the most suitable for this purpose. Its erastian character marked it out for this role. Anglicanism allowed the state to control religion. As long as bishops and many priests were appointed by laymen, the religious spirit would be contained within what was seemly and rational. As far as Melbourne was concerned, this was the great work of the Reformation. He bluntly informed

his nephew, 'I do not care a damn what they [critics] say of the religious part
of the Reformation, but the political part of it I am for standing by to the
Death.'[102] Similarly, Parliament was assured that he was 'sincerely and
devotedly attached to the principles of the Reformation; I am sincerely and
devotedly attached to the spirit of free enquiry and the right to private judgment—principles which I consider characteristics of the Reformation.'[103] A
sensible politician kept the religious instinct of men under surveillance,
because history proved that, unrestrained, it could work great mischief. The
Church of England offered the best means of effecting such surveillance.

Predictably, Melbourne disliked the idea that churchmen should attempt
to regulate the charmed routines of Whig life. Priests should not attempt to
influence elections, because if they did, as he had witnessed in Ireland, the
results were pernicious bouts of sectarian violence.[104] He thought sabbatari-
anism comic,[105] and he disapproved of proselytizing in all its forms.[106] The
Whig world was always careful not to make men more religious than they
could reasonably be. Above all, religious prescriptions should have no influence in determining the distinctive morality of the Lambs. After being on
the receiving end of a highly evangelical sermon, Melbourne famously
announced that, 'Things have come to a pretty pass when religion is allowed
to invade the sphere of private life.'[107] Whiggery had been born in the seventeenth century. One of its greatest achievements was to overcome the reli-
giously based excesses of Cromwell and James II. Since then, man had come
of age. Religion was now a calm system for exercising the mind and soothing the spirit. For these reasons, 'L'd Melbourne expressed a strong preference of (sic) the Church of England to all other sects.'[108]

Like so many of his contemporaries therefore, Melbourne was a passionate defender of Anglicanism, without in any way being conventionally religious. Archbishops were regularly consulted and reassured about the many
religious changes that came in during Melbourne's prime ministership.[109]
Similarly, he took enormous trouble over ecclesiastical appointments, and, in
promoting men, it was always 'a recommendation to me, that I know it will
be agreeable to the Clergy'.[110] He asked surprisingly little of his appointees.
Political support in the Lords would be welcome, but, as he explained to
Bishop Butler, he did not insist on slavish devotion; 'I looked for some general agreement in political opinion and a general disposition to support the
measures of the present Government, and that, if such existed, I did not wish
to bind him down to support upon every question.'[111] Being a strong Whig
was not in itself a sufficient qualification for the Bench, while some of his
nominations were barely Whig at all.[112] He turned down a protégé of Lord
Lansdowne because 'the appointment would be satisfactory in no point of
view except a political one'.[113]

Above all, candidates for high office in the Church had to be as orthodox as any Anglican could reasonably be. Melbourne enjoyed giving potential bishops an oral examination to search out their views. One such was left in no doubt of what was required:

I only wish you to understand that I don't intend if I know it to make a heterodox bishop. I don't like heterodox bishops. As men they may be very good anywhere else, but I think they have no business on the Bench. I take great interest in theological questions, and I have read a good deal of those old Fellows [the Church Fathers]. They are excellent reading and very amusing; sometime or other we must have a talk about them.[114]

He refused to promote Dr Arnold of Rugby, because he suspected him of being a unitarian. He irritated Lord John Russell by declining to make his younger brother a bishop. According to Melbourne, the young man in question was 'a Conventicler which I dislike'.[115] Most remarkable of all, he twice braved the wrath of Lady Holland in refusing to give Sydney Smith a diocese. Quite simply, the man was too 'facetious'.[116] No prime minister was more solicitous in making sure that the Church of England was governed by men of real worth.

Further, Melbourne was a friend of Anglicanism in sharing a distrust of its enemies. He had supported the removal of most civil restrictions on Dissenters in 1828 and on Roman Catholics in 1829, but for a rather idiosyncratic reason. For him, it was not a matter of rights and the lifting of oppression, but rather that the state was being denied the services of useful citizens. In arguing for the relaxation of laws against the Jews, in 1833, he first suggested that all disabilities were 'injurious, and in most instances, ineffectual', and then went on to assert that, 'it was not the privileges and advantages of individuals which they had to consider . . . the complaint was, that the privileges of the State, the welfare of the country, and the advantage of the community, were seriously injured by those restrictions'.[117] Melbourne thought in terms of utility as much as he considered rights. The toleration of religious minorities was sensible, because such groups no longer represented any danger to the state, and therefore it was silly to be denied their services. None of this made the theology of Dissent and Catholicism attractive, however. Remembering the seventeenth century, Melbourne saw both traditions as representing that narrow bigotry that could so easily overtake religious instincts, if they were not snugly tucked up in Anglicanism.

Given these views, it was right in 1829 to relieve Roman Catholics from the restrictions of the Test Acts. There was no reason why they should not take civic offices. When the Duke of Newcastle suggested, in 1837, that the concessions made eight years earlier should be revoked, Melbourne dismissed the suggestion as idiotic. At the same time, he told Parliament that he had no wish to improve on the 1829 settlement: 'If there were anything of a dangerous tendency at this time, or if there were any vice which ought to be guarded against more than any other, it was that disposition which existed for further changes in measures which had already been adopted after great consideration and carried with great difficulty.'[118] More strikingly, he disliked anything that suggested his administration might countenance Catholicism. It was too controversial to put a Catholic into a post at the Admiralty,[119] and the proposal to send Roman Catholic chaplains to the British Army in India at public expense was, in his view, 'rather startling'.[120] It was better that Catholics should enjoy their new-found freedoms out of the limelight.

If Catholicism was unattractive, Dissent was positively disliked. It was a view Melbourne formed early in life, telling his mother in 1800 that

I do not like the dissenters . . . They are more zealous, and consequently more intolerant, than the established church. Their only object is power. If we have to have a prevailing Religion, let us have one that is cool and indifferent and such a one we have got. Not that I am so foolish as to dread any fire and faggots and wheels and axes but there are other modes of Persecution. Toleration is the only good and just principle and toleration for every opinion that can possibly be formed.[121]

It was right to extend toleration to Dissenters, even though they themselves would deny it to others, given half the chance. He discouraged the building of a chapel on his own estates, not seeing the point of 'encouraging meeting houses'.[122] In public, he spoke vigorously in favour of giving Dissenters access to all universities.[123] In private, he thought that they should be satisfied with London University only. As he pointed out to Russell: 'the universities are so formed upon the principal of their students being members of the Church of England that Dissenters can hardly be admitted without a complete change of their whole form.'[124] Toleration was a device for emancipating the individual and releasing his talents for the service of the state. It had nothing to do with undermining Anglican institutions or the privileged position of Anglicanism within the state.

In fact, Melbourne patronized Anglicanism in both senses of the word. On the one hand, he guarded the Church's interests in selecting its personnel and in regulating the toleration of its competitors. On the other, he saw fit to save Anglicanism from itself, if there was any hint that it might deviate from the path of commonsense into bigotry. For this reason, Tractarianism or Puseyism worried him. Oxford academics such as Newman, Keble, and Pusey seemed to be arguing for a return to priestcraft and Church control over secular life. Pusey himself sent Melbourne a copy of *Tracts for the Times*.[125] His reaction was cool. He would admit that Manning was 'a good man',[126] and that 'the

Puseyites have the most learning or rather have considered the points more recently and more accurately, than their opponents'.[127] Melbourne, the reader of patristics, knew scholarship when he saw it. But he was not sure that it all added up to much. 'Is it', he asked, 'any more than the square cap . . . that the Puseyites wear.'[128]

Puseyite argument was difficult to follow. There was too much mysticism for Melbourne. Writing to Holland, he asked,

Do you think Puseyism as it is called is a threat and is it our interest to take any particular pains to discountenance it? I hardly make out what it is.—either I am . . . dull or its Apostles are very obscure. I have got one of their Chief Newman (sic) upon publication with the appendix 443 pages. I have read 57, and I cannot say that I understand a sentence or discern any idea whatsoever.[129]

So cloudy were the Puseyites' views, that Melbourne was inclined to believe that it would all evaporate as so much theological dew. There was certainly nothing to be gained by giving it the publicity of persecution.[130] Even so, to muddy the Anglican waters in this way was an irritation. Melbourne jealously guarded an Anglicanism that was common sense written up as theology. If Anglican clerics in Oxford or elsewhere were determined to foul their own nest, regulation by secular authority would be entirely in order.

For this reason, he became embroiled in the Hampden affair. In 1836, Richard Hampden was appointed Regius Professor of Divinity in Oxford by Melbourne, even though he was widely suspected throughout the University of holding unorthodox opinions. It is virtually the only occasion when Melbourne elevated a man with such a reputation. Hampden's distinction as a theologian seems to have overcome his doubts on the subject. Oxford protested vigorously, provoking a major crisis in Melbourne's prime ministership. His response to this academic cyclone is illustrative of his whole approach to religion. On the one hand, he refused to back down. Secular authority in matters of appointment was not to be overturned by clerics muttering in Oxford common rooms. On the other hand, he quickly realized that he had, wittingly or unwittingly, fired religious enthusiasms, which were never helpful and frequently tiresome. He therefore publicly defied Oxford and privately moved to defuse the crisis.

Replying to anxious Puseyites, Melbourne boldly defended Hampden:

Uniformity of opinion, however desirable, may be purchased at too high a price. We must not sacrifice everything to it; soundness of opinion, reasonableness of opinion, extent of knowledge, powers, intellectual and physical, must also be taken into account . . . I do not myself dread bold enquiry and speculation. I have seen too many new theories spring up and die away to feel much alarm upon such a subject. If they are founded on truth, they establish themselves and become part of the established belief. If they are erroneous, they decay and perish.[131]

He bluntly told Parliament that he found nothing alarming in Hampden's writings, and that majority opinion in Oxford should not be followed blindly. It had, after all, opposed the Reformation and persecuted John Locke. If Oxford had prevailed historically, 'everything liberal, everything noble, everything free and ingenuous in this country, would undoubtedly not have been established in it'.[132] Recalling his days at Cambridge, he claimed that there was more bitterness and prejudice in universities than 'ever there was in any public assembly or popular club'.[133] It might even be time to review the statutes that governed these institutions, since they 'never reformed themselves'.[134]

Hampden himself could only feel reassured. Melbourne, in February 1836, wrote 'to acquaint you that in justice to ourselves and to you, for the sake of the principles of toleration and free enquiry and for the interests of the University and Church themselves, we consider ourselves bound to persevere in your appointment to the Regius Professorship'.[135] In June, he was told that he had 'nothing to do but to stand your ground'.[136] Melbourne also began to use him as a consultant, asking him if he knew of any Oxford men, who might make a bishop.[137] In all of this, Melbourne publicly confirmed his belief in a secular control of religion. It was the justification for elevating and cherishing Anglicanism.

In private, all was different. Melbourne was temperamentally inclined to retreat, as soon as a religious issue took fire. He feared its power to move men. In the Hampden case, he could totally change his mind within twenty-four hours. On 10 February 1836, he thought it 'very doubtful whether consistently with the interests of the University', it was prudent to proceed with the appointment.[138] On 11 February, he assured Howick that he would never give in to 'the rebels of Oxford'.[139] Holland noted in his diary that Melbourne was both informing the King that the Hampden appointment was a resignation issue, and, at the same time, cautioning everyone against ecclesiastical nominations that might raise the dust.[140] Melbourne's ambivalence is neatly caught in a letter of advice to Hampden. It was both understanding and admonitory. Hampden should

give a series of practical elementary lectures, to which no objection can be taken. The fact is that in digging into the early history or indeed into any part of the History of Christianity since the Apostolical times, you turn up so much filth and rubbish, that it is almost impossible to avoid the appearance of casting some of the dirt upon Christianity itself.[141]

Theology in a study was one thing, public controversy was quite another. If Anglicans were to indulge in mystical acrimony, they defeated their own purpose. Melbourne profoundly believed in a controlled society. Both religion and politics were better left to those who knew best.

The generation that came to maturity before 1789, that lived through the Revolution and Napoleonic empire, and survived both, was a generation that was subjected to intolerable pressures. Born into a world of secure values, they saw everything undermined and overturned. They were invited to reinvent everything. Accepted institutions, such as monarchy and aristocracy had to be given new justifications. Religion and its relationship with civil society had to be re-examined and newly regulated. Notions of popular sovereignty were now firmly on the agenda, and politics was to be under the scrutiny of the people at large. Industrialization fractured old formulas based on ideas of communal responsibility, and sharpened competition between economic interests. It was an altogether shocking combination of events.

Someone like Melbourne was psychologically distanced from change. He was intellectually aware of it, and found the discussion of its consequences deeply fascinating. At the same time, he adjusted his prejudices little by way of response. The Whig sense of caste insulated him from so much that was in flux. His profound suspicion of politics being opened up to a wider constituency was a consistent feature in this thinking. Newspapers, lobbying, and even the extension of the franchise were unpleasing in an almost aesthetic sense. By contrast, his continued preference for landed England, and the tightly controlled social systems that it invoked carried the pre-1789 world into the second quarter of the nineteenth century. Equally, he always disliked an argument too warmly advocated, be it in old religions like Anglicanism or new religions like Socialism or Chartism. All such movements tended to invite the participation of people, who would be better advised to follow the lead of a rational, dispassionate élite. There was less violence and persecution in cynicism, than in enthusiasm.

All of this has a material bearing on the question of the extent to which Melbourne was a Whig and how much he owed to a Whig upbringing. If the term is defined in politics only, the result is ambiguous. Melbourne disagreed with Lansdowne about the Poor Laws, with Lord John Russell about the need for further religious toleration, with Brougham about educational reform and the franchise, and with most of his Cabinet about the advantages of a secret ballot and the Corn Laws. Who then was the true Whig? All sense of definiteness seems to become blurred. Clarity is only restored by seeing Whiggery in a wider context. What united them was a sense of belonging to a cousinhood from which others were excluded. Melbourne often disagreed with his friends, but they were conscious of debating in a club, whose doors were firmly closed on the outside world. The rules of the club were their own.

Newspaper editors, educationalists, much of industrial England, the religious enthusiast, and, of course, the Chartist would not be put up for membership. Whiggery was an extended family, in a famous phrase 'a great-grandmotherhood'. Melbourne could not always agree with his cousins, but he recognized them as people like himself, who were not like other people.

3

A Whig Education, 1779–1805

FOR the first three or four years of her reign, Victoria often found herself ensconced on a sofa in Windsor Castle, listening spellbound to Melbourne's accounts of his youth. So much had happened between the 1780s and the 1830s, that his tales had the quality of describing a foreign country. It is on these stories that an account of Melbourne's early life has to be built. Inevitably, they are partial, coloured, and no doubt much elaborated to tease the imagination of his young audience. Victoria was happy to believe most of what he said, and to credit him with an astonishing memory:

After dinner I sat on the sofa alone, and Lord Melbourne sat near me the whole evening. He is *so* agreeable, and kind and good. He has a very good memory and astonished us all by saying that he remembers from *thirteen months old*! He said, 'No one will believe it but I remember perfectly well being inoculated at 13 months old,' and 'I am convinced I can recollect the Riots in '80; I remember being sent out of Town then; I was only fourteen months old then, for I was born in '79.' This is incredible! But he certainly has an excellent memory, for he is like a book, if you ask him anything about History; and he remembers all he reads.[1]

Such is the nature of the surviving evidence that Melbourne and his memory are the major witnesses to his early years.

His account encompasses much unhappiness. Often the adult world 'contrived to annoy me so, and had made me cry so much, that I had lost all appetite'.[2] Worse, having discovered that he had an aversion to boiled mutton and rice pudding, he was put on this diet every day. Victoria sympathetically thought this 'a bad system'.[3] Melbourne was clear that 'boys should have a woman about them till they are five or six years old', but, in his case, the woman in question was 'a Swiss Guernsey' nurse, who was 'very ill-tempered'.[4] She did, however, contrive to teach him to read before the age of 4.[5] He was then handed over to a Mr Cuppage, who taught writing and the rudiments of Latin. According to Melbourne, the régime imposed on him was hard, and he recalled looking out of the classroom windows at agricultural labourers at work, and wishing he 'was one of those happy fellows in the field'.[6] In 1785, he was sent to board with the Revd Thomas Marsham in Hatfield, 'to be prepared for school'. Once again, the routine, by his account, was rigorous: 'I was forced to sit before my book until it was conquered. I have often thus remained with very short intervals during the whole day, or a great part of the night.'[7] He was also subjected to beatings, which had 'an amazing effect on me; quickened my understanding'.[8] In sum, Melbourne concluded that 'no boy *really likes* school, but they put a bold face on it'.[9]

This picture is almost certainly overdrawn. Reading between the lines of his own account, a more nuanced description becomes possible. If his masters were severe, they succeeded in inculcating into their young pupil 'a most decided taste for reading'.[10] By the age of 8, Melbourne, somewhat improbably, claimed that he was already reading Voltaire, Robertson, Plutarch, and Cook's Voyages. He knew Shakespeare already, and borrowed Ariosto from a footman.[11] Such cultured servants must have been quite rare. Further, if tutors were tiresome, doting parents always seemed to take the boy's side:

When my father and mother were in the country, their fondness naturally led them to have me with them, once every week; but these interruptions of study were nothing compared to the longer ones which I contrived to procure for myself by feigning sickness, and thus playing upon their anxiety and affection. I soon learned all the symptoms, which were considered the most alarming, pain in the head, weight at the stomach, and had no objection to swallow any potion.[12]

Parental affection, the capacity to dissimilate, and the company of well-loved siblings must be allowed to modify the penny-dreadful account of his childhood that Melbourne gave to Victoria. The most damaging influence in the long term may have been the beatings to which he was subjected by tutors. It set up an interest in flagellation that becomes a marked feature of Melbourne's private life. The theme recurs again and again in correspondence, and it is a point that has to have some prominence in any discussion of his extraordinary marriage.

'At Xmas in the year 1788', Melbourne was sent to Eton, where he remained until the summer of 1796.[13] Again, he liked to suggest to Victoria that 'he didn't like Eton much'.[14] He regaled her with tales of spartan living and physical violence. Breakfast was a roll and butter, with either milk or water to drink. Melbourne chose water. He was to complain that Etonians in the 1830s would be offered a choice of chocolate, tea, and coffee.[15] He had nine guineas a term in pocket money, and this was spent at the pastry cook's, or given as tips to 'Dog-fighters, rabbit catchers, boatmen etc.'.[16] Bullying, the threat of corporal punishment, and bouts of fisticuffs were, he claimed, the ingredients of everyday life. On at least one occasion, Melbourne was forced to fight, but resolved the problem in a way that would characterize his whole approach to life:

He pummelled me amazingly, and I saw I should never beat him; I stood and reflected a little and *thought* to myself and then gave it up. I thought it one of the most prudent acts, but it was reckoned very dastardly. After the first round, if I found I could not lick the fellow, I said, 'come this won't do, I will go away; it is no use standing here to be knocked to pieces.'[17]

Melbourne early acquired a reputation for walking away from anything unpleasant. Sometimes he thought a problem was simply unsolvable. Sometimes, his thin emotional resources could not cope.

In fact, Melbourne spoke of Eton repeatedly and with increasing affection. He and Victoria were to be regular visitors for the 1st of June celebrations. He enjoyed cricket and shooting, and, above all, he acquired a taste for the theatre that equalled that of his brother George. In 1792, he 'joined with several other boys of the same taste with myself in setting up a theatre, and in a room thirty feet long and ten wide we represented Heroes and Heroines, opera, comedy, tragedy and farce'. Enjoyably, there was lots of 'envy, jealousy and all the various passions, which produce intrigue and disunion in other theatres'.[18] Rehearsals and casting were taken seriously,[19] and though the theatre 'gave to those boys, who acted the Women's parts a character of effeminacy, which they very likely might never in after life be able entirely to shake off', it was much to be preferred to the alternative of heavy drinking.[20]

Further, Eton gave him two benefits which he highly prized, a taste for friendship and a love of Classical learning. Melbourne acknowledged that, 'Friendships formed at School are never forgotten. They may be disregarded or violated by the unfeeling or self-interested, as all ties may and will be, but they are never forgotten.'[21] Fellow Etonians of his generation included John Sumner, the future Archbishop of Canterbury, Beau Brummell, and Lord Kinnaird, 'my most intimate friend at school'.[22] As for the Classics, Melbourne was a scholar of note, or, as he modestly put it, 'I had obtained some reputation by my Latin verses.'[23] He also emerged with enough Greek to read the Church Fathers in the original, and to translate Xenophon.[24] At the cost of one or two bruises, Melbourne was a successful and popular schoolboy.

Writing his autobiography in 1812–13, Melbourne candidly admitted that he had left Eton 'after more than seven years of as much enjoyment and satisfaction and as little vexation and discontent, as can fall to the lot of the years of childhood'.[25] Certainly, he became an exemplary old boy, subscribing to building projects and taking trouble with appointments. In 1838, he was content that Dr Keate should be thought of as Provost of Eton, even though he was a notorious Tory, because 'being an Etonian myself, I should be sorry to do anything very contrary to their feelings'.[26] In one thing only did Eton fail. Its Tory predilections made no impression on the family Whiggishness. For his leaving oration in 1796, William Lamb chose to declaim the speech uttered by Strafford on the ingratitude of princes in general and Charles I in particular. Quite possibly, this may have been a covert, Whiggish comment on the persecuting nature of contemporary Pittite legislation.[27]

Interspersed with school terms was the noise and bustle of Melbourne House and that distinctive family circle. There was always a crowd. Even when the Melbournes decamped to the seaside, they so feared the danger of being bored that they took most of London with them. Melbourne recalled that, wherever they were, his father tried 'to make it as much like London as possible'. Rented houses on the coast could become so crowded that William and Frederick were frequently forced to find lodgings nearby. They used 'to live out anywhere'. It was all 'very good fun'.[28] It was also education in a larger sense than Eton could offer. The Melbourne coterie, free-thinking, professionally sceptical, and fast-living, must have provided the perfect contrast to the Latin grammars and bread-and-butter of Eton. One was Whiggish, the other Tory. Melbourne venerated both,[29] and, in his more candid moments, admitted that his childhood had not been so very bad. Indeed, it had been, in every sense of the word, deeply privileged. Melbourne liked to pretend that 'of my childhood I recollect nothing, which even to myself appears worthy of being recorded',[30] but once again he was deliberately throwing dust in the eyes.

Leaving Eton represented a real caesura in Melbourne's life. Verses attributed to him in 1797 suggest a profound awareness that one rite of passage had been negotiated safely, but that another lay immediately ahead:

> A year has pass'd—a year of grief and joy—
> Since first we threw aside the name of boy,
> That name, which in some future hour of gloom,
> We shall with sighs regret we can't resume.
> Unknown this life, unknown Fate's numerous shares,
> We launched into this world, and all its cares;
> Those cares whose pangs, before a year was past,
> I felt and feel, they will not be the last.
> But then we hailed fair freedom's brightening morn,
> And threw aside the yoke we had long borne;
> Exalted in the raptures thought can give,
> And said alone, we then began to live;
> With wanton fancy, painted pleasure's charms,
> Wine's liberal power, and beauty's folding arms,
> Expected joys would spring beneath our feet,
> And never thought of grief we were to meet.
> Ah! soon, too soon is all the truth displayed,
> Too soon appears this scene of light and shade.[31]

Consonant with this mood, Melbourne always liked to claim that, as a young man, he had been hopelessly shy. Indeed, 'there never was a shyer man'.[32] For such a creature, the world of 'light and shade' held fears. Once again, however, Melbourne's memory constructed a pathos that was far removed from historical fact. Facing the adult world was no doubt daunting, but Melbourne was good-looking, well-born, and clever. He could face the future with more confidence than most. In a letter of 1800, he described himself to his mother as 'dancing through life'.[33]

Entering Trinity College, Cambridge, on 17 October 1796, he was not short of intellectual self-confidence. In his manuscript autobiography, written sixteen years later, his Cambridge career is dealt with at length. Candidly, he described himself as leaving school, 'compleatly (sic) conceited, presumptuous and self-confident' with 'a contempt for most of the rest of mankind'. He arrived in Cambridge, firmly believing that he was 'endowed with a practical genius far superior to any of the writers of the present day and likely to become equal to the most admired Authors of former times'.[34] Like other students, he was sometimes drunk, and keen 'to rail at the place and make clumsy attempts at satirising the studies there'. Like other students he went hunting, and fashionably 'affected amours which in fact would have turned me sick with disgust'. These frolics were only interrupted by the contraction, in the summer of 1797, of a severe illness, whose effects were still being felt when the autobiography was written in 1812.[35] Speculation about veneral disease is inevitable, but ultimately profitless, with the want of any corroborating evidence.

Academically, Cambridge was a trial. Melbourne only scraped through examinations, because he fought a losing battle with mathematics. A certain Mr Sanderson had coached him in the subject before he went up, but he 'like many other mathematicians . . . had no power of explaining the grounds and reasons of his own science'.[36] He tried to master the rules of algebra, 'but never understood them well'. As for Euclid, the man was so boring that Melbourne 'relinquished even the design of paying any further attention to the subject'.[37] Instead, he went in for a great deal of undirected reading. Hume, Chesterfield, Sterne, and Rousseau are specifically mentioned. He failed to understand *The Wealth of Nations*, but *La Nouvelle Héloïse* produced such 'sensations of delight and enthusiasm', that he set about writing a novel. Predictably, his declamations in English and Latin were well-received.

In retrospect, Melbourne was unimpressed with his own career as an undergraduate: 'They were very useless years to me . . . but that was not their fault; the time when I was at Cambridge . . . was the time of my life when I attended least to study.'[38] As a highly intelligent man, he should have taken more advantage of the place. Instead, he simply followed the crowd. His

claim, in later life, that he 'never relished the dissipation of a university, altho'
I engaged in it to a certain degree',[39] rings true. By nature, he was a bookish man. The fast living that was deemed to be natural in a young man in
his set was something that had to be superimposed on his intelligence. These
two characteristics of the man then had to come to an accommodation.
Cambridge should have imposed a great discipline on him. Even so, he
retained a residual loyalty to the university, for, when asked to draw a distinction between Cambridge and Oxford, he replied that the former was 'best
for clever people, and the other for people of no talents'.[40]

Since the English universities, in Melbourne's generation, offered so little,
young Whigs were dispatched to Scotland. At the universities of Glasgow and
Edinburgh, the pupils of Adam Smith were teaching at a level that could not
be matched elsewhere. In June 1799, one of the most prominent of these,
John Millar, was asked by the Earl of Lauderdale to take William and
Frederick Lamb on as pupils:

There is a young man who wishes much to reside in your house next winter. He is
the younger son of Lord Melbourne's. He has the reputation and I believe really possesses uncommon talents. He means to go to the English Bar with a view to follow
the law as a profession. He is the only person I have ever yet recommended to you
of whom I think I could with any safety say that you will have real comfort and
satisfaction in having him as a pupil.[41]

Offering your mind to Millar's moulding was a serious business.
Singlemindedness in study was absolutely required. As an earnest of his determination, Lamb attended the London lectures of Sir James Mackintosh on
law,[42] and finally finished reading *The Wealth of Nations* on the journey
north.[43]

John Millar was one of the most remarkable teachers of his day. Totally
devoted to Hume and Smith, he 'believed all knowledge to be found in them'.
His own books, *The Origin of the Distinction of Ranks* and *Historical View of the
English Government*, extended the ideas of these masters, and became standard
Whig texts. Through Millar, Melbourne was exposed to the full glare of the
Scottish Enlightenment. Under Millar's tutelage, Lamb 'entered upon a
course of study and exercise of debate, doubt, contradiction, and examination such as I had never witnessed nor been engaged in before'.[44] As long as
fees were paid in advance,[45] Millar's devotion to the education of his pupils
was total. He was an intellectual empire-builder, who, in the custom of the
day, sought to hand on the maxims of his masters on history, law, and politics to a new generation. His teaching was not so much dialogue as prose-
lytism. He demanded hard work. Frederick Lamb, writing to his mother,
described a day that began at 8 a.m. and that was spent entirely in study;

'There is nothing heard of in this house but study' on week days, while, 'on Sunday we have examinations in Millar's lectures.'[46]

After the diversions of London and Cambridge, the Lamb brothers found the change of pace a little unnerving. It was, for example, tiresome that the women of their circle should be so infected with things academic: 'Ladies here are contaminated with an itch for Philosophy and Learning . . . William quotes poetry to them all day, but I don't think he has made any impression yet.'[47] As for Millar himself, Frederick described him as both a 'stupid, slow, lumbering mathematician' and as 'a little jolly dog and the sharpest fellow I ever saw'.[48] Such attributes are the common coin of student assessments of tutors. Significantly, William Lamb was less equivocal. When speaking of Millar, he was always happy to admit how 'deeply' he was 'impressed and sincerely attached in that Quarter'. When news of Millar's death reached him, he burst into tears.[49]

Of course, in letters home, William played the metropolitan figure in exile, making modish criticisms of Glasgow provincialism. The eating habits of Glaswegians were distressing, and 'from the company and meanness of this place, I do not see much difference in them from the company and manners of any county town'.[50] He warned his mother that his friend, Kinnaird, would need polishing up when he returned to London. There was too a strain of dottiness in the clever men around him. When Millar expressed the hope that Bonaparte might successfully invade England, Melbourne marvelled at just how silly a clever man could be.[51] Lamb concluded that learning was an admirable thing, but it had to be worn lightly, and mixed with liberal quantities of common sense:

No place can be perfect, and the truth is, that the Scotch universities are very much calculated to make them vain, important and pedantic. This is naturally the case where there is a great deal of reading. You cannot have both the advantages of study and of the world together. The way is to let neither of them get too fast a hold of you, and this is done by nothing so well as by frequent changes of place, of pursuit and of companions.[52]

It was a balance which he always took care to maintain.

Melbourne's criticisms of Glasgow were, however, always outweighed by his deep sense of gratitude. As Prime Minister, he was always anxious to offer help to Scots professors and their widows.[53] He believed that Glasgow had knocked a lot of silliness out of him, even if he temporarily became a slave to new orthodoxies. He noted that he 'had entirely lost the conceit and prejudices of Eton and Cambridge, but in their place I had adopted the conceit and prejudices of Scotland and Mr. Millar'.[54] Classical learning for example, which had been so much a part of his early schooling, was swamped by the

mysteries of natural law and political economy. Conversations with Charles
James Fox would restore the Classics to a place in Lamb's mind, but, for the
moment, Millar's pronouncements had no rival. Young men who have little
emotional contact with their fathers often look for other heroes. For a time,
Millar fulfilled this role for Melbourne, conferring on him in the process an
enviable, intellectual legacy.

Lamb's surviving notebooks show him to be a committed and interested
student.[55] Although they sometimes contain remarks on Greek particles, they
are overwhelmingly concerned with the study of law, history, and politics.
Crucially, they are informed by one idea; that progress could be discerned in
the development of human society, and that this wonderful movement was
predicated on the recognition that property-holding was the basis of civil
society. By 1800, this idea was a commonplace among younger Whigs, and
Melbourne accepted it without qualification. It was the stock-in-trade of the
Scots, but, before arriving in Glasgow, Lamb had some of the ground already
prepared. In 1798, he won a prize at Cambridge for his *Essay on the Progressive
Improvement of Mankind*, a work which had the distinction of being quoted in
the House of Commons by Fox himself. In this piece of juvenilia, Lamb
sought to establish a firm chronology of human development. There was first
an Ancient World of rising and falling civilizations, and no guarantees of irre-
versible progress. Then, from the eleventh century onwards, the pattern
changes. As 'knowledge advanced with a slow and timid step from the cells
of the monks', and as more complicated systems of commerce led to interdependence between individual and individual, and between nation and
nation, so man began to go forward. Improvement in spiritual and material
life was everywhere, and 'the creature who has done these things, can do
more'.[56]

Under Millar's direction, these thoughts took on depth and definition.
Now, four major phases of human development come under scrutiny in
Lamb's notes:

1—Hunters and Fishers—Natives of America—Little or no property—small societies—
2 Shepherds—Tartars—Arabs—Ancient Germans—Property in Herds and Flocks—
Society enlarged by greater facility of subsistence—3 Husbandmen—Several tribes on
the southern coast of Africa—in the East Indies—Towns and villages of Greece and
Italy—Gothic nations after their settlement in the Roman empire—These have
Property in Land and subsist in still larger societies from the greater abundance of
food—4 Commercial or polished nations—The inhabitants of modern Europe—
Improvement of arts and manufactures, exchange of commodities—refinement of
manners.[57]

He then investigates these four ages of man under such subheadings as 'Of
Property', 'Marriage', 'Male and Female', and 'Master and Servant'. The

idea of a society in movement was indelibly imprinted on Lamb's mind. In later life, as has been noted in the previous chapter, he came to suspect many aspects of industrial society, but he never challenged the notion that change was inevitable, and that to try to check it was absurd. That, in Whiggish minds, was a Tory nonsense. No one with a Scots education could fail to see civil society as anything but the product of moving history.

In particular, the state of property-holding at each stage of man's development was the factor determining everything else. The possession of property gave man the leisure and education to qualify him for active citizenship. Further, it interested him vitally in the success of the community to which he belonged, and led him to resist all forms of tyranny. There was therefore a direct correlation between the widespread ownership of property and the existence and stability of representative government. Under such headings as 'The advancement of Commerce and Manufactures tends to produce a spirit of independence in the People', Lamb discussed differences in property-holding in primitive and advanced societies. In the former, property is owned communally or by a very few people. The result is authoritarian or oligarchic forms of government. In the latter, property-holding is so widespread that many people demand a voice in politics. Here, representative government is the norm. To use Lamb's words: 'in a rude nation the lower classes of people are entirely dependent upon the higher, in a civilized nation commerce arts and manufactures give every man the providing for himself.'[58] With property, 'independence becomes easy and indeed almost unavoidable'.[59]

If further evidence was required, Lamb only had to look to recent English history. Whig dukes and earls had an assured place in politics by reason of the great property they held. In the seventeenth century, these families had led the fight against the attempts of Charles I and James II to introduce absolutism, quite often at the cost of martyrdom. While Lamb was in Glasgow, Charles James Fox had persuaded the Whig party to secede from Parliament, as a protest at what they believed to be George III's attempts to undermine the constitution.[60] If history showed anything, it showed that most rulers disliked constraint, and that the defence of property drove men to resist them. Lamb's investigations assured him that, over time, property became more extensive and more individually owned. Representative government was therefore more and more secure, with all the civil rights and material benefits that went with it. This, for him, was progress.

None of this was original. The Glasgow student was simply absorbing intelligently what his Scottish mentors had laid down. These ideas were infinitely congenial. They could be called up-to-date, even 'scientific'. They confirmed the prominent role of Whigs in history. They offered them long-term prospects of government. The young Lamb repeated his lessons as though

involved in a new religion. Thirty years later, as Prime Minister, youthful
hopes would be much eroded by age and experience. Opening up politics to
popular involvement looked less attractive. Mass education, mass literacy,
mass anything was not always to Whig taste. Yet, significantly, he teased
reformers, but never vetoed their efforts. He complained endlessly about
reforms of all kinds, but, if pushed to the wall, voted for them. Scotland cast
a long shadow. It left him with the firm idea that change could not be fought.
History was in movement. It might be a matter of joy or regret, but it was a
fact of life. Lamb would be a reformer in at least the limited sense of recognizing that human society never stood still. For the man who was to lead government in the difficult decade of the 1830s, this was an invaluable lesson.

When Lamb left Scotland in May 1801, all his bookish proclivities had
been confirmed. He began the biography of Sheridan that Thomas Moore
was to finish, and, until he took office in 1827, he sometimes contributed to
journals, notably the *Literary Gazette*. Glasgow reinforced his voracious appetite
for reading.[61] When Home Secretary, he asked for books to be sent to him
from the British Museum.[62] As Prime Minister, he not only took great care
about academic appointments, declaring that he would 'sacrifice every thing
else to politics, but I will not sacrifice learning', but also astonished his colleagues with his capacity to keep up with new works. Lord Hatherton, a duti-
ful but not scholarly member of the Cabinet, was thunderstruck by the range
and quality of Melbourne's conversation at Holland House dinners.

I had never before witnessed a greater display of learning on any subject. But what
surprised me still more was his almost universal acquaintance with the literature of
the last six years during which he has been in office—No matter whether profound
or superficial, British, European or American, he seemed to know what was going on
under every press—Deep readers are seldom practical men—few men can find leisure
for contemplation and practical pursuits. But it so happens at the moment that the
two best read men in high life in England are the leaders of the two Houses of Parlt.[63]

Melbourne came late to political office, and was a bookman before he
became a politician. As a result, his judgements had range and perception.
Decisions were not day-to-day matters, but were rather informed by wider
historical and sociological perspectives. This might make him fatalistic, even
passive, in the face of events, but it would never lead him to be precipitate.

Nothing that he had imbibed in Glasgow conflicted with the Lamb family's
Foxite loyalties. If the central theme in that creed was that Whigs continually
had to restrain would-be tyrannical kings, Glasgow history simply put that
battle into a wider, chronological context. Lamb was Foxite before coming
into the presence of the great man himself. He claimed that in 1784, at the
age of 5, he had taken part in Fox's famous victory in Westminster, 'having

a fox's brush in my cap, for Mr. Fox'.[64] In the same election, Lady Melbourne was one of a band of Whig women, who splendidly, but notoriously, traded kisses for votes. While at Cambridge, to make public his support for Fox, Melbourne dressed his hair in a style that was denominated republican. Clipped 'quite short', the hair was unpowdered.[65] His father refused to follow suit.[66] He was deeply flattered when, in 1798, Fox used quotations from his undergraduate essay on progress in a speech. In return, he attacked Fox's detractors from *The Anti-Jacobin*:

> With jaundiced eyes the noblest Partiot scan;
> Proceed—be more opprobrious if you can;
> Proceed—be more abusive ev'ry hour!—
> To be more stupid is beyond your power.[67]

He scribbled eulogies of Fox in Beau Brummell's album,[68] and was proud to follow a family friend 'of whose opinions and character I had always professed myself a warm admirer'.[69]

Fox clearly thought Lamb a young man worth cultivating. In 1799, Lamb was invited to spend some time at St Anne's Hill, Fox's home in Surrey. The young man was captivated:

There I witnessed for the first time, what I had often opportunities of seeing and enjoying afterwards those rare endowments and those irresistible attractions, which made that man the idol of every younger person who approached him, and bound his friends to him by ties, which neither Poverty nor the influence of relations, nor the frowns of Power nor long exclusion from the great objects of pursuit, nor hopes repeatedly disappointed had any strength to dissolve.[70]

For a time, Lamb was Foxite not only in politics but in everything. The study of history was to be preferred to that of poetry, which was 'more for Boys and Women'.[71] He carried Fox's prejudices against Wordsworth and Scott into old age, loathing the latter's 'sneaking, flattering, sycophantish manner'.[72] Glasgow education and Foxite preference were as one in being unsympathetic to writers, 'who regret the simplicity of the state of nature their own imaginations have formed'.[73]

In politics, Lamb intoned the Foxite creed to whomever would listen. He argued that in 1800, England and Europe were not threatened by France and its Revolution, democratic whistlings, and murderous equality. Rather, incompetent and malevolent monarchs were responsible for every disaster. At home, George III was both incompetent and malicious. The American colonies had been lost because policy had been based 'neither upon prescription nor common sense'.[74] The King was compared unfavourably to Washington. Undaunted, George then turned his efforts to undermining parliamentary government. Fox had nobly resisted this project, but was now in sad exile at St Anne's Hill. George III had so weakened the representative system, which had been at the heart of England's prominence in the eighteenth century, that the country was increasingly of little international significance.[75]

Worse, he believed that rulers had diverted the French Revolution into violence. Louis XVI refused to be a constitutional monarch. Catherine the Great, together with sundry kings and princes, had come together to coerce the French. Naturally, the French had had to defend themselves and the result was the Terror. Left to themselves, the French might have found their way to constitutional government. Violence was not inherent in the Revolution from the start, but was provoked by kings. Lamb's lecture notes on the Revolution were impeccably Foxite. This event was 'the most terrible and awful change that . . . has ever been witnessed by Man . . . The man who fears and hates the worst of the French revolution cannot but admire the grandeur of the nation . . . what can we do but admire the Energy of a People who have maintained a now successful war at times against a combination of the greatest powers of Europe.'[76] Undergraduate letters to his mother record joy at French successes,[77] and sadness at allied triumphs.[78] At Cambridge, he wrote a Latin ode to Bonaparte, some months before his hero became Consul.[79]

Following the Foxite canon, Lamb always linked English and European politics. He was outraged when, in January 1800, the English government rejected peace overtures from France. Their motives in doing so were transparent. Pitt and his friends wished to use the wartime emergency as an excuse to smother civil liberty. England 'was fixed in Bigotry and prejudice'.[80] The political system had become so corrupt, that Fox was quite right to secede from Parliament. It was the only way of advertising the demise of that institution. The English were 'panic struck'. They were so entirely fearful, that they were unwilling to consider any Whiggish constraints on the exercise of power. The results would be disastrous: 'If they [the Ministry] hold together and resolve to stand out to the last it is impossible to conceal from oneself that nothing can ever overthrow them, but the greatest and most important event, such as the failure of the Funds, or the rising of the mass of the People.'[81]

Within a very few years, many of these views would change. Statements of a Foxite character become more shaded with qualification and nuance. Young men's views are amended by experience and responsibility. For the moment, however, William Lamb, returning to London from Glasgow, could afford to be confrontational. His family upbringing bred in him a Whig suspicion of kings, even if they were near-relations of sorts. Tutorials with Fox confirmed these notions. In addition, the efforts of Millar had allowed Lamb to see the battle between king and parliamentarian as part of a much greater sociological movement over time, as property and its owners made increasing claims to government. Foxite commonplace and Glasgow learning fused. William Lamb had a formidable, intellectual armoury, with which to face adult life in London.

First and foremost, there was the question of finding a career. Younger sons like William Lamb had to shift for themselves. Even so, his inertia was such that a year's sabbatical seemed in order. For much of 1801–2, he did nothing. There was time for an amorous adventure, characteristically remembered with himself passively being taken up by a woman of determined personality:

I had fallen into the power of a Lady of no very strict virtue and was entirely devoted to her. Morning, noon and night I was at her house or pining after the moment when I should be there. All my hours were passed in attending upon her, in flattering her vanity by exposing myself in public with her, in gratifying her fancies and obeying her caprices.

Soon, the lady began to be emotionally and financially demanding, and Lamb thought himself 'very fortunate to have escaped with only the loss and abuse of a few months'.[82] The identity of this woman is unknown, but it may or may not be thought significant that the notorious Harriette Wilson claimed that both William's brother and father had been numbered among her lovers. Whoever she was, Lamb was sufficiently taken to inscribe adolescent verses in Beau Brummell's commonplace book:

> But oh! those beauties of my fair,
> Which I alone must e'er reveal;
> Come Painter, with the strictest care
> Beneath the purple robe reveal.
>
> Yet sometimes let the skin of snow
> Through the thin garment's covering shine
> And faintly tell what beauties glow
> Unseen by any eyes but mine.

This was, as Lamb himself recalled, 'a very awkward' age.[83] In the summer of 1802, he fled to Scotland with Kinnaird. Theatricals and pencil-and-paper games at Inverary Castle were less demanding.

This incident is not of itself important, but it sets a pattern which was often to be repeated. William Lamb's relations with women were governed by certain rules. Sexually abstemious compared to his father or brother Frederick, he liked the company of amusing women of determined character. He liked to be diverted. As his mother and sister knew well, William's emotions were on offer to any woman who would direct them. In this area, as in most others, he had no will of his own. Further, Lamb was quite unable to cope with difficulties. Women were never to be an embarrassment or troublesome. If they became so, his inclination was always to turn away, even if this involved considerable cruelty to those for whom he had expressed great affection. His flight to Scotland in 1802 becomes a metaphor for his whole life. In private life, Lamb wanted his emotions to be led down pleasant paths. He resented trouble. Outside his family circle, none of the women who touched his mind or heart were to be happier for the experience.

When the danger had passed, Lamb finally had to think of a career. With characteristic passivity, he allowed Egremont to push him into the law. In November 1802, he began to study in the Special Pleaders office, where he was taught his trade by a Mr Roberts. In the Michaelmas Term of 1804, he was called to the Bar, with Chambers at No. 4, Pump Court. Early in January 1805, he went on circuit in Lancashire with James Scarlett, the future chief baron of the exchequer. Allegedly, a solicitor in Salford sent him a guinea brief.[84] It is the only indication that he ever secured any financial or other benefit from his new calling. From beginning to end, the study and practice of law was 'a thraldom'. Having been excited by Glasgow's ability to open up the secrets of history and philosophy, he was now confronted by 'arbitrary rules, technical forms of action, processes of various sorts which, as it was impossible to unravel, so it was necessary to learn'.[85] The law was for minds that were narrower and more given to detail than William Lamb's.

Life for the reluctant law student between 1802 and 1805 was only made tolerable by mixing study with the full enjoyment of his social birthright. The doors of the great Whig salons were open to him as a matter of course. The fact that he was good-looking and clever merely eased the process further. As a result, Lamb decided to 'bless the admiring world with his presence a little oftener'.[86] Two houses in particular defined his manners. Devonshire House was presided over by Georgiana, fifth Duchess of Devonshire, one of the most remarkable women of her day. She was the centre of a coterie of relations and dependants that kept the scandal-sheets filled for two decades. She was the confidante of Lamb's mother and the aunt of his future wife. Reputedly, the mistress of Grey, Fox, and the Prince of Wales, her circle was deeply compromised in the public mind, but its tone was much to Lamb's taste. He later confessed to Victoria that, though the dissipation of the Devonshire House set had grown in the telling, he 'used to go there every night, and very pleasant and gay it was'.[87]

Equally compromising and equally diverting were the dinner parties at Holland House. The third Baron Holland was the nephew of Charles James Fox. His wife, Elizabeth, denied access to much of society by reason of being divorced, decided to demand that society come to her. Her temperament was so imperious that the project worked. From 1797 to 1840, Holland House was the foremost salon in London, peddling literary and political gossip, and patronizing Whig intellectual life. It became a second home for William Lamb, except for those years when he, like everyone else, quarrelled with Lady Holland. Such contests hurt all participants deeply but were always resolved. Like so many other women of character, Lady Holland saw William Lamb as someone in need of direction. Even when he was Prime Minister, she was inclined to treat him as her protégé.

The association began in February 1799. Lady Holland had been so impressed by Lamb's translation of twenty-eight lines of Juvenal, that she decided to recognize this 'rising star'[88] by inviting him to dinner. On that occasion, she found him 'supercilious',[89] but later decided that he was 'very clever and pleasing, and will improve when he gets out of his love for singularity'.[90] When Lamb lay ill in Lincoln's Inn, Lady Holland condescended to visit.[91] This was a mark of real distinction, for she hated illness and preferred London to come to her. Quite simply, as she admitted to Lady Melbourne, she had 'a *Penchant* for *young men*', who she wished to 'polish', and William Lamb was now her 'friend'.[92] There would be periods of estrangement, but the Hollands were to be two of Melbourne's closest friends throughout their lives. In retrospect, Melbourne looked back on these years with some 'remorse' for having passed so much time 'in idleness, in sleeping and sauntering',[93] but remorse never ran deep in him. As he confided to his commonplace book, he 'never can feel repentance or regret for the hours which I have passed in pursuits which really amused me at the time, although they were pursuits of folly or vice'.[94] The sentimental education acquired at Devonshire House and Holland House had been too formative and too much fun to deny.

Unlike many other young men of talent who found themselves swimming in these waters, Lamb had little need of guides and mentors. By birth and education, he had been programmed for performance in Whig salons. Yet, he was so psychologically deferential that a strong personality could always have an influence. In these bachelor years in London, 'Monk' Lewis and Beau Brummell both exerted this power. Matthew Lewis and William Lamb met in 1799. Lewis was the elder by four years and already an established novelist, having published *The Monk* in 1795, from which he took his nickname. A deep and sudden friendship was formed. In the spring and summer of 1799, Lamb was never out of Lewis's company, whether in London or, theatrically, in a cottage near Leatherhead, where both men retired 'from the world and all its mockeries' to study philosophy.[95] Briefly, an intense association ensued. Lewis was anxious to show off his protégé, telling Sir Walter

Scott that Lamb was 'in truth and without partiality . . . a very superior style of young man'.[96] In return, Lamb was grateful for Lewis's criticisms of his first attempts at poetry, though they initiated a salutory deflation in self-esteem: 'he pointed out so many faults that my faith in my own extraordinary genius, altho' not overcome, was considerably staggered.'[97]

Then, quite suddenly, in January or February 1800, the friendship was broken off, with Lamb complaining that Lewis was 'always upon the strain'.[98] Some sort of emotional involvement had been ruptured. Lamb darkly referred to a female friend of Lewis's, 'who will make him shed more tears and look more doleful in assembly rooms than ever I did'.[99] Contact was maintained, but it was of a startlingly one-sided nature. By 1810, the Lambs found Lewis 'greatly boring',[100] whereas Lewis continued to sing William's praises to Lady Melbourne: '*you know*, it would be impossible for William not to do everything better than any one else . . . I have some difficulty not to be of the above opinion myself.'[101] When Lewis died unmarried in 1818, he left 'a very odd will'.[102] William Lamb was left his entire library, but he 'cares so little for the Compliment paid Him that he is actually going to *sell* it, tho' the books are allowed by every one to be a most valuable Collection valued at 3,000'.[103] Speculation about the relationship between Lamb and Lewis cannot be taken far. The surviving evidence simply will not sustain it. That there was a homoerotic element in the friendship, at least on Lewis's part, is possible. Certainly the association developed quickly and cooled in a sudden argument. Unfortunately, it is not clear how far Lamb himself was touched by it, though his reported determination to dispose of Lewis's bequest might suggest a wish to expunge this episode from his life.

There were no such complications in his friendship with Brummell. They had been contemporaries at Eton, and now the carelessly contrived dandy-ism that was Brummell's kingdom greatly appealed to the young William Lamb. Throughout his life, he was a fastidious man. In youth, 'no one ever *happened* to have coats that fitted better'.[104] As Prime Minister, he always took half-an-hour to dress for dinner, because 'a man can't be dressed properly in less.'[105] By the same token, he always put a little eau-de-cologne on his pocket handkerchief, and liked 'perfume in hot weather and when he is fatigued'.[106] None of this was very remarkable behaviour for men of his generation, but Queen Victoria, who was an indefatigable recorder of Melbourne's personal habits, was amused to note instances where fastidiousness slipped into vanity. He dyed his hair 'with a little orange flower water' and a pomatum called 'Arnold's Imperial Cream'. The result was to make his hair 'so black', that the Queen was inclined to be critical.[107] Eyebrows were equally a matter of concern: 'Of Lord M's eyebrows, and whether he ever cut them; "I don't meddle with them," he said, "I'm afraid to cut them, it makes them ropy;

one ought to comb them" (as I said they got into his eyes), "somebody gave me a small comb for them once, but I've lost it." '[108] It was not unusual for men to use perfume and cosmetics extensively, but Lamb remained so loyal to the rules of Brummell's fastidiousness, that it might have become a factor of importance in his private life. He would become the husband of a woman who would slip away into dirt and drunkenness, and the father of a mentally retarded son. Temperamentally, Lamb was ill-equipped to deal with either situation.

At the beginning of 1805, William Lamb was the perfectly moulded product of Whig society. From Fox himself, he had been lectured on the wickedness of kings and the Whigs' historical defence of representative government. In Scotland, he had absorbed the very latest ideas about progress and the development of civil society. Eton had given him his Classical credentials. Good-looking, well-dressed and quick-witted, he had shown he could survive in the jungles of the great salons, even if a dependent spirit was always looking for direction. He had served his apprenticeship with women and may possibly have had a brush with homoerotic feelings. It added up to a formidable inheritance. Now, at the age of 26, only one thing was lacking, namely an assured income. Without it, he could not seriously consider marriage or any large role in public life. The single briefs offered to young barristers suggested a bleak future.

In January 1805, however, William Lamb's elder brother, Peniston, died. William Lamb was now heir to the Melbourne title and estates. The situation had been transformed. Now a seat in Parliament would be his for the asking. Having already acquired the reputation of being a young man of promise, he could look forward to a political career without limits. No one had ever been more clearly groomed for public success. The seat in Parliament was promptly secured, but he would have to wait twenty years before there was any prospect of office. He would be 48 before he became the member of a government. The reason for this serious delay was less that his political views were unacceptable, than that he had decided to marry Lady Caroline Ponsonby. Politics and virtually everything else was put on hold, as he attempted to cope with a marriage that became the determinant factor in his future career and personality. It was a trauma, whose scars he would carry for the rest of his life.

4

Marriage and Catastrophe, 1805–1816

THE marriage between William Lamb and Caroline Ponsonby was one of the most extraordinary unions of the whole nineteenth century. It was a catastrophe for both parties. It generated so much heat and noise that it became the stock-in trade of novelists. Benjamin Disraeli, Mrs Humphry Ward, Bulwer Lytton and his wife, and Thomas Lister were just a few of the writers, who allegedly drew on the Lamb marriage for copy.[1] Notoriously, Lady Caroline Lamb did the same thing. The pain of this marriage was never private, therefore. Over and over again, Melbourne was confronted by its failure. Newspaper owners and booksellers ensured that his marriage was always in the public eye. For a man of fastidious sensitivities, such publicity was odious. In response to it, his instinct was to retire from public view. Any thought of a career in politics had to be abandoned. Lamb simply withdrew into himself. When he once again became a public figure, after Caroline's death, he was a changed man. A carapace of cynicism shielded him from any further emotional commitments. He was in many ways damaged beyond repair.

As a young man, Lamb filled his commonplace book with fashionable doubts about marriage. There was the problem that 'two minds, however congenial they may be, or however submissive the one may be to the other, can never act as one'. It put intolerable restraints on personal inclinations: 'By taking a wife a man certainly adds one to the list of those who have a right to interfere with and advise him, and he runs the risk of putting in his own way another very strong and perhaps insuperable obstacle to his acting according to his own opinions and inclinations.' Above all, women were difficult to cope with: 'A woman is exactly like a mare; very good to ride, but apt to kick in harness.'[2] Drawing-room witticisms have their place, but probably a more reliable guide to Melbourne's views is provided by student lecture notes, when an altogether different tone is struck. Marriage is here regarded with total seriousness: 'Marriage is dissolved either by Death, or by Divorce—with regard to the latter, small discords will scarcely be reckoned a sufficient cause for dissolving a union so serious as marriage . . . In luxurious ages divorces become very common. The Passions of sex are irritated and stimulated to a degree of violence which breaks through all natural affection.'[3] This last remark could be seen as prophetic in terms of his own marriage. It is a matter to which Sydney Smith's joking accusation that William Lamb was in reality a serious and thoughtful man could easily be applied.

With terrible inevitability, William Lamb's marriage was a family affair. Frequenting the Devonshire House circle, he could not avoid the company of Ponsonbys as well as Cavendishes (see Fig. 4). It was a House full of eligible girls, though, oddly, according to one source, it may have been his future mother-in-law, Lady Bessborough, who first attracted his attention. The story has some plausibility, in that she had a proven reputation for starting *affaires* with much younger men.[4] When Lamb proposed to her daughter, Lady Bessborough described him as 'her natural son'.[5] Odd too are the discrepancies in the accounts of when William and Caroline first met. According to one, they met at Devonshire House in 1800, when Lamb immediately announced that 'of all the Devonshire House girls, that is the one for me'.[6] According to another, Caroline had come to love William before actually meeting him, simply through reading his poetry, sentiments that were confirmed when she finally saw him for the first time in 1797 or 1798. She was then 12 or 13.[7] The truth may have been a little more prosaic. In 1801, for example, Caroline noted that Lamb was 'not amiable' and 'seemed as if he had drunk more than was quite necessary'.[8] In fact, both of them indulged the theatrical possibilities of their situation.

As courtship began in earnest, it was noisy, eye-catching, and a little unreal. 'There was an extraordinary flirtation between William Lamb and Caro Ponsonby, and they seem, I hear, mutually captivated. When the rest were at games, etc., William was in a corner, reading and explaining Poetry to Car., and in the morning, reading tales of wonder together on the *tither-tother*.' According to the same report, she 'roared' and was 'the oddest compound of sentiment and oddity' and he was grown 'very vociferous and boisterous'.[9] There was just a suggestion of a false note in their behaviour.

There was no harm in any of this, because William's poverty put marriage out of the question. Then, in January 1805, Peniston Lamb died. William proposed by letter in May, and waited 'with cold hands' for a reply.[10] Lady Bessborough gave him the news of her daughter's acceptance behind a box in Drury Lane Theatre, 'whereupon he said "thank Heaven!" and so saying, threw his arms around me, and kiss'd me'.[11] Family congratulations poured in. Duncannon wrote to say that 'nobody can be more happy' to hear the news than himself.[12] The Prince of Wales pronounced himself well-pleased,[13] and Lady Melbourne informed her Derbyshire agent that the whole family were 'extremely happy'.[14] Interestingly, other people thought the engagement was yet more play-acting. Lord Carlisle thought it one of the best jokes of the season, and William himself told his fiancée: 'the surprize is universal as nobody had seen anything of it in the World, and they look upon you as only 5 years old.'[15] Significantly too, Lady Bessborough had doubts. She suspected Lamb levity. Somewhat hypocritically, she worried about Lamb morals. Above all, she was concerned about the effect of these events on Caroline's health. In the end, she suppressed her misgivings, taking refuge instead in one of Lamb's throwaway remarks: 'People shouldn't trouble themselves about why they are loved.'[16]

My poor Caroline's fate is probably deciding for ever. I have long foreseen and endeavour'd to avoid what has just happen'd—W. Lamb's proposing for her . . . but . . . she has preferr'd him from childhood, and now is so much in love with him that before his speaking I dreaded its affecting her health . . . his letter is beautiful— amongst other things, he tells her: 'I have lov'd you for four years, lov'd you deeply, dearly, faithfully—so faithfully that my love has withstood my firm determination to conquer it when honour forbad my declaring myself—has withstood all that absence, variety of objects, my own endeavours to seek and like others, or to occupy my mind with fix'd attention to my profession, could do to shake it.'[17]

They were married on 3 June 1805 at Lord Bessborough's house in Cavendish Square,[18] by 'a drunken old clergyman', called Mr Preedy.[19] Once again, histrionics were in evidence. After the ceremony, Caroline had to be told that 'W.L. would think it unkind if she was unwilling to go with him'.[20] It was alleged that she had to be carried to the waiting carriage by force.[21] Two days later, William reported that, though Caroline was still 'nervous and shy', she was now behaving 'like an angel'. Significantly, he also voiced the opinion that her mother should not visit her until she was more composed. This may have been prudent. Lady Bessborough thought her daughter looked 'well, but so unlike a *wife*, it is much more like a School Girl'.[22]

In retrospect, both William and Caroline insisted that they had very much wished to marry, and that they had been moved by the deepest affection. He told the young Victoria that, although he considered that he had married young, 'you don't marry out of reason, you marry because you fall in love'.[23] Equally, Caroline protested that she 'had *married for love* and love the most romantic and ardent—my husband and I were so fond of each other that false as I too soon proved he never would part with me'.[24] However, it may or may not be significant that in her novel, *Ada Reis*, the heroine is so 'per-secuted' by the addresses of 'her kinsman Giullano, she had the weakness to give him her hand in marriage'.[25] More important than these protestations were the reactions of the Lamb family. None of them believed that William had been a willing participant in the marriage. His sister, Emily, bluntly told

Victoria that 'it was most unfortunate that Lord M ever married her, and that *she* in fact married him'.[26] A Lyttelton cousin was equally clear that the affection only flowed one way. Caroline was 'amazingly in love'. William, when told of it, merely acted 'the gentleman's part' and married her 'from a point of honour'.[27] Lord Egremont furiously accused Lady Melbourne of failing in her duty of protecting 'poor William' from the consequences of his own lack of will:

it really is afflicting to see him chained to that nasty infamous mad woman . . . for it not only depresses him in his own estimation and exertions but it lowers his character in the world to see him submitting patiently to be the talk of the town for such a little detestable weasel when it is well known that with the least attention sufficient proof might have been had last spring to emancipate him from her for ever and I really thought that you and Ld M. and George and Ld and Ly Cowper and all the rational brains of the Family ought to join in stating it to him fully and strongly and so put an end to that foolish reserve of his which has hitherto been her preservation . . . I hope you will not sacrifice your son to any regard for that affected old Baggage the mother of the Monster. I am sure you have done enough in letting or rather *making* . . . him take such an incumbrance off her hands.[28]

The central thrust of this letter was misdirected. Relations between Lady Melbourne and Lady Bessborough were far too cool, for the one to be doing favours for the other. Lady Bessborough referred to her new relation as 'The Thorn'.[29] What is striking about Egremont's remarks is that he, like so many others, denied that William had knowingly married, as an act of will. Despite William's protestations to the contrary, it is a judgement that was much in the mind of contemporaries as the story of the marriage unfolded.

Between June 1805 and January 1806, there was a harmony of sorts. Caroline claimed that she had married 'not a Man but an Angel—take from him his beauty (which by the by increases every day) his being the cleverest and most sensible of all men and yet I say if you look all over the world you will never find his fellow—he is kinder more gentle more soothing more indulgent talks nonsense better and coaxes me more than a woman could and with all that he is in short perfection'.[30] There was only the occasional qualification of happiness reported in letters: 'You told me the happiest time in your life was three weeks after being married. I am not quite arrived at that period but am much contented with my present state and yet I cannot say I have never felt happier.'[31] An unexceptional routine of walking and reading seemed to suit both parties, and, under its benign influence William believed his wife to be 'growing quite good'.[32] Caroline was allegedly finding favour with her Melbourne parents-in-law,[33] and for Caro George, it was difficult to express 'how delightfully Caro and William are going on, it is perfection in every way'.[34]

Optimistic prophecies seemed to be fulfilled when Caroline almost immediately became pregnant, though the naïvety displayed on this occasion was
startling. Caroline had to ask Georgiana Morpeth what the symptoms of
pregnancy actually were, and whether 'it is bad for you to *sleep* with your husband at the time in the most significant sense of the word', even though she
still found him 'very beautiful'.[35] The news hugely pleased Lamb, who 'loves
her *much* better than ever, and they are if possible more like lovers even than
before their marriage'.[36] Tragically, the child was born prematurely and died
on 30 January 1806. It was a cruel 'disappointment',[37] and attempts to accept
the loss philosophically had a hollow ring.[38] A further miscarriage in 1809[39]
and the birth of a mentally retarded son in 1807 added misery to disappointment. One can only speculate about the impact of such a series of
tragedies on a psychology as fragile as Caroline Lamb's. Her later practice of
'adopting' children almost in the street may well have had its roots in a sense
of failed motherhood.

Even in this first six months, however, the Lamb marriage was a source of
unease to some of their more sceptical relations. Harriet Cavendish detected
a possessiveness in Caroline that boded ill.[40] She was 'too exigeante and with
so good a husband might spare herself the trouble'. She demanded his presence at all times, and became agitated if he left her briefly to use the lava-
tory.[41] The same source reported a violent quarrel in October 1805, which
led Caroline to flee to Devonshire House. There she 'covered herself with all
my aunt's Trinkets; rouged herself up to the eyes, sent home her wedding
ring and went with us to the play'.[42] Even at this early stage, to be able to
report that the Lambs were 'at peace' was 'contrary to custom'.[43] It became
a matter to boast of for Caroline that 'Wm and I have had no quarrel of any
consequence since I fancied myself with child.'[44] She protested, no doubt sincerely, that she wished to be a good wife, but she describes this undertaking
rather in the manner of an actress learning a role. The theatricality of the
Lamb marriage, noted at the outset, seemed to become more and more pronounced. On one level, William and Caroline Lamb played at being man and
wife.

Even if the Lambs had been more balanced, the marriage was bedevilled
by other factors. Quite apart from Caroline's highly strung nature, there were
relatives who were destructively hostile. The Melbourne clan never liked
William's new wife and made the fact plain. Equally, the Devonshires were
so emotionally involved themselves with both William and Caroline, that
their well-intentioned interventions usually misfired. Money troubles were
endless, and the young couple was financially dependent on Lord
Melbourne's largesse. Finally, their failure to produce healthy children
sharply divided them. This combination of circumstances would have tested

minds that were stronger than Caroline's and characters that were less passive than William's. It was an unenviable inheritance, and its exact nature must be set out before any judgement is passed on the notorious public behaviour of Caroline Lamb. The escapades that shocked and delighted London society probably resulted from a marriage that had little chance of success.

First and foremost, the Lamb family closed ranks against Caroline. William's brothers and sister could do nothing but sneer.[45] As Caroline observed, 'these Lambs are the best of Masters. They can teach everything but not to love them.'[46] Worse, Lady Melbourne saw no reason to give up the direction of her son's life. She became the regulator or umpire of the marriage. It was she who lectured Caroline against 'laxity' that 'not only compromises her own honour and character but also that of her husband—but you seek only to please yourself'.[47] A pattern of reprimand and apology established itself. It must, however, have been galling to accept moral direction from someone of Lady Melbourne's reputation. Not surprisingly, Caroline often fled Lamb family gatherings, 'by escaping too often to her own room'.[48] It became one of her standard defences that she had been debauched by contact with the Lamb world: 'Oh those Lambs how they do enlighten one's mind.'[49] She never breached the Lamb sense of exclusiveness, and her husband belonged to a family circle which she could not enter.

In moments of stress, Caroline began to develop the habit of fleeing back to the protection of her mother, who was unflatteringly described by Byron as 'the hack whore of the last half century'.[50] The Lambs found this behaviour absurd: 'L\ B. does Caro a great deal of harm by her unlimited indulgence, and yielding to every whim. Her passions ought to be treated like all other nervous disorders which require scolding, or at least a firm decided manner, but both her and William indulge her till she is naughty.'[51] As usual, William, who had always admired Lady Bessborough, not only could not find the energy to remonstrate about her indulgence of his wife, but rather encouraged it. Her death in 1821 was deeply felt by both daughter and son-in-law.[52] As Lady Melbourne had lectured, so Lady Bessborough had consoled. After her death, Caroline looked to her brothers for the same protection. It would be a role which Duncannon would play with reluctance and William Ponsonby with uncritical vigour.

If Melbourne–Bessborough relations were strained, the Devonshire clan presented even greater problems. As a child, Caroline had shared a nursery with her Cavendish cousins; William, Marquess of Hartington and later 6th Duke of Devonshire, Georgiana, later Countess of Carlisle, and Harriet, who married Granville Leveson Gower. Georgiana became her principal confidante and correspondent, which is odd because, one month after her marriage, Caroline confessed that William Lamb had loved her cousin before herself, and probably more so: 'he does not scruple to say he loved you very sincerely. How after that confession you ever happened to chuse another I cannot pretend to guess.'[53] On another occasion, Caroline wrote: 'seriously you do not know my Dear Dear G how very much I love you and my husband I fancy would confess as much if he dared but that is a sore subject with him.'[54] This potentially embarrassing situation was compounded by Caroline's openly expressed affection for Hartington. Just two weeks after marrying, Caroline Lamb penned an extraordinary poem, now to be found among the Chatsworth manuscripts:

> The wand was broke her elves dismiss'd
> The Deamons (sic) yell'd—the serpents hist
> The skies were black the thunder round
> When sad Titania left her lord
> And thus in plaints both loud and long
> To stones address'd her mournful song.
> To Oberon a long adieu . . .
> To mortal scenes of deeper weight
> My steps alas are doomed by fate
> and all the ills that wait on life
> attend me since another's wife . . .
> Thus spoke Titania then she sigh'd
> Doomed to become a mortal bride
> What since befel her no one knows
> but certain 'tis overwhelmed with woes
> she deeply mourns her broken vows.[55]

There can be little doubt that she was casting herself as Titania and Hartington as Oberon. It is a sombre production for a bride of eighteen days.

Over the next twenty years, her affection for and dependence on Hartington is confirmed in prose and more poetry. She endlessly 'flummeried up a certain young Marquis'.[56] He was assured that she had 'ever loved' him, and that her 'heart had . . . been yours even from your childhood'.[57] In verse, he was reminded that, 'Thy first thy earliest love was mine'.[58] Her missives began with such phrases as 'most delectable', and were signed by a bewildering series of noms de plume; 'William Rufus Rex', 'Sophia Heathcote', and 'Molly Bradley'. In talking of her husband to her cousin, she often used the term 'my Black William'.[59] Hartington would be directly involved in the Lamb marriage on a number of occasions. His company and correspondence always had a 'soothing'[60] effect on Caroline. Unfortunately, William Lamb resented the relationship. Caroline protested to Georgiana that it was unfair of her husband to question her right to 'talk to a man as he talked to you'.[61]

The Lambs had become thoroughly enmeshed in the tangled emotions of the Devonshire House set. Both of them, from the very outset of their marriage, were acutely aware that they might have married each other as a second-best option. Deeper emotional involvement should have led them to make other choices. It was an uncomfortable situation.

Equally unpleasant was an endless shortage of money. On his marriage, Lamb was allowed £1,800 a year, and Lady Caroline pin money of £400 a year.[62] On this they either could not or would not afford an establishment of their own. They were forced to live at Melbourne House and Brocket, where relations with the first viscount were mercurial. Sometimes, Caroline was 'really useful and attentive' to him.[63] Sometimes, the quarrelling was intense. On one occasion, she sent her father-in-law 'a shocking letter, and said she hoped his deathbed would be one of agony—he enclosed it to William, who with his usual infatuation took her part'.[64] The old man seemed torn between allowing the Lambs enough to live on, and having them as house guests, between avarice and convenience. In 1819, he complained so much of 'Lady C's violence' and of her 'breaking some more Heads with Candlesticks', that he determined to raise their allowance to 5,000 a year 'as the means of getting rid of this nuisance'.[65] In his view, Caroline exercised a 'despotic and grinding authority' over his son, 'without his making any effort to liberate himself from it'.[66]

There is some question, however, about whether this new money was actually forthcoming. William Lamb continued to fret about his financial position. In 1824 Brocket was let to a Sir William Rumbold.[67] The crashing of banks in 1825 terrified him.[68] He attempted to bridle Caroline's total disregard for expenditure but largely failed. Disputes about money punctuated the marriage. She turned his worries into parody. In April 1823, for example, Princess Lieven found her

planted on the pavement, on horseback, parlaying with a cheesemonger. I knew that, that very morning, in a fit of temper, she had broken two hundred pounds worth of glass and crockery. Repentance had been immediate. She had promised her husband not to break anything else, to cut down her expenses and to busy herself with her household; and, as a preliminary expiation of her sins, she was going round the shops herself to enquire the price of groceries. 'Par l'odeur alléchée', she was beginning with the cheese.[69]

Lamb himself evolved rules to keep creditors happy that would have done service to Alfred Jingle. It was, for example, always better to pay something to four or five tradesmen than to satisfy one completely. All of these men might then extend credit a little longer. These tactics worked to some degree, but, according to an early biographer, Lamb was once served a writ for debt

by Francis Place, the future Radical politician, who was then his tailor.[70]
Clearly, neither William nor Caroline were good at dealing with money. An
income, which other couples might have found handsome, left them complaining of poverty. Not surprisingly, when there was a question of the marriage ending in a judicial separation, the financial aspects of such a rupture
would be particularly thorny.

Emotional and financial problems were compounded by terrible sadnesses
about children. Babies died in 1806 and 1809. The only one to survive was
Augustus, born on 29 August 1807. William reported the birth rather clinically: 'Caroline was brought to bed about an hour ago of a very large boy
. . . for so small a woman, which quality of the child made the labour very
hard and painful, tho' it was very short lasting.'[71] Initially, the baby was the
reason for rejoicing. As her sister-in-law noted, Caroline 'deserves her happiness by enjoying it so fully. She exclaims whilst she is sucking, I am too
happy, this is perfect joy, and every thing every body does is perfection.'[72] It
was a source of pleasure, and no doubt of relief, that the boy looked so much
like William:

> His little eyes like William's shine—
> How then is great my joy,
> For while I call this darling mine,
> I see 'tis William's boy.[73]

He had 'the Lamb manners', namely 'a satirical smile and seems on the point
of rubbing his hands and swearing at one',[74] with the result that the family
were for once prepared to give Caroline the benefit of the doubt.[75] It seemed
that the child would guarantee the marriage. It was an image that Caroline
liked to project. In 1811, she described her family situation in terms of total
contentment: 'Wm Lamb chases the fox and pheasants—I ride a great deal
and see much of the neighbours—Augustus is my bosom Friend speaks
French and reads courament (sic) he is also Wm Lamb's delight—we are
united like 3 frames or 3 oaks or what you will.'[76] In fact, this idyllic picture
was nothing but fantasy.

When the child was just over a year old, his mother noticed the first signs
of a mental backwardness that would become more and more pronounced in
later years.[77] He was 'like a lamb' in being 'en beau and fat' but in nothing
else.[78] As he became older, he began to become boisterous and uncontrol-
lable,[79] so much so that Caroline seems to have delegated his upbringing for
much of the time to Lady Holland.[80] When the child began to have fits, his
mother had resort to all kinds of fashionable, medical quackery, including
scaldings and magnetizings.[81] Nothing worked, and Augustus became a permanent problem in the Lamb household.

A man as fastidious and as emotionally guarded as William Lamb was quite unable to cope with the challenge of a mentally retarded son. He never felt real affection for the child. The best he could manage was a cold reserve. Two months after the birth, his wife hopefully observed that 'William is growing very fond of him', but had to add that he was 'less so than I am in outward demonstrations'.[82] Soon, William referred to the boy as 'a hideous fellow'.[83] His surviving letters to his son are few. They have a headmasterly detachment and are always signed 'William Lamb'. It must have been chilling for an 18-year-old to be reminded 'to clean your teeth both night and morning, and remember your hair',[84] or to be admonished by the thought that, 'if you do not make yourself agreeable by a little freedom and absence of reserve nobody will much care for your society'.[85] Lamb was endlessly trying to make his unfortunate son look presentable. In childlike handwriting, Augustus replies, calling his father 'Mr. Lamb' and promising to improve at his lessons and in general conduct.[86]

It seems that Lamb was reluctant to accept the fact of the boy's condition. In 1817, he employed Robert Lee for five years to teach him Latin and Greek, when it must have been clear that such studies were beyond his capabilities. Lee befriended Augustus in a way that his father never could, and was rewarded ultimately with a Regius Professorship at Glasgow University.[87] Lamb himself only saw his son 'occasionally'.[88] When he separated from his wife in 1825, Augustus became his sole responsibility. He shouldered it with something close to repugnance. Emily Lamb, who referred to her nephew as 'Frankenstein', sympathized with her brother's discomfort:

I am afraid he will find a drawback to his comfort in Augustus whom he has taken with him. I am glad he has taken him for he ought to make acquaintance with him and see what can be done with him but it is a sad case. The boy is very strong and healthy but with the mind of a child always in mischief and rolling the maids about . . . his fits are as bad as ever and more frequent.[89]

When Augustus died in November 1836, Lamb could show little remorse. The boy had been a living symbol of a marriage that was immature, even unhealthy.

Under the weight of these unpropitious circumstances, difficulties in the marriage arose almost immediately. In November 1806, Caroline, in a temper, thrust a ladder through William's favourite painting, a portrait by Cosway. This action led his family to call him a 'jerry sneak', or hen-pecked.[90] For the first, but not for the last, time, Caroline would be accused of unmanning him. A month later, she dressed as a man to visit the Commons when William moved the Address, thereby provoking that kind of public scandal and notoriety that would punctuate her whole life.[91] By 1807, a pattern of violent arguments had established itself. Harriet Cavendish reported that 'they all worked one another up', and that Caroline 'stood in a corner . . . flinging cups and saucers at William's head (a pretty pastime for him, poor man)'.[92] Unsuccessful pregnancies, unsupportive relatives, and money problems no doubt made for trouble, but there was something darker in these quarrels. There was a real wish to wound. Caroline's letters between 1807 and 1810 show real evidence of a deteriorating mental condition. Long, rambling disquisitions in agitated handwriting are signed 'Citizen Lamb',[93] and are accompanied by doodlings of pierced hearts and sketches of her husband and son.

These letters begin to display the astonishing swings in mood that become so marked a feature of her later life. On the one hand, submissive paragraphs are coyly signed 'your own faithful Wiffins',[94] and promise amendment:

I think lately my dearest William we have been very troublesome to each other which I take by wholesale to my own account and mean to correct leaving you in retail with a few little sins which I know you will correct . . . condemn me not to silence, assist my imperfect memory and occasionally call me friend-girl, Darling . . . and all such pretty names as show great love. I will on other hand be silent of a morning—entertaining after dinner.[95]

She protested to her Cavendish cousins that she adored her husband and would always look up to him.[96] At other times, she ruefully noted 'the difference between a lover and a husband'.[97] She complained of neglect, of illtreatment, and of being morally undermined by Lamb values. In these moods, she was impelled to take attention-seeking remedies. In October 1807, as one of her 'absurdities', she went to the theatre 'tête-à-tête with her Page, and the first thing she saw was Lord Egremont in the opposite Box, who must have enjoyed it much more than the Farce'.[98] She began to be incautious in the company of other men in a way that brought ridicule on her husband and that, as she herself admitted, was 'not very decent for one of my Cloath. I am like the song of Rosa in love with every body and am always abused for it.'[99] This see-sawing between virtue and flirtation reflected the heat and cold in relations with her husband.

Then, in 1810, shortly after the termination of her last pregnancy, she slipped into adultery. When she did so, she could hardly have chosen a more unsuitable lover. Sir Godfrey Webster, apart from showing an almost conscious deficiency in personal qualities, was Lady Holland's son from her first marriage. The incident therefore so soured relations between the Lambs and Holland House, that communication was broken off for a time. William's political prospects were thereby damaged. When the *affaire* became public,

Caroline once again begged her mother-in-law's forgiveness: 'on my knees I have written to William to tell him not any falsehoods not as you say any stories to conceal my guilt but the whole disgraceful truth. I have told him I have deceived him.'[100] Contrition came easily to Caroline Lamb. In January 1811, she threw herself on Lady Holland's mercy. Somewhat incongruously calling her 'the Mother of Heroes',[101] she assured her that 'my adoration for William and my gratitude and interest for him are not all hypocrisy and words'.[102] She meant 'henceforward to be a Pattern wife'.[103] In May 1811, she seems to have started a flirtation with Sir Godfrey's brother, Henry.[104] Unpredictability, involving savage changes of mood, began to stamp everything she did. Cousins hoped that 'the learned could explain the incongruity of her behaviour', but admitted that 'They would be put to it indeed'.[105]

The Webster *affaire*, or *affaires*, set a pattern that would be repeated over and over again. There would be scandals of an increasingly public kind. Pleas for forgiveness and protestations of love for William would follow. Throughout, Caroline was probably sincere in both adultery and penitence, in the sense that her life became increasingly theatrical and she believed fully in the part she was playing at any one time. She would dismiss servants and page boys at the behest of her relations and promise amendment. In June 1811, although she had been snubbed in public by her brother Duncannon and her father-in-law,[106] she could turn the incident into doggerel humour, as though no damage had been done:

> I am at home with William Lamb
> And he I think is rather better
> He says he does not care a d—n
> Whether I prate or write a letter.[107]

It seemed that a marriage that had, from the start, contained a large measure of fevered artificiality, had been so strained by unsuccessful pregnancies and family hostilities, that Caroline's fragile mental health could no longer cope.

Anonymous letters informed William Lamb of his wife's infidelity.[108] According to Caroline, his reaction was to reaffirm his love and to join in pleas for understanding:

I have not entreated him to retain me or used any arts to bind him—he has however sacrificed himself for me—and will my friends bear nothing for the sake of a man so noble and generous—if you all villify (sic) and degrade me—you stamp upon him that disgrace you wish to fix alone upon me . . . do you think he does not feel bitterly the whole of this—indeed he does—but at the point when he saw that I had brought ruin on myself he resolved and promised to share it.[109]

The truth, however, was a little different. Lamb had been deeply hurt, but his reaction to unpleasantness was always to retreat into himself, to flee before the expression of someone else's will. There was no way he could exercise any control or authority over the extravagant and demanding character of Caroline Lamb. By 1811, however, the marriage was in one sense over. On their sixth wedding anniversary, William left a ballroom alone, after reminding his wife 'of the vows and protestations I had then made, and are all changed in a few years'. Caroline went on waltzing for three hours after her husband's departure.[110] A few months later, she met Byron.

The *affaire* between Lady Caroline and Byron began in March 1812,[111] and lasted only for three or four months. Yet it was one of the most publicized and public scandals of the early nineteenth century, and it cast long shadows. In retrospect, Caroline liked to give the impression that Byron had been responsible for undermining a hitherto, happy marriage: 'I was the happiest and gayest of human beings . . . *I had married for love* and love the most romantic and ardent—my husband and I were so fond of each other that false as I too soon proved to be he never would part with me.'[112] William 'uniformly expressed the feelings of a gentleman'.[113] Once again, memory was defective. The *affaire* had been sudden, violent and, as ever, somewhat theatrical, involving such well-known episodes as Caroline attempting to slash her wrists in the middle of a ballroom. She was reported to have put Byron 'upon a Pedestal', the better to do him 'Hommage'.[114] She pursued him all over London, and may have gone through some sort of mock marriage ceremony.[115] An unpublished poem by Caroline is full of her delight in fantasizing about virtue eventually succumbing to overwhelming odds:

> Love seiz'd for her his sweetest dart
> And plunged it in her guilty heart
> Even while entwined within his arms
> She gazed upon his matchless charms
> Even as she pressed his lips of rose
> And heard the music of his vows
> The subtle poison through her frame
> Burst like the old insatiate flame
> Remorse—despair and agony
> Mingled with every extasy
> One kiss—one last forced kiss he tried
> She gave him what he wished—and died.[116]

Coming so soon after the Webster *affaire*, the liaison with Byron destroyed whatever social credit remained in Caroline's account.

The *affaire* lasted a few months. The recriminations went on for four or five years. Threats and mutual abuse followed one upon the other. Caroline accused Byron of seduction, of destroying her marriage, even of sodomy.[117] In return, Byron characterized her as Phryne, or procuress.[118] She was 'an adder in my path',[119] a Desdemona who richly deserved to be smothered.[120] Significantly, he accused her of being 'not feminine'.[121] She had *'no sex'*.[122] He addressed her in the masculine form of 'Carolus'.[123] In all of this was the suggestion that she dominated William Lamb, who was bound to her precisely because of her masculine qualities. Byron believed that the Lambs were 'a cuckoldy family'. Both William and his brother George were incapable of satisfying women sexually, and were therefore wise to be complaisant about their wives seeking out lovers. He referred to 'William and his "Corni Cazzo da Seno" (as we Venetians say—it means—Penis in earnest)'.[124] There was no reason to feel remorse or guilt.

To compound Lamb's humiliation, his mother had also become involved with Byron, who later claimed that she had been 'my greatest *friend*, of the feminine gender'.[125] Sometimes he denied that she had also been his mistress, and sometimes that he had become her lover immediately after abandoning Caroline, 'to be more wicked than other people'.[126] Whatever the real facts of the case, Caroline was not alone in believing that her mother-in-law was 'infatuated about Lord B'. Certainly, Byron's behaviour towards her son in no way bruised Lady Melbourne's friendship with him. She remained on close terms with him until her death.[127] In argument, she always took Byron's side both against Caroline, whom she dubbed 'canting' and 'hypocritical',[128] and against her niece, who had the misfortune to be Byron's wife (see Fig. 5). She agreed that Caroline should go on living at Melbourne House, even though she had begun to attack servants with pokers and broomsticks,[129] but was clear that there could be no real solution in the long-term except a formal ending of the marriage. In letters to Byron, Lady Melbourne blames all difficulties on her daughter-in-law, and shows less sympathy for her son than irritation that he could not summon the energy to disencumber himself of a terrible wife. She accused Caroline of being able to 'manage him more easily than she can any other person, and she thinks it as well to give it ye appearance of fondness, if she determines to remain'.[130]

Predictably, this bizarre situation began 'occupying the beau monde far more than anything else'.[131] William Lamb's humiliation was of the most public kind. Byron had debauched, it was believed, his wife and his mother. Neither woman had regarded his views or feelings as matters of importance. He neither influenced nor controlled events. The experience scarred him for life. In old age, his detestation for Byron poured out in conversations with Victoria. Byron was 'crooked and perverted'.[132] He was 'treacherous beyond conception'.[133] He was 'quite the Poet of the Devil'.[134] Among Melbourne's personal papers is a critical essay on Byron's poetry. While admitting that his early work retained a kind of innocence, most of his verse 'cast of [sic] all sense of the Beauty of moral truth', and 'embraced the cause of all that is base and criminal in our nature'.[135] Byron had held him up to public ridicule, had dripped poison into his family circle, and, as he believed, had put an end to all hopes of a career in politics.

Throughout the whole episode, Lamb's sense of emotional isolation must have been intense, and it is perhaps not surprising that he drew near to the other principal victim in the case, namely his cousin, who was also Byron's wife. Initially, Lady Byron had found his manner off-putting,[136] but her opinion soon changed. In a poem entitled *Lord Melbourne*, she later portrayed him as neglected by the whole world, with only her own affection to give him any comfort:

> Save when some heart that answered to his own,
> Perchance too humble, or perchance too high,
> To yield, in life, the ministries of love,
> Shall bring a liegeman's homage to his tomb.
> .   .   .   .
> That high Ideal, pregnant with despair
> Casting upon the sea of human life
> Its own reflection, to be broken there
> By turbid waters; and lost in scatter'd wrecks.[137]

An enamel-portrait of Melbourne became one of her most treasured possessions.[138] In return, Lamb gladly offered friendship. When Thomas Moore was writing a life of Byron, Lamb insisted that Lady Byron's side of the story be fully covered, and that certain passages offensive to her should be expunged. He frankly admitted, in 1830, that he helped Lady Byron, because 'so much remains of resentment, as would make me rather glad than otherwise of any thing that should tend to unmask his [Byron's] real character'.[139] In office, he was 'very anxious' to respond to her suggestions about patronage.[140] She was a fellow victim of a man he detested.

The shadow of Byron never quite lifted above the Lamb marriage. In 1823, Caroline published a novel called *Ada Reis*. The overtly didactic purpose of the book was to exemplify 'the dangerous power of the evil agent, if his influence be once admitted'.[141] The evil agent in question is a corsair who is 'a strange compound of every excellence and every vice'.[142] He takes up with an English woman who dies for love of him.[143] This tale of unrequited passion is set amidst a gothic backcloth of shipwrecks and earthquakes. The moral is clear: 'To hate is wiser than to love; but the wisest is to do neither. Better is it to pursue our course upon earth as the blind mole does beneath its surface, working our way, without seeing or attaching ourselves to ought, that like ourselves, is dust.'[144] Byron too wrote about corsairs, but literary clues such as this were hardly necessary to convince contemporaries that Caroline Lamb was yet again rehearsing the Byron *affaire*.[145] Her husband disliked the book. There were too many 'manifest faults' and he would have preferred a lot of rewriting before publication.[146] What he most resented was Byron's lingering influence. By awful coincidence in 1824, the Lambs met Byron's funeral cortège as it passed through Hertfordshire. At the time, William sensibly failed to tell his wife whose coffin they had seen. When she later discovered the truth, she became distraught.[147] William too, however, had been terribly damaged. The beginning of the Byron trauma coincided with a crisis in his political life. Its repercussions ensured that any serious career in public life would have to be postponed.

Throughout his life, William Lamb saw difficulties as things to escape from rather than confront. In 1812, having lost his parliamentary seat and, in some sense, his wife, his instinct was to hide. For a term of years, it was reported that he 'endures a life as solitary as that of the Hermit'.[148] Escape was geographical as well as psychological. He wished, above all, to remove himself and his wife from the mocking eyes of London society. In the autumn of 1812, he took Caroline off to Ireland, where she melodramatically announced her intention of living forever, because her 'whole constitution is so irritated that Wm says he does not know what to do with me'.[149] She acknowledged over and over again that 'Wm Lamb has ruined himself by excess of kindness for me' and that she would do 'anything to clear him',[150] but, on infrequent visits to London, she immediately began the pursuit of a 'lost Dandy' called Dawson.[151] The Hollands began to compare her with typhus.[152] As for Lamb himself, the Byron episode was a determining experience. He frankly told his mother-in-law that, with regard to Caroline, 'no middle course can be pursued, no advice, no scolding, no threats have any effect, and that he must therefore bear everything or part with her'.[153] Storms inside the Lamb household were now frequently 'little exceeded in violence by the storm of thunder and lightening without'.[154]

In 1815, the defeat of Bonaparte made the distraction of a European tour possible. The Lambs were in Brussels from June until the end of August, and then in Paris for the next five weeks.[155] On this his first visit to France, Lamb was accorded the usual pleasantries. Visits to the battlefield of Waterloo and a wounded brother-in-law were followed by Parisian entertainment stage-managed by Talleyrand.[156] Even so, he was right to doubt that Paris could provide the anonymity he so badly needed. Paris was not a place in which to hide. His diplomat brother Frederick answered his anxious questions with some irritation: 'as to Paris being agreable (sic) to a woman that must depend entirely on the taste of a Lady. The folly is that they are decided to come.'[157] Normally, the indigent and the morally-stricken could sink into shadow in a provincial French town, but Paris was made to take notice of Caroline Lamb. The Hotel Meurice reverberated to the sound of smashing crockery and furniture.[158] The scandal sheets ran stories that she was waiting for Byron to join her, or that she had eloped with him to Switzerland, with her husband in hot pursuit.[159] As a cousin reported, the Parisian interlude did nothing to alleviate Lamb's distress nor to diminish its very public nature: 'Nothing is agissant but Caroline William in a purple riding habit, tormenting every body . . . Poor William hides in one small room, while she assembles lovers and tradespeople in another. He looks worn to the bone.'[160]

Worst of all, Caroline Lamb began a serious flirtation in Paris with Michael Bruce, a wealthy adventurer in the Byronic mould. She advertised herself to him as 'not very feminine and gentle something like Catherine the shrew before she was tamed'.[161] It is not clear how far Bruce took up the challenge of taming his new friend, but he becomes a regular feature in the Lamb marriage, being used as a go-between and confidante. The Byronic parallel was exact in another sense. Once again, Caroline Lamb competed for Bruce's favours with her mother-in-law. It seemed that the two women had always to compete sexually. As Caro. George reported,

to crown all my gossip and scandal there is my belle mère très sérieusement amoureuse de Monsr Bruce who is neither handsome nor pleasant, but very conceited, and I am doomed to hear her's and Caro's mutual confidences of how the other makes up to him. Caro says the 'truth is he wants me, but I am not to be taken in, so he comforts himself with her.' This family is enough to make one sick.[162]

In 1815 therefore, William Lamb was once again the public cuckold. Desperate efforts to keep his wife in seclusion at Brocket or abroad had hopelessly failed. Reacting to situations created by his wife and mother, he never really controlled events or made any mark of his own. Little wonder that, at the age of 36, he took the opportunity of being in Paris to have all his grey hairs plucked out. Even that process was 'exceedingly painful'.[163]

Yet the worst ordeal was yet to come. In May 1816, Caroline published *Glenarvon*, a novel which figuratively threw buckets of ordure into the faces of the whole Whig world. Vicious portraits of its leading figures, such as Lady Holland and Lady Melbourne, became the talk of London. Further, if anyone was still in doubt about the details of the Lamb marriage, they were now set out in the plainest possible terms. The author received £500 for the manuscript, but financial reward was not her first priority. Above all, she wanted publicly to give her version of events, a self-justification by novelwriting. She positively wanted a sensation, suggesting to her publisher that the title might be followed by three exclamation marks. To ensure notoriety on a European scale, free copies were to be sent to Mme de Stael and the Duchesse de Coigny.[164] Caroline Lamb often tested the patience of her circle, but it was for this public exposure of their values that she was never thereafter forgiven.

The novel tells the story of Calantha, a young woman of much innocence, who marries a certain Lord Avondale, in whose society initially 'every hour brought her joy'.[165] In return, she dominated him: 'whilst Calantha could make him grave or merry—or angry or pleased, just as it suited her, he pardoned every omission—he forgave every fault.' He was 'a willing slave'.[166] The word 'slave' is then repeated at intervals throughout the novel. Only the blindest of contemporaries could fail to identify these two principals as Caroline and William Lamb. If further evidence were needed, Calantha, like Caroline, was, on her wedding day 'torn from her father's bosom' with 'shrieks of despair'.[167] The young couple are beset by Avondale's cold and cynical relations, who proceed to undermine Calantha's sense of religion and morality: 'A strong party spirit prevailed . . . [Calantha] though she loved and admired the individuals, she felt herself unfit to live among them. There was a liberality of opinion and a satiric turn which she could not at once comprehend; and she said to herself daily, as she considered those around her— "They are different from me—I can never assimilate myself to them".'[168] No more savage revenge on Lamb family exclusiveness could have been devised.

Debauched in values by Avondale's family, Calantha falls an easy prey to the brooding figure of Glenarvon, who, in Byronic fashion, carries her off, and 'a dream of ecstasy for one moment fluttered in her heart'.[169] The much misunderstood heroine never quite forgot Avondale, and rebuked herself for 'the injustice her imprudence and wanton prodigality had caused'.[170] At the end of the book, she returns to her husband to expire in his arms.[171] Avondale then challenges Glenarvon to a duel and is shot. At this point, imagination overcame fact. Lamb, the Etonian schoolboy who saw little point in fighting, never challenged Byron. Perhaps Caroline resented this reticence. Like Melbourne, however, Avondale was the owner of a bottomless pit of forgiveness. This cautionary tale is played out in a world of vicious men and women, all easily identifiable, against whose machinations the virtue of Calantha stood no chance. Women like Lady Holland, memorably depicted as a dark-skinned Princess of Madagascar presiding over Barbary House, cynically destroyed true feeling. *Glenarvon* was Caroline Lamb's plea of not guilty. There were overwhelming, mitigating circumstances. No one could run straight in Whig society. It stood formally indicted. Caroline Lamb was innocent because Whiggery was guilty. Both she and her husband were victims, because neither had skins thick enough to move within its dangerous society.

The novel's publication provoked outrage. Byron could hardly find expletives enough to express his feelings. *Glenarvon* was 'that damned novel' written by 'my evil Genius',[172] who has now 'damned herself'.[173] A couplet in questionable taste gave a clue to his feelings;

> From furious Sappho scarce a milder fate
> —by her love—or libelled by her hate.[174]

Lady Holland, too, was enraged. Every social norm had been violated. The novel was a

singular libel published by Lady C. Lamb against her family and friends. It is a *plaidoyer* against her husband addressed to the religious and methodistical part of the community, accusing him of having overset her religious and moral (!) principles by teaching her doctrines of impiety, etc. . . . The words about Mr. Lamb are encomiastick, but the facts were against him, as she insidiously censures him not fighting a duel which her fictitious husband does.[175]

Lord Holland, normally the most easy-going of men, broke off all contact, an event that seems genuinely to have surprised the author.[176] Not for the first time, she was really shocked to discover that those who she tried to wound by satire should actually be hurt, and should react accordingly.

The reaction of the Lamb family itself was predictable. They felt sorry for themselves and, now, very sorry for William. Lady Melbourne gave an airing to her resentment in a letter to her niece;

Of Glenarvon I have only read the first Vol and it is so disagreable (sic) to me that I don't feel as if I had courage to proceed. I never can excuse ye falsehoods she tells about Willm and ye acct she gives of a society in which she had lived from her childhood. She knew them perfectly, unfortunately they did not know her, and Wm ye least of all, and to this hour she has the art of deceiving him as to her real character.[177]

It was bad enough for newspapers and scandal-sheets to pass judgement on Whig society. For one of their own number to lift the veil was simply inexcusable. Further, at the very centre of the disaster was William Lamb. His sister found it 'distressing to see Wms character in the world utterly and entirely blasted by it, his name held up to ridicule and contempt, and himself the sport of every Club where the Book is laid upon the Table . . . it makes my heart bleed to see him walking up and down the street when I know what people are saying of him—and if he has no feeling for himself, at least his family are bound to have some for him.'[178] His sister-in-law ruefully noted that, whenever he appeared in company, 'there is a whisper and laugh. He is abused for having allowed her to publish it.'[179] The cuckold lacked the character to prevent his wife publishing his dishonour all over London, and dramatizing his failure to fight for either his good name or hers.

Lamb found himself in an intolerable situation, as a result of 'the late cursed events'.[180] As he explained by way of apology to Holland, they had led to 'an unwillingness to see any body . . . I could only exculpate myself from any previous knowledge . . . I am sure you will feel for my situation.'[181] He did summon up the energy to tell Caroline at one point that he would 'never see her more', though his resolution only lasted four days.[182] He also tried to stop the novel being widely advertised,[183] and to suppress any thought of subsequent editions. He frankly told the publisher that, since objections had been started to some passages of the work, and others certainly being liable to some objection, it was his determination to stop sales of the book.[184] Even so, further editions were brought out, with Caroline's full approval. His apparent inability to suppress the novel merely confirmed the impression that London had formed of him since 1812. William Lamb could not control his wife, could not command the loyalty of his mother, and could not act like a gentleman in defence of his honour. Contemporaries were justified in asking whether there was any belief or affection in his life that could overcome his preference for simply accepting events and bowing before them.

Since William, as usual, found it difficult to act, his family, as usual, felt compelled to act for him. In their view, the Byron *affaire*, Parisian adventures, and *Glenarvon* made it imperative that he and Caroline should be formally separated. Byron heard a rumour that this was being considered in the spring of 1815.[185] A year later, Caroline was warning her mother-in-law that any attempt to have her declared insane would be resisted.[186] After the publication of *Glenarvon*, Caroline complained that the family 'write to advise William to part from me'.[187] Lamb was under intense pressure to act in a resolute manner, but the separation scheme came to nothing for two very good reasons. First, there was no question of Caroline quietly slipping away. She made it clear that her severance from the Lamb family would be both messy and noisy.[188] Quite simply, the scandal would go on through interminable lawsuits. Secondly, William could not be brought to any final decision. At one point, in 1816, articles of separation were actually awaiting signature. When, however, Lady Melbourne brought them to her son and daughter-in-law, she found them at breakfast, contentedly buttering muffins for each other.[189]

The Lamb family attributed William's lack of resolution to his inability to cope with distressing or embarrassing occurrences. He always preferred to concede. As his sister lamented, he 'has not courage enough to stand against scenes and entreaties'.[190] This, however, was only half the story. Lamb would always prefer peace to acrimony, would always try to hide from embarrassment, and would rarely stand and fight. As a result, Caroline's capacity to cause acrimony, embarrassment, and friction gave her powerful weapons. But there was a deeper chemistry at work. Much as they wounded each other and publicly complained of mistreatment, there survived a strange underlying affection and bonding. Each traumatic episode is punctuated by anti-cyclonic periods of muffin-buttering. There is no reason to doubt Caroline's endlessly expressed regrets for the damage she had wreaked on her husband's career and personality. Equally, William's endless expressions of forgiveness were solemnly pronounced. They could neither live with each other, nor could they live apart. It is a point of some significance that, throughout the whole of his married life, William never sought consolation in the arms of another woman. By Whig standards, he showed an almost unbelievable chastity. There was a terrible alchemy in his relationship with his wife, and she was 'fixed to him for life'.[191]

5

Marriage and Nemesis, 1816–1828

AFTER 1816, William Lamb's marriage was something to be endured. His wife became increasingly slovenly and drunken. His son grew physically, but not mentally, stronger. London life became a terrible burden, so refuge was sought at Brocket. In its library, Lamb read voraciously and found a little peace, even if the price he paid was an inability to pursue politics seriously. Contemporaries wondered that the marriage survived at all. The diarist Greville noted that the Lambs had had 'a sort of half-laughing, half-resentful reconciliation. They lived in this queer way.'[1] The pattern of extravagant behaviour followed by a penitence that some saw as self-indulgent reasserted itself. In 1817, Caroline assured Michael Bruce that 'wicked as it may be I should not so much mind errors of the wandering heart, if I had been gentle and made William happy but as it is I am miserable and when I die he will not even be able to love my remembrance'.[2] At this time, both William and Caroline claimed that they had no wish to go on living.[3] They implored their friends to pray for them.[4] There was no career, no acceptance in society, and little sympathy from friends or relations. Nor would there be any respite. From 1816, until her death in 1828, Caroline Lamb endlessly rehearsed her misery before the public by writing more novels and by provoking outrage. *Ada Reis*, giving a loosely veiled account of the Byron *affaire* appeared in 1823. A year earlier, *Graham Hamilton* had been published. It tells a familiar tale. Hamilton loves and marries a cousin. Both young people test their innocence and virtue against the decadent values of London society, and both are corrupted by it. They become victims of the 'censorious, officious, intermeddling world'.[5] The wife dies of grief and remorse. The husband flees to the New World. As in her earlier productions, Caroline portrays herself as destroyed by vicious social conventions against which an amiable but ineffective husband could not defend her. It was a version of events to which William Lamb to some degree assented. He read the manuscript of *Graham Hamilton* and corrected proofs, as 'an occupation to him in his lonely hours'.[6] He did not censor the content, only asking that, when the book was published, no mention should be made of *Glenarvon*. In the circumstances, it was a mild request to make.[7] Caroline reported that, 'I am proud in having Mr. Lamb's sanction for Grayham (sic) Hamilton.'[8]

Unfortunately, Caroline Lamb's itch for self-vindication was not confined to literary efforts. Whenever she was in London, attention-catching incidents occurred. It seemed that 'her only object is to push herself on in the world, which is . . . very uphill work'.[9] In view of her recent history, it was less than disarming to attend a masquerade ball dressed as Don Juan, with all its Byronic implications.[10] In 1819, she notoriously canvassed for George Lamb in his Westminster constituency. She freely entered taverns, drank heavily, and exchanged kisses for votes. As Princess Lieven archly observed, 'what else she did is shrouded in obscurity'. She was 'that madwoman'.[11] Byron angrily announced that he would like to have 'f——d Caroline Lamb out of her two hundred votes although at the expense of a testicle'.[12] Five years later, she tried to brawl with the sergeant on duty at the Horse Guards, and had to be forcibly restrained by her husband and brothers. After this incident, 'she is kept low, which means being limited to one bottle of sherry daily'.[13] There seemed to be no end to the humiliation. There is no doubting Caroline Lamb's contrition or her affection for her husband, but her behaviour robbed him of all self-respect and all prospects.

After 1816, William attempted to hide his family at Brocket, even at the cost of immersing himself with a drunken wife and a retarded son. According to his sister-in-law in 1824, living there was 'really like being in Bethlem [i.e. Bedlam], such a scene of confusion, and such a wife and son, as that poor William has got. I pitied her more than I have done lately for she appeared to me not to know what she was about and quite like a person out of their mind . . . Augustus is better but very near an idiot.'[14] The household reverberated to the sound of flying crockery, and no servants stayed long. They passed through 'like figures in a magic lantern'.[15] Of those who did stay for any length of time, the most important were Robert Lee, Augustus's tutor, and a certain Dr Walker, who was widely believed to be Caroline's new lover. Emily Lamb thought it 'a low-lived thing to take a Scotch doctor for her lover, and Wm looks so like a fool, arriving with them and looking as pleased as Punch'.[16] Predictably, Brocket was not a house that many chose to visit.

Perhaps the oddest characteristic of the Lamb household was the presence of an endless series of boys and girls, recruited or adopted at random. After two miscarriages and the pathetic inadequacy of Augustus, both husband and wife may well have known a desperate need for children. Certainly, the pattern was consistent. As one of the consequences of the ending of the Webster *affaire* in 1810, Caroline's relations had insisted on her dismissing two 'pages'.[17] In 1817, she was entangled with a 'boy' called Rushton in a man-

ner that caused her husband 'great bitterness'.[18] Referring to yet another
'page', she assured her relations that it 'was an idle whim of mine more for
the love of educating a boy and having something to do than from any other
motive'.[19] She was capable of offering to take into her household boys who
she met by chance on the seashore.[20] None seem to have stayed long, but,
as personal attendants to Caroline, each attracted such notoriety that the
Lamb and Bessborough families could demand their dismissal.

Girls seem to have had a more permanent place in the Lamb household,
though their exact role and function remains shadowy. In 1817, Caroline
wrote of having 'adopted' a certain 'orphan child' called Ellinor Mowbray.[21]
In 1826, she was actively seeking a governess for yet another 'adopted' girl.[22]
The child about whom most is known was a certain Susan Churchill. Born
illegitimately in 1818 to Harriet Spencer and a relation of the Duke of
Marlborough, she was, for some unknown reason, taken in by the Lambs.
Her education was supervised by them, and, after Caroline's death, William
sent the child to Switzerland under the care of one of his ex-mistresses, Lady
Branden, who was also seeking anonymity abroad. The girl eventually married a Swiss named Aimé Cuenod. Melbourne took an intense interest in the
marriage, providing a dowry of £500 himself.[23] In gratitude, the new Mme
Cuenod named her children William and Caroline, and continued to write
to her benefactor until at least 1841.[24]

It is only possible to speculate about the role these children played in the
Lamb household, but their number and constant presence suggests that they
were of importance. On one level, the Lambs were accused of using these
children as nothing more than a diversion of which they eventually tired.
Referring to Miss Churchill, Mrs Norton remarked to Melbourne; 'Seriously
to speak, I think you are weary of this self-imposed burden of a little girl who
must be fed, clothed and grow into a woman. When you weakly allowed her
to be domesticated as *a plaything* in your house, you consulted your own
caprice or that of Lady Caroline, and not the good of the child.'[25] The notion
that these children were human dolls gains some credence from their often
being dressed up in exotic costumes. A more sinister possibility is that they
were somehow involved in Melbourne's pronounced interest in flagellation.
This topic will be dealt with elsewhere, but it may be of significance that it
plays a significant part in the few surviving letters between him and Susan
Churchill. After all that the Lambs had suffered and were suffering, there was
no reason to expect that their relations with children would be orthodox. The
page and the orphan girl merely added yet another strange ingredient to a
household that was eccentric and frightening in nearly all its parts.

Nor was country-living free from scandal. The Lyttons were Hertfordshire
neighbours, and Bulwer Lytton, the future novelist, had early in life become

an habitué of the Lamb circle. In 1820, at the age of 17, he began to visit
Brocket regularly, ostensibly to show his poetry to William Lamb.[26] In retrospect, Lytton described his association with Caroline in innocent terms:

a very intimate friendship grew up between this singular woman and myself. We corresponded regularly on my return to Cambridge; and in our correspondence there
was a great deal of sentiment and romance which looked like love, but it never came
to that.[27]

Even so, at the time, she was his 'unique Caroline', while he was never quite
sure that he liked her husband.[28] He bombarded her with pimply verse:

> Daughter of Feeling, Queen of Love!
> 'Tis to thee these lines are due
> Beauteous as the Cyprian Dove
> Hast thou her nature too.[29]

In return, Caroline kept up a correspondence until at least 1826, flattering
his poetic efforts, and asking him to go on writing with his old 'affection, boy-
ish affection'.[30]

It is profitless to speculate about the exact nature of the relationship,
though Caroline Lamb would hardly repel the adoration of a moonstruck
adolescent. Equally, it is clear that Lytton was deeply jealous when, in 1824,
Caroline imported into Brocket a natural son of the Duke of Bedford, known
simply as 'Mr Russell'. He then accused her of being a 'coquette', who
derived pleasure from playing Russell and himself off against each other.[31] In
writing of the episode later, Lytton saw Caroline as someone who 'delighted
to bring men to her feet, and when she had succeeded in enthralling them,
she commonly hastened to pass on to fresh conquests'.[32] If indeed she was
the model for the heartless Lady Melton in his novel *De Lindsay*, then he had
felt deeply enough for her to make the taking of revenge sweet. It may also
be important to note that Bulwer Lytton's wife also discussed the Lamb marriage in novel form by way of attacking her own husband. *Cheveley or The Man
of Honour*, published in 1839, once again refreshed the public memory of what
the Melbourne marriage had been. William Lamb never escaped the long
shadow of this degrading publicity. Much as he and his family deplored the
'bad style . . . of bringing all their own histories before the public',[33] the
Lytton *affaire* would do nothing to aid the cause of anonymity.

Further, at the same time that she was enjoying the spectacle of Lytton and
Russell locking horns, Caroline was still intent on justifying her behaviour in
the Byron *affaire*. In 1824, she threatened to publish Byron's letters, upon
which Lady Holland could only comment that, 'It is pleasant for Wm. Lamb
to have the degree and extent of Lord Byron's love for his wife discussed by
the public.'[34] A year later the rumour that she was writing her memoirs led

her husband's family to seek legal advice. Frederick Lamb asked the family solicitor if the scribblings of this 'infernal woman' could not be stopped by an application to the Lord Chancellor.[35] They could only be 'of the most libellous nature'.[36] For whatever reason, neither letters nor memoirs were published, and William Lamb was spared further anxiety. Significantly though, his escape had been organized by his family. There had been no initiatives of his own.

Then came blackmail. In March 1826, Lady Byron warned the Lamb family that a certain Washington Fleming[37] had contrived to borrow Caroline Lamb's journals. Extracts had been made. Unless the family chose to buy his notes, poverty would force him to publish them.[38] Typically, Caroline tried to cast herself as the only aggrieved person in the case. She had trusted Fleming only because she had been abandoned by everyone else. She had been 'miserable and cared not what became of me'.[39] She deserved sympathy because she was 'dashed to destruction'.[40] It is not known whether Fleming's attempts at extortion were bought off or faced down. Whatever the outcome, it would not be Lamb's last brush with blackmail. In 1831, a certain John Burn threatened to publish material relating to the Byron *affaire* if he was not given a job. In 1837, a Mary Simpson tried something similar.[41] All of this can only have been horrific to someone who detested the idea of his private life and private thoughts being masticated in public. William Lamb had 'a greater dislike than anybody to the smallest circumstance in which he is concerned being repeated'.[42] Yet, again and again, the detail of his humiliations was on public display. Retreating from London had not provided any respite. Not surprisingly, he confessed to a friend, in 1827, that he knew 'enough of domestic disquietude not to be surprised at any step, which a man may take under the pressure of it'.[43]

The consequence for the Lambs of these bizarre circumstances was social ostracism. In Derbyshire, Melbourne Hall was 'the most dismal place in the world', 'a gloomy den' in which 'the two Lambs damn and whistle . . . with their hats on'.[44] In Hertfordshire, Brocket was in social quarantine. Entertainments were offered to a hundred guests, of whom only a handful would appear. Such social disasters made William 'miserable, fretted to death, flying into passions continually and letting her have quite her own way . . . There never was such a Woman!!!'[45] There was every chance of William Lamb becoming 'the laughing stock of his County'.[46] More hurtful still was Emily Lamb's attitude. Married to Lord Cowper, she lived at Panshanger, only a comfortable drive from Brocket. By the early 1820s, however, William could only visit his sister alone. His wife was no longer received. Emily Lamb had come to detest Caroline, and Lord Cowper had a 'horror' of her.[47] Socially marginalized, the Lambs took refuge in the company of others who found themselves in social shadow. William Godwin and William Blake became protégés and were helped financially. Artists of the establishment like Sir Thomas Lawrence found themselves dining at Brocket with the fathers of anarchism. Their company clearly meant a great deal to Lamb himself. They were not forgotten when he became powerful, but were instead comfortably pensioned.[48] In later life, Melbourne's sympathy with outsiders, like Robert Owen, may owe a great deal to his own loneliness in the 1820s.

By force of necessity, William Lamb spent months in solitary introspection. He escaped to the library at Brocket as often as possible. Reading was the major consolation. It was undertaken on such a scale that he became a regular contributor to William Jerdan's *Literary Gazette*.[49] Very significantly, he never transferred affection to another woman, an astonishing fact given the values of his circle. In the whole period 1805–27, there was mention of only one 'flirtation' which 'did not go very far' with a woman so ignorant that she was appalled to discover that Desdemona was smothered at the end of *Othello*.[50] It seemed that all emotional responses had been frozen by the chilling association with Caroline Lamb. Quite possibly, he never trusted anyone fully ever again, certainly not to the point of making an emotional commitment Instead, his only resource was to cry on his sister's shoulder:

Wm. came over here the other day and talked to me more openly and more freely about Caroline than he had ever done before; he says he is quite miserable, and does not know what to do about her, that he never has a day's peace, and that her violence increases so much that he is always afraid of her doing some serious mischief . . . He says she is the greatest bore in the world . . . He is a *great* ass, for having borne her as he has done, but one cannot help feeling for him just part[icularly], when it appears that he is not blinded about her.[51]

According to Emily, her brother's cursed marriage had put him 'quite out of the question' with regard to political office. It had also socially 'separated him from the society of all those with whom he would naturally have associated and . . . everybody is considerably influenced by the opinions of those with whom they live and I think nobody more than him'.[52] His marriage had made William Lamb a social and political cypher.

In fact, for fifteen years or so, the extraordinary circumstances of the Lamb marriage provided matter for the table-talk of London. It was publicly dissected. Everyone felt free to apportion blame. Caroline herself always insisted that, though her husband had never stopped loving her, he and his family had debauched her. He was her 'Black William'. He had called her religion 'superstitious enthusiasm'. Further, and more sinisterly, 'he called me Prudish said I was straight-laced, amused himself with instructing me in things I should never have heard of or known'.[53] On more than one occasion, she accused him of beating her. This accusation was dismissed by the Lamb family as the raving of a madwoman, but, in view of William's interest in flagellation, it may deserve some credence.[54] Caroline apologized for drinking heavily, but that too was her husband's fault: 'Being unhappy today I have drunk a whole bottle of wine which I bought for myself all at once . . . I did it upon hearing Mr Lamb wished to speak to me. I still was able to do every thing he wished.'[55] Quite simply, in her view, William Lamb, spoilt by upbringing, was so self-absorbed that he never freely gave affection and never could cope with difficulty. As Caroline expressed the point in verse:

> A little Lamb there was that from its birth
> Had cropp'd the daintiest fruits and flowers of Earth
>
> . . . .
>
> Trust not its bleatings nor its looks of love
> Ne'er long will faithful to another prove.[56]

It was a version of events that William himself almost accepted. He admitted to being 'very selfish, both Boy and Man', and 'always anxious to escape from anything of a painful nature'.[57] He did not find consolation from a terrible marriage by transferring his affections elsewhere. Instead, he shut himself up in his own feelings.

In particular, Caroline came to believe that her husband could not accept women of independent views. In 1809, she read Mary Wollstonecraft's *Vindication of the Rights of Women* and 'became a convert'.[58] She now numbered herself among those 'liberal-minded women who . . . stand up for the rights of the sex and wear our shackles with dignity'.[59] There is no evidence to indicate how William responded to his wife's claims. However, much later in life, he enjoyed shocking people with blimpish remarks, which, under the guise of humour, betrayed real opinions. In 1835, he assured Lady Lichfield: 'a wife should have neither country, religion or politics; she should adopt those of her husband.'[60] He lectured the young Victoria on why 'the wife is always in the wrong'.[61] On this reading, Melbourne was a man who both allowed his life to be ordered by women of determined, even masculine temperament, while deeply resenting it at the same time. Caroline Lamb's defence was that her behaviour had been provoked by an immature man, who found it hard to give affection, and who abused her physically by beatings and psychologically by lecturing on the worthlessness of her values.

This unflattering picture seemed just to some contemporaries. Greville believed that Melbourne carried cynicism to destructive lengths. He was 'a sensualist and a Sybarite', someone 'of the lowest morality', who regulated life 'by thoughts and opinions fraught with the most cold-hearted mockery and sarcasm'.[62] According to Lady Charlotte Bury, all Caroline Lamb's *affaires* were basically William's fault: 'as he is careless of her, her disposition which is naturally *aimante*, leads her to attach herself to others.'[63] This case was most dramatically presented by Lady Lytton in her novel, *Cheveley or The Man of Honour*. Here Melbourne is shown as Lord de Clifford, a man who gives up 'the science of manners for the art of tormenting, which he has practised on his wife ever since'. In this, he was assisted by a 'calculating machine' of a mother and a family before whom all must 'bow down'. In his opinion, every woman was 'ignorant and inferior'.[64] This savage account is to some extent supported by the record of Melbourne's involvement with women after his wife's death. There are not more than half-a-dozen individuals and they are of a type. Strong-minded, amusing, and undemanding, these women were for diversion, not emotional entanglement. Any of them would be abandoned at a hint of trouble. Caroline Lamb effectively claimed that, in a sense, she was the first to suffer abandonment.

Others saw William as the real victim of these hard years. Lady Holland disliked Caroline's attempts to humiliate her husband by emphasizing his sheeplike, will-less qualities. She bleated his name in introductions, calling him 'Williaaaam'.[65] A footman in a great house was dismissed for retaliating by calling her 'Lady Caroline Wolf'.[66] On this reading of events, William had always been 'very quiet and patient', arguing that 'that's the only way in which a man can have any power with a woman'.[67] Such forbearance only meant that he was endlessly 'teazed'.[68] His sister observed that he 'must have been an angel to have borne it',[69] and Victoria, admittedly listening to very partial evidence, had no doubt that the real suffering had been his. His wife's behaviour had 'quite embittered his life . . . He has now the greatest horror of any woman who is not as she should be and who is extravagant.'[70] This was the sadder because Melbourne never believed that Caroline's behaviour was to be attributed to what the doctors called 'the higher form of insecurity'.[71] According to him, mental disorder was a function of bodily malfunction and intemperance. He was so sure of this that he lectured fashionable medical men on the subject.[72] As a result, he concluded that 'all Madmen are also rogues'.[73] He saw himself therefore shackled to a wilful and libidinous wife, whose absurd antics had damned his career and destroyed him as a social animal.

It is difficult to know where to anchor truth amid the flow of accusation and counter-accusation. Clear perspectives are not to be expected from people who lived so intensely. Both parties to this terrible mismatch found it a draining experience. As her mother feared before the marriage took place, Caroline Lamb had a fragile mental health that was only sustained by endless reaffirmations of affection. Her demands in this respect were not lessened by the lowering experience of miscarriages. Unfortunately the fastidious temperament of her husband could not cope with her claims. To some this was selfishness, to others a nature that had difficulty in unfolding. The result was that Caroline sought consolation in flirtation and alcohol, as a consequence of which her husband shunned her company more and more. A vicious cycle set in. Caroline's instinct was to bleed her disappointments in public, while William's was to seek the obscurity of shadow. He hated her publicity-seeking, and she despised his unwillingness to fight. Underlying everything was a basic affection that made the idea of separation unattractive. It was an impossible chemistry. They were damned to each other, to their mutual destruction.

In 1825, Caroline heard rumours that the Lamb family were once again trying to push William into a formal separation. Since women had little or no legal standing in the early nineteenth century, she immediately sought the protection of male relations. First, she tried Hartington, now sixth Duke of Devonshire, assuring him that William himself was 'miserable' at the prospect of separating from her, and 'did not wish it'.[74] He expressed sympathy but declined to act. Significantly, he saw 'unlimited indulgence' as the cause of her troubles, but thought she yet deserved 'kindness'.[75] When her elder brother, Duncannon, also refused to become involved, Caroline found a champion in her younger brother, William Ponsonby. He refused to allow his sister to 'be trampled on', by telling the world that all the trouble stemmed from William's 'alternate violence and indulgence'.[76] Lamb met these accusations with customary fatalism: 'What will happen, what she will do, or what Wm Ponsonby will do, it is out of my power to conjecture in the slightest degree.'[77] As usual, he simply dodged unpleasantness. George Lamb, lamenting 'the weakness of William's determination', reported that he had gone away, leaving Frederick with full powers to act on his behalf.[78]

Early in the proceedings, the Lamb family solicitor informed Frederick that a separation would only be possible with the consent of both parties. The alternative of going to law was too public and too costly.[79] There was the further problem of finding trustees for the financial aspects of the settlement. By law, such men would be liable for any expenditure made by Caroline Lamb over and above the sum settled on her. Given her prodigality, this was an unattractive proposition. Earl Fitzwilliam, when asked to act, prudently consulted a lawyer, who was sure that 'it would not be prudent to accept the trust with this liability'.[80] Fitzwilliam promptly withdrew from the matter. Viscount Althorp warned the Duke of Devonshire about the same point. Caroline's conduct was so 'strange', that it would be dangerous to put oneself 'so completely in her power'.[81] In the event, Althorp's conscience overcame his scruples and he agreed to act, with William Ponsonby as the other trustee. In June 1825, negotiations about the financial aspects of the separation could now begin.

An even greater obstacle to separation was William Lamb's irresolution. Duncannon simply hoped that 'Lamb will make up his mind to something soon'.[82] In May, while negotiations were under way, he was 'foolish and used to go and see her and listen to her stories and laugh'.[83] The Lamb family decided that there could be only one remedy. William's decisions must be taken for him. While Frederick therefore supervised financial arrangements, Emily decided to tackle Caroline head on. At the end of May, she had an interview with her sister-in-law and scored a success: 'I have bullied the Bully and told her Wm is now prepared to go to court. This was sobering and Caro Lamb immediately agreed to negotiate.'[84] After that, 'Wms affair' was 'settling very fast'.[85] In July, Emily reported to Frederick that, although William 'has not strength and decision to resist this sort of warfare',[86] at least he had come to feel 'disgust' for Caroline, who had relapsed into drunkenness and changeability.[87] Although she was exasperated by 'so irresolute a person, every trifle turns his purpose and makes him wander', he had at last accepted that a separation was for his own good.[88] His health had broken down under the strain of events, but the main point seemed to have been gained. He just needed 'somebody at his back to push him on'.[89]

Swiftly and clinically, William Lamb was removed from his wife by his relations. Caroline was to be given an allowance of £3,000 a year,[90] and William was assured that this settlement released him from all other liabilities.[91] He thought the sum offered 'unreasonably large, but it is the general opinion of all that it would not be wise to let considerations of money stand in the way of the conclusion of the business'.[92] Emily agreed. Though 'it is certainly a great deal more than she deserves', generosity to Caroline offered the possibility that 'this great work' would be completed without undue publicity.[93] Quite simply, it was worth it 'to get rid of her'.[94] Final details were still being worked out in the autumn of 1825, largely concerning the question of whether Caroline should be allowed a London establishment, but the main point had been won. For the moment, she was sent off to Brocket with a Dr Goddard and two nurses.[95]

Predictably, William Lamb experienced an unaccustomed freedom from responsibility. In August, his sister could report that he had 'no regrets', but was rather as 'gay as a lark; what an easy Man he is to live with, and what a foolish Caroline she is to have thrown away such Cards'.[96] There followed a short visit to Paris by way of recuperation.[97] By contrast, Caroline was bitter and angry. At the end of October, she had still not been brought to sign the deed of separation, complaining that she had been a fool, 'in trusting to William's honour'.[98] She formally cursed Emily and Frederick Lamb, who she accused of spiriting her husband away. Above all, she loaded her husband with recrimination:

My conduct spirit and pride shall prove to you that I deserved more mercy at yr hands than you have shewn—your cruelty will one day recur to your mind and may my curse bitter and entire fall upon the rest, as for you I will never curse you but if it be permitted me to return I will come and look at you even as Ld Byron did at me— the more I think of the mean barbarous manner in which I have been sacrificed the less I can understand how *you* could bring yourself to sanction it . . . I would not be you for all your present momentary Happiness—cruelty even in this World is ever punished—and you are cruel—cowardly—and selfish.[99]

The Lamb family had closed ranks and Caroline was finally excluded from their company. As they saw it, William had at last been rescued from the consequences of his own irresolution.

For the next two and a half years, Caroline lived at Brocket or in hired houses in London. She was now always attended by nurses from Bedlam,[100] and she had 'not many opports. of plaguing William'.[101] To the exasperation of his relations, William made a point of visiting her from time to time. When his sister heard of these visits, she not unnaturally asked, 'when will that child cut his wise teeth'.[102] Worse, he offered no objection to Caroline proposing a journey to Paris, only meekly suggesting that she should 'avoid making scamps of acquaintance, which is your great fault and danger'.[103] This journey was never made, but Lamb's reaction to its possibility suggests a less than robust attitude to the separation. In fact, once the sense of immediate liberation was over, he felt intensely lonely. In 1826, he spent the summer in Hastings, where 'he stayed quite alone in the Hotel; I had my horses there and rode all day, it did very well in the day, but in the evening—it will not do to be alone'.[104] Caroline herself noted that William seemed 'less happy' without a wife than with one.[105] Legal ties had been severed, but residual emotions had value if the alternative was loneliness. In 1826, Caroline offered William verses full of nostalgia, regret, and hopeless affection:

> Loved one, no tear is in my eye,
> Though pangs my bosom thrill,
> For I have learned when others sigh
> To suffer and be still.
> Passion and Pride and Flattery strove,
> They made a wreck of me,
> But o, I never ceased to love,
> I never loved but thee.
>
> My heart is with our early dreams,
> And still thy influence knows,
> Still seeks thy shadow on the stream
> Of memory as it flows;

Still hangs o'er all the records bright
Of moments brighter still,
Ere love withdrew his starry light,
Ere thou hadst suffered ill.[106]

Caroline Lamb died in January 1828. She had been taken ill the previous November, and William followed the progress of the disease from Ireland, where he had been serving in an official position since April 1827. He was thus 'cruelly situated'.[107] He felt himself 'harassed to death with domestic calamity'.[108] Three weeks before she died, Caroline received a letter from William, informing her, in words mingling affection and a kind of irritation, that he could not easily come over to England: 'My heart is almost broken, that I cannot come over directly . . . How unfortunate and melancholy that you should be so ill now, or that it should be at a time when I, who have had so many years of Idleness, am so fixed and chained down by circumstances.'[109] In fact, as the disease took on a terminal character, Lamb decided that the journey from Ireland to England had to be faced, and he was with his wife when she died.

Opinion was sharply divided about the real nature of William's reaction to the loss of his wife. William Ponsonby, his highly critical brother-in-law, was satisfied that 'Mr Lamb has felt and acted as I knew he would, upon this sad occasion.'[110] William himself described Caroline's death as a 'blow' that was 'severe'.[111] Returning from the funeral, he was relieved that 'everything had been done that could be and every duty paid'.[112] He was left with 'a sort of sense of desolation, solitude and carelessness about every thing, when I forced myself to remember that she was really gone'.[113] Unfortunately, these expressions of grief are contained in letters to an Irishwoman, Lady Branden, who had become his mistress a few months earlier. Paragraphs about Caroline's death are followed by discussions about how his relationship with Lady Branden was to be regulated. Unsentimental as ever, Emily Lamb reported to Frederick that William 'was hurt at the time and rather low next day, but he is now just as usual and his mind filled with Politicks'.[114] According to another relation, Caroline Lamb died 'unregretted'.[115] Years later, Melbourne insisted, when speaking of his wife, that 'in spite of all, she was more to me than anyone ever was, or ever will be'.[116] In one sense, this was true. Lamb almost certainly never cared for anyone more than his wife. In another sense, it is a half-truth. In 1834, Lord Egremont found a sketch of Caroline Lamb by Hoppner among his papers. He thought of sending it to Melbourne, but then changed his mind. Quite simply, he did 'now know whether Melbourne would prefer to have it or to have it burnt'.[117]

His marriage was the determining, and possibly deforming, experience of Melbourne's life. From 1805 to 1828, he could do nothing but respond to the behaviour of a most remarkable wife. He had no spirit or resource for anything else. To his natural father, Lord Egremont, it was clear that the whole arrangement had been damaging. His son's 'only blunder that he could never understand was his mad choice of a wife . . . I always thought he had better judgment and taste.'[118] In his commonplace book, William Lamb soliloquized about the nature of foolishness. His remarks on the subject easily translated into a commentary on his own life:

Neither man nor woman can be worth any thing, until they have discovered that they are fools. This is the first step towards becoming either estimable or agreeable, and until it be taken there is no hope. The sooner the discovery is made the better, as there is more time and power for taking advantage of it. Sometimes the great truth is found out too late to apply to it any effectual remedy. Sometimes it is never found out at all, and there form the desperate and inveterate causes of folly, self-conceit, and impertinence.[119]

Lamb was accused of foolishness by his family and the world for over fifteen years.

Inevitably, he came to see marriage as a kind of grotesque lottery. His own was so painful that Caroline Lamb was only accorded one paragraph in an autobiography begun in 1812 or 1813. By definition it was a confrontational arrangement, a contest of will: 'Mr. L. thought there could be no doubt that it was most advisable to marry, but that those who are not rich ought not to marry at all. People who are forced to live much together, are confined to the same room, the same bed etc, are like two pigeons put under a basket who must fight.'[120] Adultery was almost to be recommended as the only relief from this emotional imprisonment, though significantly Melbourne never took this option himself.[121] Inevitably, the true character of a wife or husband was something 'we must always take our Chance of'.[122] There was always the danger of marrying one person and then finding that you were living with another. In old age, Melbourne had argued himself into a fatalistic neutrality. In 1843, he congratulated a nephew on becoming engaged, but quixotically added that happiness was 'neither in marriage nor in celibacy', but in 'a settled and satisfied mind'.[123] His own marital experience had certainly not provided that.

More generally, the emotional legacy of these years was to choke the channels for expressing affection in a man who was always fastidious in such matters. If he withdrew his love from Caroline Lamb, he never obviously transferred it elsewhere. Women were to talk intelligently, to amuse, and to distract. He never dared to love again. The women, who filled his life after Caroline's death, Lady Branden, Mrs Norton, Emily Eden, and Lady

Stanhope, were all of a kind. Strong-minded, even masculine in temperament, quick-witted and undemanding, they were agreeable companions until they came too close or caused embarrassment. Then they were simply dropped. To some extent he feared them. Women had 'violent and ungoverned passions which made them in the moment of love the most devoted and disinterested Friends and in that of hate the most bitter, determined and malignant enemies'.[124] Such phrases could be taken as a description of his wife. Half-jokingly, half-seriously, he always claimed to sympathize with Henry VIII, because 'those women bothered him so'.[125]

Prolonged emotional disturbance reinforced in Melbourne a tendency to look for distraction and diversion. Talk should be clever and inconsequential. He hated the conversation of Macaulay, which seemed to come out in lecture form. He 'would prefer to sit in a Room with a Chime of Bells, ten Parrots and one Lady Westmorland to sitting in a Cabinet with Mr Macaulay'.[126] He retained a nostalgia for bachelor days, free of all responsibility:

> Then give me back the scorn of care
> Which spirits light in health allow;
> And give me back the dark brown hair
> Which curled upon my even brow.
>
> And give me back the sportive jest
> Which once could midnight's hours beguile,
> The life that bounded in my breast,
> And joyous youth's becoming smile.[127]

A disinclination to impose himself on events led to an all-pervasive passivity. One of his sister's many worries, in 1826, was that he 'eats and drinks too much and gets too full and fat'.[128] He held life at arm's length. Above all, he had a terror of being bored. He disliked going into any issue too deeply for fear of it becoming tedious. Real commitment to an issue could prove as painful as real commitment to an individual. It was better and safer therefore to deflect challenging situations with an epigram.

The pursuit of politics, too, was a distraction. It filled the time. He could never sympathize with ideals or the politicians who peddled them. He lounged his way through difficulties. Guizot, arriving in London as French ambassador, was quite shocked to meet a prime minister, who was so little engaged with events: 'Lord Melbourne . . . was impartial from clear sense and indifference; a judicious epicurean, an agreeable egotist, gay without warmth, and mingling a natural air of authority with a carelessness which he took delight in proclaiming. "It is all the same to me", was his habitual expression.'[129] Others detected a determined hardness in response to human misery which they attributed entirely to a disastrous marriage: 'Lord Melbourne . . . has shown more of his hard ironheadedness as to human suffering than he ever did before. Originally, he was not so, but Lady Caroline's infidelity scathed his sensibilities. There is in Lord Melbourne the sarcasm of the wounded spirit.'[130] William Lamb had been so injured that he could not believe that political action could heal. The role of government was limited to regulating the worst excesses of men and women who could never ultimately trust each other. It was a distinctive stance for someone who was to become prime minister.

Above all, Lamb's family were convinced that his marriage had plunged him into terrible introspection, from which he never fully emerged. Writing a most illuminating memoir of his uncle, William Cowper, called the Lamb marriage 'an unmitigated evil',[131] because 'for twenty years his life was embittered, his ability repressed, and even his credit with the world temporarily impaired'.[132] A natural preference to run before the face of difficulties led to a withdrawal from normal social and political intercourse. Quite simply 'he was driven into seclusion'.[133] A corrosive cynicism came to overlay generous qualities:

There was indeed in his remarks and in his whole character not only a wayward recklessness which was natural to him, but a touch of cynical bitterness which contrasted strongly with the nobleness and generosity of the original man. The nobleness and generosity were, I say, original. The scenes which surrounded him in his early years, and still more that unhappy married life . . . may account for the remainder.[134]

By the time that William Lamb took government office for the first time, in 1827, at the age of 48, his character had been well and truly moulded by events that were not political. His attitude to politics, so often infuriating to those with whom he was called upon to act, had been determined by experiences in private life. Indeed, a serious public career only became possible after his wife's death. William Lamb did not grow in politics. He entered it fully-fledged. He brought to it the flexibility and the rootlessness of someone who had been taught to trust in, and believe, little or nothing. As Lord Houghton observed, 'By the time, therefore, that Mr Lamb attained any political eminence he was practically alone in life.'[135]

Just possibly, near the end of his political life, this pattern was interrupted. In 1837, the young Victoria expressed a need of him and an admiration of him that was irresistible. He, who 'had long suffered from want of an object for which he really cared',[136] now saw a way of easing the emotional isolation that had been forced upon him by a mismatch of a marriage. In some sense, he decided to trust Victoria. Tragically, in trusting once again, he would once again be cruelly disappointed.

PART II

6

Apprenticeship in Politics, 1806–1830

WILLIAM LAMB entered Parliament in January 1806, six months after his marriage. For the next twenty-two years, with the exception of 1812–16, he was in theory a House of Commons man, representing seven different constituencies. Initially, his prospects were excellent. Lady Holland, a talent spotter of some distinction, hailed him as 'one of the most rising men in public'.[1] Unfortunately, William Lamb failed to rise. Until 1827, he was a political nonentity, with no offer of office and a blasted reputation. Even when he took on a junior post in Ireland, contemporaries might well have thought that this would be the ceiling of his ambitions. He was a minor figure, whose existence as a politician at all was entirely a matter of inheritance. He had the benefit of being born in influential circles. There was little else to recommend him. His catastrophic marriage was the major factor in his political eclipse, but there were others.

First and foremost, he lacked ambition. The unwillingness to impose himself on events, which had been so marked a feature of his domestic life, made him an unlikely politician. Indeed, he believed that 'most mad people grow mad out of ambition'.[2] He admired men like Charles V and Diocletian who had abdicated from positions of great power. The slightest set-back was enough to make Lamb think of retiring from politics altogether. As late as 1826, he was seriously thinking of exercising this option.[3] His first two decades in Parliament are marked by long periods of non-attendance and inertia, and this lack of interest was only partially to be explained by a preoccupation with his wife's behaviour. As Albany Fonblanque observed:

The one thing needful and wanting in him was the spur to exertion. Had he been born to bread-and-cheese, he would have risen to the top of whatever profession he had made his choice. His capacity was of the highest order, but there was something which prevented its full development; not indolence, though it bore the appearance of indolence; but the ruling idea that nothing was worth its trouble, the *non tanti* answering to too many a suggestion.[4]

In old age, he expressed surprise that anyone should be so interested in politics as to record its ebb-and-flow in a journal.[5] As a young man, he kept such
a journal, running from March 1807 to February 1808, November 1808 to
July 1810 and, sketchily, from 1811 to 1812. These volumes are completely
self-effacing. Parliamentary matters are reported, but little or nothing is
recorded of the author's own views.[6]

Secondly, William Lamb's political range was dangerously narrow. His suspicion of mass literacy and mass education carried over into a suspicion of mass
politics. He was a pocket borough man. For all but seven years of his time in
the House of Commons, he sat for seats with tiny electorates which followed
the preferences of a patron.[7] Only from 1819 to 1826 did he represent a constituency with a large electorate, Hertfordshire. Significantly, he was driven
from it in 1826 after conducting a campaign that demonstrated a complete
inability to come to terms with a mass audience. His sister lost patience;

Wms election is awkward and will be hard even. I believe he could certainly carry it
if he would exert himself but I never saw such a want of energy or they say a worse
canvasser. He never talks the people over but takes an answer at once, always seeing
things in the view of his opponents as he did in politicks and too candid and doing
the thing only by halves and always despairing.[8]

Altogether, he made a 'foolish figure' on the hustings.[9] Everything was 'shilly
shally'.[10] His opponent, Thomas Duncombe, won the seat by exhorting the
voters in Hertfordshire to rise up against 'the condescending protection of
noblemen'.[11] Lamb took refuge in Newport, a borough on the Isle of Wight
with twenty-four voters. He was not prepared to contend for votes 'against
difficulty, ill-will, and opposition'.[12]

Thirdly, William Lamb was a terrible parliamentary speaker. Before
becoming Home Secretary in 1830, he had no oratorical reputation at all,
speaking less often and less well than his brother George. Between 1806 and
1828, seventy-nine parliamentary interventions are recorded, but many of
these run to only a paragraph in the Commons journals. Between 1820 and
1828, he spoke only nineteen times. There are no speeches at all in 1808,
1820, and 1827, and less than four in 1806, 1807, 1809, 1816, and 1821 to
1826. He practised his speeches in the 'shrubbery . . . at Brocket', but, as
soon as he rose to speak in the House, he was paralysed by a nervous apprehension: 'a torpor of all my faculties almost always comes upon me, and I
feel as if I had neither ideas nor opinions.'[13] Caroline Lamb was always
'frightened to death' when her husband summoned up the courage to
speak.[14] He himself observed, about 1812, that

I had upon me the load of some reputation; I was always nervous, and I was too vain
to expose myself to what I considered the disgrace of speaking in a hesitating manner

and I had not taken the measures necessary for a more fluent and thinking performance. In this manner I acquired the evil habit of sitting silent, until my Fears of course
increasing became so strong, that seven years hardly got the better of them in any
considerable degree.[15]

Even when he had specifically researched a topic, his courage could fail him
at the last minute.[16] When newspapers failed to report his 'bothering, tan-
gling' speeches, he could only think this just.[17] Strangely, for a future Prime
Minister, he never improved very much. Few holders of that office can have
spoken so infrequently or with such brevity. In an obituary of Melbourne, the
Gentleman's Magazine recorded: 'he had the habit of floundering along, seem-
ing to speak without making any real progress.'[18] For much of his life,
Melbourne simply lacked the confidence to give his intelligent and literate
views oral expression.

For someone of such a reticent temperament, it must have been comforting that his political views were, initially, genetically determined. He
had no choices to make. For someone brought up in the Holland and
Devonshire House circles, Foxite Whiggery was the only possible creed. As
has been noted above, this predilection was confirmed by the personal interest that Fox took in him. Lamb visited Fox at St Anne's Hill regularly, and
was proud to remember that the famous statesman, 'took great notice of
me'.[19] Fox sponsored him for Brooks's Club, the Whig party's favourite
watering hole, and showed an 'almost paternal interest about him which I
know to have been stronger than about any young man now in
Parliament'.[20] Fox's death, in 1806, was deeply felt. Lamb had 'admired
and loved' him.[21] He had been 'almost his best friend'.[22] Not surprisingly,
at the funeral, it was noted that William Lamb was the mourner who
'seemed most to feel'.[23] Part of his grieving was to compose an inscription
that might be added to a bust of Fox:

> Live, Marble, Live! for thine's a sacred trust—
> The patriot's face, that speaks his noble mind;
> Live, that our sons may kneel before this bust,
> And hail the benefactor of mankind.
>
> This was the man, who, midst the tempest's rage,
> A mark of safety to the nation stood,
> Warn'd with prophetic voice a servile age,
> And strove to quench the ruthless thirst for blood.
>
> This was the man whose ever-deathless fame
> Recalls his generous life's illustrious scenes.
> To bless his fellow creatures was his aim,
> And universal Liberty his means.[24]

As a young man, Lamb uncritically accepted the Foxite creed intoned by those around him.

Central to this faith was the idea that parliamentary government was threatened by tyrannical rulers in general and by George III in particular. By dispensing places, pensions, and sinecures, the Crown gradually corrupted the consciences of members of the Lords and Commons. Slowly but surely, the executive infiltrated the legislature. Representative government was snuffed out and a royal autocracy took its place. Sinecures, Lamb told Parliament in 1810, 'had a tendency to introduce into the House a set of men, who could not be expected to give an unbiased suffrage upon any discussion'.[25] Once kings controlled parliamentarians, they could make or break ministries at will. In 1807, the Ministry of All the Talents, of which Foxite Whigs formed a part, was removed from office. According to the party view shared by Lamb, their offence had not been incompetence, but merely that they had been uncongenial in the eyes of George III. In public, he expressed concern 'to see removed from the councils of their sovereign, the men who were such able props to the constitution'.[26] In private he was much sharper. Referring to the end of the Talents in his journal, he tartly observed that: 'the short history of the matter is that He [George III] was determined upon the first opportunity to get rid of an administration, which acted upon principles and maxims, which it has been the study of his reign to counteract and destroy.'[27] Lamb wholeheartedly accepted the Foxite view that English parliamentarianism was seriously at risk from a king who had never accepted the constraints that it imposed on his wishes.

Accordingly, Fox's political opponents became Lamb's enemies too. He had absolutely no regard for Castlereagh,[28] and actively opposed the setting up of any kind of public monument to Spencer Perceval.[29] As for the long administration of Lord Liverpool, its principles were so suspect that each of its proposals had to be carefully scrutinized, to the extent that ministers could be threatened with the cutting off of public supplies.[30] In 1819, he had no hesitation in voting for a Committee on the State of the Nation to be set up, because the performance of the government substantiated the gravest doubts.[31] This early, Foxite suspicion of kings would be much modified as Lamb grew older but it never entirely disappeared from his political make-up. As a minister of the Crown in due course, he was always acutely aware that kings had to be kept within bounds. Piously, he kept up with Fox's widow, who in turn assured him that he was 'so beloved by him who was all to me'.[32] Gladstone, writing in 1890 and puzzling about how Melbourne had 'found his way into the Liberal Party of the day', believed that Fox had bequeathed Lamb three profoundly Whiggish attributes which never left him: 'he did not love national quarrels. He was incapable of religious intolerance.

And he had a real sympathy for Ireland.'[33] If doubt about kings is added to this list, it would represent a complete account of Melbourne's debt to a Foxite youth.

Yet, right from the beginning, there were points on which Lamb's views were not Fox's. In particular, he never showed his leader's almost unqualified Francophilia, which he described as amounting to a 'contempt of the feelings and habits of his own country'.[34] Lamb spoke rarely on foreign affairs, perhaps aware of the differences which separated him from his friends in this area. His views have to be culled from his private journals, in which he observed that the disagreements about 'the accursed French revolution' had a habit of leading to 'a general breakup of political connexion and friendship'.[35] The student of Glasgow and Cambridge, who had taken up Bonaparte as a hero, gave way rapidly to a politician deeply suspicious of everything the French did. The more this mood settled in, the more Lamb set himself at a tangent to Foxite politics. By 1842, he could assure the House of Lords that the French Revolution had been 'the greatest calamity that ever befell the world'.[36]

By 1806 or so, it was clear to Lamb that Bonaparte was less a liberator of oppressed peoples than the latest representative of the standard French desire to dominate Europe. He wrapped himself in the *tricolore* rather than the fleur-de-lis of the *ancien régime*, but the ambition was the same. Incidentally to this purpose, he could bring benefits to backward parts of Europe like Spain by doing away with 'the enormous and galling privileges of the nobility',[37] but such gains scarcely mitigated the enormity of the overall design. He was the old Adam. In 1808, Lamb vigorously supported the Spanish resistance to Napoleon, because when 'one contemplates his resources, when one thinks of in how many rich and populous countries he wields the power and the strength, it is impossible not to tremble'.[38] It was right to lend all assistance to the Spanish guerillas,[39] and it was right to take such extreme measures as allowing foreigners to join the British army, if 'the necessity of the times' demanded it.[40] The lingering admiration for Bonapartism, which could be sniffed in the air at Holland House, and which led its owners to try to help Marshal Ney in 1815, was specifically repudiated by Lamb.[41] He could even rise to a kind of blimpish verse that made Fox and the Hollands turn pale;

> The soul of Britain thro' that awful night,
> Shed on the waves a calm and splendid light,
> And from her sacred Isle's commanding steep
> Streamed Life and safety o'er the labouring deep.[42]

In Lamb's view, the only way to secure a permanent peace with France was to put that country into such a disabled condition that it would have

neither the will nor the resources to cause trouble. Otherwise, as he told the
Commons in November 1806: 'It was soon discovered that if any peace consistent with the honour of this country could be made, France would soon
find it in their interest to break it.'[43] This warning stands in stark contrast to
the exuberant, even schoolboyish, joy with which he had welcomed the Peace
of Amiens four years earlier. In May 1802, he wrote an epilogue for Miss
Berry's play *Fashionable Friends*, which begins

> Amidst these different tastes, may I advance
> The grounds on which I vote for peace with France.[44]

Foremost among these was the frivolous idea that London would be an amusing place again. Within a very short space of time, this Foxite trust of France
had been replaced by a more doubting position.

Of equal importance in distancing Lamb from Foxite orthodoxy was his
cynicism in evaluating the parliamentary credentials of people in Europe who
called themselves liberals. Such men also gave evidence of being totally lacking in commonsense. While Holland House endlessly offered shelter and
encouragement to liberal movements all over Europe, Lamb was unsure
whether violence in Europe 'ought to be attributed to the continental sover-
eigns, to the wickedness of their ministers, or to the impracticable designs of
that very liberal party, who now lamented over the evils by which the conti-
nent was afflicted'. In particular, 'to attempt to relieve a country from arbitrary power, without the least chance of success', was in fact a folly.[45] Too
much of European liberalism was the prerogative of idealistic conspirators
huddled in garrets. Their pipe-dreams led to violence in which they had no
hope of success. It was madness for England to think of intervening in Europe
on their behalf.[46] Even if, by some fluke, a liberal uprising succeeded, it was
unlikely to change the realities of power politics:

The case with all foreign powers is that they never take our advice . . . they treat us
with the utmost contempt; they take every measure hostile to our interests; they are
anxious to prove that we have not the least influence on them. And then when by
their misconduct they have got themselves into an inextricable difficulty, they throw
themselves upon our mercy, and say, 'For God's sake re-establish us . . . that we may
run again the same course of domestic error and hostility to England.'[47]

Lamb knew Europe much less well than many others in Whig circles.
Travelling between 1789 and 1815 was admittedly difficult, but many managed it. He in contrast only visited France twice, in 1815 and 1825. He met
foreigners at Holland House and other salons, but knew them far less well
than Fox, the Hollands, or Lord John Russell. He preferred to see liberal,
parliamentary states in Europe, and disliked autocratic ones, but a passive
fatalism governed his response to both.[48]

Further muting Lamb's mumbling of the Foxite creed was his response to domestic unrest. In this area, once more, fatalism broke in. Since orthodox Whiggery tended to believe that riot was almost always the result of misgovernment or the consequence of dearth and hunger, it also advocated action by government to rectify the situation. Government could behave better and government could succour those in need. Lamb disagreed. Economic cycles, man's improvidence, and acts of God always had and always would produce trouble from time to time. Governments could do little to change the situation. When, in 1819, his agent in Derbyshire reported terrible distress among the frame-knitters in Melbourne village, Lamb agreed to subscribe to a fund for their assistance, though he felt compelled to add that, 'this is in the nature of things which no human law can by any possibility alter, though they may in some degree perhaps modify it . . . They must also recollect that society is not in reason bound to find a man employment any more than it is bound to find him assistance for nothing.'[49] Disgruntled manufacturers looking for assistance were told the same thing. They should look to their own resources. Economic dislocations were to be suffered fatalistically, like bad winters or bouts of influenza.

These differences between Lamb and the Foxites on why riot occurred naturally led on to disagreements about how it should be dealt with. Foxites tended to see political protest as provoked by incompetent or malevolent government. Those who engaged in it therefore often deserved sympathy. Lamb agreed that protest of all sorts was perfectly justified, but insisted that it had to stay within legal bounds. If it strayed outside those limits, it should be severely put in its place. The future Home Secretary told the Commons, in January 1817, that

he reverenced popular meetings, which were regularly and quietly conducted; . . . but when they led to breaches of the peace, he was for vigorous and immediate repression. . . . He deprecated all breaches of the peace, disturbance, and riot . . . Tumult for liberty and right was not only dangerous and destructive, but was a liar, and never kept its promises. It led in the end, through scenes of anarchy and blood to a political tyranny, or military despotism.[50]

The last sentence is redolent of memories of events in France in the 1790s. As a schoolboy and undergraduate, he had welcomed them. Now, he saw them as a vicious precedent. To the dismay of Holland House and other Whig friends, Lamb, a month later, agreed to serve on a Committee of Secrecy to consider the extent and nature of seditious activities. Convinced that the Hampden and Spencean Clubs were intent on violent revolution, he went along with the Committee's recommendation that Habeas Corpus should be suspended. He was sorry 'to differ with so many of those, whose persons I esteem and whose opinions I respect',[51] but he had no choice. Although 'he was not a very old person . . . it had been his lot to see war upon war, revolution upon revolution'.[52]

Two years later, the pattern repeated itself. While most Whigs were so appalled by the massacre of people attending a public meeting at Peterloo, that they demanded an inquiry into the conduct of the magistrates, Lamb regretted the deaths but doubted the proposed remedy. He therefore supported the idea of an inquiry in public,[53] and questioned it in private.[54] Lamb was Whig in the sense that he 'would rather see the country revolutionized than enslaved',[55] but if protest was fully allowed within the limits of the law and punished outside those limits, perhaps both these extremes could be avoided. To ignore violence completely was to threaten liberty rather than to defend it. Lamb's actions in 1817 and 1819 established his reputation in the area of law and order. He was clearly not as libertarian as many of his Whig friends. It was a comfort to a Cabinet colleague, in 1836, to 'remember the eloquent manner in which Lord Melbourne expressed himself at that time against those Revolutionary Proceedings'.[56] His speeches on the subject are among the best of his early career, but they won him scant praise in Holland House circles. On the other hand, his nomination as Home Secretary in 1830 was a little less strange if a memory of these years is taken into account.

The last point of divergence from the straight Foxite path in these early years concerned Parliamentary Reform. This was the least important departure, not because the issue itself lacked substance, but because the Foxite myth was not clear on the matter. Tradition hailed Fox as a reformer. Those who had known him were aware that his views had been more equivocal. Lamb's hesitation on the issue was not therefore damning. Many Whigs had doubts about Reform, though few, perhaps, had as many as William Lamb, who thought, as early as 1813, that 'any great alteration in the general complexion of society is always to be viewed with apprehension'.[57] On this view, the need for change had always to be demonstrated. It should never be a matter of altering hard practice to fit mere speculative theory: 'Whenever you meddle with these ancient rights and jurisdictions it appears to me that for the sake of remedying comparatively insignificant abuses you create new ones and always produce considerable discontent.'[58] If new forms of commercial and industrial property claimed a place in politics, it was 'of extreme importance that correct notions should be formed by such persons',[59] by which he meant that they should accept the rules of the political club they wished to join, and should not seek to invent new ones. If new property claimed the franchise, it had to accept the principles laid down by old property.

In particular, the admission of new property-owners into the political process must not be taken as a bowing towards democracy. On this his views were clear. In a draft speech, he observed that 'The fault of Democracy is, that you can get nothing good done by it in cool blood or upon consideration—The people will make no effort, unless they are excited, and when excited they are of course liable to be misled by their own passions and the artifices of others.'[60] If pushed to the wall, he would prefer democratic to despotic government, but even so, he half-thought that 'the Sultan of Constantinople, the Shah of Persia, or the Dey of Algiers, were subject to more efficient responsibility than the leaders of a democratic assembly'.[61] As has been noted, he hated the idea of Parliament being pressurized by mass politics in the form of meetings and petitions. He admitted that such things were perfectly legal, but found the process noisy and vulgar. Not infrequently, he refused to present petitions to Parliament, even if they came from his own tenants and neighbours.[62] None of this made William Lamb psychologically receptive to the idea of major, constitutional reform.

Further, he much disliked those who did advocate change. As far as he cut any parliamentary figure in these years, it was as a baiter of Radicals. Cobbett, whatever his disclaimers, only had one basis for his politics, which was to 'call upon the poor to seize upon the property of the country'.[63] In 1810 and again in 1817, in opposing Burdett's motions for Parliamentary Reform, he lectured that Radical baronet severely. It was outrageous to suggest that parliament, as then constituted, failed fully to represent the people.[64] It was monstrous to argue that great property should not have great influence,[65] and it was absurd to think that the motley army of persons who attended public meetings and signed petitions expressed 'in any degree the cool, deliberate, well-understood sense of the people of England'.[66] Burdett and Cobbett lived by speculation not experience, and 'to determine this question, we must not have recourse to mere theories, and visionary ideas of perfection; we must look at the actual state of things, and at the working of the machine'.[67] Invoking yet again, 'that great repository of woeful experience, the French revolution', he declared himself, in 1818, an enemy to all the changes proposed by the Radicals.[68] If necessary, in a way that prefigured his tactics as Prime Minister, Lamb was happy to invoke Tory assistance against Radicals. In 1820, he implored the Tories to make common cause with the Whigs in the Westminster constituency to defeat the Radical candidate Hobhouse, and 'the distinct principles of revolution upon which he stands'.[69] Frederick Lamb derived 'real joy' from seeing his brother 'in a towering passion with Burdett'.[70] When William thought or spoke about Radical programmes for constitutional change, it seemed, for once, that he was genuinely moved. Lethargy, uncertainty, and a practised disdain for enthusiasm all slipped away. The issue gave evidence that he had more than ice in his veins.

Yet, to record his voting and speaking against Reform motions in 1810 and 1817 is not to tell the whole story. Lamb was Whig enough to admit the theoretical proposition that, if the people, meaning the propertied, demanded change, it would have to be conceded. Equally, he was flexible enough to see the 'defects in the representation'.[71] In 1820, on balance, he was inclined to vote to unseat the Members for Grampound, as a punishment for corruption on an heroic scale:

What do you think of the Grampound business? The disfranchising the borough *entirely* is a new and unprecedented step . . . and is an admission of some of the main principles of the reformers, and cannot be considered as anything less than the commencement of a reformation of the present system of representation . . . At the same time, considering the state of the Borough of Grampound, and of others like it, and considering the feeling and opinion of the country upon the subject, I for one am not unwilling to take these steps, important and considerable as I know them to be.[72]

He could swallow small adjustments to the system, but he baulked at any more extended schemes, because they could not be 'moderate nor limited'. If once the Reformers' criticisms were admitted, no half-way remedy would be acceptable. All would be overturned.[73] In 1826, only six years before the great Reform Bill passed into law, William Lamb voted against Lord John Russell's motion for change in a speech which led his sister to note that 'all the Whigs are furious with Wm'. According to her, he had now formally 'left' that party.[74] On this view, Parliamentary Reform had become the point of separation of Lamb and the Whigs. This is too apocalyptic, but Lamb caricatured the views of his friends by listing in his commonplace book the names of those Whig reformers who sat for rotten or pocket boroughs. It amused him to think that they were so anxious to cut their own throats.[75]

Between 1806 and 1827 therefore, Lamb started as a protégé of Fox and developed into a politician with views of his own. He still felt comfortable in Whig salons and shared all of their social assumptions, and many of their political prejudices. As Gladstone had noted, he was incapable of understanding jingoism or religious intolerance, and he took a sympathetic view of Ireland. On top of which, and importantly, Hollands and Devonshires remained his cousins. Yet, more and more, William stepped out of line. He thought Bonaparte a real threat to England; he was determined to suppress protest that went beyond legal bounds; and he profoundly distrusted schemes for Parliamentary Reform. His long absences from Parliament and his long silences in Parliament masked the true extent to which he had diverged from the Whig norm. In terms of society and habits of thought, he was true to his upbringing. In politics, he had become more distinctive.

Crucially though, in becoming a little less Whig, he never became a little more anything else. Looking for a label to hang round Lamb's neck by 1827, many historians have called him a Canningite. Brougham thought this likely,[76] and Emily Lamb noted that her brother was 'completely devoted' to Canning.[77] Those, however, who listed the members of the Canningite group without mentioning William Lamb were nearer the mark.[78] In fact, Lamb had a low opinion of Canning's abilities and motives. In 1807, he observed that Canning's politics were marked by 'pettishness, querulousness and littleness'.[79] His speeches were often 'brilliant', but 'fake and inconclusive'.[80] After Canning's death, Lamb's judgement was severe: 'Canning was a Schemer, witness all the projects, some of which he entertained, and some actually adopted upon his accession to office, one more absurd than the other. He had none of the straightforward simplicity, which belongs to a Great Man, altho' he could sometimes assume the character of it.' With true Whig hauteur, Lamb thought that Canning brought into politics 'the tone of a clerk'.[81] Canning's presence in a Cabinet was no guarantee of either stability or a principled approach to policy-making.[82] His quixotic behaviour offered promising opportunities for bets in clubland, but was otherwise unattractive.[83] In 1822, both William and Frederick Lamb turned down offers of employment in Canning's Foreign Office, fearing 'abuse and misrepresentation, and the imputation of the most sordid and interested motives'.[84] Not surprisingly, there was little correspondence between the two men. A dozen letters survive, only one of which is dated before 1827, and that was concerned with only a minor point of patronage. Both men denied political association with the other. Canning called Lamb his friend only 'in a private sense'.[85] Lamb begged Brougham 'not to call me a Canningite, or a follower of the Canning Party . . . I . . . never acted with him, nor was in his confidence.'[86]

It is true that Lamb had a Canningite cousin in William Huskisson (see Fig. 5), but this connection had little of politics in it. William was distressed to hear that Huskisson had defeated a Foxite in a Cornish election in 1804.[87] The two men rarely corresponded. Among Huskisson's papers, there are less than ten letters from Lamb, and all of those are of an entirely formal nature. Huskisson frequently referred to a Canningite group consisting of himself, Palmerston, Grant, and Dudley, but never mentioned Lamb. The latter was distressed to hear of his cousin's death in a railway accident in 1830, but pointed out that the tragedy in no way changed his own political options.[88] As far as William Lamb had any real contact with the Canningite world, it rested on his deep affection for Emily Huskisson. The cousins had grown up together. Mrs Huskisson 'had learned to consider William Lamb as a brother, and have never ceased to love him as such. Our ages were nearly the same, and our early years spent much together, for even when he went to school, I eagerly awaited the returning holidays, as joyous ones for myself.'[89]

Remembrance of things past, exchanged with an amiable cousin, was, however, too infirm a foundation on which to base a transfer of political allegiances.

Never a Canningite and not strictly a Whig, William Lamb demanded the right to private judgement. He seemed to find it as difficult to make a commitment to the corporate identity of party as to freely give emotional responses. His distancing of himself from hard choices informed both his political and personal life. Further, the two could not be kept separate. Stepping back from the Holland House creed was the easier if the two families were embroiled in the consequences of Caroline Lamb's behaviour. At the very outset of his career, Lady Bessborough worried that William Lamb was 'too scrupulous and conscientious for a good party man'.[90] Party, perhaps like a wife or clinging mistress, closed options, made demands, and was generally noisy and tiresome. Lamb liked to be as fastidious in politics as he was in dress. From the beginning, he liked to balance alternatives and to nuance decisions. He adored Fox, but he was happy to admit Pitt's 'transcendent talents'.[91] He disliked Pitt's heirs, but thought that the Foxites were too 'short-sighted, prejudiced and erroneous' in judging their achievements.[92] Some of his political friends were so full of 'presumption', that they were 'guilty of every species of misrepresentation'.[93] This remark was written as early as 1810. Even by this date, politics had really become a matter of choosing between evils. Pitt and Lord Liverpool had many, many faults, but their opponents were too often 'factious'.[94]

In these early years, complaints about Lamb's performance as a party man abound. Too often he missed votes because 'he durst not vote either one way or the other'.[95] His sister-in-law described his speeches as 'half and half', and added that this was 'usually' his style.[96] Emily Lamb more trenchantly called them 'such milk and water' stuff. She heartily wished her brother 'would join one side or the other'.[97] By 1819, the Duke of Bedford gave up the unequal struggle of defining Lamb's politics at all. He thought that they could be summed up by the phrase, 'God know's what!'[98] In the same year, Lord Althorp thought that, in spite of 'doubt', Lamb should be supported by Whig grandees in his Hertfordshire election, even though he had spent the whole of the previous session voting against them.[99] Whiggery was always more of an association of like-minded cousins than a party, but William Lamb's lack of team spirit was straining patience. It was too easy to draw analogies between the passivity and indecision that marked his turbulent private life and the same qualities demonstrated in politics. William Lamb had no capacity to go beyond himself. He could not join others, cope with others, accept others, or perhaps, love others.

There was a price to be paid for this diffidence. To the social ostracism that followed marital derangement was added the political isolation that was the consequence of an almost wilful aloofness. A man of fortune, who could meet his own electoral expenses, might have acted as Lamb did without risk. But he claimed the privileges of an independent income without actually possessing one. For most of his House of Commons career, Lamb was dependent on the goodwill of patrons. To claim to be a man free of all influence and constraint was therefore ungrateful. Equally, to demand the privileges of party without accepting the corresponding responsibilities was asking a great deal. In 1811, he was mortified to be offered only minor office in a projected Grey–Grenville administration, but this can hardly have been totally surprising. Only a short time before, he had proudly told his mother-in-law that he was unwilling to 'bind himself by a place to an Administration form'd of such discordant parties, and when he knew many things might be brought forward he should dislike, that for the present at least he was determin'd to remain unpledg'd'.[100] Such a manifesto had a brave ring to it, but it could hardly have made its author an attractive, potential colleague. If he denied party, party might deny him.

Just how exposed he had become was demonstrated by the 1812 election. Lamb lost his seat and was out of Parliament for four years. He felt this reverse bitterly:

It is impossible that any Body can feel the being out of Parliament more keenly than I feel it for myself. It is actually cutting my throat. It is depriving me of the greatest object of my life at the moment . . . I have no money—I am embarrassed to a certain degree by circumstances which I am willing to explain, my income is insufficient, I am deprived of many things which I wish to have, and in many things in which I might be facilitated, I receive no assistance.[101]

In accounting for this set-back, which came in the middle of the Byron *affaire*, Lamb was inclined to blame everyone but himself. He accused his family of not helping him to come in for St Albans.[102] When the Duke of Bedford offered him a seat, he declined it on the grounds that this nobleman had 'too *narrow* a view of the present state of politics'. His mother-in-law, reporting this remark, concluded that he disliked all forms of political dependence. Quite simply, 'he dislikes extremely the thoughts of being brought in'.[103]

Under the weight of these many disappointments, Lamb became intemperate. Still claiming the right to an independent opinion, he yet argued that the Whig party should have taken more care of him. To Charles Grey, he poured out his bitterness:

I cannot but feel that my friends have failed me at the most critical moment of my political life, and perhaps at the only moment which may afford them an opportunity of shewing any attachment or conferring any obligation. I have never before stood in need of aid. Perhaps I may never stand in need of it again, but it will be difficult for me to forget that when I did stand in need of it, it was not afforded me.[104]

Both Grey and Holland offered sympathy, but Lamb refused to be consoled.[105] The loss of his seat and the failure to find another was 'a perverse interruption of my career'.[106] He had been the victim of 'abandonment'.[107] Shortly after, he began an autobiography. It was both a self-justification and a valediction to politics. For a man of 34 to begin an autobiography suggests a feeling that most important aspects of life had already come to an end. It was to be 'a short review of the course of my life',[108] as though it had almost run its course. Nearly all of this was unfair, unkind, and lacking in perspective. The combined impact of the Byron *affaire* and what looked like the termination of a political career that had hardly started was too much for him. In every sense, he felt totally isolated.

The mood did not change quickly. In 1814, he claimed that to be out of Parliament was 'utter extinction and annihilation', but went on still to demand that party should regard him while he remained free of party: 'much as I wish for a seat in the House of Commons, I could not accept any but a perfectly Independent one . . . I could not possibly bind myself to agree with any party or to follow the lead of any Individual now existing in either House of Parliament.'[109] He was asking the impossible. A year later, Holland found a political patron for Lamb, but was snubbed for his pains.[110] He resented any 'conditions and restrictions' being put on his views. The Foxites had not helped him in 1812, and were now only trying to shackle him.[111] When he did return to the Commons, in 1816, the sense of distance between Lamb and the Whigs, complicated by Lady Caroline's behaviour, was mutually felt.[112] On one or two crucial issues, his views were diverging from Foxite Whiggery, without finding an anchorage in any other political tradition. But this was only part of the problem. For a number of years after 1812, Lamb was so traumatized by a combination of extraordinary experiences that he was inclined to break off contact with all his previous connections. For the moment, he liked and trusted no one.

Given this studied aloofness from obligations of party, Lamb's prospects could not be considered promising. Yet, in April 1827, he was appointed Chief Secretary to the Lord Lieutenant of Ireland. It was his first taste of office and he was already 48 years old. Inevitably, the circumstances which wafted such a marginal figure into some kind of prominence were extraordinary. The appointment of George Canning as Prime Minister had created confusion in all parties. Some Tories agreed to work with him and some refused. Equally, some Whigs offered full co-operation, some a benevolent neutrality, and some defiance. With all party loyalties under strain, a man with little party loyalty like Lamb had a chance. As Canning desperately searched around for anyone of talent and unexceptional views, William Lamb seemed suddenly less inconsequential. He had few personal interests in Ireland, and would no doubt welcome a Dublin posting as putting distance between himself and his marital difficulties. He himself was in favour of religious toleration,[113] but he was also happy to work with those who found this notion hard to swallow.[114] In his view, lobbies like the Catholic Association had every right to press their views legally, and should have every expectation of being silenced if they did so illegally.[115] Above all, as has been noted, he was a sceptic who admired Anglicanism. Therefore, he was in favour of that degree of religious equality that was 'compatible with safety both to the Doctrines and to the superiority of the Protestant establishment'.[116] In being partly friendly to all religions, Lamb might at least give the Irish pause.

The appointment delighted his family. Emily Lamb reported to Frederick that 'Wm . . . always wanted employment, and was in a *fausse position* about Politicks. Now he has everything open to him and is in his proper station.' It all proved the wisdom of parting 'with that Woman', who had been 'a mill stone round his neck'.[117] Her brother's politics seemed to be acquiring more definition, 'having been so long no how'.[118] The only discordant element in the whole business was that William had been, as usual, 'terribly supine about putting himself forward',[119] and had actually left London at the very moment that ministerial arrangements were being discussed. In fact, Lamb had been very keen to come in from the cold. He later admitted that he had been mildly irritated at not being offered a Cabinet post,[120] although in the circumstances that would have been out of the question. There was nothing in his career to date that could have suggested such a move. As it was, he accepted the Irish job joyfully. To pretend that office had been won reluctantly would have been 'pretence and affectation'.[121]

Whether William Lamb could cope with an Irish appointment was debated by friends and relations. Holland optimistically reported that many thought him 'best suited to Irishmen',[122] though he was wonderfully ignorant of Ireland's politics. He himself admitted that he had never 'paid the least attention to any of the reports or debates upon Irish subjects',[123] and that it was 'more than probable, that in the outset I shall commit many errors'.[124] For once, however, he had steeled himself to some commitment and hard work. With a rather self-conscious girding of loins, he thought he could 'manage it'.[125] Though it was, as his sister pointed out, 'a troublesome employment', it was also his first opportunity to show his paces in 'a place of great consequence'.[126] After years of enforced idleness and isolation, William had at last secured something that could at least divert him, and might even lead him to a real interest in public affairs.

As for the Irish themselves, Lamb's political credentials were so indistinct, that his suitability for the job was questioned by both Catholics and Protestants. The latter were so suspicious, that the new Chief Secretary was denied the usual honour of being offered the Freedom of the City of Dublin. Throughout his stay in Ireland, Lamb frequently had cause to worry about Orangemen tampering with his mail.[127] When Catholics sought a clarification of Lamb's views, they were simply told to have 'confidence, though we cannot do much, or worse men will come'.[128] This unappetizing formula led the Catholic leader, Daniel O'Connell, to conclude that it was 'idle to expect anything of Mr Lamb'.[129] Even if he himself was happy to indulge Catholic claims, his political associates would assuredly block his initiatives:

There are to be sure some individuals in that administration perfectly free of guile and too honourable themselves to believe in the existence of duplicity. Such I unequivocably believe Mr Lamb to be. Besides, his rank and station in society place him on a superior level. But all the acts of the Administration convince me that they are determined to give us good words as long as they can delude, but their acts, *their acts*, are unequivocal.[130]

In the other words, William Lamb, probably unconscious of his own position, was seen as the unthreatening face of a government that was in fact full of hostility to Catholic pretensions.

Cheerfully inexperienced in office and inexpert on Irish affairs, Lamb began work with one principal only. There were to be no exclusions. Anyone, of whatever religious or political persuasion, was welcome to a meal or an interview. Whig enough to believe that a good dinner was the answer to most problems, he began to give three or four such parties each week, asking 'every body right and left'.[131] After three months in Dublin, he reported to Canning that he had 'done nothing but dine out since I arrived'.[132] His accounts show that he was spending over £100 a week on entertainments. After the sombre years in the seclusion of Brocket, this re-entry into a full social life was exhilarating. Crucially, Catholics were as welcome at Dublin Castle as Protestants had ever been, a fact that led some officials to think that 'Mr Lamb keeps a lot of bad company'.[133] Lamb was impervious to remarks of this kind, however. In fact, he wished to extend this spirit of inclusion beyond dining and dancing. There was no reason in his mind, by 1830, why O'Connell himself should not be offered high legal office, 'perhaps even the Mastership of the Rolls'.[134] Given his background and education, it was inconceivable to Lamb that differences of religion could be a bar to forming a friendship or appointing a colleague.

Lamb was to hold his position in Ireland until June 1828. In these fifteen months, he showed a capacity for hard work that surprised his family and may have surprised himself. By September 1827, he was writing letters that suggested a mastery of such Irish problems as tithes, education, customs, and land reform.[135] Though there were topics like 'police, goals, hospitals, penitentiaries', which he had 'little or no taste for', he worked away at them, and modestly thought his situation 'enough for me, who have been so long used to do nothing'.[136] He developed a good working relationship with two Lords Lieutenant, Lords Wellesley and Anglesey, and positively liked the latter. On leaving Ireland, he kept up an interest in Irish affairs and this was of importance for his own prime ministership. There were few areas of policy that Melbourne could speak on with the confidence that comes from detailed and expert knowledge. Ireland and its problems would be one of them. For once, he came close to having the unaccustomed feeling of not being an amateur.

The major problem faced by the Irish administration in which Lamb served was undoubtedly presented by Daniel O'Connell and the Association movement. Demands from Roman Catholics that they be accorded full religious toleration were not new, but now they took institutional form. The Association, as an organization, believed itself capable of coercing government by promoting electoral chaos and the non-payment of taxes. As lobbyists, O'Connell and his friends seemed prepared to threaten as well as persuade. Lamb responded to this challenge predictably. Protest and arguments for change must always be given a fair hearing. Roman Catholics, in particular, were, in his view, entitled to every sympathy. To exclude significant groups from the *pays légal* was to lose the services of talented people, and to create unnecessary friction. If Catholicism ever had been politically dangerous, it clearly had ceased to be so. As far as Lamb was concerned, the case was clear. Even so, Catholics had to operate within the law. Protest was legitimate as long as it was legal. He had taken this view in response to Radical disturbances ten years earlier. He would adopt it again as Home Secretary. Lamb was all affability as long as the conventions were observed. He would dine with anyone as long as they refrained from shouting.

By family upbringing and education, William Lamb was for toleration, not simply because he himself was indifferent to particular creeds, but rather because there was something coarse about persecution. To hate religious dissenters involved a level of religious enthusiasm that was in itself distasteful. Before accepting the post in Dublin, Lamb had tried to secure guarantees that policy would be determined 'upon the most rational, sensible and liberal footing'.[137] If he had any doubts about Wellesley as Lord-Lieutenant, it was that he was too 'irresolute and indecisive' in this respect.[138] He was clear from the start that the Catholics deserved more patient handling than the

Protestants, because 'the former are labouring under a galling exclusion, whilst the latter are striving to maintain an unjust superiority'.[139] To principle was added practicality. Until the Catholic majority in Ireland was accommodated, Protestants could never feel secure, and that country would continue to offer a base from which England's enemies could mount an invasion. The memory of the Irish rebellion of 1798 must have been still fresh, when he noted that 'Ireland has always been the weak point of England'.[140] Therefore, Lamb had no doubt that 'policy as well as justice' demanded concessions to the Catholics, particularly as O'Connell was 'kicking up a Devil of a dust'.[141] He pointedly disassociated himself from an anti-Catholic petition promoted by his own tenants in Derbyshire.[142]

Yet, the process by which toleration would come had clearly defined parameters. As he told Anglesey: 'by reason moderation and common sense the Roman Catholics may effect their object, notwithstanding the serious difficulties in their way, by threatening, blustering and trying to bully they never will.'[143] The Whig in him hoped that change would come through the irresistible logic of informed opinion. Appealing to a mass audience was, as ever, unfortunate. He disliked O'Connell's Association and he disliked the Protestants' Orange Lodges. Marches and meetings provoked nothing but noise, and that drowned debate. It was a pity that such things were 'such an inveterate habit . . . in Ireland'.[144] If, however, they operated within the law, they had to be tolerated. Banning them merely drove dissent underground. What had been open became dangerously secretive. Confronting the Duke of Wellington, Lamb bravely told him that a ban would 'have no other effect than to produce useless and unnecessary exasperation . . . He [Wellington] looked staggered and with that air, which he always has, of a man very little accustomed to be differed from or contradicted, . . . changed the subject.'[145] Lamb half-believed that O'Connell was a French spy.[146] He absolutely believed it was wise 'to be on your guard' when dealing with the Protestants.[147] Yet, a strict adherence to legality was the only proper response to both: 'if an Association or any other body be legal in itself and formed for legal purposes, there is, I apprehend, nothing either in the common or statute law which prevents such a body from taking measures to procure information, or to promote its aims.'[148] If government obeys the law, it exposes those who take other courses.

In some ways, Lamb saw the Protestants as more threatening than the Catholics. As he reported to Canning: 'objectionable as the Roman Catholic Association undoubtedly is, and indeed incompatible with the supremacy of the Government of the Country, its evil consequences are still comparatively remote, nor does it tend to immediate disturbance of the peace, violence, and bloodshed, as these Orange processions do.'[149] The threat of coercion definitely came from two quarters, not one. With luck, a balance could be struck between the two, particularly if Protestants could be assured that being just to Catholics did not subvert their own position. If, however, violence did erupt, then Lamb had clear priorities. It was essential 'to crush dangers'[150] at their first appearance. It was also necessary to admit that, unpalatable as it may be, the Protestants were the ultimate guarantee of the Union with England. The conclusion that, 'with respect to the Protestants of the North, I have always felt that it is to them that the Government must look for support in circumstances of difficulty',[151] was hardly congenial to Lamb's sensibilities, but it says something for his hard-headedness. When and if dialogue broke down, the connection between England and Ireland rested on 'the Protestant Yeomanry of the North'.[152] In promoting Catholic claims, Lamb never lost sight of Protestant susceptibilities. As far as there was an answer to the Irish problem, it lay in listening to everyone, dining with everyone, allowing what was legal, stamping vigorously on what was not, and, above all, in treating Ireland 'as a branch of the United Kingdom'.[153] The Irish should be encouraged to feel themselves to be part of a unitary state whose citizens enjoyed the even-handed protection of government. The alternative of operating exclusions and hounding dissenters by law was always misguided. Lamb's few months only confirmed a Whiggish predilection that, tiresome as it might be, it was better to associate with people rather than to shun them.

William Lamb served in Ireland from April 1827 to June 1828. When he returned home, there was more reason to take his political pretensions seriously. A troublesome wife was dead. He was on the point of inheriting his father's titles and estates. Above all, he had proved himself not to have been as incapable in office as some had predicted. True to form, he had found the detail of many Irish issues boring, but he had mastered a brief when required to do so. He had not made the situation worse, and, if few Irishmen became his friends, few ended up disliking him. As a first attempt at office, the record was promising. Unfortunately, his stay in Ireland had done nothing to clarify his position in politics. In these few months, he had served under three Prime Ministers, Canning, Goderich, and Wellington,[154] all of whom represented varying shades of Toryism. Since Lamb never called himself a Tory and despised the word Canningite, his ability to work with men from these traditions was a matter for comment. The young Foxite, the *habitué* of Holland House, seemed to have developed into a politician, who was not too nice about the company he kept.

Worse, he openly expressed pleasure in working with them. When Wellington asked him to stay at his post in Ireland, on becoming Prime Minister, Lamb told his brother that he had every intention of doing so, because 'Nothing could be more satisfactory or in fact more agreeable to my own opinions than the language and views of Peel and the Duke, and under the circumstances in which I stood there was nothing to preclude me from giving them any assistance I could.'[155] Peel fulsomely returned the compliment, declaring that there 'were few things that I look forward to in public life with more satisfaction than a cordial union with you'.[156] Importantly for the conduct of his own administration, Lamb established an understanding with both Peel and Wellington in these years that would greatly facilitate the politics of the 1830s. All this camaderie between Lamb and the Tory grandees deeply irritated Whigs, who came to look on him as a lamb that had wandered.[157] It was not reassuring to them that, at one and the same time, Lamb could admire Peel and Wellington, while admitting that they had 'got such a damned Character for intolerance'[158] that no honest man could work with them. Apparently, Lamb's answer to tangled loyalties was to be loyal and disloyal to everyone at the same time.

Even when Lamb resigned from Tory government at last, there was little clarity about his decision. William Huskisson resigned office after disagreeing with Wellington over the relatively trivial matter of whether East Retford should or should not be disfranchised for corruption. With bizarre logic, Lamb voted with the Duke and resigned with Huskisson. His attempts to explain his conduct were rationalizing the illogical:

It was all temper and irritation on both sides, each party suspecting the other of views and intentions which in my conscience I believe neither of them entertained. The Duke of Wellington expected Huskisson to retract the resignation which he had hastily tendered. Huskisson expected the Duke to retract the step which he had hastily taken in submitting the resignation to the King . . . For myself the real cause of my resignation is that under the circumstances I felt that I could not abandon Huskisson. It has always been a maxim with me that it is more necessary to stand by ones Friends, when they are in the wrong, than when they are in the right . . . at the same time I must say that I never took a step with deeper regret and less satisfaction.[159]

This was all perfectly Irish. Lamb had resigned from the government he claimed to respect, for an issue on which he agreed with government. Allegedly, this was done out of loyalty to Huskisson, but Lamb denied elsewhere that he was of his cousin's connection.[160] The larger question of why a man of Whiggish upbringing and temperament should be consorting with either Wellington or Huskisson was not even addressed. In the circumstances, it must have taken a large dose of sisterly affection for Emily Lamb to claim that her brother 'stands higher in character with all the parties than anybody else in Engd, so that I think we shall still see him some day prime minister'.[161] In fact, he would be Prime Minister six years later, but not even the most intrepid gambler at Brooks's would have risked money on such a prophecy in 1828.

Between May 1828 and December 1830, there was no label that could fix Melbourne's politics or give a clue to his future actions. He had officially parted company with Wellington, but he was still sufficiently close to the Duke to be the subject of tempting offers. In September 1828, July 1830, and October 1830, he was formally invited to rejoin the government, in the last two negotiations with a seat in the Cabinet.[162] His answer was to think this a perfectly plausible line of argument, as long as Grey, the leader of the Whigs, and Huskisson, the heir of Canning, were invited into government as well. In other words, Lamb wished to dissolve party distinctions in a common effort. With little or no feeling for long-standing political traditions, he merely wished to see all those he respected in office together. Conceivably, this demand was a convenient excuse for not rejoining Wellington. More likely, the idea, preposterous in itself, looked plausible to a man who could work with men from all political traditions, being rooted in none of them himself. The independent voice in politics, which he had claimed since 1812, still seemed to be his preference. He could not see why Grey and Wellington should not resolve their differences by a conference or two, where they 'were to agree upon the main principles of action'.[163] Whatever happened, he relished his lack of party commitment: 'God in Heaven knows what will come out of it, but at least it is something to keep one's self free from embarrassment and degradation.'[164] Much of Lamb's behaviour in these months fuelled speculation about whether he was ever prepared to take politics seriously.

No Tory but an admirer of Wellington and Peel, no Canningite or Huskissonian, a Whig in society but not always in politics, Lamb trod his own path. If a label is required, it must be Lambite. If he had a political loyalty, it was to the other members of a family group that had sustained him through a terrible marriage and had won his trust. In November 1829, William and George Lamb met with Palmerston, their sister's lover, at Brocket. There, they declared that they followed no one's lead in politics, but, 'in a state of great pugnaciousness', were prepared 'for fighting everybody and everything'. Their views were 'free and unshackled'.[165] This manifesto sounded more like a nostalgia for the family-based politics of the eighteenth century than the party-based politics of the nineteenth. When in doubt, Whigs simply trusted their own. No doubt this was reassuring for Melbourne, but it was not behaviour to make his clan attractive to other politicians. Collectively, they had little experience of office. When they had been in office, their willingness to find friends anywhere had given them a mongrel reputation at best. Worst of all, to claim a freedom from the loyalties of party was unhelpful to those looking for stable government. Yet, in December 1830, all three became members of Grey's government, with Melbourne himself in the high office of Home

Secretary. It was a measure of the most unusual nature of the politics of that
year, that such a thing could come to pass.

Quite simply, between 1827 and 1830, party was not in fashion. As a
result, men like Melbourne were. The Whig party of Lord Grey had had no
united response to the formation of Canning's ministry, or to the pressing
question of Parliamentary Reform. Equally, those who had followed Lord
Liverpool in what might loosely be called the Tory tradition, had also fallen
out. They, too, differed on whether Canning was to be supported or opposed,
and this difficulty was compounded by the decision of Peel and Wellington
to sponsor Catholic Emancipation. Severe fault lines opened up in both the
main political groupings. As a consequence, the administration that Grey
cobbled together, in November 1830, was Whig only in the sense that he led
it, and that a number of Fox's disciples held prominent posts. It should more
properly be called a coalition, stretching across the political spectrum from
the Radical Brougham to the ultra-Tory Duke of Richmond. In its breadth,
it was, oddly enough, exactly the sort of government that Lamb had been
calling for since 1827. Events had conspired to make Lamb's indifference to
party not only chic but useful. As Grey contrived to hold together colleagues
from such disparate, political backgrounds, a man like Melbourne, who had
proved that he found all of them congenial, was invaluable. In these strange
circumstances, William Lamb, with only fifteen months experience of office,
became Home Secretary.

7

The Home Office, 1830–1834

MELBOURNE was Home Secretary from November 1830 to July 1834. For most of that period, he employed his brother George as Under-Secretary. Few holders of this office can have faced more turbulent situations. In addition to the grave disturbances that punctuated the years in which the first Reform Bill was debated and passed, protest was taking institutional form. Political Unions and Trade Unions presented the Home Office with new challenges, which could not be ignored. Inevitably too, the Irish, like the poor or bad weather, still demanded attention. Emancipation in 1829 had not drawn the sting of Catholic protest. It had merely diverted it into other channels. For all these reasons, Melbourne was suddenly in the full glare of public scrutiny. As the minister responsible for law and order, he had much to do. His reputation as a political *flaneur* would either be confirmed, or abandoned in favour of something a little more complimentary.

He brought to the office certain guiding principles that had served him well in Ireland. First, when in doubt, it was essential to cling to legality. Government must always do so, and what was not illegal had to be tolerated. Secondly, government could only make a limited response in the face of riot and disturbance, both because its resources were finite, and because heavy-handed tactics only made the trouble worse. For this reason, he always showed an absolute preference for action by local agents rather than by central government. The Justice of the Peace and the Lord Lieutenant knew their localities, and could gauge the mood of the people who lived in them. Their standing in their own neighbourhoods should guarantee them all the deference and respect that was needed to deal with trouble. This Whiggish distaste for any enhancement of central government is the basis for Melbourne's reputation for inactivity. This was not indolence. He simply believed that government should not act. As he ironically observed to his brother, government measures usually ended in 'a killing of the People, which is always awkward in this country where there is so much law'.[1] It was better to put up with a little rick-burning than to overreact. Justices should do their best, by 'adhering strictly, firmly and dispassionately to the rules and principles of the law'.[2]

This relaxed attitude should not be read as a condoning of violence. Riot was always tiresome, not least because it usually undermined the cause it had espoused. It always 'persuaded and convinced very few'.[3] Worse, in tumultuous times, too many people took refuge in hysteria. For example, reports about the Captain Swing Riots in his own county of Hertfordshire were hopelessly 'exaggerated' and were 'in fact nothing'.[4] In the disturbed months of the autumn of 1831, news of trouble in Bristol and parts of the capital did not 'make him half so gloomy as an hours conversation with Abercrombie'.[5] If the bubble and froth of protest failed to subside, however, then something would probably have to be done,[6] preferably by forms of local authority. In 1820, he had stood ready with his Hertfordshire Yeomanry in the face of the Queen Caroline Rioters,[7] but, on this occasion, as on so many others, nothing needed to be done. Philosophically, he believed that just as a human body is periodically visited with a distemper, so political systems were sometimes overheated. Whig insouciance in the face of violence, which so impressed Alexis de Tocqueville and other visitors, was based on the belief that disturbance was endemic in the system, an almost annual occurrence. Melbourne drew on a long memory in 1832 to describe the phenomenon and to prescribe the remedy:

I have seen, during my life, the Country twice mad—in a paroxysm of madness—. . . once with Anti-Jacobinism, and now with something very like Jacobinism. I still, however, trust that we shall get through it, and . . . our best chance of doing so is to adopt in time the necessary reformations in the Church and State. But we must not trust to conciliation alone. Nations cannot be governed solely by force, neither can they be managed entirely by concession. There must be a mixture of both.[8]

This fatalism was reinforced by one other factor. Melbourne seriously doubted whether punishment had any effect on the inclination of the criminal to be bothersome. As a student, he had noted in a lecture that as men grow more civilized, 'the great severity of punishment is rendered unnecessary'.[9] Over thirty years later, the House of Lords received the same lecture:

it must be recollected, that crime had existed in all ages and all times. All nations had employed themselves for the purpose of repressing it, but all attempts at eradication had hitherto been found ineffectual . . . Persons addicted to criminal courses had minds so constituted, that they could not be understood by those who had not so unfortunately devoted themselves.[10]

As a result, over-severe sentences were 'unwise', merely making martyrs out of law-breakers.[11] In his early parliamentary career, he had supported Romilly's attempts to cut the number of capital offences,[12] though he significantly approved of hanging for those who had committed serious crimes against property.[13] Even so, for a Home Secretary to believe that in most instances government should not act, and that punishment had very little impact on the level of crime, did not suggest that he would be among the most crusading of his kind.

A man who believes in literally doing nothing runs the risk of being accused of indolence. Nearly twenty years later, some of Melbourne's obituarists dismissed his performance at the Home Office as passivity raised to the level of a system:

> While he held the seals of the Home Department, his measures were sometimes unskilful and always late. He loved procrastination, and even gravely contended in the House of Lords that the general rule of official life was 'never do anything till a man could not possibly help it.' To this theory his practice at the Home Office was perfectly conformable; but, fortunately for that department, his administration of its affairs did not continue much beyond three years.[14]

Tories sarcastically wondered whether Melbourne would lose office to a more determined man before he lost Brocket to rioters.[15] In reply, friends thought that, after his Irish exertions, he had every right 'to lay on his sofa and read a romance'.[16] Melbourne himself, reviewing the duties of a Home Secretary, concluded, no doubt a little ironically, that, although it was not quite true that '*anybody cd. do the duties*', there was in truth 'very little required' of any man of intelligence.[17]

Certainly, throughout the Grey ministry, Melbourne was the most anonymous of his colleagues. In spite of the intense topicality of the policy areas directed by the Home Office, there is virtually no mention of Melbourne in Whig newspapers like the *Morning Chronicle*. Equally, his long-established reticence about speaking in Parliament continued. On Parliamentary Reform, there are only two speeches of any length or substance. Even on riot and disturbance he spoke only half-a-dozen times a year, and then with the greatest economy. Only on Irish issues did he intervene with some frequency, though again with an embarrassed brevity. As far as he had an area of expertise, it was Ireland. In 1833, for example, Melbourne spoke on twenty-four occasions. Only two or three of these contributions concerned domestic disturbances. The rest dealt with Ireland. In *Hansard*, Melbourne spoke in paragraphs rather than columns. It was not surprising, therefore, that Grey should try to demote him to Lord Privy Seal or to return him to Ireland, claiming that his 'indolence' could not be tolerated. Holland resisted such moves by telling Grey to distinguish between Melbourne's 'careless nonchalant Manner' and the reality of his performance as a minister, but the Prime Minister was not reassured.[18] In these years, Grey came to the view that

Melbourne suffered from a basic incapacity for office, and, as a result, he was to be bullied and patronized. A tension was created between Grey and Melbourne that was to bedevil the politics of the whole decade.

In fact, Melbourne was an assiduous minister. His papers suggest that he read everything that came across his desk, annotating reports and draft legislation, and frequently writing replies to incoming enquiries in his own hand. His sister complained that her Home Office brothers were so industrious that they had withdrawn from her social circle,[19] and other friends feared that William Lamb was 'overworking himself'.[20] The diarist Greville, no friend of Melbourne's, was forced to admit the same thing:

> The only one who has had anything to do is Melbourne, and he has surprised all those about him by a sudden display of activity and vigour, rapid and diligent transaction of business, for which nobody was prepared, and which will prove a great mortification to Peel and his friends, who were in hopes he would do nothing and let the country be burnt and plundered without interruption.[21]

It was, as Lord Holland had indicated, all a matter of separating manner from substance. In conversation, Melbourne deflected any point of seriousness into irony, paradox, and sarcasm. These were his defences against a world he had come to distrust. People like Grey, who could see nothing more, were naturally irritated. Those, who dug deeper, knew a man of industry and clear vision of what government could and could not do.

The most public test of Melbourne's ministerial abilities was the deeply disturbed state of England.[22] The Captain Swing riots among agricultural labourers, extensive rioting in such urban centres as Bristol and Nottingham, and talk of reform campaigns backed by non-payment of taxes, seemed to many to threaten revolution. Melbourne was subjected to a massive correspondence on these issues. His Under-Secretaries, George Lamb and John Philips, dealt with most of these letters, but Melbourne himself seems to have answered enquiries from local officials such as Justices of the Peace and Lords Lieutenant. In these answers may be discovered the ideas which governed his response to civil disturbance. In their coolness, in their acceptance of violence as an unfortunate fact of life, they are quintessentially Whig.

Crucially, Melbourne refused to believe that, in essence, the rioting of 1830–4 was any different to the rioting that he had heard of throughout his life. Rioters were people with not enough to eat, insufficient wages, or on the point of losing their employment. Slogans about Parliamentary Reform or Catholic rights were imposed on these basic grievances by self-seeking demagogues, but it was vital to distinguish between what caused riots and the language in which rioters expressed themselves. Commenting on riots to Grey,

Melbourne observed: 'I expect we shall have them wherever there are real or imaginary grievances, and that is everywhere—however it appears perfectly clear that neither reform nor any other political feeling has anything to do with them.'[23] As harassed Justices were told, therefore, the best way of defeating agitators was to ensure that the poor were supported effectively in the traditional way.[24] The Poor Law, not the military, was the effective prophylactic against disturbances. Local authorities should keep their heads, resist the lurid and exaggerated talk of spies, and do their duty by their social inferiors. Endlessly referring back to a memory of the period 1815–21, Melbourne was inclined to attribute the troubles of those years to hysteria on the part of the authorities as much as to malevolence in those joining various forms of agitation.[25]

Further, even if a situation degenerated so far that force had to be exerted, it was a mistake to look to the army. With a peacetime establishment of only 29,000 men, the army could not hope to police the whole country, and anyway 'it was always safer to allow violence to proceed somewhat too far rather than to run the risk of being accused of uncalled for interference'.[26] Recalling that Peterloo had been a terrible business, Melbourne observed to Lord Derby that force was 'a most unsatisfactory way of maintaining order'.[27] If the use of troops were to be largely ruled out, local authorities were encouraged to explore different options in their own neighbourhoods. When Wellington proposed to raise a company of Volunteers in Hampshire, on the precedent of the Napoleonic War years, Melbourne had no objection, though he confessed that he was 'a little afraid of being hurried by the vehemence of the moment into the adoption of an expensive and comparatively inefficient system which it may not be easy afterwards to get rid of'.[28] Similarly, he asked the Duke of Richmond to think of ways of making the militia and the parish constables more effective in keeping law and order.[29] Beyond these Dogberry-based proposals, however, Melbourne refused to go. For government to set up national police-forces would be 'over legislating'. For parishes and counties to raise and pay for their own constabularies would be 'viewed with great jealousy' and give rise to 'the imputation of jobbing'.[30] No new structures were needed. The disturbances of 1830–4, severe as they were, would subside as those of the 1790s or 1810s had subsided. Various forms of local peace-keeping might, temporarily, need reinforcement, but it was absurd to cover England with armed men in a range of uniforms.

Behind all these ideas was the notion that law and order was a function of propertied gentlemen doing their duty. Government could not cure riot. Justices of the Peace, faithfully executing the Poor Law and enforcing the Riot Act with militias and constables, could. In Melbourne's view, propertied England seemed to be suffering from a crisis of confidence. It needed to be reminded of its obligations. Local authorities, who sent in panic-stricken appeals to the Home Office, quite often received brusque answers. Sir Thomas Gooch was reminded that, 'it is impossible, and if possible would be highly objectionable to post Troops in every town the neighbourhood of which may be threatened with riot'.[31] When the Earl of Airlie asked for troops to be sent to Dundee, he was told that 'the Citizens of the Place' were perfectly capable of helping themselves.[32] Edinburgh's city fathers were told the same thing. They were to rely on 'the firmness of the Magistracy . . . to repress any similar ebullition of popular feeling'.[33] Even Bristol's sad experiences were to be attributed to a paralysis within the propertied and party divisions within the city.[34] By contrast, Melbourne much approved of magistrates like Colonel Wodehouse in Norfolk, who did what men of property should do in an emergency, namely organize their kind in the vigorous application of the law.[35] The tumultuous experiences of 1830–4 were not evidence that central government was lax, but that local government had for a moment lost its self-respect.

None of this comforted those who accused Melbourne of inaction in the face of violence. Factually, this was largely true, but it stemmed from a belief that this was the proper, governmental response, and not from congenital indolence in the Home Secretary. The proof of this is that, when crisis really threatened, Melbourne acted swiftly and decisively. JPs were assured that: 'To force nothing but force can be successfully opposed, and it is at once evident that legislation is impotent and ridiculous unless the public peace can be preserved, and the liberty and property of individuals secured from outrage and invasion.'[36] His first act on taking office was to draft a Circular to Magistrates, which instructed them to meet threats of violence firmly, and on no account to buy off trouble with the promise of improved wage rates. Such concessions could only have 'the most disastrous results'.[37] A complementary Proclamation warned 'persons engaged in illegal acts against the danger of their proceeding'.[38] If proof of violent conspiracy was forthcoming, Melbourne was happy to send troops to reinforce beleaguered local authorities.[39] Property could be protected by spring-guns and mantraps.[40] Those who took part in notorious rioting, like that which shook Nottingham in the autumn of 1831, were to be punished 'in the most exemplary and speedy manner'.[41] So too were those who attempted to reinforce claims for reform by organizing campaigns for the non-payment of taxes.[42] In all of this, Melbourne showed little or no sympathy with the poor or those who rioted. If they persisted in being tiresome, troops would be sent against them. The only reason for restraining the power of central government in this area was that the enforcement of law and order by local authority was simply more effective. Poverty should be relieved, but it should know its place.

Traditional forms of violence could be countered with traditional insouciance. More worrying were new, organized expressions of the same phenomenon. Political Unions pressing for Parliamentary Reform and Trade Unions moving for betterment in wages and conditions were both seen to have the intention of coercing rather than persuading.[43] Melbourne was under continual pressure from William IV and Grey to take action against them.[44] In reply, Lamb once again took his stand on the principle of legality. He told Parliament that the setting up of a Political Union for the purpose of advocating reform was not in itself outside the law. Outraged JPs, demanding that Unions set up in their neighbourhoods should be disbanded, were simply informed that the mere existence of such a body was not illegal, though its actions might make it so in due course.[45] As long as Union leaders abstained from advocating violence and did not attempt to set up national bodies in a conspiratorial network, they were to be regarded as irritating by-products of the operation of English liberty. Melbourne was happy to lecture Wellington on this point: 'These societies are of course responsible for any illegal language, which they hold, or acts which they commit—otherwise I am not aware of any law which renders their existence illegal, whilst they continue separate and independent.'[46] He was clear that, if government stayed within the law, its opponents would always be wrongfooted by being clearly seen to wander into illegality.

Very sensibly, Melbourne looked beyond the Unions to a wider constituency. When William IV plagued him with demands for action, Melbourne patiently responded by arguing that if the government won the good opinion of the propertied, the Unions would wither away without recourse to the law:

It is the public feeling which is dangerous, not the political unions. If the latter should adopt any of the measures mentioned in my former letter, such as the resistance of the payment of taxes, unless they are supported by a large proportion of the middle and even of the better classes of society the attempt will be abortive and ridiculous. If they are so supported it is unnecessary to say how critical the state of public affairs will become . . . the best mode of meeting and foiling these unions is . . . not to interfere with them while they confine themselves within the boundary of the law. If we act otherwise we shall only give them strength.[47]

He was acutely aware that the Unions were not exclusively 'composed of the rabble'. To move against them by force would alienate a wider opinion. Even to invoke the law 'would only end in giving them consequence and importance, and would perhaps constitute them the acknowledged organs of public feeling, of which at present they are only the symptoms'.[48] Let the actions of government be scrupulously legal and opinion would not be affronted. Sooner or later, if not challenged, the Unions would adopt a language that would frighten the very supporters they needed to have any significance at all. Melbourne's inaction, once again, was not the product of indolence, but of policy. Masterful inactivity was built on the idea that government is difficult to attack, if it threatens no one.

The pattern was repeated when Melbourne came to confront Trade Unions. They were not in themselves illegal, though it was no doubt cold comfort to a Manchester JP to be reminded of the fact: 'Unions and combinations for the purpose of raising or of lowering wages, provided they do not resort to violence, forced intimidation, illegal riots or acts in themselves illegal, are legal . . . You will naturally ask me, are we to wait with our arms folded whilst this combination spreads itself throughout the peasantry and prepares undisturbed the most dangerous results. I am compelled to answer, that in the present state of the law and of the public feeling I see no safe or effectual mode of prevention.'[49] He simply entertained 'great doubt whether it is possible to devise any legislative measures which would be effectual against them'.[50] Fending off the King, Parliament, and many of his own Cabinet colleagues on this point, Melbourne insisted that the question could only be approached with superabundant caution.[51] Once again, a legalistic stance by government would immediately expose any illegality on the part of the Unions.

Further, Melbourne refused to believe that, ultimately, Trade Unions were as dangerous as Political Unions. The latter dealt in plausible ideas for reforming the electoral system, many of which were shared by members of his own social circle. Trade Unions, by contrast, dealt in nonsense. They were bound to 'break up and dissolve . . . from the false principles upon which they are founded, and the unattainable nature of the objects which they propose to themselves'.[52] Calling on his Glasgow education, Melbourne was clear that wage rates were determined solely by the rise and fall of the demand for labour. Any attempt to meddle with this iron law was at best futile and at worst destructive. He complained to his brother that Trade Unions 'bother us to death', but comforted himself with the thought that they 'must break up by reason of absurdity'.[53] Wage rates could not be artificially imposed on an economic situation. If the threat of violence led to such an attempt, it would quickly unravel in the face of harsh realities. Further, he was well aware that working people had conflicting aims and objectives. In settling wage rates different trades, the skilled and the unskilled, fought each other as much as they fought the employer. Working people had such 'different . . . objects, views, motives and modes of acting, and consequently how difficult it will be to reconcile all these, and to unite them into one body for the purpose of any general and simultaneous movement'.[54] Trade Unions were self-contradictory bodies pursuing economically unattainable ends. The conclusion was obvious. Once again, they were to be allowed to founder through internal inconsistency rather than harried to death by the law: 'under these circumstances it appears to me to be questionable whether it would be discreet to incur the hazard of outrunning the public sentiment by any strong measure adopted now against the Trade Unions.'[55]

Of course, a stand on legality involved the firm handling of illegality. When agricultural workers at Tolpuddle in Dorset were accused of taking secret oaths and of seeking to set up a national organization, thereby transforming unionism into conspiracy, Melbourne was for a harsh response. A local JP was told that he thought 'these proceedings in your County are a part of the general system, which is now attempted to be established in many parts of the Kingdom . . . Generally speaking measures of spirit and firmness are highly desireable [sic] in such circumstances.'[56] Melbourne took an intense interest in the labourers' trial,[57] and asked local magistrates for as much detail about the case as they could furnish.[58] When the men were found guilty, he was clear that the sentence of transportation should indeed be put into effect, and that there should be no early reprieve.[59] The Tolpuddle men had wandered beyond the law, and therefore the law must take its course:

I am well aware of the obstinate fidelity with which the lower classes cling to one another . . . at the same time I trust that the convictions which have lately taken place in Dorsetshire will have some effect in proving to them the illegality of their combinations, the power which the law possesses of punishing them, and the determination of the Government to carry the law into effect.[60]

No inhabitant of Tolpuddle would share the contemporary view of Melbourne as either indolent, indifferent, or passive in the face of significant challenge.

On the other hand, a stand on legality also involved the toleration of everything that was legal, tiresome and time-consuming though it might be. Delegations of all kinds had open access to the Home Secretary, though they might be received by him lying on a sofa in a silk dressing gown. They were likely to be addressed in a 'coarse but easy and plain manner', which 'frightened their leaders without offending them'.[61] Mass meetings which disrupted the life of the capital were irritating, particularly if held on a Sunday, but there was nothing to be done about them.[62] In April 1834, a march showing support for the Tolpuddle men was organized in London. Melbourne refused to ban it as a threat to public order. Men had a right to march. Instead, he stood at the window of the Home Office as the procession past by, visibly representing an unconcerned authority. For this subtlety of approach, he was applauded in the Whig press. According to the *Morning Chronicle*, 'no man will say that Lord Melbourne did not act wisely in confining himself to watching the procession, instead of interfering with it . . . The English are in the habit of marching in processions in considerable numbers.'[63] Palmerston, generally much more alarmist about the likelihood of violence, could only marvel at Melbourne's 'odd ways', which 'seem on this as on most other occasions to have answered admirably'.[64]

Facing down violence by greeting it from a sofa represented a type of sang-froid which deeply impressed foreign visitors, who, like Tocqueville, frequently identified it as specifically Whig. On 16 January 1834, a delegation of allegedly 3,000 men arrived at the Home Office at ten in the morning to protest about the way the Assessed Taxes Bill was being put into effect. Lord Howick explained that Melbourne had not yet arrived for work, but invited the leaders of the delegation to wait. They did so for an hour, after which they marched to Melbourne's home in South Street. There, they found him still breakfasting, but were told civilly that he would see them at the Home Office at two o'clock. At that interview, all was frosty legality; 'he apprehended, that having placed the Resolutions in his hand, the object for which they were deputed was at an end. He regretted that they had been kept waiting so long, and this would not have happened if they had given him any previous intimation of their intention of calling upon him.'[65] Drawing on a Whig sense of caste, Melbourne confronted protest and violence with the law and lessons in good manners. The combination had a disabling effect on Radicalism that astonished those whose imaginations could not go beyond the advocacy of systematic repression.

There were other Whiggish elements in Melbourne's response to Radicalism. Like his early hero Charles James Fox, he thought it should be talked to and dined with. He was in the habit of dropping in on Sir Francis Burdett, Chairman of the Political Union of London and Westminster, to urge him to lead Radicalism along constitutional paths.[66] In 1831, after what he described as 'a devil of [a] riot at Bristol', Melbourne, assuming that Brougham had a better nature, appealed to it, and asked him 'not to encourage agitation' for fear of having 'the whole Country in a blaze'.[67] Through the agency of Thomas Young, Melbourne's personal secretary, regular channels of communication were kept up with Radical leaders like Charles Napier and Francis Place, who fortuitously had once been the Home Secretary's tailor. These men were asked to use their influence to control and moderate protest, and to restrain the Radical press. It was later revealed that these men did 'great service to us in preventing riots and meetings'.[68] Young himself, 'a cleverish sort of fellow with a vulgar air of frankness',[69] had established himself as Melbourne's factotum. A former purser on the Duke of Devonshire's yacht, Young's influence over Melbourne was thought strange.[70] Odder still was the fact that the last month of Melbourne's life was soured by Young publishing his letters to Napier, which led Melbourne formally to disassociate himself from his former secretary's conversations with 'Revolutionists' twenty-five years earlier.[71] It is not known why this repudiation of Young's efforts should have been so important to Melbourne in his last illness. What is clear is that keeping open channels of communication with Radical leaders between 1830 and 1834 was of the first importance. In the Whig tradition, it had never been enough simply to repress Radicalism. It needed to be coaxed, and made to feel that it was not excluded from a voice within official politics.

Equally Whiggish was Melbourne's belief that, if half the cause of violence was poverty and cyclical distress, the other half was the stupidity endemic among Tories. In Whig historiography, unrest was more often provoked by rulers than engendered from below. Too often Tory ignorance created trouble, which Tory panic then exacerbated. It was, for example, grotesque that, in May 1832, Tory leaders should agree to set up an anti-Reform administration, against the declared wishes of both Parliament and the electorate. When this happened, both Melbourne and Palmerston were 'frightened at the public determination shown but at the same time feel spiteful with the Tories for having tried to play the trick and made them less able to assist themselves'.[72] Brougham had a sympathetic audience in telling Melbourne of his anger at the 'brutality and greater obtuseness of understandg. of such men as you see in the H. of Lords'.[73] Tory peers demanding that the Home Secretary make provision for the protection of their property received dusty answers. The Duke of Buckingham was told: 'it is impossible to guarantee any one against broken windows.'[74] The Ultra-Tory Duke of Newcastle, whose anti-Reform speeches had been widely broadcast, received even less sympathy for the damage suffered by his property in the Nottingham riots of the autumn of 1831. Ironically consoling the Duke for 'the difficulty under which Your Grace must necessarily labour, in distinguishing false Rumours from all well-founded intelligence', Melbourne refused to put him on a commission to try the rioters, thought his claim for damages exorbitant, since his house was nothing but an 'old ruin' anyway, and resolutely refused to allow him the use of arms.[75]

In his handling of the terrible disturbances of 1830–4, Melbourne was thoroughly Whiggish in temperament. With limited force at its disposal, there was little that government could do. If the essentials of English liberty were to survive, there was perhaps little that government should do. Suffering a little violence was better than suffering repressive government. For the same reason, it was always better that law and order should be the responsibility of local authorities. JPs could be relied on to respect both order and liberty. Soldiers could not. Protest was, after all, an honoured aspect of the freedom that marked Englishmen out as a special breed among Europeans. Its legal expression was always to be tolerated, even if any slippage into illegality had to be firmly dealt with. Even then, it was important to remember that violence was endemic in the system, and so traditional and conservative in many of its forms, that it was bad form to overreact in response to it. Only Tories took this line, and nothing could be expected of people, who took no trouble to look for the causes of violence, and who had no Glasgow training in the dislocations that were bound to occur within a society moving from an agricultural to an industrial base. Nearly all these assumptions recommended inaction rather than action. To accuse Melbourne of personal indolence, therefore, is to miss the point. Passivity could be well thought out policy. As even some Tories later came to admit, it also in the end seemed to work.

If Melbourne's reaction to the violence of these years was minimalist, on the central issue in politics, Parliamentary Reform, he is virtually invisible. He spoke on the issue rarely,[76] had no part in drawing up the measure, and had to be carried along like a dead weight by his more enthusiastic colleagues. By 1830, Melbourne had established a reputation for voting against Reform measures. As has been noted, he believed that an electorate should represent a country's property. Ownership, a stake in the country, made a man a responsible and independently-minded voter. To change this rule was to enfranchise irresponsibility and ignorance. It was one of Melbourne's major criticisms of O'Connell that he would insist on meddling in constituencies in which 'he has no property or natural connection'.[77] Rotten boroughs were unobjectionable if they performed their traditional function of representing great property. His own tenure as MP for Peterborough in the Fitzwilliam interest was a perfect example of how the system should work. With respect to his own tenants, there was a slightly menacing ambiguity. On the one hand, he would 'never ask whether they voted, or stayed away or how they voted'. On the other hand, 'If I do I shall of course feel obliged to those who voted according to my wishes but not in the least offended with those, who act otherwise.'[78] Someone, who saw the exercise of the franchise as part of the interplay between deference and condescension that should mark the ownership of property, was unlikely to be an enthusiastic Reformer.

Change was a fraught business. It raised expectations which could not always be satisfied.[79] His Scots education had convinced him that the process of industrialization produced new forms of property that would properly claim a voice in Parliament, but, as he noted in his commonplace book, the most important task was to teach new property the dangers of changing too much too quickly:

Great increase of persons who think upon and take an active part in politics, and great rise into political power of merchants, manufacturers, and person raised into consequence by the increasing trade, etc, of the country. Extreme importance that correct notions should be formed by such persons, and that they should not immediately think that nothing is so easy as to reform the system and to exclude every evil which has heretofore been admitted.[80]

It would have all been easier if Melbourne could have brought himself to like the new voters, but his Whiggish nose caught the smell of factory and counting-house: 'I don't like the middle classes. The higher and lower classes, there's some good in them, but the middle class are all affectation and conceit and pretence and concealment.'[81] He could have added religion and morality to this list. Worst of all, Melbourne was sure that if Reform was taken up, it would have to be on an extensive scale. Tinkering with the system would not meet the expectations inevitably raised.[82] For Melbourne, therefore, Reform was both inevitable and disagreeable. It was thoroughly uncomfortable.

As the Reform debate unfolded between 1830 and 1832, no one was much surprised by Melbourne's equivocations. In November 1830, he had specifically come out against Reform.[83] Holland knew him not to be 'a reformer by choice',[84] and Lord John Russell complained that he was 'very slack'[85] on the issue. His brother, Frederick, even more determinedly against change, accused him of 'only deceiving your own conscience in going along with Cabinet decisions'.[86] Melbourne would be 'a reluctant convert' to the idea of Reform, if he ever came to believe in it at all.[87] On good days, Melbourne, on looking at the small print of the Reform Bill, thought that he might be able to 'reconcile' himself to its objectives,[88] but such occasions were few. For most of the time, he was 'wretched at having been led so far, and tossed backwards and forwards between opposite sentiments and feelings'.[89] As far as Greville was concerned, it was positively diverting to see Melbourne ensconced among Reformers, mumbling words that must have been dust in his mouth:

It is curious to see the working and counterworking of his real opinions and principles with his false position, and the mixture of bluntness, facility, and shrewdness, discretion, levity and seriousness, which colouring his mind and character by turns, make up the strange compound of his thoughts and his actions.[90]

To open up élite politics, even to new forms of property, was almost more than he could bear. In particular, he resolutely refused to countenance any dilution of the aristocratic principle expressed in the House of Lords. A mass creation of peers to see the Bill through that House was unacceptable.[91] Only ten days before the Bill passed, he was prepared to resign rather than sanction such a move.[92]

In view of all this, it was not surprising that Melbourne made only two major speeches on Reform, on 4 October 1831 and 9 April 1832. In these, he stood by his Cabinet colleagues, but the tone is embarrassed and the arguments not entirely convincing. Insisting that no one could more strongly wish 'that the affairs of the country might have gone on without our being forced to incur the hazard and responsibility which must result from so great and fundamental change', he told the Lords that he had changed his mind because popular wishes could no longer be resisted. As he put it: 'although it may be our duty to resist the will of the people for a time, is it possible to resist it for ever? Have we not in this case resisted it enough?' By the people, he meant 'men of opulence, of spirit, and intelligence'. He was careful to deny that the democratic emphasis on mere numbers influenced his thinking in any way.[93] His villagers at Melbourne in Derbyshire were told the same thing. Reform had to come because it was 'demanded by a great majority of the respectability and intelligence of the community'.[94] To stand out against it any longer would destroy the Grey government and lead to 'a general convulsion'.[95]

If these few public statements suggest a man looking for an argument, his private remarks confirm the full extent of his embarrassment. In these, the bowing to an overwhelming popular opinion is not thought necessary. True, the Grey administration had come in with a 'transient, phrenetic and epileptic' fever for Reform,[96] but by April 1832, Melbourne thought that 'there was no strong feeling in the country for the measure . . . "Why then", said he, "might it not be thrown out?" '[97] By thus directly contradicting in private what he had claimed in public, Melbourne looked ridiculous. As Greville observed: 'It was a pretty avowal for a man to make at the eleventh hour who has been a party concerned in this Bill during the other ten.'[98] Tory commentators accused him of being an accessory to a criminal act. Everyone knew that he 'hated the Reform Bill',[99] yet he so contributed to its passage that he could be called 'a *particeps criminis*'.[100] He found himself in the absurd situation of being tied 'to a party which, as it seems, he cordially hates and insincerely serves'.[101] The constraints of party had been imposed on Melbourne at last, with grim consequences.

If Melbourne felt that anything positive could come out of the Reform Bill, and this is doubtful, it narrowly concerned the relationship between Parliament and Crown. There was just enough of the Foxite left in him to see that a House of Commons with fewer rotten boroughs, and elected on a wider franchise, would be better able to resist attack from the executive powers of the Crown. Kings would no longer be able to destroy Whiggish governments as they had in 1782, 1783, and 1807. When, at a Holland House dinner party, his host declared that the Reform Bill would 'throw the

Government of the country' into the House of Commons, 'Lord Melbourne agreed that it was most desirable that it should be there.'[102] As a very young MP, his notes for possible speeches on Reform often return to the point that the Commons must be independent of both popular and royal pressure.[103] He was still Fox's protégé in thinking that William IV's attempts to obstruct and delay the Bill were 'indiscreet and imprudent'.[104] When the Bill finally passed, he thought it mean of the King to refuse to celebrate the fact by allowing illuminations in the Royal Parks and fireworks in Leicester Square.[105] However much Melbourne wished the people to know their place, he was just as anxious to apply the same maxim to kings. If Melbourne had been the final arbiter of the situation in 1832, there would probably have been no Reform Bill at all. Since there was one, it was some small comfort that the Foxite vendetta against kings had been significantly advanced.

After 1832, Melbourne steadfastly refused to argue that there could never be more movement on the franchise issue. It was all a matter of 'circumstances, prudence and expediency'.[106] He was never 'a finality man', and there is some evidence to suggest that he was contemplating further adjustments to the franchise in 1839.[107] Yet, it is hard to imagine circumstances in which reflections of this kind would lead to action. In thinking about the Reform Bill debates in retrospect, he was clear that 'there never was a question so well-argued on the adverse side'.[108] Equally, the whole episode 'ought never to be mentioned without the word *necessary*. If it was not absolutely necessary, it was the *foolishest* thing ever done.'[109] He told his brother that he now foresaw 'the prevalence of the Blackguard interest in Parliament and I fear there will be no inconsiderable portion of members of that description'.[110] He never loved the Reform Bill, either in 1832 or subsequently. It was conceived in necessity and born with pain. When the 1832 Parliament was dissolved, he was frankly glad 'to get rid of it',[111] and for the rest of his political life 'nothing is so much dreaded as the recurrence of the circumstances and the demands of 1832'.[112] Whatever sophistries were employed, there was, in Melbourne's opinion, no escaping the fact that the defences, on which élite politics stood, had been breached. One reform bill would lead to another. Mass education, a popular press and, the flow of history would bring more and more people into politics. Policy-making in salons would be overtaken by the tactics of the populist. In 1837, Melbourne agreed with Lord John Russell when the latter admitted he had 'always thought that the Whig party as a party would be destroyed by the Reform Bill'.[113]

In terms of parliamentary performance, Melbourne's real interest in those years was not Reform or law and order, but Ireland. It was, after all, the only topic on which he could claim any expertise. Quite uncharacteristically, there were moments when he came near to enthusiasm. In an Irish debate, in July 1833

up started Lord Melbourne like an artillery rocket. He began in a fury. His language flowed out like fire. He made such palpable hits that he floored the Duke of Wellington as if he had shot him. But the moment the stimulus was over his habitual apathy got a-head. He stammered, hemmed, and hawed. But it was the most pictorial exhibition of the night. He waved his white hand with the natural grace of Talma; expanded his broad chest, looked right at his adversary like a handsome lion, and grappled him with the grace of Paris.[114]

In exchanges such as these, Melbourne could demonstrate what a talented fellow he was when his attention and interest were fully engaged. Unfortunately, as many contemporaries observed, such occasions were few. Odder still was the fact that this interest was sustained alongside his usual fatalism. He was doubtful, as usual, that anything helpful could be done. The Irish were 'in short half or rather whole Barbarian'. They were 'the most conspiring people on the face of the earth'.[115] The Protestant and Catholic camps were both equally 'outrageous', and their quarrels were to be likened to those between Hurons and Iroquois.[116] The only factor that provoked any sympathy for the Irish was that their troubles were not of their own making, but resulted from 'the violence with which the laws and religion of England had been attempted to be forced on that country'.[117] Harassed Lords Lieutenant, confronted by the difficulties of governing Ireland, were unhelpfully reminded of the fact that 'the dependencies and provinces of great monarchies have always been apt to grow too great and too strong to be governed by the mother state'.[118] Melbourne, the pupil of John Millar, passively accepted that empires rose and fell.

In his view, no one set of concessions had any hope of settling Ireland.[119] None of those enacted since 1829 had 'in any respect attained their end'.[120] One concession merely became the jumping off point from which to demand another. In endlessly complaining and petitioning, Catholic behaviour, 'since the passing of the relief bill, has been most abominable'.[121] The remorseless whining of the Catholics merely discredited their friends in England. The Dublin government was advised to operate 'strictly equal and impartial Government',[122] but it was also charged to make it clear that concessions had a limit. In particular, the Union with England was not negotiable.[123] Melbourne was impatient to assert that Ireland could not set the agenda for English parties forever. Its problems had no guaranteed priority over those of the rest of the kingdom.

Further, Melbourne's suspicions about O'Connell had hardened significantly. Once he had thought that the Irish leader might have been a candidate for a government post. Now O'Connell had put himself beyond the pale by effectively advocating the end of the Union. Such a challenge to sovereignty was unacceptable. Melbourne instructed Anglesey to fight this idea, with the real or implied use of force: 'The question is now brought to issue, whether O'Connell or the King's Lieutenant is to govern Ireland, and it is a question, which in my apprehension it is worthwhile to try at any risk which can possibly be apprehended from bringing it to a decision.'[124] Negotiating with O'Connell was to be discontinued, because such conversations had 'no result but that of enabling him to take advantage of it by further misrepresentation and falsehood'.[125] As in the 1820s the Irish leader was organizing Associations on a national basis, from which delegates were to meet in a kind of impromptu Irish parliament. To Melbourne, this was an attempt 'to establish an Irish in opposition to the Imperial Parliament', and a direct challenge to Westminster sovereignty.[126] This could only represent an illegal conspiracy, and the Dublin government was encouraged to prosecute.[127] Such Associations were 'all of them more or less . . . usurpations of legislative and executive powers'.[128] In return, O'Connell accused Melbourne of betraying his reforming past, and now it was only realistic 'to expect the worst from him'.[129]

Between 1827 and 1831, Melbourne's perceptions of Ireland changed markedly. The Irish had moved on from legitimate pleas for religious toleration to illegitimate demands for a repeal of the Union, backed up by the implied threat of violence. O'Connell had followed and led this shift of emphasis. The logic of the situation was inescapable. In Melbourne's view, if the Union was threatened, Ulster's Protestants were his only allies: 'with respect to the Protestants of the North, I have always felt that it is to them that the English Government must look for support in circumstances of difficulty, and what is now taking place sufficiently proves that feeling not to have been erroneous . . . Distant and prejudiced, irritated and offended as they are.'[130] As this last phrase indicates, Irish Protestants were uncongenial allies. Historically, they had systematically deprived Catholics of land and status.[131] Melbourne saw Orange Parades on 12 July and 5 November as mere 'acts of vengeance'.[132] Orange Lodges and Protestant processions should be banned if they continued to aggravate 'the old animosity', and to involve 'much conflict and blood'.[133] Intellectually and psychologically, Melbourne had nothing in common with an Ulster Protestant except a wish to preserve the Union. No marriage had ever been more contracted for convenience rather than love: 'I have for a long time thought that we shall either lose Ireland, or hold her by means of the Protestants, and I hardly know which alternative opens to us the most melancholy and appalling prospect.'[134] The contract was sealed with Melbourne's embarrassed formula that Protestant interests would be protected, 'as far as we can do so without sacrificing to them the rights of their fellow Citizens and the authority of the law'.[135]

Between 1827 and 1834, Melbourne's warm feelings for Ireland's Catholics cooled. Any sympathy he felt for the Protestants was a matter of convenience. The Irish question was therefore increasingly a matter of preserving the Union, and of refereeing disputes between the two communities to this end. He increasingly seemed to agree with Anglesey that, with this purpose in mind, taking a stand on determined policies was 'the true way to work'.[136] Irish disturbances began to be compared with the revolutions that were challenging legitimate governments all over Europe. As he assured Stanley, 'it is all the same spirit which influences all Europe at present'.[137] As in other contexts, when protest was seen by Melbourne to transform itself into sedition, the response of authority should be merciless. Anglesey, as Lord Lieutenant, was offered the use of increasingly coercive powers, up to and including the proclamation of martial law.[138] The imposition of curfews in disturbed areas was thought particularly beneficial, and all the provisions of the Coercion Bill of 1833 won Melbourne's full backing.[139] If a Lord Lieutenant in Dublin could convince the Home Secretary that the Union was in danger, it was quite likely that full powers would be forthcoming.

Unfortunately, this clear expression of policy was, to the irritation of Dublin government, almost always immediately subjected to Whiggish qualifications. Whigs never felt comfortable in responding to protest with the use of force alone. It had to be accompanied by a respect for the law and by the offering of reasonable concessions. Melbourne was happy to allow a suspension of Habeas Corpus, though reflecting that it was usually 'a measure, which subjected the Government to more odium, than it gave it strength or power'.[140] The Coercion Bill of 1833 was acceptable, but he hastened to tell Parliament 'that the necessary measures of coercion were to be accompanied by others of concession and salutary improvement'.[141] He had no doubts about proclaiming martial law in certain circumstances, but then wondered if the authorities had 'force enough to carry it into effect'.[142] Above all, no measure would work if it was denied by the opinion of propertied men:

The murders, outrages etc are dreadful and will unfortunately sooner or later compel the adoption of measures stronger than the ordinary law. I have long foreseen this; but such measures must not be prematurely proposed. You must carry along with you the public feeling and the general conviction. The evil must be so glowing as to be seen even by the blind.[143]

This is pure Whiggishness. The exercise of power was always a qualified, never an absolute, right in government. A ministry must never be afraid to act, but all its measures would be futile, if not backed by the opinion of the natural leaders of society. Their good offices were won by government always remaining within the law, until such times as the dangers to public order were so gross and so manifest that extraordinary measures could be enacted.

Melbourne's nuanced approach to Ireland is best illustrated in the tithe question. Between 1830 and 1834, the requirement that Roman Catholics should pay tithes to Anglican churchmen in Ireland was increasingly challenged, not least by a very successful non-payment campaign run by O'Connell. By 1833, 'it is impossible to overstate the anxiety', with which Melbourne viewed the issue.[144] On the one hand, the non-payment of a lawful tax was a challenge to the authority of the Westminster Parliament. It might also encourage similar campaigns in the rest of the United Kingdom, putting Anglicanism everywhere at risk. As has been noted, Melbourne, though not religious, was a friend to the Church of England. On the other hand, Melbourne thought it absurd and provocative that Irish Catholics should be compelled to support Anglicanism. For them, these were, understandably, 'vexatious proceedings'.[145] There was the practical problem of finding the means of enforcing payment. Stanley in Dublin was told that the tithe question boiled down to mere practicalities: 'If it be local and limited, it may be put down; but if it be widely diffused and increasing, your force, which is already represented to be fatigued and harrassed [sic] will be found insufficient to accomplish its object.'[146] Officials in Ireland were, as a consequence, given an ambiguous brief. Landowners and clergymen were to be encouraged to assert their property rights in the collection of tithes, but they were to be given no guarantees of assistance or protection while doing so.[147] It was a logical, if unhelpful, prescription.

Melbourne's defence must lie in his appreciation of the fact that the tithe question was only a small aspect of a much larger problem. After Catholic Emancipation, the relationship between Irish Catholics and the Anglican Church in Ireland had to be readjusted. It was simply no longer possible for a religious minority to enjoy a privileged status. Ireland was an overwhelmingly Catholic and, in Ulster, Presbyterian country. The Anglican supremacy was artificial, and would not hold when challenged. Melbourne's apologia was therefore that there was little point in tinkering with the tithe question, when that would be subsumed within a much larger settlement. Such a defence merely leads to a larger criticism, however. Melbourne saw the need for a larger settlement, and yet did nothing. Partly, this might be explained by his reverence for the Church of England that has already been discussed. Partly, the magnitude of the problem simply paralysed him. To Anglesey he wrote:

I agree with you that the question of the established Church requires to be settled in such a manner as is likely to be final, and I also agree that a provision should be made for the Roman Catholic Clergy. But it appears to me that in the present state of Parties and of the Houses of Parliament, no reasonable expectation either could or can be entertained, that measures for these purposes can be adopted easily and expeditiously.[148]

In private, he would admit that it would be right 'to pull down the edifice' of the Church settlement in Ireland and 'rebuild it',[149] but he ducked the issue. Plausible excuses about inappropriate timing and unhelpful individuals barely masked the perception that Melbourne knew what needed to be done, but failed to do it.

These well-modulated, Home Office policies were not what harassed Lords-Lieutenant wanted to hear. Sitting in Dublin Castle, trying to contain crisis on an almost daily basis, these men wanted more definite decisions. They wished to be told what government could do, not what it might be prudent to avoid. Melbourne quarrelled with both the men who led the Irish administration in his time, the Marquess of Anglesey and the Marquess Wellesley. With the first he had served in Ireland in 1828 and had established an amicable working relationship with him. Five years later, the friendship was in ruins. Anglesey, never having 'thought Melbourne stout',[150] gave up consulting him on Irish affairs. Instead, he made his views known to the Cabinet through Lord Holland. This confusing of the smooth flow of opinion and information between London and Dublin was constitutionally irregular, and eventually became so tangled a system that it played a large part in bringing down Grey's government in June–July 1834.[151] For his part, Melbourne accused Anglesey of assuming the airs of 'a kind of extra Royal Duke'. As Lord Hatherton recorded, meetings between the two men after 1833 were frosty:

When he [Melbourne] joined me I had been riding with Lord Anglesey, to whom I made a fine bow, taking off my Hat when I left him. Melbourne said, 'who the devil was that you were so civil to?'—'What is the use of being so obsequious?'—'Oh, you know he likes it—he is a great Man and affects magnificence and state'—'It seems to me that any man may be what he likes—He has only to assume, and every one concedes.'[152]

To have a Home Secretary and Lord-Lieutenant at loggerheads opened government policy up to derision and misrepresentation.

Exactly the same pattern was played out with Anglesey's successor, although this time the antagonism was even more bitter. Once again, Melbourne complained that Wellesley and his friends neglected him:

They never thought it necessary to consult me about any thing. On the contrary, if they thought I should disapprove of any step which they were determined to take . . . [they] took the step without asking me; altho' I was the only person with whom they ought to have consulted. . . . The consequence of Lord Wellesley's conduct was no less than the dissolution of Ld. Grey's Government . . . Events which may have been good or bad, but which ought not to have been brought about in that manner.[153]

In reply, Wellesley accused Melbourne of never reading dispatches, and of failing to answer them if he did read them. If it was administrative muddle that destroyed the Grey government, the fault lay in the Home Office. He told Melbourne that he was 'the offender; I am the victim', and accused him of an 'unjust, treacherous and cruel act', by which he was 'expelled' from the public service.[154] Neither Anglesey nor Wellesley were men of an accommodating nature, but to so anger both suggests how far Melbourne's reservations on Irish policy seemed opaque to men on the spot. Undeniably, this lack of rapport deeply compromised the expression of policy.

The experience was so bruising that it became the basis of a long-standing grudge. When he became Prime Minister, Melbourne refused to allow Wellesley to remain in Dublin, and offered him the largely honorific post of Lord Chamberlain instead.[155] This was indignantly refused, and 'the storm that burst from him against Lord Melbourne was terrific. It lashed at the full stretch of his voice for exactly an hour by the Clock on his Mantlepiece.' Melbourne was 'this Puppy', 'this damned Scoundrel'. Wellesley seriously contemplated calling Melbourne out in a duel.[156] In due course, a measure of political co-operation was resumed, but without any degree of personal warmth.[157] When Wellesley died, in 1843, he instructed Brougham to use his papers to protect his 'character from the aspersions of Ld Melbourne and his associate Daniel O'Connell'.[158] As far as Wellesley was concerned, his quarrel with Melbourne would go on after his death. Neither he nor Anglesey had any regard for a man, who, as Home Secretary, had seemed to them to be vacillating and almost paralysed by doubt. For those who thought like them, these years merely confirmed William Lamb's reputation for lounging his way through politics. This is too hard a judgement. His doubts were well founded, and he gazed into the depths of a problem. Unfortunately, he could not work with men of action like Anglesey and Wellesley, and the coherence of government policy suffered grievously. The Irish dimension of his Home Secretaryship did little to enhance Melbourne's reputation. But then, it had buried that of many others.

Melbourne's performance as Home Secretary had been undemonstrative. Given the political agenda of these years, the occupant should have been a major influence in government. Instead, Melbourne never enjoyed the weight or reputation of Grey, Palmerston, Russell, Althorp, or even perhaps of Duncannon and Lansdowne. He had not improved very much as a parliamentary speaker, and was ignored by the press. In the Reform Bill drama, he had been little more than an onlooker. The threat of Political Unions and Trade Unions had been met with indulgence. On Ireland, Melbourne had informed and deep perceptions, but these, too, seemed to argue for inaction. It was not altogether surprising that Grey should have attempted to move him to a more ceremonial office, or that Anglesey and Wellesley should have tried to find ways round his doubts and hesitations. Critics like Greville enjoyed the spectacle of Melbourne wriggling with discomfort as he voted for measures he disliked in the company of men he never quite trusted. To those who had always accused William Lamb of lacking any real belief, and any will-power of his own, his performance in office had been all of a piece. His private life had been regulated by mother, wife, and sister. His political life was determined by men of vivid and determined personality. If Melbourne accepted this situation uncomplainingly, it was because he sought nothing from politics but to be diverted and amused. It filled the hours of the day for a man, whose decision to take no more emotional risks left him much alone.

An alternative reading of Melbourne's views would centre on the point that, on many occasions, doing nothing is a right policy for government. The *Morning Chronicle*, in assessing Melbourne's Secretaryship in July 1834, sensibly commented: 'what he has *not* done during his administration of the important office recently held by him has always appeared to us a distinguishing merit in a modern statesman.'[159] Melbourne was intensely aware that, unless both the army and the bureaucracy were significantly enlarged, there were firm limits to what government actually could do. To be effective, its efforts would have to be supplemented by the voluntary services of county and parish officials. Further, government was constrained by the law. If its own actions were above reproach, and if it tolerated what was legal, those who challenged it could be exposed as traffickers in illegality. Such people, like the Tolpuddle Martyrs, would then be shown no mercy. Most important of all was Melbourne's fatalism. As his notebooks make clear, his Glasgow professors had convinced him that society was always, and properly, in motion. Many of the factors that determined this movement were beyond the reach of any government, lying as they did within the gaunt and inflexible laws of economics. At best, politicians could regulate on a limited scale, moderate consequences, and be aware that much that happened was unavoidable.

Melbourne's passivity was not, therefore, simply a bruised personality refusing to take decisions. Inaction was something that could be positively argued for. In fact, the disturbances of these years passed off without undue violence. Even so, few contemporaries would have thought that Melbourne's reputation had been much improved by his years in office. The fact that he became Prime Minister of England, in July 1834, was therefore little short of miraculous. Only an odd configuration of politics gave him a chance of office in 1830. Only an even odder configuration could have wafted him to the chief place in politics.

8

Prime Minister, 1834–1841

WILLIAM LAMB became Prime Minister only as the result of an extended, political crisis that so muddled loyalties and affiliations that he found himself in charge of the government. Difficulties started in May 1834 with the resignation of four members of Grey's Cabinet over Irish policies. In July, Melbourne was appointed Prime Minister. In November, he was dismissed even though he still enjoyed a majority in the House of Commons. For five months, Peel attempted to lead a minority government, but, when this experiment failed, Melbourne was reinstated in office in April 1835. For nearly a year, there was turmoil right across the political spectrum. The confusion of 1829–30 was re-enacted. Many Tories had never forgiven Peel and Wellington for their role in Catholic Emancipation, and the antipathy was reciprocated. Many Whigs thought that Grey had been ousted by conspiracy, and Grey himself certainly thought so. Irish MPs had come to distrust the Whigs without warming to the Tories. Radical leaders like Brougham seemed to prefer a maverick system of politics, and that made their behaviour totally unpredictable. Fault lines ran through nearly all the major, political groupings. In this situation, Melbourne discovered that his history of detachment from party suddenly became an asset. His career in office had been so short, that he had not had the opportunity to offend too many people. Being unobjectionable is normally to claim only faint praise. In 1834, it was the most prized quality.

Throughout the convulsions of 1834–5, Melbourne's conduct could hardly be called decisive. He followed events rather than led them. The reticence, about which his mother, sister, and wife had all complained, was still very much in evidence. He was reluctant to accept greater responsibilities. He consulted everyone about everything. In particular, he was hesitant about taking any step without Grey's approval. At crucial moments, he was hardly a player in the game at all. The Lichfield House agreement, for example, was arranged without any contribution from Melbourne. He was endlessly disregarded and bullied. Grey and his son, Howick, lectured him mercilessly on

PLATE 1 William, 2nd Viscount Melbourne by Samuel Diez, 1841.

PLATE 2 Marginalia of a letter from Lady Caroline Lamb to Lady Holland (*c*. Nov. 1810).

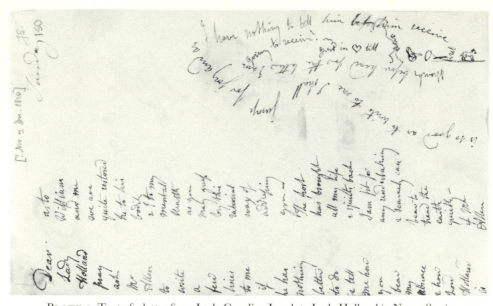

PLATE 3 Text of a letter from Lady Caroline Lamb to Lady Holland (*c.* Nov. 1810).

PLATE 4 Lady Caroline Lamb by Eliza Trotter (*c.*1810).

PLATE 5 John Doyle, 'Receiving the Fatal News', Dec. 1834. Melbourne announces his dismissal to his Cabinet colleagues.

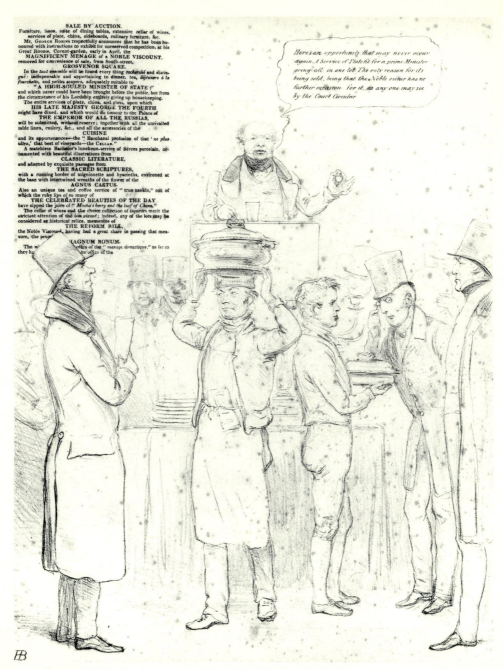

PLATE 6 John Doyle, 'Auction Extraordinary' Feb. 1838. Melbourne's Administration is put under the hammer.

what was and what was not acceptable to Foxite Whiggery. In fact, Grey continued to think of himself as Prime Minister, in substance, if not in name. Holland House regarded Lamb as a protégé who was to take dictation. People as diverse as Brougham and William IV thought that he was a man to be manipulated. Few contemporaries gave Melbourne the credit of being his own man. Most thought he was someone else's mouthpiece. After all, he was 'a queer fellow to be Prime Minister'.[1]

The story of the collapse of the Grey administration has been well told.[2] It turned on the question of whether, in the new Irish Coercion Bill, clauses banning public meetings should be renewed. Wellesley, writing from Dublin on 11 June, thought that it would be prudent to retain the clauses, and, acting on his advice, the Cabinet agreed this policy. Brougham then persuaded E. J. Littleton, the Chief Secretary in Ireland, to talk to Wellesley again about the matter. After this conversation, Wellesley changed his mind. Once more acting on Brougham's advice, Littleton told O'Connell of his superior's change of mind, who promptly announced it to the whole world. As a result, Grey's Cabinet found itself committed to an Irish policy, which had been repudiated by its officers in Dublin. The government was so compromised by the incident that Grey renewed the controversial clauses, and promptly resigned.[3]

Grey and many others believed that the government had been destroyed by a Brougham–Wellesley plot, and even if these men had not been keen 'to worm out Lord Grey', their behaviour had been constitutionally unfortunate, to say the least.[4] For a moment, Brougham was 'in fact, first Minister'. The Radical leader's reputation never quite recovered from this accusation, and he spent much time and ink in later life trying to establish an interpretation of the events of 1834 that exonerated himself.[5] Almost certainly, the crisis was produced by administrative muddle rather than conspiracy, but, if there was a plot, Melbourne had no part in it. His only contribution to these events was his flawed relationship with Wellesley, noted in the previous chapter, which may have played a part in interrupting the smooth flow of information between London and Dublin. Otherwise, Melbourne had not foreseen trouble. He was not prepared for the resignations of Stanley and Graham over Ireland in May, nor did he think that the Ministry had been unduly endangered by their departure.[6] When the crisis came, he thought that Littleton had been incompetent rather than conspiratorial. He seemed to live 'in a fool's paradise'.[7] He had talked to O'Connell in good faith and had been betrayed. His bad judgement merely underlined his insignificance.[8]

So far was Melbourne from being involved in a plot to destroy Grey, that he was reported to be 'very angry', that the Ministry had been brought down.[9] He blamed Brougham entirely for causing the crisis, and told him to his face that his itch to meddle had had calamitous results:

It is true as you state that the immediate cause of Lord Spencer's and Ld Grey's resignation was the communication made by Littleton to O'Connell of Ld Wellesley's
. . . opinion upon the Coercion bill but the whole originated in your urging Littleton
to induce Ld Wellesley to express that opinion in a formal despatch and to urge it
upon the Government.[10]

When he came to form Cabinets himself, Melbourne steadfastly refused to
give Brougham office. He liked the man's company, but his behaviour in
1834 justified the use of the blackball on any suggestion that he could be
accepted as a colleague. The dismissal of Grey opened up totally unexpected
possibilities for Melbourne, but he had neither foreseen them nor welcomed
them. Indeed, it was not immediately clear to him that the Irish crisis should
have necessitated Grey's resignation at all.[11] In these weeks, Melbourne's
tone is bewildered rather than machiavellian.

   When Grey did resign, few people saw Melbourne as his successor. In the
first two weeks of July, Melbourne was little more than an errand boy for the
King, as William IV searched about for an alternative administration. Lamb
simply had conversations with 'some leading Members of the House of
Commons', and reported them to the King. Also by royal request, he wrote
to Wellington, Peel, and Stanley about the possibility of forming a cross-party
administration, but had to report that the obstacles in the path of this proposal were 'insurmountable'.[12] None of these men gave the idea a second
thought, even though Melbourne himself insisted that he had 'no personal
likes or objections'.[13] Being employed as a kind of human poste restante by
the King and leading politicians was a wearing business. On 12 July, he complained: 'it is very inconvenient to continue to be the medium of communication, and maybe liable to misconstruction.'[14] He was reported, on the same
day, to be 'sulky' about politics,[15] and he sought diversion by taking a party
of ladies for a picnic on the river.[16] Two days later, he told the House of
Lords that he had been appointed Prime Minister.

   No one was immediately impressed. Frederick Lamb told his brother that
he had taken on 'a rum task', and that he would have preferred to hear that
'you were out and coming to Carlsbad'.[17] The appointment had such an *ad
hoc* quality that all the details of a working relationship with the King had to
be worked out after the announcement was made.[18] Grey had patronizingly
suggested Melbourne as a possible successor, 'as one who might fill his office
with less danger of divisions than most publick men',[19] while Durham, the
Radical leader, agreed that Lamb might do, because his lack of weight in politics made him 'the only one of whom none of us would be jealous'.[20]
Melbourne might win acceptance, but only because he was not a number of
other people. The new Prime Minister himself was hardly more confident.
He told the Lords, on 14 July, that 'it was impossible to be more sensible of

the incapacity of the individual to whom this difficult and delicate task was intrusted than he was himself'.[21] Allegedly, he accepted office only when Thomas Young pointed out that it was something to be Prime Minister, even if 'it only lasts three months'.[22] His elevation seemed to prove the validity of Melbourne's belief that, 'much of what is attributed to design is accident; the unknown cause leading to the unknown end'.[23]

The announcement that Melbourne was Prime Minister was greeted with rudeness and incredulity from friend and foe alike. Howick thought that he had shown 'no very nice sense of political rectitude nor very high standards of morality'.[24] Holland found his attempts at political conviction and passion 'ludicrous rather than injurious'.[25] Edward Ellice advised him that any thought of trying to form a government would be 'madness'.[26] For once, the Lamb family were not very helpful or supportive. Mrs George Lamb thought that Melbourne's strongest motive for staying in office should be his clear need of a salary.[27] Emily Lamb worried that the cares of office would 'kill William'.[28] Within four days of becoming Prime Minister, Melbourne was described as 'a melancholy instance of the cares of office—notes coming in to him every two minutes and his gay laugh completely stifled'.[29]

People further removed from the centre of London politics found the changes even harder to take seriously. Not infrequently, they turned to theatrical metaphors to describe the situation. Metternich observed that it reminded him 'of the Comedie Française when in summer the parts are acted by *doubles* [understudies]'.[30] The professional wit, Joseph Jekyll, reported: 'we have had a famous political pantomime, and our theatre was in danger from a flare-up of the actors, but we have patched up the scenery, got a new harlequin, and trust a generous public will permit us to play through the season.'[31] The comic potential of the apparition of Melbourne as Prime Minister was confirmed by reports that he used the Great Seal as the object of search in games of hunt-the-thimble, and that he had appeared at a race meeting, dressed as the Lord Chancellor, and quite considerably the worse for drink.[32] It was hard to believe that William Lamb would ever acquire the necessary gravity for the office he now held. He was 48 when he took up his first appointment in Ireland. He had had only four years of experience in the Cabinet. His willingness to work with men from different parts of the political spectrum had a mongrel quality. Yet, a set of extraordinary political circumstances had contrived to make him Prime Minister. When the Hollands first visited the new Prime Minister, they 'found him extended on an ottoman *sans* shirt, *sans* neckcloth, in a great wrapping gown and in a profound slumber'.[33]

The most charitable explanation offered was that Melbourne was a mere figurehead, with real authority being exercised by Grey from behind the scenery. As far as Peel was concerned, the whole arrangement was under 'the sanction of Lord Grey'.[34] The dispensation of patronage and titles confirmed this belief, as did Melbourne's anxiety to consult Grey on almost everything, and to acknowledge continuity between the old Ministry and the new.[35] As Melbourne informed the Lords, his 'was not in any respect a new Government, that it was in fact only a renewal of the old Government, with the loss of one member, whose loss all must deplore'. Policies would be unchanged, because 'there was nothing for him to do but to follow up those principles, suiting them to the circumstances of the times, and to the events that might possibly arise'.[36] So widespread was the belief that Melbourne had no programme of his own, that this interpretation seemed wholly credible. Grey's control of government was undiminished. It was now exercised through an elevated office-boy called William Lamb.

A less charitable view saw the new Cabinet as nothing but 'a lath-and-plaster' affair.[37] It was a botched and hurried arrangement, without firm principles or direction. Aberdeen told Wellington that from William Lamb, 'I am satisfied that we have nothing to expect, and that he will sacrifice every principle without scruple or hesitation to suit the convenience of the moment.'[38] Melbourne himself seemed to think that the composition of his government was so disparate as to make unequivocal policies hard to come by:

A Cabinet . . . is at all times a delicate and fragile Machine—it is very difficult either to secure its regularity of action or its coherence. This is still more the case, when it has recently been shaken and broken and repaired with new materials. Its weakness and liability to accident is much increased by such an operation. Those who stay in are anxious to appear not to have conceded every thing to their new allies, and those who join are equally desirous of obtaining as much concession as possible . . . Such a body is not to be approached but with the utmost care and even alarm.[39]

Running true to form, Lamb seemed to be fortifying himself with good reasons why government should do nothing. As a result, Greville was not alone in thinking that the new government would not last long.[40] It seemed too obviously a stop-gap, whose only function was to keep government ticking over, until such time as William IV accepted that Althorp was the only man of consequence, and raised him to the leadership of affairs. Sooner or later, the King must 'come back to Althorp'.[41]

Melbourne's first administration lasted for four months, and for most of this time Parliament was not sitting. Its caretaking quality seemed confirmed. The lack of respect accorded the new Prime Minister was startling. From the beginning, everyone agreed that Althorp was the only man of importance in the Cabinet. On the day the Ministry was formed, Melbourne himself had jokingly admitted 'that Althorp is the Tortoise on which the world now rests'.[42] Only he had the capacity and reputation to hold the government's majority in the Commons together. His elevation to the Lords on the death of his father, in November 1834, was therefore bound to provoke a crisis. Melbourne, before setting out to see the King in Brighton, sent a letter ahead in which he 'stressed that the Government had been mainly formed upon the weight and influence of Althorp in the House of Commons and that now it was for his Majesty to consider whether he would empower me to make fresh arrangements, or whether he would take other measures'.[43] No Prime Minister has signalled his own insignificance with more clarity. In view of this admission, he was not in a position to complain when the King dismissed the government on 14 November: 'What will be the consequences, God knows; at the same time I am not surprised at his decision; nor do I know that I can entirely condemn it.'[44] He was sure that William IV had acted 'conscientiously'.[45] Grey agreed,[46] and even Holland thought the King's action 'not altogether *unjustifiable* though very foolish'.[47] All of them were conditioned to think that Melbourne's government had never been anything but a passing convenience, and now it had ended.

What transformed the situation was not what the King did, but how he did it. First, he failed in the courtesy of seeing the outgoing Ministers. Some of them read of their dismissal in their morning newspapers. Secondly, his attempt to set up another Wellington administration was simply provocative. The Duke was so compromised by his anti-Reform attitudes, that there was no hope of the sitting Parliament accepting him. William IV seemed to be directly challenging the House of Commons. A crisis between executive and legislature seemed unavoidable. If Melbourne had been dismissed because he could not guarantee a majority in the Commons, it was quixotic of the King to think that Peel or Wellington could do better. People began to talk of a royal *coup d'état*, aimed at the destruction of parliamentary life. He had at least been impolite, and those, who had suspected George III of being a would-be tyrant, transferred their suspicions to his son. Greville observed that, 'It is long since a Government has been so summarily dismissed—regularly kicked out, in the simplest sense of that phrase.'[48] Foxite memories of kings destroying Whig Ministries in 1782, 1783, and 1807 were vigorously stirred. Holland House thought the King had made a 'fatal' mistake. The *Morning Chronicle* spluttered outrage, and insisted that 'Englishmen must be up and doing'.[49] When Kings attacked Parliamentary majorities, Foxite Whigs were recalled to their duty.

Melbourne's reaction to the termination of his attempt at government was altogether different and typically passive. He had admitted that Althorp's elevation had created a new situation, in which the King had clear options. He also seemed to have so little confidence in his own powers that leaving office was almost a relief. The day after his dismissal, he went to Drury Lane and laughed heartily at a play called *The Regent*, whose plot involved a Ministry being turned out. Greville noted that Melbourne, 'who does not care a button about *office*, whatever he may do about power, was heartily amused'.[50] Illegitimately related to William IV, Melbourne felt sorrow rather than anger, and, in his resignation letter, promised all assistance, 'not merely as a matter of duty, but with all the warmth of the most grateful feelings and the strongest personal attachment and devotion'.[51] There was no fight in Melbourne. He had not willed himself into office, and he lacked the energy to stay there. As his mother and sister had prophesied, decisions were taken for William Lamb, not by him.

Indeed, being out of office was almost therapeutic. Melbourne told Holland: 'I hardly ever felt so much relaxed and in such spirits in my life. I know by experience, that after a time one gets tired of being out and longs for office again, but at first nothing can be more delightful.'[52] Partly, this mood was set by a fastidious reluctance to whine in public: 'I do not like to be considered ill-used; nothing looks so foolish as ill-used People from a blubbery seduced girl to a turned out Prime Minister.'[53] More importantly, the King's cavalier behaviour towards the Cabinet was not directed against Melbourne. The outgoing Prime Minister was offered an earldom and the Garter, both of which he refused.[54] He admitted that he had been treated 'with every expression of kindness and consideration', and so Wellington not unreasonably concluded that he was 'delighted to be relieved'.[55] Over and over again, Melbourne insisted that he had no complaint to make: 'They may say what they wish upon the imprudence and want of wisdom in the King's determination, but I think it cannot be said to have been personally unfair and injurious to those whom it offended.'[56] Admittedly, 'the experiment was rather fearful', but he thought that 'it may be got through without serious and permanent evil'.[57] Those, who wished to cast Melbourne as an abused and tragic hero,[58] were to be disappointed. Melbourne had never had a great belief in his own administration. Few people had given it the chance of a long life. Now, having been very decently treated by William IV, he was not unhappy about returning to a less stressful way of living.

Lamb's family heartily agreed with the line that William had taken. They closed ranks. Emily was sure that her brother had acted 'with great dignity. They don't say anything against the King or his Court—there is nothing on this occasion to explain.'[59] Egremont, too, was proud of the 'propriety' of his son's behaviour.[60] The clan had no sense that their favourite son had been in any way disadvantaged. Fortified by this approval, Melbourne firmly disapproved of any attempt to use his exit from office as a device to attack the monarchy. Efforts 'made to raise a flame in London seem to me quite contemptible, and to proceed from the lowest quarters'.[61] Editors, who tried to raise a dust, were instructed by Melbourne to print statements exonerating the King. Their tactics were productive of nothing but 'mischief'.[62] In late November, he spent a week among his tenants in Derbyshire, where he was continually besieged by delegations of well-wishers from surrounding towns and villages. His sister-in-law thoroughly approved of the statesmanlike way he addressed them:

Lord M. cannot bear it to be talked of as personal ill-usage, he says when the interests of a great Empire are at stake, it is low to descend to that and so he told the people today, who have been in crowds to present him an address—it was really a very good one, and he spoke beautifully in reply. He looked so well, standing out among them, without his hat and his action so earnest I was quite delighted.[63]

In these domestic surroundings, he could speak well, and she began to think that 'he is quite made to be the Minister of a great Country'.[64] Warmly supportive, his family was unanimous in believing that nothing had so dignified William's tenure of power as the manner of his giving it up.

Others were less accommodating. Some former Ministers thought that Melbourne had been absurdly indulgent towards an unconstitutional king, and that he had damaged parliamentary traditions by not taking a stronger line. Lord Lyttleton, for example, observed that:

You told the Melbournians and Derbyites the other Day that you did not consider yourself *personally aggrieved*: but you must allow me to say, that nonetheless His Majesty behaved about as scurvily to you, as he did to the Constitution—and hang, draw and quarter me if I ever forget either, or fail to act practically upon the Recollection.[65]

Emily Eden, much in Melbourne's confidences at this time and a woman of some intellect, thought that 'anything equal to the ill treatment of Lord Melbourne never was known'.[66] Holland House 'badgered and bullied' him on the subject, and urged him to speak out.[67] To many friends and political associates, Melbourne's complaisance in his removal from power did him little service. If his family saw it as statesmanlike, many others saw it as gutless. Once again, William Lamb had failed to impose himself on events.

Under pressure from criticism of this kind, Melbourne gradually shifted position. A harder tone creeps into his pronouncements. On 6 December, he made a speech to a delegation of Derby Reformers. This time, while reiterating that he had no 'just cause to feel personally aggrieved', he added the opinion that: 'the dissolution of the Cabinet had occurred abruptly, and at a time when the public mind was in a state of especial calm and quiet.'[68] This change of tack was noted. Now, Lamb was accused of lacking the resolution to take a line and hold it. He had been bullied out of his own thoughts:

Melbourne's two speeches at Derby, and the history connected with them, exhibit him in a very discreditable and lamentable point of view—compelled by the menaces and reproaches of Duncannon and the rest to eat his words; and all this transacted by a sort of negotiation and through the mediation of his vulgar secretary, Tom Young and Mrs. Lane Fox. Such a thing it is to be without firmness and decision of character. Melbourne is a gentleman, liberal and straightforward, with no meanness, and incapable of selfish trickery and intrigue, but he is habitually careless and *insouciant*, loves ease, and hates contests and squabbles.[69]

By the end of December, the change of government was described as being made 'in direct opposition to the known opinion of the House of Commons'.[70] In February, Melbourne had reinstated himself as a Foxite Whig. The Lords were treated to a thesis, which linked 1784, 1807, 1831, and 1834 as examples of royal assaults on parliamentary values: 'They were bold, dangerous, desperate measures all of them.'[71] In ten weeks, Melbourne had first exonerated William IV and then condemned him. Not surprisingly, some thought him pathetic in his willingness to leave office, and others accused him of lacking consistency, as he was harassed into shifting from one interpretation to another.

Therefore, Melbourne played little or no part in the movement to punish the King which gathered strength within the Whig ranks in January and February 1835. He had to be pushed and pulled into action, always following and rarely leading. He agreed that the Peel government was a 'claptrap administration',[72] but hesitated about whether it was proper to bring it down, if it enjoyed royal backing. He expressed his doubts in a letter to Grey, adding, astonishingly, that his brief premiership had not compromised his freedom from party ties in any way: 'Are we, or am I justified in declaring a decided opposition to the present government, unless we see a reasonable prospect of being able to form another . . . this is a new point of departure. I consider myself now free, entirely free, to choose both the principles upon which and the men with whom I will consent again to join.'[73] Holland was told the same thing. Bringing Peel down would be too much of 'a Plunge',[74] and, after all those who opposed the Tories were nothing but 'a discordantly composed majority'.[75] The prospect of stable government did not necessarily lie with them. Once again, William Lamb had found a very plausible argument for postponing action.

For those who thought that the November *coup* had been an outrageous insult to Whiggery, and that the very existence of Peel's government defying a majority in the Commons made a mockery of constitutional procedure, Melbourne's passivity was incomprehensible. Holland told him frankly that he had to vindicate the record of his own premiership by attacking Peel.[76] Otherwise, any claim to high office in the future would be forfeit: 'In considering these matters Fabius himself must take into his calculations the extent of his authority over his troops.'[77] Even Grey was more adventurous in his views, and tried to assure Melbourne that there was no shame in defending the events of 1830–4, or in continuing to advocate 'the necessary reforms, which the state of our institutions may require, upon safe and moderate principles'.[78] In reply, Melbourne admitted that his views were 'not likely to be very popular with our friends and supporters',[79] but he had no wish to see the King 'prostrate',[80] and he feared that a new Whig ministry would be so battered by Tories on one side and Radicals on the other that it would not stand.[81] Therefore it might be better to leave Peel undisturbed, even if this implied the meek acceptance of the unpleasantness of November 1834. This was a distinctive point of view, and few of his friends agreed.

Predictably, Melbourne played little or no part in the construction of the Lichfield House Compact of February 1835 between Whigs, Irish, and Radicals, by which they agreed to bring Peel's government down. The idea came from Hobhouse, and Melbourne followed events at a considerable distance.[82] His only contribution seems to have been a letter to O'Connell, which, while hoping that they could 'cooperate generally until the Tory measures are defeated', added the important qualification that he thought it 'necessary to explain that while I do not ask you to give up any of your opinions on public questions, you will of course understand that I do not renounce any of mine'.[83] Given his opinion of O'Connell, this was a chilling remark. Confronted with the stark choice of tolerating Peel or allying with O'Connell and Durham's Radicals, Melbourne was not in a happy position. He had worked with Peel in government in the late 1820s. He had never been able to work with O'Connell. It was literally the Devil or the deep blue sea. He was forced to choose the first when every instinct led him to prefer the second. This embarrassment gave all his actions and remarks a lack-lustre quality that threatened once again to return him to the margins of politics. He had shown himself to be 'a Man created by the Times, hardly equal to them'. Quite simply, he 'was not the most likely person to lead the Whigs back to power'.[84]

When Peel's government fell in March 1835, a second Melbourne administration as a possible successor was barely thought of. Spencer or Grey were seen as the most likely new Prime Minister. Melbourne's claims were ignored, and he cheerfully seems to have acquiesced in his own abasement. On 28 March, Ellice reported that Melbourne pledged his unreserved support for Grey,[85] and, on 11 April, Melbourne joined other colleagues in formally asking Grey to resume political life, adding that 'it would naturally be our wish that you should place yourself at the head of the treasury'.[86] The King was happy to accept this idea, and, as in July 1834, Melbourne was used as a post-boy for exchanging letters between Grey and the Court.[87] It was as though Melbourne had never been Prime Minister himself. His brief period in office had clearly done little for his reputation. He was seen as a caretaker, while Grey enjoyed a sabbatical from office. Only when Grey declined to return to political life did the King once again fall back on Melbourne, as the least awful of a number of evils.[88] The offer to resume government could hardly have been less flattering.

Not surprisingly, Melbourne was 'half-inclined'[89] to turn it down. He thought he had 'a right' to do so.[90] Quite apart from his candidature being clearly a second-best option, he conjured up so many phantoms that doing nothing once again became reasonable, as he tried to explain to Lord Spencer:

You must feel that everything is at stake, that we have fearful odds to bear up against, the inclination of the King, the House of Lords, three-fourths at least of the gentlemen of the country, and such a preponderant number of the clergy as may be fairly called the whole of them, and if this attempt on the part of the Whig and Liberal party should fail, that party will most probably sink into insignificance, or be only able to aspire to a share of power in conjunction with, or in subordination to, its opponents.[91]

William Lamb could only rarely rise to the heroic, but this assessment of the chances of his second administration was peculiarly dismal. This time, Palmerston hurried him into accepting office, pointing out encouragingly that, 'It is wonderful how difficulties sink before one, when one sets to work to scale them.'[92] Melbourne found it hard to agree. It was all going to be a matter of 'shuffling'.[93]

There were reasons for Melbourne's despondency. William IV was widely known to respect him personally, but, equally, he told everyone that his new Prime Minister 'had no position either at home or abroad to be compared with Lord Grey, and that as to the rest of the government, they were *nobody*'.[94] King and minister had been thrown together by circumstance, not political affection. Formal treaties had to be worked out between the two men in the early days of the ministry, covering the many areas of possible disagreement, particularly Irish affairs and patronage arrangements.[95] Still more bothersome, from Melbourne's point of view, was the behaviour of colleagues who should have been helpful. Grey had declined office, yet still insisted on being consulted about everything, thereby claiming power without responsibility. Holland, whom Melbourne now dubbed 'a fatiguing old woman',[96] tried to dictate the composition of the new Cabinet,[97] and Palmerston flatly refused to consider anything but the Foreign Office, which he already regarded as a personal fief.[98] Only Lord John Russell and Lansdowne were totally co-operative.[99] Melbourne's relations with all these men would remain on substantially the same footing for the next six years. As he had predicted, keeping them all in harness would indeed be a matter of endlessly skipping from one expedient to another.

Gladstone, writing in 1890 an account of Melbourne's career, defended him against charges of inconsequentiality by arguing that he 'could not have been a small man who took by consent the office of Prime Minister in a Cabinet which . . . still numbered among its members . . . Lord Lansdowne, Lord Palmerston and Lord John Russell'.[100] This is too kind an assessment. Both in July 1834 and April 1835, Melbourne was not the first or even the second choice for the prime ministership. The office was his because others declined it, or were unacceptable to the King. He had fewer enemies than most of his competitors, and his professed detachment from party was an asset, when party loyalties were in a muddle. It was all the work of Fate, malevolent or benevolent as the case may be. In his Commonplace Book for 1833, Melbourne transcribed lines from Voltaire's play, *Henriade*, describing the fortuitous way in which Henry IV had become King of France. They could just as easily cover his own rise to political prominence:

> Mais Henri s'avançait vers sa grandeur suprême
> Par des chemins cachés, inconnus à lui-même.[101]

He had no great programmes to promote, no deep beliefs to vindicate. He set little store by the actual exercise of power, except to use it to observe other men's natures, and to divert himself. High office came to him uninvited.

No one thought that Melbourne's second attempt at government would be any longer-lived than his first. The French ambassador reported to Paris in this sense: 'C'est alors que commenceront les embarras des Wighs qui, unis pour combattre un ennemi commun, se divisent pour constituer un gouvernement.'[102] Tories looked at the new government and waxed sarcastic: 'literally and in point of form Lord Melbourne is Prime Minister . . . but such is the want of confidence in that Government on the part of the people . . . that substantially I consider Lord Melbourne and his party only holding office, until the Conservatives choose to take advantage of any one of the several grounds of difference which must arise between the Unholy Alliance, and then the Whigs are out for ever.'[103] When news of Melbourne's appointment reached Whig ears in Brooks's Club, all were in 'high glee', but whether in amusement or political contentment is not clear.[104] Those anxious to write the government's obituary had their pens poised from the very start of its life. Significantly, Melbourne himself shared nearly all their gloomy prognostications.

Melbourne was to survive as Prime Minister until the autumn of 1841, no mean achievement given the despondency which had greeted the birth of his administration. Its prospects were a matter for speculation throughout its existence. Odd political circumstances had brought it into being. The same odd circumstances dictated its distinctive character. As the most recent historian of the Melbourne government has pointed out, 'Whiggery was more a large faction in government than a unified party controlling half of the political world', and was based on 'the mutual need of Melbourne and Peel to deny influence to their respective dogmatic and ultra supporters'.[105] As long as Radicals and Ultra Tories had to be denied influence, moderate men in the middle ground of politics looked for a figurehead. Melbourne, with a reputation for working with anyone, was an obvious choice. He had no interest in party or its organization. Government was more a dinner party among friends than anything else. Tories like Peel preferred him to the Ultra members of their own party. Radicals and Irishmen swallowed hard, and acknowledged that he offered more than a Tory government could. Among Whigs, he was plainly perceived to be one of their own, by family, by upbringing, and by his dining habits. The secret strength of the Melbourne government lay in the fact that, when politicians contemplated the figure of the Prime Minister, they could always imaginatively compare him with someone worse. He was rarely admired, but he was not feared. The record of his private life and his brief career in politics made him the least menacing of men. Nearly everything about him was negative, but then there had been much in the period 1827–34 which had been too positive.

Melbourne viewed the prospect of office with dismay. Ten days into the Ministry, he wrote:

I did not wish to undertake this task at all. I thought the support we could calculate upon insufficient; I think so still, but I have never said so . . . The Radicals can blow us out of the water at any moment. They did so before and they may again . . . success is hardly upon the Cards. I do not wish to use the language of menace or any thing like it but . . . I have not the usual motives for office. Most people suffer more pain from seeing their Enemies in power than they receive pleasure from seeing their Friends there. I have none of those feelings. It is no mortification to me to see Peel Prime Minister. I had as lief see him there as any one else.[106]

He complained that, in order to construct an administration out of very disparate materials, he had been forced to offer posts 'to men in whose opinions I do not concur and for whose characters I have no great respect'.[107] At social gatherings he often described his colleagues in ways which 'if repeated would be greatly to his detriment'.[108] Throughout his tenure of office, he wriggled under the pressure exerted by party men, and loathed being bullied by such leaders of populist politics as newspaper editors and demagogues. He was profoundly aware of the anomaly of his own position. Party and popular opinion were everywhere and growing, yet he detested both: 'Popular governments never have been, and I believe never can be conducted except upon the principles of party, and these principles of necessity injure the public service by frequently excluding from it those, who are the best qualified to perform it with ability and efficiency.'[109] By temperament and preference, he talked the language of the élite politics of the late eighteenth century. In the 1830s this gave him something of the attraction of a raree-show.

With party considerations at such a discount in Melbourne's mind, it was not surprising that many contemporaries found it hard to decide where the centre of gravity in the new government lay. William IV was happy to think of his Prime Minister as 'a Conservative in the truest sense of the word, and to as great a degree as his Majesty himself'.[110] Melbourne himself described his administration as 'avowedly Whig', while admitting that others saw it as 'Radical'.[111] His preferred metaphor, however, was to describe politics as a tide that ebbs and flows: 'It is like the tide, it comes on with great violence and then recedes as violently in an opposite direction. It gains ground perhaps with every wave, but it is far from always keeping the ground which it temporarily occupies.'[112] The years 1829–34 had seen a flood-tide. It was now time merely to tidy up the consequences of this experience, and to consolidate. In this sense, the agenda of the Melbourne government was pre-arranged. It was to deal with the results of what had gone before. It was not its duty or responsibility to move on to new ground. Referring to 'the scope of change and the restless spirit of the time', Melbourne was clear that 'our measures did not create it, on the contrary it produced our measures'.[113] Being reactive, not proactive, had always suited Melbourne's character, and now it was high politics. His objective was the 'maintaining as much and as many of our present institutions' as possible.[114] His Glasgow education had taught him that to resist change was futile, and a progressive Cabinet colleague recalled that, 'on every occasion on which a degree of rational change was discussed in the Cabinet at that time, Ld Melbourne had always sided with him'.[115] Yet changes had to be consolidated as well as introduced, and institutions should be reformed, not undermined. This formula could be Whig, Tory, or Radical, if viewed from different points of the political spectrum.

Such ambiguities meant that government could only function if run on unconventional lines. Cabinets in particular were much at a discount. Tensions between Ministers were so pronounced, that it was often wishful thinking to hope that policy could be made round a table. In his experience, Melbourne thought that '*A Cabinet* is a *bad machine to work great affairs with*'.[116] Two such meetings a week were as much as he could tolerate.[117] Sometimes, he presided over them with what his colleagues called 'sagacity and prudence, and that extraordinary mixture of good humour with quick sensibility, which is so peculiar a characteristic in him'.[118] Sometimes, they were reduced to the level of farce, with the Prime Minister reading the newspapers while others spoke, and merely contributing 'a few of his sceptical remarks'.[119] Not infrequently, Cabinet meetings were held before or after dinner parties. At these, Melbourne sometimes slept.[120] Members of the Grey family complained that Cabinets had lost their purpose. They were no longer meetings at which policy was debated and decided. They had become occasions for rubber-stamping decisions taken elsewhere: 'Cabinet meetings are merely an idle waste of time in desultory or inconclusive conversation or a mere form to adopt a decision already formally come to.'[121]

Lack of Cabinets made Cabinet solidarity unlikely. Ministers felt little sense of common purpose, but rather ran their own departments as independent kingdoms. In pursuing their own line of policy, Ministers had little compunction about reporting governmental conversations to interested parties. Palmerston's Foreign Office was almost a law unto itself, but he was not the only culprit. The Hollands were so keen to preserve the French alliance that Guizot could report to Paris their anxiety 'me donner les indications et les conseils qui peuvent mener au succès'.[122] From time to time, even Melbourne was moved to protest against his government being committed to lines of policy, worked out by individual Ministers chatting to outsiders.[123] In particular, 'the talking at Holland House is inconceivable'.[124] His brother, Frederick Lamb, now Ambassador in Vienna, complained, in 1840, that information about the Cabinet's views came to him from Metternich, who had it from a French banker, who had been told by a French politician, who had been taken into Lord Holland's confidence.[125] It was certainly a worryingly round-about way for an English ambassador to be told of the political situation in a country he was allegedly representing. A Melbourne Cabinet was very short of what might be called team spirit.

If it was unhelpful to bring Ministers together round a table, then policy had to become a departmental matter only, with the Prime Minister as the coordinating agent between different areas of policy. There were precedents for this way of arranging things in the Liverpool and Canning governments, and Melbourne was well aware of them. He reminded Russell that,

When Canning succeeded . . . he, for I had a Conversation with him upon the subject, who whether from consciousness of his inferiority or from more generous feelings had no jealousy of anybody, at once determined . . . to make each Minister transact his own Ministry, to obtain as much assistance as he could, and only himself to exercise a general superintendence and to come forward when he was required. This was the right state of things and this may surely be restored. There are some advantages in doing all yourself, particularly which is not the case at present, if you have any sulky, refractory, discontented or crotchety Colleagues.[126]

To critics, such a scheme looked chaotic. It was a formula for 'a government of departments without unity or pervading plan'.[127] Melbourne did not agree. For him, government could properly be the sum total of departments. The quality of an administration could only be gauged by assessing the effectiveness of each of its separate units. It was an almost mathematical point of view. Quite simply, as he told Edward Ellice, 'If more of the Departments in your opinion are bad than good, the ministry is a bad one, if the other way round, then it was good and should be supported.'[128] Equally, a government could look idle, while its individual departments were feverishly busy.[129] For a man like Melbourne, who had always suspected corporate identities found in parties, policy-making by individual Ministers was a perfectly comfortable idea.

Such a system depended very heavily for its effectiveness on the capacity of the Prime Minister to play the roles of coordinator and referee. In discussions with individual Ministers, he had to suppress initiatives that were politically inept or that had no chance of finding favour with the government as a whole.[130] He also had to resolve disputes between departments. In doing so, he would encounter bureaucratic rivalries, which he likened to 'the pride of Lucifer'.[131] For better or worse, the Prime Minister had to be everywhere, exercising what the *Quarterly Review* called the 'paramount share in the measures of every department of his government'.[132] Melbourne was not a policy-maker himself. That would have been too forward a stance for a man of his temperament. Rather, he facilitated the making of policy. His Ministers often had no great liking for each other. Their efforts could only be made fruitful, if filtered through the unexceptional mind of the Prime Minister. In this task, Melbourne seemed to have found his true vocation. Using a 'trop camarade' style mingled with 'sufficient talent', he moved easily across the political spectrum. His relationships with individual Ministers made him 'invaluable and invulnerable'.[133] Indeed, some contemporaries came to 'doubt whether anyone else could have preserved the concord necessary to the existence of the Government for a session'.[134] Melbourne literally held the ring.

Operating merely as a facilitator of politics, what Palmerston described as Melbourne's 'indifference' to most policies and events became one of his strengths.[135] He could umpire because he was often not emotionally or intellectually involved. Critics like Disraeli found this insouciance infuriating. He asked Melbourne to 'cease to saunter over the destinies of a nation, and lounge away an empire'. Metaphorically clasping his head, he noted that when he recalled to his 'bewildered memory the perplexing circumstance that William Lamb is Prime Minister of England, it seems to me that I recollect with labour the crowning incident of some grotesque dream'.[136] Though it was true that Melbourne was not averse to transacting business while lying full length on a sofa,[137] this kind of attack missed the mark. After all, the government was not lacking in talent. Rather, its existence was endangered by clever men coming into conflict. Disasters in private life had made it nearly impossible for Melbourne to be committed to any idea or any person. He found men of commitment to be objects of suspicion. As he told Ebrington:

almost all those who either have possessed or do possess extraordinary and unusual powers either of speaking or of writing have generally either in their character or their method of thinking some twist, some deformity, some mal-information, which at least balances and neutralises their other great and splendid facilities.[138]

There was interest, even a kind of ironic amusement, in managing the talents of Durham and Russell, Howick and Palmerston. Looking as though 'he had been born smiling', he coaxed and wheedled. At one level, this was a major contribution to making politics work. At another, it exposed him as nothing more than 'a brilliant social electrotype. There was nothing solid in his pretensions, and of this he could not help sometimes becoming aware.'[139]

A further, and very public, indication of how loosely strung the Melbourne government was came with the acknowledgement that many issues were not to be collectively decided by Cabinets, but were to be 'open' questions, on which all could follow conscience. After the fever of 1830–4, Melbourne was determined to allow the pulse of politics to return to normal, but even he had to cope with some policies of importance, and on these he knew he could not command the loyalty of his colleagues. When Macaulay joined the government, in 1839, he was explicitly reassured on this matter: 'You are well aware of the principles of the Administration, of the questions which are left open to the private judgment of its members and of those in support of and in opposition to which they are united and act together.'[140] Taking comfort from reviewing many historical precedents for governments allowing open questions, Melbourne yet had to admit that such instances were almost always 'a manifest proof of instability'.[141] On great issues of the day, like the future of the Corn Laws or the institution of the secret ballot, Melbourne's government had no common policy. Its fragility was thereby proclaimed.

Predictably, too, the political history of 1834–41 is peppered with resignations or, more usually, the threat of resignations, all of which the Prime Minister had to take seriously. In answer to Ministers who complained of colleagues interfering in matters outside their jurisdictions, Melbourne begged, 'For God's sake, let nobody resign or we'll have everybody resigning.'[142] To him, it seemed 'that people always die and resign at the most inconvenient moment'.[143] Lord Howick, Grey's son, had raised the threat of resignation to an art form, using it as 'the ultima ratio on all occasions'.[144] Patching and mending by the Prime Minister usually averted trouble, but occasionally, and more so as the administration aged, all his efforts proved vain. In 1839, Glenelg was dismissed by Melbourne against his better judgement, bowing to resignation threats from other Cabinet members. He found the whole thing 'very awkward'.[145] He told Victoria that 'such forced changes' were 'an admission of weakness'.[146] Melbourne's letter dismissing Glenelg was firm enough,[147] but it was observed that he was also 'a little ashamed of himself'.[148] A sympathetic French ambassador concluded that, 'Le ministère anglois ne se repose pas sur un lit de roses.'[149] Not even the policy of running open questions and departmental rather than Cabinet responsibility could make Ministers work together. Resignations and forced dismissals gave the government a tottering character. At the same time, the fact that it survived at all depended on the happy accident that the Prime Minister had few axes to grind himself, and that, from indifference, he was able to talk to almost anyone.

In these circumstances, holding a government together was a wearing business, and Melbourne suffered for it. He was repeatedly ill, and his correspondence with his doctor, Sir Henry Halford, suggests a concern for his health that came close to hypochondria. In the summer of 1836, he was prostated by gout and biliousness.[150] Three months later, he was 'quite unable to move' with lumbago, and took to wearing flannel.[151] In 1837, he complained of insomnia.[152] In January, June, and December 1838, he was stricken by a bowel condition that made it impossible for him to attend Cabinets.[153] He himself was clear that these illnesses were caused by 'worry of mind',[154] and his family agreed. The letters of his brother, sister, and other relations are full of concern that William was working himself into a major illness. Caro George found him looking thin 'from work and anxiety'.[155] From his post in Vienna, Frederick Lamb's letters express mounting concern about his brother. In January 1838, he told his sister Emily that he was 'anxious about Wm. Every body tells me he has grown old.'[156] Three months later, he declared his willingness to return to London immediately if William needed him: 'I shall be ready to come to him whenever He wishes it in as far at least as it depends on me. No human strength can go on Session after Session without breaking down.'[157] By April 1839, he had convinced himself that his brother was in real danger:

I do not at all like yr account of Wm; for some time back I have not felt easy about his health and fear He will have an illness. Nothing can be done, so there is no use talking about it, but it is well to know that when health breaks down . . . a year passed in the South, winter and summer also generally renovates and adds ten years not of life only but of health. I think he will be brought to it, and if He is I shall constitute myself nurse, and do nothing but take care of him.[158]

Protecting William from the consequences of his own actions had always been a family priority, but in this case their concern was well founded. William Lamb enjoyed being Prime Minister at a cost.

There was no doubt that, in part, illness had been brought on by overwork. To the world, Melbourne presented an image of lounging indifference. The reality was very different. A government run by departments, not in Cabinet, pivots on the ability of a Prime Minister to co-ordinate and harmonize. Hard work was unavoidable. Further, the task was made more onerous by such a shortage of 'clerks and copywriters' that his brother thought Melbourne severely 'harrassed' (sic) by being denied the most elementary forms of assistance.[159] Handwritten replies and instructions involved the Prime Minister in hours of labour. His official papers are substantial and give evidence of a closer attention to politics than his public image would allow. Memoranda were read and frequently annotated. Most subjects were commented on, even those like the fiscal and economic on which he felt least at home.[160] If a criticism is to be made of Melbourne's working practices, it is not that he was idle, but that he wasted effort by giving almost as much attention to the trivial as to the serious concerns of state. He acknowledged resolutions passed by the Liberal Club of Glasgow University, a scholarship application from a Cambridge student, and complaints from the Jockey Club about the breaking up of the Royal Stud. He was fascinated by the internal wranglings of the Scottish Churches, was happy to give the boys of Rugby an extra holiday in celebration of the birth of the Princess Royal, and took a lively interest in how far Queen Victoria should be kissed at her Coronation. No doubt, the attraction of these issues lay partly in their being resolved through his own efforts, without the need to consult troublesome colleagues. Even so, all this involved labour. Noting the disparity between public image and political reality, Sydney Smith ironically observed that, 'I am sorry to hurt any man's feelings, but I accuse the Prime Minister of honesty and diligence.'[161]

Hard work did not mean, however, that William Lamb had suddenly become a committed politician, or that the pattern of his early life had changed. Rather, working at politics filled a terrible vacuum in his life. His family were relieved that being Prime Minister gave William something to do. The amusement he derived from watching men scramble for patronage, when he himself refused the Garter, was diverting. To settle differences between squabbling Churchmen, or to pronounce on the Byzantine intricacies of Court etiquette was entertaining to a man with little religion and not much respect for kings. It was all done with good sense and not too much malice. But it was all done too from the lofty heights of a profound indifference. Melbourne feared boredom more than the weary task of coaxing impossible people to agree in politics. When he lost office, it would be less difficult to resign power than to discover another occupation. The sourness of his last years was, in part, a result of this. For the moment, politics provided diversion, and the distraction of hard work.

Inevitably, there were, too, factors that lightened the burden of office. First, against the resignation threats and inter-departmental wrangling could be set the good sense of Lansdowne and, in particular, the support of Lord John Russell. Coming from the same Whig stable, Russell and Melbourne were connected by much more than politics. They had known the same people in the same contexts. They had the camaraderie of nostalgia. Russell was the man, with whom Melbourne could reminisce about personalities and old politics.[162] From this, it was natural to make him the Prime Minister's amanuensis. Russell was regularly consulted about appointments,[163] and particularly about any redistribution of Cabinet portfolios.[164] If a point of special difficulty presented itself, Russell would be an inevitable member of the sub-committee appointed to suggest a solution.[165] The crisis over the future of the Turkish Empire in the summer of 1840 was almost unresolvable because, for once, Russell was a combatant and not a seconder of prime ministerial arbitration. Educated in Scotland and trained at Holland House, Russell was probably the man for whom Melbourne felt the closest, political affinity. In his whole career, he had trusted few others. His support and approbation helped Melbourne through difficulties that might otherwise have overwhelmed him.

Secondly, there were aspects of office that were promising of fun. A very significant percentage of Melbourne's official correspondence concerns the distribution of patronage. Having refused an earldom, the Garter, and other 'gewgaws' himself,[166] the Prime Minister's caustic views of human nature were reinforced as he watched others scrambling for distinction. Refusing preferment was as pleasurable as giving it. When a doctor asked for a knighthood in recognition of serving abroad, his patron was told that, 'to go abroad is hardly a sufficient reason. If he is ashamed of calling himself "Doctor", let him call himself John Yellowby Esq. or whatever his name may be. There must be some end of Knights.'[167] An importunate peer was reminded that 'one Title is enough for one generation',[168] and the spectacle of dukes sulking for being denied ribbons and orders was not unwelcome to someone of Melbourne's temperament.[169] In fact, the prodigality in distributing titles and honours had become, in his view, so extensive that it threatened to dilute the value of real distinctions. In the Whig mind, when everyone was somebody, then no one was anybody. In talking of the granting of titles, he was clear that he wished 'to discontinue and diminish them rather than otherwise'.[170] Melbourne's Whiggish preference for élite politics led him firmly to take the view that an honours system was a device to exclude as well as to reward. Every time an unworthy claimant was denied a request, the social order was the stronger. Every time real property and merit were honoured, deferential systems would be reinforced. This was work that Melbourne undertook with relish. It was some consolation for the tiresome nature of most other aspects of politics.

Given all these difficulties, Melbourne's style of government was bound to be distinctive. It was in no sense innovative. It tidied up matters left over from the Grey administration, and it dealt with issues as they arose. There was no overall programme. Indeed, parliamentary sessions could begin without Russell and Melbourne discussing the nature of its business.[171] In Melbourne's view, the passing of one major bill each year was as much as any government ought to contemplate: 'In the session of 1834 we passed the English poor law act pretty well for one session considering the effect it has had and the row it has made. In 1835 the English Municipal bill, pretty well too. In 1837, the Irish tithe bill and the Irish Poor Law, the effects of which are yet to be seen, but which hitherto promises well.'[172] Facing Parliament at all was not particularly welcome, because it 'was a bore to be badgered'.[173] There was merit, in Melbourne's mind, in acting while Parliament was in recess, even in areas like arms expenditure.[174] Such a procedure might be constitutionally dubious, but it was the line of least trouble. Foreign governments negotiating with England over the Turkish crisis of the summer of 1840 were astonished that Melbourne saw no reason to recall Parliament, even though war threatened.[175] Guizot, a harassed French ambassador, found it difficult to track down Ministers. Melbourne had allowed all of them to leave London, and showed no wish to recall them or Parliament. As a result, Guizot plaintively described his situation as taking 'des voies détournées pour faire arriver à ces esprits légers, très légers par préoccupation ou par insouciance, un peu de vérité et de sage crainte'.[176] Melbourne seemed to have a distaste for facing Cabinets or Parliaments.

When Parliament was sitting, the Prime Minister spoke frequently but rarely at length. On two issues only, the reform of English local government in the Municipal Corporations Bill of 1835 and he question of Irish Tithes, did he speak with real authority.[177] He had little to say on foreign policy and on a whole range of other issues. In keeping with the departmental nature of his government, these were left to individual Ministers. This was notoriously true of the Foreign Office, which Palmerston viewed as his personal empire. Disarmingly in debate Melbourne could cheerfully admit to a total ignorance of the matter in hand, 'declaring himself totally uninformed on the Evidence—no possibility of reading a word of it'.[178] When he spoke, he rarely addressed the detail of an issue, but rather chose to confine himself to broad generalizations of a philosophical nature. As a Cabinet colleague noticed, Melbourne 'hated details in business—indeed he had practically no knowledge of them. His course of life and of study had led him to philosophical reflection and to generalize—and his speeches especially on opening Questions in Parlt. frequently contained passages very striking from their enlarged and philosophical character.'[179] It was dinner-table conversation transmuted into a parliamentary speech.

In these circumstances, the transaction of business in the Lords took on a very distinctive character. While the Commons debated and voted, it seemed to contemporaries that affairs were settled in the Upper House by a peculiar kind of horse-trading between Melbourne and the Tory opposition. In August 1838 for example, Lord Hatherton recorded the following spectacle:

H of Lords . . . Amusing discussion on Commons amendments on I. Municipal Corporation Act Amendment Bill—Lyndhurst standing on one side of the Table with his spectacles on, and Melbourne holding his glasses to his eyes on the other, talking over the matter of each amendment from a printed paper, which Melbourne seemed never to have read (I believe his Counsel had talked them over with him this morning) and disposing of each as they thought best. Lyndhurst had to be sure two Aides de Camp in Ellenborough and Redesdale—but Melbourne had none and had solicited none. They looked to mere spectators like two men driving quiet bargains for various small articles.

The conversation was of this kind:
M: 'Here's "payable". What do you say to that.'
L: 'Oh, I cannot take that—Really I cannot take that.'
M: 'Umph! Well, what's next?'
L: 'Three clauses about Commission of Charities—we can't take them—will you give me your assurance that you'll treat these Irish Charities the same as the English? Will you engage to do for Ireland what you've done for England?'
M: 'Why, that you know is "equal justice" (the cant phrase decided by the Tories) 'we can't refuse that.'
L: 'Very well, then let us go on.'
And so it went on for 4 hours—each Party very much fagged—all the Peers sitting by and talking.[180]

It seemed that government policy was simply what the Prime Minister chose to say it was, and, though this was a caricature of Melbourne's style, there was enough truth in it to irritate Cabinet colleagues, men who dealt in the detail of measures, or anyone who thought that the political process was deserving of more attention.

With little or no agenda of his own and endlessly reacting to the initiatives of others, Melbourne gave an impression of being 'indefatigable in doing nothing'.[181] The *Quarterly Review*, in 1839, took pleasure in reminding its readers that, in the previous parliamentary session, nineteen Bills had foundered without, apparently, unduly distressing the Prime Minister.[182] It was a 'poco curante' government.[183] One of his Ministers observed that Melbourne hated the months of June and July, because, in those weeks, 'Bills came up by dozens from the H. of commons, and the unpleasant things that had been delayed will admit of no longer delay.'[184] If affairs became pressing or tiresome, Melbourne had an extraordinary capacity to take refuge in sleep. At City dinners, 'bored to extinction', he slept.[185] In the Privy Council, he slept, 'but as nobody was hanged and the rest were awake, no matter'.[186] Above all, he slept soundly in the House of Lords and set a pattern for others. In July 1836, for example, 'Lord Londonderry spoke an hour and a quarter on a petition about the surplus revenues of the See of Durham. He kept addressing Ld Melbourne, who, with Ld Duncannon by his side, were both fast asleep the whole time, while the Dukes of Wellington and Cumberland were asleep behind them; and three out of 7 Bishops equally happy.'[187]

The defence for such a somnolent system was put as part of the obituary of Melbourne that appeared in the *Morning Chronicle*. It was a piece of writing that those who had known him recommended to others, as doing most justice to his character and government.[188] In this, the obituarist came close to taking up Melbourne's own tidal metaphor to describe politics. Events ebbed and flowed. Consolidation followed change. The tumultuous politics of 1830–4 had to be assimilated, made workable, and allowed to become familiar. Marking time became a policy in itself:

the period during which he was at the head of affairs in this country must ever be memorable in its annals, as having witnessed the general dissipation of the democratic forces by which the great question of the Reform Bill was carried; and the restoration of the executive power, and a dominion over public opinion, to those Conservative classes of the community, who, from their combining amongst themselves the elements of National stability with the instincts of National progress, may, without invidious comparisons be declared the legitimate inheritors of the Government.[189]

Melbourne ran a government based on 'the principle of no-principle',[190] and that was appropriate. Politics had surfeited on principle for four or five years, and now needed time for digestion.

To a large extent the character of the Melbourne administration was determined by the nature of its birth and composition. It was put together out of two constitutional crises, in both of which Melbourne had not been the first choice for Prime Minister. Only the wounded pride of Grey and the reticence of Althorp gave him his chance. Though he was able to exclude known troublemakers like Brougham from office, Melbourne had to deal with men of disparate political backgrounds and very thin skins. As a result, Cabinets gave way to departmental independence. The Prime Minister became an umpire and arbitrator. Resignations and the threat of resignations were regularly invoked. Facing Parliament became an unpleasant duty, not least because such a government lacked the cohesion to initiate large, legislative programmes. To keep such an administration in being at all demanded levels of activity and hard work, that the political world knew nothing about. Publicly, Melbourne was inert, and sometimes comatose. He knew little of the issues in politics, and was bored by detail. Privately, the Prime Minister worked hard to keep his colleagues together. Arbitration between departments meant a close reading of papers and memoranda. Interviews with colleagues were draining experiences. He was denounced as idle because he was not a legislator, nor much of a Parliament man, but then he never had been. In fact, he was a brilliant facilitator of politics, creating the circumstances in which others could act. At this, he laboured hard and long, to the detriment of his health. Watching politics move, and observing the frailties of human nature when in close contact with the exercise of power, gave interest and diversion to a man, who had long since ceased to be capable of emotional involvement with a person or a principle.

9

Tories, Radicals, Irishmen, a King, and Lord Grey, 1834–1841

FROM its inception, the Melbourne administration attracted the attention of those keen to write its obituary. It was seen to be terminally ill from the moment of its birth. It was to be dismissed as terminally ill for the next seven years. After all, the Tories were against it, and that meant that the government would always face a hostile majority in the House of Lords. The King was barely for it. Earl Grey and his family were in theory supportive, but in fact acted in a manner that was disruptive. By so doing, they allowed the trusteeship of Whiggery to be disputed. As a result, Melbourne was forced to rely on the votes of Radicals and Irishmen, skittish creatures with a tendency to bolt. Over the period 1834–41, Melbourne saw his majority in the House of Commons steadily evaporating, and, after the election of 1837, it sometimes sank to single figures. When the 1841 election was finally lost, he ironically observed that he 'was sure it would be so for we've always been losing since 33!'[1] In these circumstances, it was hard to think that Melbourne would be long in power. The prospectus was not convincing.

At the beginning of Melbourne's second administration, in May 1835, his old friend Lord Holland gave him only a modest chance of success, because 'a Ministry with a decided majority in the Lords against it, without the appearance certainly, and the reality possibly, of any Court Powers and with a bare majority in the Commons cannot be sure of commanding success'.[2] Eight months later, the French ambassador thought he could detect an improvement in the Ministry's condition,[3] but his optimism was not shared by the Prime Minister. Melbourne himself was almost uniformly gloomy about the likelihood of staying in power beyond the next Session. In September 1836, he felt 'no security'.[4] The survival of his government was 'perfectly incredible'.[5] In April 1840, he thought himself 'exposed to all sorts of chances and accidents, and he nowhere sees a guarantee for its stability'.[6] Dependent on the votes of men he could not much care for, he wondered 'whether it was right and becoming to go on with the government in our present condition . . . with nothing but an insignificant majority in the Commons in our favour, and even there it was only on doubtful and unpopular questions that we outnumbered our opponents'.[7] He worried that his administration 'was formed upon too narrow a basis', and fretted as resignations and sulks eroded the ground on which he stood still further. Brougham jokingly observed that Melbourne 'wants to remain in till he can get a majority in both houses'.[8] It was uncomfortable, even undignified.

Yet, talk of the unlamented death of Melbourne's government was premature. It lasted nearly seven years. Paradoxically, each of the groups in opposition to Melbourne had good motives for keeping him in office. All of them preferred him to any alternative. This was not very flattering to the Prime Minister, but then Melbourne had always been everyone's second choice. The configuration of politics was such, that, though Melbourne was not much respected, he was unavoidable. In his brief experiences of office, he had proved that he could work with almost anyone. His lack of a personal agenda allowed him to be receptive and flexible. Above all, he had never threatened anyone. For Radicals and the Irish, Melbourne was better than the Tories; for Peel, he was to be preferred to the nastier elements in his own party; for the King, he was at least a gentleman, to whom one was illegitimately related twice over. Tories would accuse him of being 'reckless', Radicals of being 'feeble',[9] but, uncomplimentary though this was, Melbourne was seen by everyone as the alternative to something worse. It proved a surprisingly successful formula.

In spite of the constitutional implications of the 1832 Reform Bill, any Prime Minister still had to cultivate a sound working relationship with the Crown. King and Parliament, executive and legislature, had to be kept in step, and made to march to the same tune. Unfortunately, William IV never fully reconciled himself to accepting his defeat in the crisis of 1834–5 or the government that was born out of it. He had no objection to Melbourne personally, but that was not enough to allow him to welcome his tenure of power. In 1838, Victoria noted in her diary that, 'The King [William IV] wasn't at all open with Lord M., he said, though very civil; he *liked* him, no wonder; that the King *couldn't help*; "he liked me", said Lord M., "he liked me as much as anybody could, under the circumstances; that was a very disagreeable affair in 34".'[10] In interviews, the King was always 'civil' to Melbourne, but such occasions were 'always very short'.[11] Worse, Queen Adelaide, who exercised considerable political influence over her husband, refused to talk to Melbourne at all. He recalled that he 'never used to go near her, but used to talk with the Maids of Honour . . . I used to go and talk with the girls.'[12]

If Melbourne's reception at Court was frosty, his Cabinet colleagues were barely acceptable at all. They were deliberately snubbed. Invitations to Windsor and Court functions were withheld.[13] Only Melbourne and Palmerston were occasionally asked to social events. The King's hatred for all the Ministers was said to be 'excessive'.[14] It was all very public and premeditated. The King explicitly informed the Duke of Grafton that 'since Ld. Melbourne's Government had been forced on him last spring, he had been studiously cold to all who supported it . . . Accordingly . . . scarcely a Whig nobleman or gentleman was seen near the King.'[15] The same metaphor was used by the French ambassador. He talked of 'toutes les froideurs de la Cour, qui sont très marquées'.[16] In the Drawing Room assemblies, 'toutes les prévenances étoient pour les Torys . . . Les Wighs eux mêmes n'ont pas de confiance et s'en expriment librement. Cependant, ils sont et ils restent.'[17] For royal approval to be so openly withheld from a Ministry was not only deeply wounding to its individual members, but it was also profoundly damaging to their political prospects. Historically, kings had chosen and dismissed ministers. Whether they could still do so after 1832 and 1834 was debatable, but certainly the fact that William IV had no love for the Melbourne government would encourage anyone who contemplated attacking it. At the very least, Melbourne was weak because the failure of the King to support him did not make him strong.

At the beginning, William IV saw Melbourne's elevation to high office as part of his personal defeat in the crisis of 1834–5. As far as he was concerned, the new government was nothing but a stop-gap arrangement. It was 'the King's object . . . merely to use the Party to enable him to tide over a crisis'.[18] As has been noted earlier, his negotiations with Melbourne about the composition of his administration had been chilling. The new Prime Minister could find no kinder words to describe his efforts than to call them 'the best that it is in his power to put together'.[19] His conversations with the King about Cabinet-making have the formal character of a treaty between warring factions. When they were concluded, Melbourne was under no illusions about the nature of the contract that had been agreed. As he acknowledged to Holland, it was 'damn'd Irish in many of its parts, but the best that could be agreed upon amidst conflicting opinions and prejudices'.[20] No one could doubt for a moment that the new government was viewed with anything but distaste at Court.

Until his death in 1837, William IV never changed his mind. For Melbourne, he was always a nuisance, and frequently a menace. Endlessly intervening, he attempted to amend, modify, or undermine government measures. In 1835, for example, he first tried to circumscribe Palmerston's foreign policy by insisting that: 'The King never can consent, while he is

Sovereign of this Country, to engaging in a General war as the Ally of France.'[21] He then proceeded to mount a clause-by-clause attack on the central feature of the government's legislative programme, the Municipal Corporations Bill.[22] The fact that the King was, in many instances, claiming powers he no longer possessed, allowing him to be ignored in the last resort, hardly made Melbourne's task any easier. Long hours were spent trying, usually through the agency of the King's secretary Sir Herbert Taylor, to persuade William to co-operate and not to obstruct. If persuasion failed, Melbourne was prepared to offer no quarter in the defence of his colleagues[23] and his policies, but it was wearing work.

Vist Melbourne like all other public men, has more than once acquiesced in propositions, with respect to which he himself entertained doubts, in compliance with the opinions of others, the circumstances of the times and the general feeling of the public, but with respect to the Corporations it has always been his own strong and sincere opinion, that a thorough reformation of them was required, if it was intended to prevent abuse and corruption and to restore unanimity and concord in those great communities.[24]

Clearly, Melbourne could manage forthright words, but they cost him dear. Not surprisingly, he would complain to Taylor of being 'somewhat wounded by some apparent want of confidence'.[25] These polite words in fact described sustained guerrilla warfare mounted by the Court against the Melbourne government.

Even worse than William IV's meddling in day-to-day politics was the threat of being dismissed from government by royal fiat. Such a possibility hung over politics like a dark cloud as long as William lived. In 1835, Sébastiani reported to Paris that the King had decided to rid himself of Melbourne at the end of August.[26] About the same time, Hobhouse recorded that William had publicly announced his intention of having the whole Cabinet impeached, concluding that he had finally followed his father into madness.[27] In the autumn of 1836, the King suggested to a visiting German prince that he might stay in England a little longer, because he was on the point of turning Melbourne out, and 'a Change of Government was always a curious event for a foreigner to witness'.[28] None of this unduly surprised those with Whiggish upbringings. Princes and monarchs were never to be trusted, and all of them were would-be autocrats. Holland noted that William IV 'was no doubt like all Princes, especially Germans, lofty and arbitrary in his notions of Government'.[29] Thereby placing William IV within an historical experience of difficult kings brought the consolation of familiarity, but it did little to make Melbourne's position, in a practical sense, any easier.

In fact, however, the King's hostility was no threat. In the last resort, he could not act. If he dismissed Melbourne, the obvious alternative was a Tory government, but the Tories, for reasons that will be discussed below, were not in a position to undertake the assignment. As Holland noted in his diary, the King's 'fears that the Tories would not undertake the government, or that undertaking it they would be beaten, alone, restrained him no doubt from repeating the experiment of 1834'.[30] In these circumstances, the loss of Melbourne would probably mean the elevation of Lord John Russell, whom the King positively loathed. However much he harassed and threatened Melbourne, therefore, William had of necessity to keep him in office for fear of worse. The King's death, in June 1837, finally removed a considerable embarrassment, but, even before that event royal hostility could not bring Melbourne down. As the fiasco of 1834–5 had demonstrated, a reformed House of Commons would not accept that kings could make or break governments. Melbourne had never been a keen Reformer, but, ironically, he was one of the earliest beneficiaries of the reformed system.

More complicated and just as threatening was Melbourne's relationship with his predecessor, Earl Grey. In theory, there should have been no problem of any kind. Grey had refused to return as Prime Minister, and, at the age of 70, could be expected to take a less and less active role in politics. He sent Melbourne an encouraging letter, 'wishing you every possible success in over-coming the difficulties with which you are beset'. In return, Melbourne offered to store some of Grey's furniture.[31] Further, everyone was clear that Melbourne's administration was based on a continuation of Grey's policies, and not on a repudiation of them. His son and heir, Lord Howick, would have a prominent place in the Cabinet, and his extensive family connection would be accommodated. Lady Holland was not alone in being pleased that Melbourne had been happy to construct his government according to Grey's specifications: 'You see all matters are adjusted, and the Govt. is entirely Ld. Grey's. *All* that has been done is in compliance with his wishes . . . In short, this Govt. is Ld. Grey's legacy.'[32] Grey had the option of an honoured retirement.

Unfortunately, this option was not taken. Grey could not rid himself of the suspicion that his departure from office had been the consequence of a plot, and, even if Melbourne could not really be accused of being part of the conspiracy, he was visibly its chief beneficiary. Like William IV, Grey never recovered from the events of 1834. Queen Victoria was very aware of this problem, and her diary entries often return to it: ' "Lord Grey is very hostile", said Lord M.; but he *resigned*, I said; "Yes, and recommended me to the King", said Lord M.; "but it caused immediately a comparison to be drawn between his Government and mine, in disfavour of his,—which nearly drove him mad".'[33] Determined to influence events from behind the scenes, Grey infected anything he touched with sourness and a splenetic disaffection. Melbourne's attempts to pass this interference off as a joke rang a little hollow: 'Grey is full of condemnation of the past and the present and of fear for the future. This is to be looked for. He never was contented for a moment with his own Government and cannot therefore reasonably be expected to be so with that of anyone else.'[34] At his worst, Grey became simply spiteful. In 1836, he objected to Melbourne's health being drunk at a Fox Dinner after his own and that of Fox himself, which led Lord Hatherton to observe: 'Vanity and Jealousy!—which requires hourly management by those who live with him! and which destroyed all cordial feeling towards him on the part of his late colleagues.'[35]

For many years, Grey's claims to attention were met with almost unqualified appeasement: 'Every thing is done and has been done to remove all jealousy of neglect or estrangement.'[36] Melbourne conscientiously consulted his predecessor about appointments[37] and about policy decisions.[38] Grey freely exercised the right to offer advice on any issue, whether it had been called for or not. He was so active in foreign affairs that Palmerston was moved to protest about this interference in his own department.[39] Similarly, Grey's family were flattered and employed. Howick, Sir Charles Wood, Edward Ellice, and a flotilla of cousins had no reason to complain of Melbourne's behaviour. As a backbench MP observed, 'The most melancholy reflection arises from the conduct of Lord Grey, who has never given a cordial support to Lord Melbourne; yet no man has asked and received from him so many favours for his family.'[40] Melbourne countenanced these actions because, particularly in the early years, he had a real fear of Grey. As Fox's chosen heir, Grey had a status in Whiggery that could not be challenged. With him, Melbourne's claim on Whiggish minds was strong. Without him, Whigs might feel freer to wander. Melbourne frankly told Holland, in 1834, that his government would be hopelessly damaged, 'if the Ministry should cease either in substance or appearance to enjoy the sanction of Lord Grey and the character of a continuance of his *Government*'.[41]

In response to all this attention, Grey was almost uniformly ungracious. He gave up attending the House of Lords, appearing only once in 1835 for example,[42] on the grounds that anything he might say would only 'irritate'.[43] Social contacts, too, became more and more tenuous.[44] He was not on speaking terms with Lord John Russell, and had little social contact with any of the Cabinet. According to his latest biographer, Grey sulked in his tent, because he believed that Melbourne had become the creature of O'Connell,[45] suggesting that conspiracy theories about the events of 1834 still operated as a powerful influence on his mind. Emily Lamb was more critical. For her, 'poor Grey' could not reconcile himself to his loss of power. He tried to support Melbourne, but 'he is almost sorry to see things going well and to think that he is indispensable'.[46] The temptation to try to exercise a *pouvoir occulte* was too strong. Grey's long shadow cast a pall over Melbourne's government. Fox's heir could not be ignored, but he would neither leave politics nor commit himself. He claimed great influence and no responsibility.

The instrument of Grey's resentment would be his son, Lord Howick, sitting in Melbourne's Cabinet as Secretary for the War Office. Melbourne had 'an aversion' to him.[47] He found him prim and inclined to take offence at the slightest provocation. Worse, Howick seemed to have views on everything, and this, for Melbourne was a fault, for 'nothing disqualifies a man from forming a sound opinion upon a question, as the persuasion that he has made himself thoroughly master of it'.[48] His worst fears were realized. Howick regularly complained about the Prime Minister's system of managing the government, and frequently set off bitter inter-departmental disputes by trying to interfere in the business of other Ministers. As Melbourne was forced to arbitrate and conciliate, it seemed to some that 'Howick, through Lord Grey, rules all things'.[49] When thwarted, Howick readily threatened resignation and the withdrawal of the sanction of the whole Grey clan. In June 1836, for example, he threatened to leave office over Canadian policy, complaining to Melbourne about 'ye weakness and indecisn which has marked ye whole policy of ye Govt respecting it'.[50] On this occasion, Melbourne faced down this impertinence with a mixture of firmness and conciliatory words, but it was a fatiguing business. Little wonder that he should describe Howick as 'a terrible fellow and that when he complained of not having proper influence he meant nothing short of being master of the whole administration of affairs'.[51] The Grey family represented a dull and persistent ache in government.

Howick's resignation finally came in August 1839, having been prefigured in the previous January.[52] Ostensibly, the excuse was once again the government's handling of a crisis in Canada. In fact, Howick, quoting his father's authority, complained of neglect and maltreatment over a long period. Even though Russell was held up as the main villain, Howick's letters were nothing less than an indictment of almost everything that had happened since 1834. As one newspaper observed, Howick's resignation was simply 'a decision by the Grey family to overthrow the Melbourne government'.[53] On 21 August, Howick presented the Cabinet with a memorandum that amounted to a family ultimatum. There was to be no increase in Cabinet numbers and no more Radicals in government; open questions were no longer to be tolerated; Charles Wood, not Labouchère, should be the next candidate to be promoted to ministerial office; and the whole tone of government should be more aristocratic, for 'to be a member of the cabinet when it consists of 15 of whom 8 are in the House of Commons ceases to be a distinction'.[54] No Prime Minister could accept dictation on this scale, and, with reluctance and irritation, Melbourne had to see the benediction of the Grey family withdrawn.

The separation of trust and connection was undertaken with the maximum of ill will. Grey told a friend that it would be hard for Howick 'to form new Connections or to divest himself of the feelings which he still seems to have for some of those whom he leaves behind him, among whom however I do *not* include either Lord Melbourne or Lord John Russell.'[55] As for Melbourne, he was quite clear that Grey had been the driving force behind the rupture. He told Victoria: 'Lord Grey has done it . . . he [Howick] said he couldn't show his face again at Howick, if he was to remain; that his life would be intollerable [sic].'[56] There was no doubt that Melbourne's administration was weakened by the loss of Howick and Wood. They were men of ability. Without them, Holland feared that the Ministry would soon be 'assuming the fatal character of Mediocrity'.[57] On the other hand, Grey's bluff had been called. Melbourne's government did not fall. New men were found. Howick found himself in the political wilderness, without immediate prospects. It was a calculated risk that Melbourne had foreseen a year before he took it.[58] The enmity of the Grey family damaged a government that claimed in part a Whig ancestry. On the other hand, when Victoria reflected on Howick's performance in office, she not unreasonably concluded that, 'no one ever gave such perpetual trouble as he did'.[59] William IV could not bring down Melbourne, and nor, it seemed, could Lord Grey.

If the hostility of a king and a former leader could be contained, it was not at all clear that Melbourne would be able to establish a working relationship with the legislature. The majority of the House of Lords was always against him. Here, only the fear or grudging co-operation of Tories allowed Bills to pass. In the Commons, his majorities were never large, being calculated at roughly twenty-five after the 1835 Election, and in single figures after that of 1837. He was always dependent on Irish and Radical votes, and therefore always vulnerable to their moods and skittishness. In theory, therefore, Tories, Radicals, and the Irish could have engineered the downfall of the government at any moment of their choosing. To keep everything in equilibrium, Melbourne became involved in a balancing act of theatrical proportions. Inevitably some, like most of his family,[60] thought he was too friendly with the Radicals. Others thought that the Tories were leading him by the nose. As he wistfully observed to Russell: 'By one set of People we are certainly told that we are ruining ourselves and losing support by allying ourselves with the Radicals and the Roman Catholics, by another, that we are producing the same effect by leaning too much to the Tories and Conservatives—probably

both statements are true, and we are thus losing on both sides.'[61] It seemed
that Melbourne was always losing and always on the point of being turned
out.

Yet he was not turned out for seven years. As the most recent historian of
the Melbourne administration has pointed out, Melbourne held a lot of
important cards. He made it plain to the Radicals and the Irish that, if he
were to leave office, the only real alternative was a Tory government, and a
Tory government of such a nature that it should make them pale to contemplate. As a result, he conceded little or nothing to these groups, refusing
electoral pacts with them, even when his majorities were most precarious. As
for the Tories, Melbourne's ability to work with Peel, and Peel's distaste for
the Ultras in his own party, meant that, again and again, Tory votes or
abstentions saved the day. Quite clearly, Peel thought a Melbourne government more acceptable than one in which Ultra Tories like the Duke of
Newcastle, still complaining about Catholic Emancipation and the Reform
Bill, had any serious role. Not until at least the spring of 1839 was Peel
remotely tempted to challenge Melbourne.[62] Of the two possible sources of
stability in government, a large majority or the mutual antipathy of opponents, Melbourne enjoyed none of the first but unqualified amounts of the
second. He survived because those who disliked him could imagine worse.

In theory, Radical votes were a critical part of the government's majority,
but they received short shrift from the Prime Minister. He disliked many of
their leaders, and blamed them openly for the difficulties of 1834–5. In
December 1834, he told Bulwer Lytton that the Radicals

have overthrown us by their violence, and by moving us along too far and too fast,
and now when the battle is lost, they talk of union. Pray tell Mr Fonblanque from me
that a little steady support of a Minister, when he is in office, is worth a ream of pan-
egyric, after he has retired from it . . . There is some philosophy for you, tho' I am
not à la profondeur or à la hauteur de Lord Durham.[63]

He bluntly told Radicals like Joseph Parkes to support him or face the Tories:
'I do not quite share in your confidence in the strength of the liberal party in
England and in the impossibility of the Conservatives . . . how much the
power of the liberals has always depended upon excitement and what is called
agitation—this force is like that of a fever or epilepsy, almost irresistible at
the moment, but transient and succeeded by weakness.'[64] He was happy to
dine with Radicals as a member of the Reform Club, but they were not to
determine policy. Four times in the 1837–8 Session, Tory votes neutralized
Radical attempts at rebellion.[65] When Radical defections, in the summer of
1839, really did threaten to destroy Melbourne, Radicals were rudely confronted by the consequences of their actions in the shape of a Tory govern-

ment, and came to their senses. It showed them, as Holland noted, that 'in the state of publick opinion parties Parliament and Court, the downfall of Ld Melbourne's Ministry was synonymous with an immediate and possibly permanent triumph of the Anti-Reformers'.[66] The Radicals had to live with Melbourne or content themselves with opposing a Tory government.

Throughout the 1830s, Frederick Lamb bombarded his brother with injunctions about not making concessions to Radicals,[67] but Melbourne hardly needed such advice. On more than one occasion, he was happy to consider resignation rather than to surrender to Radical demands.[68] His dealings with their leaders were businesslike, even brusque. When Joseph Hume asked for a clarification of the government's policy on further parliamentary reform, to remove 'the discontent existing in the ranks of the liberal party',[69] he was told that the Prime Minister had 'no communication to make'.[70] Sir William Molesworth and his friends were dismissed as 'fools'.[71] After the summer crisis of 1839, Melbourne told the Lords that, 'so far from evincing any disposition to make Radical concessions, he intimated with sufficient clearness that he was resolved to make none whatever, and that he would not sacrifice his conscientious convictions for any political or party purpose'.[72] The speech was cheered by the Duke of Wellington.

Predictably, Radicals became increasingly angry at Melbourne's performance. He knew of this, but could do nothing about it.[73] By 1839, John Roebuck denied that the government had any claim to 'Liberality' at all.[74] When Melbourne at last left office, two years later, Radicals were in a sense relieved by no longer having either to support a man they held in suspicion, or to oppose him and thereby to be responsible for setting up a Tory alternative. As Mrs Grote observed to Francis Place,

Things wear an aspect of disastrous change for the humbug Whigs methinks? Should dissolution occur shortly, we shall be freed from the irksome duty of figuring in the same section with these miserable quacks, void of all power to put forward improvement of any sort but the most piddling domestic . . . amelioras w[ch] are magnified into vast gains by the mouthpieces of said quacks.[75]

The Melbourne government had been a miserable experience for the Radicals. Symbolically, their distress found martyrs in Henry Brougham and the Earl of Durham. One Radical leader was not allowed into government at all, and the other resigned, without, to his great disappointment, being able to sabotage the administration by so doing. Melbourne often insisted that office should be open to anyone of goodwill, but there were to be exceptions to this rule.[76]

Taking on Henry Brougham was no mean undertaking. Immensely able and immensely difficult, he had acquired the status of Radical hero, not least for his victory against established interests in Yorkshire, in 1830. Melbourne, however, never wavered from his intention not to have Brougham in office. He held him responsible for the muddle of June–July 1834, which had destroyed Grey, and for provoking William IV to attempt his '*coup*' in November 1834; 'The experience of Lord Grey's government and of my own in 1834 had determined me never to have him again for a Colleague in the Cabinet.'[77] Having him near the centre of power 'never can be safe'.[78] He had so 'many defects', that no one could trust him.[79] Melbourne was happy to shoulder the not very pleasant task of telling Brougham that his services would not be called upon.[80] First, there was a carefully drafted letter, in which he stated plainly that Brougham's conduct 'was one of the principle causes of the dismissal of the late Ministry'.[81] Then there was an interview, in which Melbourne itemized Brougham's 'many many indiscretions'.[82] In reply, Brougham huffed and puffed about being the victim of a conspiracy organized by the Grey family or, more intriguingly, by Thomas Young.[83] Alternatively, he returned to the well-worn theme of claiming that someone of his lowly social origins was bound to be rejected by 'the mandarin aristocracy'.[84] He was condemned 'to enjoy the dust and the sweat while others had the fruit and the shade'.[85] This kind of special pleading only led the Lamb family to conclude that he was 'only fit for a mad house', or if 'not mad he is the next thing to it'.[86]

Keeping Brougham out of office was achieved at a cost. He inevitably became one of the government's most unpredictable critics. Sparring matches between him and Melbourne became so much a feature of Lords' debates, that the latter admitted to being irritated by 'the continual twitterings and punchings that Brougham every day dealt out to some or other of the Ministers'.[87] With heavy irony, he thanked Brougham 'for his active support in 1835, . . . for his absence from the House in 1836, for his less active support in 1837'.[88] Importantly, however, Melbourne only wished to be 'politically quit of him'.[89] He was publicly a nuisance, but, in the Prime Minister's view, Brougham's unpredictability was 'very natural'.[90] Both men were solicitous about each other's feelings, and, privately, remained on good terms. Occasionally, Brougham could praise the government, and the 'stoutness and gallantry' of the man who led it.[91] Equally, Melbourne could never 'forget much kindness shewn him by B'.[92] He told Victoria, in 1839, that he had known Brougham for thirty-seven years, and that, throughout those years, the latter 'has always stood by me'.[93] This remark must relate to Melbourne's personal, rather than public life. The two men had never been politically close. Almost certainly, Brougham had been helpful in easing the turbulence in the Melbourne marriage, although all detail is lacking.[94] In the last year of his life, Melbourne was much exercised to know what Brougham thought of himself and his career, 'feeling, as I admit I do, much curiosity, and much interest in your feelings and opinions, especially as they regard myself'.[95] He made Brougham an executor of his will. Brougham was liked and needed as a friend. He was not, however, to be a colleague in government.

If Brougham was one Radical martyr, the Earl of Durham was the other. Here, there was no ambiguity between Melbourne's personal and public views. He disliked him 'so much, that there is no course would please me so well as setting him at defiance'.[96] In spite of being Grey's son-in-law and the darling of the Radicals, Durham, in Melbourne's view *'had no truth in him—and was worse in that respect than Brougham'*.[97] He seemed to be professionally at odds with everyone and everything, and Melbourne had no hesitation in making this point to Durham's relations: 'Discontent is there ingrained in the Character . . . and if Paradise should be his ultimate lot, the Almighty will find it beyond his power to make him happy there. He will do nothing but complain and find fault.'[98] His clamouring for attention and status was 'quite childish',[99] but 'his usual course'.[100] For reasons that Melbourne found it hard to understand, the political world seemed to be frightened of Durham and only anxious to defer to his every whim.[101] He had therefore developed the manner of the bully. Having such a man in government would compound the severe difficulties that Melbourne already faced in holding his colleagues together. Therefore, he determined that Durham could have anything but substantial office. Quite simply it was to be doubted 'whether there can be either peace or harmony in a Cabinet of which Lord Durham is a member'.[102]

Left to himself, Melbourne would have treated Durham as he had treated Brougham, and given him nothing,[103] but such were the man's connections that he could not be quite ignored. Some appropriate wilderness had to be found, first in the ambassadorship to St Petersburg and then in the Governor-Generalship of Canada. Both jobs were designed 'to satisfy and dispose of him'.[104] Melbourne was not surprised when difficulties arose, first with the Russians and then with the Canadians, leading up to a major crisis in 1839.[105] Throughout, 'Lord Durham's conduct has been most mad and indiscreet and as far as we can see unacceptable.'[106] Much against his better judgement, Melbourne defended in the Lords the actions of a man who would not be controlled, and whose policies seemed certain to embroil the country in colonial wars.[107] When Durham resigned, claiming, as usual, that he had not been fully supported by Melbourne, the latter could not regard it as *'so great a misfortune'*.[108] Quite definitely, he had 'brought it on himself', and he had no case to make against his colleagues.[109] By being given positions of responsibility, Durham had simply been given the opportunity to demonstrate 'une vanité qui passe toutes les bornes'.[110] The Radicals were determined to canonize their fallen hero, arguing that his resignation merely proved that Melbourne and his friends were moving away from all liberal policies, but, whether Durham was man or martyr, the Prime Minister was determined not 'to be any thing but firm with the Governor of Canada'.[111] He was now out of office for good.

Much to his disappointment, Durham's resignation, like Howick's failed to bring down Melbourne's government. The Radicals now had a powerful voice in the House of Lords, but little else changed. Yet again, Melbourne had met a Radical challenge and faced it down. It was symbolic of his whole stance. There was to be no concession made to Radical programmes, even if such demands were backed up by threats of a withdrawal of support in the Commons, or of major resignations. When Radicals came close to dislodging Melbourne, in the summer of 1839, they were confronted with the prospect of a Tory government. To substitute Peel for Melbourne could hardly be viewed as a Radical achievement. Therefore, they had to put up with Melbourne for fear of worse. Eating dust became an unpleasant but necessary occupation. Small gains might be registered on issues like the secret ballot, but, for the most part, Radicals had to study patience. Their leaders' careers were abruptly halted, and their votes were taken for granted. They could in theory bring Melbourne down, but in practice were an irritant rather than a threat.

Exactly the same circumstances conditioned Melbourne's relations with the Irish bloc of MPs, led by O'Connell. On the one hand, there was no hiding the fact that they were a crucial element in providing Melbourne with his slim majority in the Commons. He acknowledged 'the fact which tells the most against us viz. the great proportion in which our majority consists of Irish members. This is a fact . . . which it is not our business to blazon forth.'[112] It seemed that Melbourne had no choice but to dance to an Irish tune, 'parce que M. O'Connell lui donnait des voix'.[113] Like the Radicals, the Irish had the capacity to embarrass the government whenever they felt so inclined, and to bring it down if it failed to meet their expectations. Pressurizing, even blackmailing, was always an option. On the other hand, again like the Radicals, the Irish had to accept that Melbourne's departure from office would bring in some kind of Tory administration, which would either not be able to govern Ireland at all, or would only do so with the help of Orangemen. So grim was this latter possibility, that O'Connell and his friends had to support Melbourne, even though they came to suspect, even to despise, him.

For Melbourne himself, the situation was brutally clear. He told Victoria that the Irish were 'a poor set; that they were quick and clever, but uncertain, false, hippocritical [sic]'.[114] The majority of the population were 'bigotted Roman Catholics'.[115] As a result, the endless crises had less to do with particular policies or grievances, than with an ingrained, almost psychological, itch to be difficult. Trouble arose from 'the natural disposition of the People and the natural state of society . . . I have therefore no hope of any speedy amendment'.[116] The Protestants and their Orange Lodges were equally bad, sunk in 'the absurdity and unpracticality of their own objects'.[117] Yet, since Melbourne held fast to the idea that the political Union of the two islands was not a point for negotiation, he had to accept that, in the last resort, the Protestants were his only allies. As a consequence, they were to be treated 'with firmness and justice, but at the same time with caution and moderation, and with the utmost tenderness and consideration not only for their feelings but even for their prejudices'.[118] It was difficult for a Whiggish mind to enter, with any degree of sympathy, into Irish politics, when they were so informed by sectarian hatreds. Little could be done except to hold the ring among the warring parties, and to preserve the Union.

Not surprisingly therefore, Melbourne refused to let the Irish set the agenda for his government. He had played little or no part in the Lichfield House Compact, of February 1835, which had brought Whigs and Irishmen into association. He further insisted that the object of that agreement had been narrowly to remove Peel. It had not set up any long-term understanding. If the Irish chose to support him, it would be churlish not to be grateful, but there was to be no bargaining. O'Connell was not consulted about the membership of Melbourne's governments. Nothing was to be done, 'in order to satisfy him [O'Connell] or his Party', though it would be 'little short of madness . . . to reject and repudiate the support of him and those who act with him'.[119] Throughout his period in office, Melbourne was accused of having a 'mysterious connection'[120] with O'Connell, and he never tired of denying it. At the beginning of his second administration, in April 1835, he told the Lords: 'I do not know whether I shall have the aid of Mr. O'Connell. I have certainly taken no means to secure it, and most particularly I have made no terms with Mr. O'Connell.'[121] It was a message that would be repeated again and again, and that in fact reflected political reality. Melbourne was grateful for Irish support, but he never paid a great price for it.

His independence from the Irish lobby was manifested in his response to Irish issues and to O'Connell personally. He spoke on Ireland regularly, and gave it more attention than many other subjects. As has been noted, it was one of the few areas in which he could claim an expertise. But there were limits to his interest. There was little detailed work, for example. He was supplied with views and points of detail by Lord Hatherton.[122] Nor was there anything new concerning Ireland on Melbourne's agenda. His Irish Bills represented either a tidying-up of aspects of Grey's legislation on Ireland, or an applying to Ireland of measures like the Municipal Corporations Bill, which had already been brought in for the rest of the United Kingdom. Ireland was not to be different or separate.[123] Much of Melbourne's legislation was to place Ireland 'upon the same footing with this country'.[124] In this sense, Ireland lost importance as a special case. Its prominence in politics from 1828 to 1834 was not to be continued. If Irish Bills were amended or destroyed in the House of Lords, Melbourne was not much put out. After all, as he told Russell, 'there have been so many bills that I hardly recollect one from another'.[125] On no account were O'Connell and his friends to dictate the nature of legislative programmes.

Left to himself, with no Irish legacy from Grey's government to manage, it is likely that Melbourne would have demoted Irish issues even further. He had doubts about extending the 1834 Poor Law to Ireland.[126] On central questions, like the redeployment of the revenues of the Anglican Church in Ireland and the wisdom of making non-Anglicans pay tithes, Melbourne confessed that he thought these questions 'need not yet have been raised'.[127] Since they had been raised under Grey, some attempt must be made to solve them, but it was a nuisance.[128] They were topics which, as the French ambassador noted, 'consolidera ou renversera le Ministère'.[129] Therefore, only 'necessity, absolute necessity' forced him to address them.[130] On the Tithe Question, he made, for him, long and yawning speeches, which tried to inject commonsense and secular prudence into the minds of men, who were known not to relish such qualities.[131] By February 1838, he candidly announced that he was 'quite tired of reforming the Church'.[132] He had lived with the problems of Ireland for a decade. Reform had been endlessly attempted, yet the Irish were as far from reason as ever. Little wonder that the foremost historian of Ireland in the 1830s, when discussing the detail of Bills and polices, did not feel obliged to mention Melbourne very often.[133] He was grateful for Irish votes, but bored by their concerns.

His detachment with respect to O'Connell was even more marked.[134] The Irish leader was bracketed with leading Radicals as beyond the pale. In December 1834, Melbourne simply stated that, 'I will have nothing to do with Brougham. I will have nothing to do with Durham. I will have nothing to do with O'Connell.'[135] In Melbourne's view, the Irish leader's behaviour since 1828 proved that he was 'an irreclaimable blackguard, and that it is unfit for any gentleman to associate with him. It hinders one from saying a single word in his defence.'[136] All contact with 'the Beast' ended in embarrassment:

I have . . . undertaken the Herculean and impossible task of defending, or rather of palliating his most perverse and stupid conduct and language. I have found no means of doing so, except by asserting that other persons have said and are saying as bad things as he does, which is not true.[137]

The best that could be said of him is that, 'He has probably no feeling of what a Blackguard he is, nor of what people think him.'[138] In the late 1820s, Melbourne had argued that O'Connell might be made productive by being given office. By 1834, he had firmly changed his mind.[139] There was nothing to be gained by flattering O'Connell, or in trying to meet some at least of his wishes. The satisfaction of one demand merely led to the production of another. As far as Melbourne was concerned, O'Connell's ultimate aim was the dissolution of the Union between England and Ireland, and, since that was unimaginable, there was little purpose in conceding lesser points.[140] Treating with O'Connell between 1828 and 1834 had produced no lasting peace. He could now vote with the Whigs if he pleased, but he would do so only on Whig terms. As politicians, he and his followers were no longer to be particularly regarded.

In spite of receiving cavalier treatment at Melbourne's hands, Irish votes steadily contributed to Melbourne's hold on government. As Angus Macintyre has pointed out, once O'Connell's motion to repeal the Union had failed by the miserable margin of 523 to 38, in April 1834, the Irish had few options.[141] They could cling to the Whigs, or be instrumental in bringing back the Tories. Sensibly from their point of view, they chose the first of these routes. On the Tithe Question and on the Irish Poor Law, O'Connell grumbled and protested, but ultimately voted for Melbourne's measures. The same is true in divisions on Irish Municipal Reform in 1838 and 1839.[142] On all these measures, O'Connell was forced to accept that Whigs offered more than Tories ever could. In November 1834, when Melbourne was dismissed from office, the Irish leader claimed to be pleased that 'the humbuggers' had been unseated.[143] Five years later, he was a wiser man. When news came to him that the Radicals had decided to resume their support of Melbourne's government, the Irish leader was moved 'to rejoice in the goodness of God for our escape'.[144] Although Melbourne had demonstrably refused 'to be governed by Mr. O'Connell',[145] he was the only guarantee against the return of Tory government. The crises of 1834–5 and 1839 made this point inescapable. From time to time politicians cut off their noses to spite their face, but until either the Radicals or the Irish worked themselves up into such a state, they offered no threat to Melbourne. They could not dictate the agenda of politics nor force themselves into office. He depended on their votes, but, in a much more real sense, they depended on him.

Potentially, the Tories represented a much more serious threat. Controlling the House of Lords, where Melbourne's legislation could be amended or emasculated at will, the Tory party also had such strength among the propertied that it remained the natural party of government. Melbourne had no doubt of this. He told Brougham, in 1835, that, 'The Tories are in fact the strongest party in the country—strong in property, strong in station, strong in prejudice, strong in union . . . When our administration was formed in 1830 it was clear it could not have stood without the Reform Bill, which gave us a transient, phrenetic and epileptic strength. When that ceased, we were again left in a state of feebleness.'[146] Only the Tory divisions over Catholic Emancipation in 1829 had allowed the Whigs into office at all. The Reform Bill, only increasing the electorate from 14 to 18 per cent of adult males, had not significantly dented Tory hopes. Indeed, Lord John Russell thought that, in enfranchising tenants at will by the Chandos clause, the Bill had actually improved Tory prospects.[147] After 1834, it was only the continuing divisions among the Tories that kept Melbourne afloat. Peel, and to some extent Wellington, intensely disliked the Ultras within their own party, who regretted Catholic Emancipation and Reform, and who even called for the rescinding of either or both. Both men saw value in supporting Melbourne in government. He seemed to have the capacity to neutralize the efforts of Irishmen and Radicals, and his existence made the Ultra Tories powerless. It was better to amend Melbourne's measures in the Lords than to be in government, with a programme dictated by Ultras.

Melbourne was happy to accept that his existence as Prime Minister had been brought about by a kind of fluke. Only a certain configuration in politics could have made a man of his temperament and record of value. If, however, Melbourne survived because Peel and Wellington chose not to attack, it was precisely that temperament and record that was priceless. Gladstone later described the 1830s as a period of intense party warfare, when 'the struggle between a Ministry and an Opposition was so intense, so prolonged and so unremitting',[148] but this must be wrong. Had politics run on these lines, Melbourne would almost certainly never have become Prime Minister at all. Party feeling may have been fierce, but it was not reflected in Melbourne's politics. He quite liked Tories. As he confessed to Victoria,

'I don't dislike Tories,' said Lord M. 'I think they are very much like the others; I have acted with them.' We agreed J. Russell disliked being supported by them; 'I don't care,' said Lord M., 'by whom I am supported I consider them all as one; I don't care by whom I am helped, as long as I am helped,' he said laughing.[149]

When the young queen expressed the fear that she would not be able to work with Tories, Melbourne cheered her up by saying that 'the measures they propose are not so very different'.[150] He had served under Canning, Goderich, and Wellington in the late 1820s. He had kept up friendly relations with Stanley and Graham, who had left the Whigs for the Tories in 1834.[151] In moments of exasperation with party demands, he could even describe his own followers as 'more violent, more greedy, more exclusive than their opponents'.[152] In terms of organization, discipline, and creed, party lines might be hardening, but none of these things were of interest to Melbourne.[153]

His relations with Peel were respectful and amicable. There was of course the terrible drawback of his social origins. Melbourne was clear that Harrow and Christ Church had failed to polish up the ironmaster's son into something that could pass for a gentleman. He was 'an underbred fellow' and 'all gaucherie'.[154] To Melbourne's Whiggish mind, Peel was too religious, too uxorious, too prim. He was all 'prudence and calculation'.[155] There was no spontaneity in him. On the other hand he was immensely able, and, in accepting religious and political Reform, right-minded. He worked hard to soften Victoria's prejudices against Peel, reminding her that she might well have to look on him as a future Prime Minister. The French ambassador heard him remind her that, 'Sir Robert Peel était le chef d'un parti puissant, considérable, et d'ailleurs un très habile et très galant homme, avec qui la Reine devoit toujours être en bons termes.'[156] When the queen opined that Peel was a 'nasty wretch',[157] Melbourne, with magnificent, Whiggish condescension, explained that, 'he is a man not accustomed to talk to Kings . . . it is not like me; I have been brought up with Kings and Princes.'[158] In return, the Prime Minister was clear that Peel had 'no personal hostility to Lord Melbourne'.[159]

If relations with Peel were politely respectful, those with Wellington were positively cordial. He was a favourite with the whole Lamb family. Emily thought that the Duke and her brother had traits in common. Wellington was so 'Like him in one respect, that of being so honest, that even party feeling cannot prevent him saying what he thinks—When I used to live with the Duke of W. more than I do now this resemblance seemed very often to strike me, and this was one reason why I liked him so much.'[160] Similarly, Frederick Lamb thought the Duke 'a dear and noble old boy'.[161] Wellington was not particularly religious and was certainly not prim. Like Melbourne, he was illegitimate, and enjoyed a colourful private life. In his view, the Duke was quite often monumentally wrongheaded, but he was 'a very great and a very able man', with whom he could live in 'charity'.[162] In return, Wellington liked Melbourne. He assured Victoria that he understood her esteem for her Prime Minister, that he felt a 'personal friendship' for him, and that 'he hoped . . . he had done all he could to help your Government'.[163] In moments of difficulty, like the Bedchamber Crisis of 1839, the Duke was to be as solicitous of the feelings of Victoria and Melbourne, as he was of those of his own party.

The French embassy reported home, in 1840, that 'malgré son attitude générale d'opposition . . . le duc de Wellington vit, au fond, en bonne intelligence avec Lord Melbourne, et prête souvent au gouvernement son appui'.[164]

To ties of esteem and regard must be added certain common interests. There were areas of politics on which Melbourne, Peel, and Wellington found themselves in agreement. For example, they were detested by the same people. Ultra Tories such as Newcastle, Londonderry, and Buckingham never forgave Peel and Wellington for promoting Catholic Emancipation and accepting Reform. Noting that the Tory party in the Lords was split into moderate and extreme factions, the French ambassador reported, in 1835, that 'il est certain que lui [Wellington] et Peel sont devenus odieux aux Duc de Newcastle et à ses fougueux partisans'.[165] They loathed Melbourne too, keeping up a vituperative campaign of pamphlet satire and venom. For them, Melbourne ran government with 'Epicurean shrugs and nil admirari smiles'.[166] To people like Londonderry, it was maddening to see the three men co-operating to secure the passage of legislation in Lords and Commons.[167] Lord Lyndhurst, not Wellington, led the Tory attack in the Upper House, and his verbal duelling with Melbourne became a feature of the age. In these exchanges, he taunted Lyndhurst with the charge of leading an ignorant and irresponsible faction within the Tory party, just as Peel, in the Commons, refused to take seriously the views of those whose main interests lay in hunting, shooting, and fishing.[168] Ultra opinion was the articulation of stupidity, and Melbourne and Peel fought it, shoulder to shoulder.

Equally, there was to be no further truckling to Radicalism. All three men saw themselves involved in a campaign to block any further constitutional changes. The prerogatives of the Crown and the influence of Lords, Churches, and universities were to suffer no more harm. The great reforms of 1829 to 1834 had to be accepted and absorbed, but neither Melbourne nor Peel nor Wellington had been convincing reformers. All were clear that a term had to be put to further changes. In this respect, Ultra Toryism was a menace, not because it advocated reform itself, but because, in using the Tory majority in the House of Lords to thwart the wishes of the Lower House, it gave a justification to Radical arguments that further changes were necessary. With mounting irritation, and feeling 'his temper giving way',[169] Melbourne lectured the Lords on the folly of their own behaviour. He warned them against 'setting yourselves in opposition to the opinions of the people of England',[170] and begged them to 'pause' before demolishing Bills which had passed the Commons with large majorities.[171] He repeatedly pointed out that, if the Ultras voted down his moderate reforms, they would certainly face more dramatic measures in due course.[172] He took the Lords seriously, taking trouble over attendances for example, and he asked that House to act responsibly.[173] Some of his colleagues went further. Holland was clear that the Reform Bill had given the Commons a primacy in legislation, and that 'it is to be hoped that the Hse of Lords will ere long discover and act upon this undeniable truth'.[174] Stupidly, Ultras failed to see that the Lords could only be the losers in what the French ambassador called 'la collision entre la Chambre des Pairs et la Chambre des Communes, [which] devient tous les jours plus animée'.[175]

In attempting to save the Ultras from the consequences of their own policies, however, Melbourne was never tempted to play the radical himself. Like Peel and Wellington, he regarded the powers of the Lords as sacrosanct. Every Whiggish inclination led him in the same direction. After all, maddening though the Tory majority in the Lords could be, government could stand in spite of them. A defeat in the Upper House was not a matter for either a resignation or a dissolution.[176] Occasionally, their amendments actually improved Bills, diluting their radicalism and giving Melbourne arguments against his more exuberant colleagues.[177] By the same token, he was not always averse to 'a state of Inaction' in the Lords, which slowed the progress of measures, for which he himself often had little enthusiasm.[178] Above all, he could not agree with Holland that, after 1832, the Commons had somehow achieved a superior status to the Lords. To do so would be 'to change the fundamental principles of the constitution'.[179] Such a theory could only be 'rather awkward and objectionable . . . seeing that it is directly contrary to the spirit and theory of the constitution'.[180] However much the Lords amended the wishes of the Commons, no one could deny their right to do so. It might not be prudent, but it was certainly constitutional.

Melbourne's respect for the Lords was therefore everything that Peel and Wellington could hope for. In December 1835, he emphatically declared:

I am decided that there has been nothing either in the recent or the remote conduct of the House of Lords, which can justify any man in trying a change of its present constitution, or of diminishing its powers, rights and privileges. These are my sentiments, and these I shall declare whenever any fitting opportunity occurs.[181]

Two bruising Parliamentary sessions later, his views were unchanged. He refused to accept the Radical thesis that the time had come to settle the relative status of Lords and Commons. Further, if such a debate came on, he was not sure that the decision would be clear cut: 'The fact is that the Case as between the Lords and Commons is by no means so strong for the latter, as it has been represented. Many of the bills amended in the Lords were very faulty, and those that were rejected, were by no means of clear advantage and a postponement of their further consideration was by no means unreasonable.'[182]

The answer to the difficulty lay not in constitutional change, but in the active co-operation of Wellington and Melbourne to ensure that Ultras throwing stones should do as little damage as possible. Tory peers were assisted in the preparation of parliamentary questions.[183] Major Bills, like the Municipal Corporations bill, were drawn up, with Tory advice and incorporating Tory comment.[184] In particular, Wellington was so often taken into Melbourne's confidence that he could be regarded almost as an honorary member of the government. The Duke's views were valued over a wide range of issues, far beyond the military matters on which he had a particular expertise.[185] Most dramatically, for example, Wellington was asked for his opinion during the Eastern Crisis in the summer of 1840, producing a memorandum, which argued so powerfully against a war with France over the fate of the Ottoman Empire, that many people thought it the most significant factor in neutralizing Palmerston's bellicosity.[186] The French ambassador reported home, in August, that 'le duc a eu, à ce sujet, avec lord Melbourne, une longue conversation qui a fait sur ce dernier, m'a dit le Roi, beaucoup d'impression'.[187] His Prime Minister agreed: 'il a produit de l'effet, en somme lord Palmerston est ébranlé, battu de l'oiseau.'[188] As examples such as this indicate, part of Melbourne's sleight of hand, in presiding over government, was to make leading Opposition figures part of it. Equally, why should Wellington hurry to unseat a Minister by whom he was so regarded.

In view of all this, Melbourne could honestly report to Queen Victoria, and 'with tears in his eyes', that 'the Duke of Wellington and Sir Robert Peel have behaved very well; they have helped us a good deal; some of the *other* tories have not behaved so well, and have been factious; when Sir Robert Peel is not there they give trouble; but they don't dare to do so when he is there.' Wellington repeatedly assured Melbourne of his willingness 'to assist the Govt by every means in my power'; so often in fact that his own side accused him of 'leaving them'.[189] It was an arrangement that suited everyone. Tory strength in the Lords allowed Melbourne to tell the Radicals and the Irish in all honesty that their wilder notions had no chance of passing, and that was extremely convenient. For a man who looked for no new agendas, any excuse to brake expectations was to be welcomed. Equally, from Peel and Wellington's point of view, Melbourne in government, consulting and considerate, had more immediate attraction than a purely Tory administration. They for long doubted their ability to secure a majority in the Commons;[190] they worried about their capacity to govern Ireland; they were hesitant, after 1837, to force themselves into government against the wishes of a Whig Queen;[191] and, above all, they were not prepared to accept any arrangement that would allow the Ultras any real influence.

Until at least 1839, Wellington and Peel showed little or no interest in turning Melbourne out. Even when they failed to support him on a particular division, it was recognized that 'ils . . . ne veulent pas renverser le Ministère, surtout dans les circonstances actuelles'. All these men were keen to maintain 'un juste milieu en repoussant les exagérés'.[192] With no ambitions for government, Tory policy was simply 'to lye still'.[193] The understanding between this triumvirate was almost so formal, that, when it sometimes broke down, allowing the Ultras to roam free, Melbourne could invoke the language of contract. One such occasion was recorded as follows:

Melbourne's reply [was] very striking . . . standing on Tip Toe, and reaching across the Table, and striking it vehemently, in a tone and look of great indignation, full in the face of the D. of Wellington, 'Never again will I make a contract with those, who want either the will or the power to execute their agreement.' The Duke who had sat with his former colleagues all the night . . . pulled his hat over his face and looked greatly annoyed.[194]

Such spats were rare, however. Again and again, Tory votes and abstentions, orchestrated by Peel and Wellington, saved government legislation.[195] Typically, 'conciliation' on the part of Wellington and Peel was balanced by 'sérieuses concessions' on the part of Melbourne.[196] His 'opinions se rapprochent celles des Torys modérés; il n'en diffère qu'autant que cela est nécessaire pour conserver l'ascendant sur la Nation.'[197] Little wonder that the possibility of a Peel–Melbourne coalition should exercise the minds of pamphleteers throughout these years. It would be the ultimate guarantee against '*Noyades* in the Thames, and *Fusillades* in Hyde Park'.[198]

Reviewing evidence such as this, the question inevitably arises of when exactly Tory government was resumed. Officially, it returned in 1841, when Melbourne lost an election. But Radical critics of the Prime Minister had complained with increasing bitterness that, effectively, Tory values had returned to prominence much earlier. Irishmen and Radicals had to put up with Melbourne or face the Tories, but they could increasingly see little difference between the two. Their irritation was well founded. Melbourne had followed the reforms of 1830–4 without enthusiasm or conviction. He frankly admitted that he had 'concurred in all the great liberal measures of late years not from choice but from necessity'.[199] The force of circumstances had left him the responsibility of seeing through the remnants of Grey's programme, much of which he personally disliked, and he wanted no other agenda. Issues, which were bequeathed to him by Grey, and which were to occupy so much of his time, had better not been agitated in the first place. The fate of the Anglican Church in Ireland was a case in point:

You know that I always disapproved of those proceedings of 1834 and of the stirring of all those questions about the Irish Church. When they were stirred I was obliged to take upon them the part which I thought right, but I always thought [them] foolish to the utmost extent of foolishness.[200]

Melbourne was clear that after the Municipal Corporations Bill had been settled in 1835 nothing of consequence remained to be done:

With respect to the general state of the public mind and consequently of public affairs and of the Country, we are certainly approaching a difficult and doubtful point, viz, the point at which it is to be decided whether we can stand still or at least proceed somewhat more slowly in alteration and change. With the Reformation of the Corporations, which I consider to involve a similar measure with respect to Ireland . . . appears to me to terminate those measures of a popular character which it is possible to adopt with safety and with the maintenance of the present Constitution.[201]

In other words, reform was at an end.

Within a year of taking office, therefore, Melbourne had, in a personal sense, decided against changes that were not already in the pipeline. In looking for a label to describe his politics, the words 'Radical' and, possibly 'Whig', seem increasingly inappropriate. Melbourne had worked comfortably with Tory governments between 1827 and 1830, and resumed co-operation after 1834. Much that happened between 1830 and 1834, by contrast, had caused him discomfort. There is not much profit in trying to detect the Whiggish elements in Peel or the Tory elements in Melbourne, but clearly both men saw consolidation, not further change, as the central requirement of politics after 1834. All that needs to be emphasized is that, as has been noted before, to call Melbourne a Whig is to refer to his upbringing, psychology, and society rather than his politics. It was precisely this ambiguity that gave him such political strength. In crises like those of 1834–5 nearly everyone could see some point of common ground with him. As a Prime Minister he was tolerated for the same reason, and because it was easy to conjure up a more unpleasant alternative. The tabulation of the government's weaknesses—Grey, William IV, Irishmen, Radicals, and Tories—should not obscure the fact that it was actually rather strong. When it fell, it fell not through intolerable pressure coming from outside, but from tensions within government that Melbourne could not control or resolve for ever.

Collapse from Within, 1837–1841

THE real threat to Melbourne's tenure of office came not from the Left or the Right, from Radicals and Tories, but from within the ranks of those he counted as his supporters. His government had been put together in a fragmentary way: one or two Foxite Whigs, the Grey family interest, and Palmerston as a law unto himself. He kept it together by umpiring in crises between departments, and by making personal appeals to whatever better nature his colleagues had. It was political juggling of a very high order, but it could not go on forever. Issues of any kind brought on new divisions. While the agenda of 1830–4 was continued and polished, there was a chance of minimum agreement, because his friends would be bound by previous decisions. On the other hand, new points of business would be devastating. Melbourne endlessly fought to divert the attention of his colleagues from anything that would demand new responses. He knew that their formulation would put intolerable strain on Cabinet loyalty, even when it was most loosely defined. Unfortunately four issues could not be suppressed; the possibility of introducing a secret ballot; the future of the Corn Laws; colonial policy; and the problem of a resurgent France. Each of them divided Minister from Minister. Cumulatively, they brought resignations and threats of resignation. In the end, they forced Melbourne to call an election at a moment not of his choosing on issues he would have preferred to ignore.

Melbourne was acutely aware of his situation. He fought the idea of new agendas with, for him, something approaching vigour. He was 'for holding the ground already taken, but not for occupying new ground rashly',[1] or, as he put it to Archbishop Whately, 'all this reforming gives a deuced deal of trouble, eh? I wish they'd let it all alone.'[2] On innumerable occasions, Howick complained that the Prime Minister could not 'bear adopting any new measures',[3] and William Mackworth Praed made a joke of it:

> To promise, pause, prepare, postpone
> And end by letting things alone:
> In short, to earn the people's pay
> By doing nothing every day.[4]

No Whig ran headlong into reform. Change should strengthen institutions, not undermine them. It should always be conformable to the times. In Melbourne, this strain of thinking was confirmed by the knowledge that a divided government could only afford limited vision. He told the young Victoria: 'the danger doesn't come so much from our adversaries as from ourselves.'[5] It was obvious to him that 'if we hold desperate language, and if we give up or condemn our own policy, we must of course go to pieces'.[6]

Inevitably, inertia was maddening to those who saw a more active role for government. The consequences of industrialization had to be addressed. Chartism had to be answered. It was not enough for Melbourne to treat industrial society as a distasteful inconvenience. Frederick Lamb, in September 1841, attributed his brother's loss of office less to an election defeat than to a *coup* organized within his own party. Long in the making, and possibly led by the ambitions of Russell, this conspiracy broadly represented the views of those who wished for more movement in politics, against those who wished to stand and draw breath:

What I care about (if Wm does) is that I have long since been apprized of a party within the Whig party who are striving to lay all the blame upon Wm and to put forward Johnny as the future leader . . . Melbourne seems to have done every thing that could be done for good, and if this is overlooked any where it is among the Whigs themselves; whether this is confined to the most violent or is a device of the *faux frères* among them who are always aiming at mischief, I have not the means of knowing but its existence is beyond a doubt.[7]

As early as 1837, Melbourne was speculating about how his government would end. He hoped that it would 'fall in the open light, and not be dissolved by embarrassments arising within itself in a manner unintelligible and unsatisfactory to the great body of its supporters'.[8] He was not to have his wish granted.

Publicly, the cancer at the heart of the Melbourne administration was demonstrated in the increasing recourse to the expedient of making issues, officially, open questions. When a Cabinet could not agree, each Minister was free to follow his own conscience. The Ballot and Corn Law Reform were the two most prominent measures to fall into this category. Melbourne disliked both, and he fought doggedly, both to stop them being debated at all, and to prevent them becoming governmental measures. He might have to concede 'open question' status, but that was in itself a half-victory. He profoundly disapproved of Ministers making declarations on these matters,[9] and he took care, in briefings to candidates, to urge the maximum caution.[10] There was nothing heroic about calling on the device of 'open questions', but it kept government together for a time, and certainly slowed the pace of a reform movement, that, in the early 1830s, seemed to be gathering a precipitous momentum. Russell ruefully observed that, 'It is certainly for the convenience of an administration to have many open questions, but I do not think it is for their honour and glory.'[11] Melbourne, by contrast, was all for convenience, and Whiggishly sceptical of honour and glory.

The Corn Laws stood majestically to symbolize the primacy of agricultural England, and the values of county and parish, over industrialist and shareholder. By artificially guaranteeing agricultural prices, even if this resulted in high food prices and therefore high wage costs, the Corn Laws were a totem of almost magical significance. The fact that they were, by the 1830s, under attack from Chartists and the Anti-Corn Law League was something that no government could ignore. Melbourne tried to. In July 1838, he told the Lords that no immediate decision was necessary, and that he was established firmly on the fence. Temperamentally against change, he was intellectually prepared to consider it a possibility:

> he must say, that it was far from his intention to introduce any measure for altering the present corn-laws, or for disturbing the system which at present existed . . . nor would he ever introduce any new system of corn-laws, founded on a different principle from the present, unless a decided opinion was expressed on the subject by a large majority of the people. But he believed the system to have operated well, and that it would be dangerous to touch it . . . Next to change, the great evil was the fear of change, which produced effects scarcely less disastrous than change itself.[12]

Between December 1838 and March 1839, however, Chartists and Anti-Corn Law Leaguers brought the issue centre-stage, with 'démonstrations populaires très menaçantes'.[13] Melbourne thought the League 'a lot of fools', but a response had to be made.[14]

There was none. At a Cabinet meeting on 23 January, Melbourne restated his position. The dignifying of the Corn Law issue by giving it the status of an 'open question' had in itself been a concession, and it was the last that he was prepared to make.[15] On 29 January, he tried to conciliate Russell by offering an inquiry on the subject,[16] but, two days earlier, he had thought this a futile gesture, because 'we shall never agree on these points beforehand let us enquire until doomsday'.[17] A month later, he blocked all idea of an inquiry by eccentrically telling the Lords that all argument was on one side of the question, all 'practical sense' on the other.[18] He carried his point, but from the spring of 1839, the Corn Law issue was a running sore in politics. Those who had always criticized Melbourne's reluctance to act now had the argument that his inertia risked economic dislocation and civil disobedience on a large scale. It was the obvious starting point from which to question Melbourne's continuing leadership of the party. The Prime Minister himself was very aware of the danger it presented:

I dread this question. It was always a hateful one, full of . . . abuse and accusing. I feel myself placed in a great difficulty by it. I cannot pledge myself to the maintenance of the present system, because I think there is much objection to it, and I cannot bear to face the blind and violent clamour for altering it, especially as I think it is likely to lead to precipitate and dangerous courses.[19]

Equivocation and an unwillingness to decide were marked features of Melbourne's character, but, in this case, he had arguments to justify a drifting policy.

First, he was clear that, once the Corn Law issue was pressed, the government would founder. Its constituent elements simply could not withstand the strain. In December 1839, he told Lady Holland that, for those who wished to bring the government down, 'the way to do it . . . decisively is to propose a measure upon Corn'.[20] Jokingly, he made the same point to Victoria: 'There are two things which I know hold the Govt. together; *not* meddling with the Horse Guards nor with the Corn Laws, and those were 2 things they were very fond of touching but which I always resisted; I knew they were 2 things that would be fatal to the Govt, either the Horse Guards or the Corn Laws.'[21] Secondly he was unpersuaded by the economic arguments for change. When industrialists argued that the Corn Laws dangerously inflated food prices and labour costs, which in turn threatened manufacturing competitiveness, Melbourne replied that the whole agitation had been got up by 'northern manufacturers, taking advantage of the present dearness of corn and with the object of lowering wages'.[22] The Leaguers were the political incarnation of selfishness, not principle. Further to leave agriculture unprotected might so discourage domestic production, as to leave the country at the mercy of foreign suppliers. Remembering Napoleonic blockades, Melbourne could only regard this as 'madness'.[23] Referring to the long years of war with France, he confessed to his peers that, 'It is, my Lords, in my humble opinion, not a desirable thing for us to be dependent for our nourishment on foreign supplies.'[24]

There were larger considerations still. Corn Law debates invariably set town against country, and, by dividing landowner from manufacturer, undermined that unity among the propertied on which all good and stable government rested. The turbulence of the early 1830s had already tested that stability severely. Melbourne doubted whether it was wise to put yet more strain upon the system. Rather, some years of healing were required. Russell was kept in line by this argument. As Melbourne observed to him, in December 1838:

I suppose the present Irish prices will make the Corn Law a serious question, which it never has been since the year 1815. I own I dread it very much; not so much for either the difficulty or danger of the question itself, tho' it is both difficult and dangerous, as from the conviction that it will not be settled either one way or the other without a very severe struggle, a struggle which will increase all the evils of the present day by leaving behind it more animosity discord and alienation than even prevails at present. Nothing is so bad in my mind as clashes of Classes of society and this question naturally produces it . . . depend upon it any advantage that can be gained is not worth the danger and evil of the struggle, by which alone it can be carried, but which may be unavoidable.[25]

In the Whiggish mind, change could be either a good or a bad thing according to its timing and management. It was possible that the difficulties attending its introduction could outweigh any benefit derived by its enactment. In Melbourne's view, the Corn Law debate could only set half of propertied England at the throats of the other half.

Importantly, if, in spite of all his efforts, such a contest came on, Melbourne was clear that his sympathies lay entirely with the pre-industrial world. Agricultural England and the deferential social systems it supported were, for Melbourne, stable, generous, and proper. As has been noted, he doubted, when Home Secretary, whether a manufacturer had the appropriate attitudes to be a JP. Melbourne disliked giving the Corn Laws a political, rather than an economic character,[26] but, if this was unavoidable, he was determined not 'to let loose upon the Landowners a rabid and ferocious hostility'.[27] On this issue, Hobhouse observed that Melbourne 'spoke with more than usual earnestness', in declaring that 'he did not believe in coercion of landholders—they had not yielded and never would yield'.[28] Within landowning society, those above performed duties to those below, and those below deferred to those above. Industrial societies simply changed expressions of mutual regard into a battle between capital and labour. Stability became confrontation. Paternalistic in his dealings with own tenants, Melbourne distrusted the social rules of industrial life. When asking the Duke of Bedford to move the Address at the opening of a new Parliament, Melbourne emphasized that this was a function for a man of 'high Character and large landed Property'.[29]

In forming these views, Melbourne was not acting entirely on personal prejudice. He was very aware that the Whig party would have almost as much trouble as the Tories in presenting a united front on the Corn Law issue. Prominent Whigs like Althorp wrote to tell him of their opposition to the Laws, and this lobby was distinguished and vocal,[30] but there was another side to the question. Great Dukes, like those of Hamilton and Roxburghe informed Melbourne that any attempt to modify the Corn Laws would lead to the end of their association with the Whig party.[31] Individual voters sent letters, explaining that they proposed to abstain or vote Tory in the election of 1841, because they believed the Prime Minister to be insufficiently stout in his defence of agriculture.[32] Quoting evidence such as this, and referring to the anger of farmers at falling prices in markets all over England, Melbourne began to discern 'a general reaction against free trade which will eventually overbear all opposition'.[33] No doubt this was to some extent a rationalization of his own prejudices, but, in 1839 or 1840, the League's arguments against the Corn Laws had not, according to him, achieved that degree of acceptance that would allow the Whigs to adopt them without taking great risks.

Indeed, Melbourne half-believed that clever Whigs sitting in Cabinets might be running too far ahead of opinion generally. To give them their head might be to split the party, as the Tories would be split in 1846. Given his doubts, the best he could do, in the face of their informed and increasing pressure, was to conduct a Fabian retreat. It was not particularly dignified, but it bought time. 'Battered by arguments and old friends', he acknowledged what one of his colleagues called 'a rational submission to the circumstances of affairs'.[34] Allowing the issue to be an 'open' question had been a concession in itself, by allowing it on to the agenda of politics. After 1839, he began to lose control of the issue altogether. In March 1840, he told the Lords that he might not be averse to a 'modification' of the Corn Laws.[35] Three months later, he described the Corn Laws as being 'no question of stubborn principle from which he could safely pledge himself not to swerve'.[36] Two months after that, he admitted that it would be 'absolutely necessary to put these laws some day or other on a more reasonable and satisfactory foundation'.[37] Even this verbal progression towards change was not enough to save Melbourne from embarrassment. In June 1840, Lord Hatherton noted that the Prime Minister was the only Cabinet Minister not to vote for a motion seeking a revision of the Corn Laws. Publicly, he 'stands alone' on the issue.[38] Melbourne and his Cabinet clearly no longer marched to the same tune.

In the last year of his government's life, from the summer of 1840 to the summer of 1841, Melbourne had effectively lost control of much of fiscal policy. He himself began to state openly that 'it's impossible this Government can go on'.[39] In May 1841, he disliked Baring's budget, which attacked protectionist duties, and only 'yielded to his colleagues unwillingly'.[40] When Baring's proposals ran into difficulties, Melbourne was against calling an election, and most definitely against calling an election in which the Corn Law Repeal would be a major issue. He told the Cabinet as much on 19 May.[41] Once again, however, he was heavily outvoted. The election came on, at a time not of Melbourne's choosing, and involved a discussion of issues that he thought wise to ignore. He registered his views with Russell: 'I feel persuaded that we shall be greatly beat at a general election, and that by giving the Tories this opportunity we shall give them a great advantage. We shall give them an appearance of strength greater than they really possess and we shall ourselves shew weaker than we really are.'[42]

London society watched, with distaste, a Prime Minister being pushed and pulled into decisions he personally deprecated. It was an unedifying sight. Some began to argue that Melbourne should have resigned. By staying on, the false nature of his position only became the more glaring. It seemed that he was prepared to cling to office 'upon any terms rather than give it up'.[43] Others began to interpret the Corn Law debate as a plot, which was intended to drive Melbourne out of office 'in the same way as Lord Grey was pushed out by his colleagues some years ago'.[44] Jokes began to circulate: 'Why is Lord Melbourne like a *very* serious young lady?—Because he won't go out *at all*.'[45] Melbourne's isolation on the Corn Law issue had indeed become very singular. It became one of the most compelling reasons why Russell should succeed him as party leader as soon as possible.

In retrospect, Melbourne never spoke of the Corn Law debate as part of a conspiracy, but he entertained a deep bitterness against those in his Cabinet who had forced the issue. He could hardly fail to be aware of the loneliness of his position, and of the fact that he had 'never condemned the present system so decidedly . . . as the rest of my late Colleagues'.[46] He found consolation in being proud of his delaying tactics, which alone had allowed the government to survive. In 1843, he took pleasure in telling Greville that, 'he had prevented any measure being proposed for above three years, and that if he had done it sooner his Government would have fallen sooner'.[47] By December 1845, when the prospect of an anti-Tory government again became a possibility, Melbourne was so far separated from his former colleagues, that he could not pledge support for them. He refused 'to come in pledged to a total and immediate reform of the Corn Law'.[48] In fact, the Queen reported that her old minister was 'not at all pleased at *any thing* being done about Corn Laws'.[49] Former warm relations with both Peel and Russell cooled dramatically. When Peel carried through the abolition of the Corn Laws, Melbourne disturbed a dinner party at Windsor by calling it 'the greatest villainy'.[50] Absolutely unforgiving on this matter, he claimed, in 1847: 'Peel's measures have pretty well effected the entire ruin of the commercial interest, and I expect that by this time next year John and Peel together will have added to this the entire extinction of the landed interest.'[51] He found it impossible to change his mind, or to forgive, on an issue which had overwhelmed him.

An exactly comparable pattern emerged when Melbourne was confronted by calls for the introduction of the secret ballot in elections. In public and in private, he robustly opposed the change. It struck at the heart of deferential social values. Not only should no honest man shrink from voting openly, but also there were to be no further amendments to the theory and practice of the constitution. He had been the most sceptical of Reformers in 1832, and he firmly considered that a line had then been drawn under the issue. He told Russell that his government had been formed on this clear understanding: 'I am ready to continue to conduct the Government upon the principles upon which it was formed and in the manner in which it has hitherto been conducted, but that I cannot consent to or acquiesce in any alteration in these respects.'[52] To concede the ballot would be to open up the whole Reform issue once more: 'it was evident that ballot was only put forward in the first instance and that all the other points, extension of suffrage, reformation of the House of Lords would be pressed necessarily in the same manner.'[53] His ability to work with Peel and Wellington to some extent rested on their joint opposition to further constitutional change. For all of them, the political system needed no further amendment in their lifetime.

Further, to open up 'this absurd question of ballot'[54] would be to give the impression that the Radicals were setting the government's agenda, and that could not be tolerated. Significantly, Melbourne chose to make this point, not to Cabinet colleagues, but to the Tory Duke of Richmond: 'The attack upon us being thus we have already given too much to the radicals, an attack by the way to which I do not feel myself greatly liable. Can we afford to take another step towards them without alienating from us more of that class of supporters who have already been divided from us by the Irish Church question.'[55] In this situation, his friends were 'fools' to give public pledges in favour of the ballot. This was particularly galling to Melbourne for he firmly believed that the mood of the electorate was moving to the Right. Whigs lost ground in the elections of 1835 and 1837 for being too Radical, not for being not Radical enough. To manœuvre in a Radical direction was therefore 'madness'.[56] He told the Lords on more than one occasion that there was little or no feeling in the country for the ballot. The idea went against 'the firm and steady good sense of the great majority of the people of this country'.[57] After the busy years of 1828–34, Radicalism was now out of fashion. Melbourne personally could not regret this.

So clear was this perception that he was even unwilling to give the ballot issue the status of an open question, as had been accorded the Corn Laws. To do so would be to bring it into political debate and respectability. It was 'imprudent' even to think of it.[58] Instead, he robustly preferred to make a public statement opposing any change, and to take the consequences: 'I am for standing firm upon [the] ballot; for making an early declaration upon the subject and putting it to the House and the Country, whether they will stand by us or have it.'[59] Radicals were to receive no quarter on the issue.[60] When individuals or corporations sent in petitions in favour of the ballot, Melbourne either flatly refused to present them at all, or explained that, having done so, he would vote against their acceptance.[61] He would do nothing that would give the issue 'a lift'.[62]

Soon, however, as with the Corn Laws, pressure began to build. In August 1837, Russell told Brougham that he saw no reason why the ballot should not become an 'open question'.[63] Thereafter, Melbourne could only regard his chief Minister in the Commons as profoundly unsound.[64] When, in June 1839, the Prime Minister expressed the opinion in Cabinet that the introduction of the ballot 'would make him hostile to representative government altogether', Russell reportedly 'smiled' at this 'strong opinion'.[65] Similarly, taking Macaulay into government in 1839 materially added to the strength of those advocating change.[66] As with the Corn Laws, the Prime Minister was increasingly isolated on the ballot question, not winning the argument but merely suppressing it. Hobhouse complained to Durham in 1838 that 'we have never had a Cabinet upon it—that Ld Melbourne did not wish to be spoken to on the subject, because if asked he should be obliged to give an answer'.[67] As more and more Whig candidates and Ministers declared themselves for change, Melbourne's position looked more and more uncomfortable. He never shifted from his view that, 'to allow difference of opinion upon the question of the ballot . . . is destruction to the Government, either immediate or more distant, but destruction to the Government as it stands and to the principles upon which it has been constructed'.[68] His stubbornness kept the ballot at bay, but the price to be paid was heavy. Radicals saw his attitude as proof positive that supporting his administration would bring few rewards, and, more importantly, it suggested to younger men like Russell that perhaps Melbourne had outlived his moment.

The same unresponsiveness marked Melbourne's attitude to colonial questions, which he found troublesome and intrusive. Problems in Canada or the West Indies failed to engage heart or mind. In July 1840, he frankly told the Lords that, 'he was somewhat indifferent as to the retention of those colonies'.[69] Born in the late 1770s, he belonged to a generation whose parents talked of nothing but the loss of America. It was a precedent to which he endlessly returned, because 'the loss of these had given us at the time great shocks'.[70] Colonies, in terms of military and civil establishments, were clearly expensive. The returns were less obvious. Areas of white settlement, sooner or later, began to mouth claims to home rule or independence. Those inhabited by black or brown men raised difficult issues about slavery, and land tenure and physical control. There was little joy in any of it. Further, Melbourne was profoundly aware that Great Britain, with perhaps ten million people, could only dominate large areas of the world's surface if luck was much in evidence. There were not enough resources for the exercise of real power. As he observed to Hobhouse: 'The Empire of Great Britain, particularly in India, has been gained with power, apparently, very inadequate to the purpose, and if it is to be maintained at all, it must be maintained in the same manner by energy skill and enterprise: but not by overwhelming numbers.'[71]

Empire was such a doubtful proposition in his mind, that he advised Victoria not to offer royal patronage to colonial projects.[72] Overseas adventures gave rise to absurd heroics, and allowed small men to acquire large pretensions. They all saw themselves as 'Scipio Africanus'.[73] In principle, colonies could have a use in providing employment far from London for troublemakers like Durham, but any such advantage was short term. Durham and his like rapidly turned themselves into self-conscious satraps, ignoring London's wishes and starving the home government of information. Too often, official policy was determined by a necessity to rescue colonial administrators from the folly of their own actions. The nagging crisis in Canada, in 1838–9, which involved Cabinet resignations and the threat of war, was blamed on Durham almost entirely.[74] There was a certain amount of honour involved in holding on to imperial possessions, but not so much as to make it a priority.[75] As the American precedent suggested, independent states made just as good trading partners as colonies.

Melbourne's letters and speeches are significantly free of references to the topical concerns that informed the imperial debate. He had no interest in promoting emigration as an answer to Malthusian worries about population growth; he found the economic arguments for empire unconvincing; and, of course, he had no interest in missionary work or the moral dimension in colonial projects. Even the continuing struggle against slavery failed to move him very much. He delighted in teasing the high-minded on the subject. Archbishop Whately was subjected to the following raillery:

I say, Archbishop, what do you think I'd have done about this slavery business, if I'd had my own way? I'd have done nothing at all! I'd have left it all alone. It's all a pack of nonsense! Always have been slaves in all the most civilized countries; the Greeks and the Romans had slaves; however they *would* have their fancy, and so we've abolished slavery; but it's great folly.[76]

He told his sister-in-law that slavery was 'a matter of necessity'.[77] His undergraduate lecture notes contained the view that slavery would exist as long as it was profitable.[78] It would stop when free labour became cheaper.[79] In his opinion, 'Religion, Morality, Laws' counted for nothing, 'when opposed to profit cent for cent and more'.[80] He was hesitant about coercing foreign governments about the slave trade,[81] and saw it as no bar to the recognition of Texan independence.[82] Above all, the wish to abolish slavery was no argument to extend the boundaries of Empire. When Thomas Buxton sent Melbourne a book, arguing for the establishment of 'posts in the interior of Africa' to secure this end, the Prime Minister studiously refused to read it.[83]

Given this psychological distancing from the preoccupations of colonial lobbyists, Melbourne saw imperial issues as unnecessarily complicating the already difficult task of holding his government together. It was on a Jamaican issue that he suffered defeat in the Commons in 1839, and it was the extended crisis in Canada, from 1836 to 1840, which brought the resignations of Durham, Glenelg, and the Grey family. When British authority in Canada was challenged by the French in Quebec and by a refusal to pay taxation, Melbourne saw that something had to be done, but worried that he might be establishing an 'arbitrary' power in the colony.[84] Throughout the winter of 1837 and the spring of 1838, his letters to Victoria reported great Cabinet divisions on the Canadian issue, which he found difficult to control.[85] Howick accused him of never taking the issue seriously: 'You will excuse me saying that, in my opinion, you ought much sooner to have given your serious attention to the affairs of this colony . . . Let me entreat you to rouse yourself from your past inaction.'[86] Melbourne feared that there was a real possibility that the administration would be brought down on the issue.[87] In the event, the crisis was weathered, but, almost immediately, Durham's appointment to lead the Canadian administration produced two more years of turmoil, ending in damaging resignations.

Melbourne's own views on Canada were unsentimental. Durham's brief was to 'make a Constitution, but for God's sake make one that has a chance of lasting. All Colonial assemblies it appears to me are always resorting to the Extreme of their Power, and if they do this, they necessarily produce their own destruction. They pronounce sentence upon themselves—Affairs must go on, and if they cannot go on with the Assembly they necessarily proceed without them.'[88] As the crisis deepened, Melbourne's letters give the impression of a man shrugging his shoulders on paper. By 1839, the situation was thought nearly hopeless:

I have not much immediate apprehension, but how these provinces are to be settled with any thing like security, I do not see—The French population entirely hostile and ready to rise whenever called upon, the frontier thronged with refugees, the Americans always exciting and ready to assist rebellion, and the English population loyal according to their own fancy, and upon condition that they have their own way in every thing.[89]

He simply could not become emotionally or intellectually involved with the issue. Virtually all the parties were unreasonable. No settlement with any long-term prospects seemed possible. Little wonder that colonial enthusiasts and men of resolution within the Cabinet should protest about a Prime Minister who seemed to react to colonial problems with an extended yawn.

By 1839, contemporaries were not unreasonably speculating about the end of Melbourne's tenure of office. The withdrawal of Radical votes led to defeats in the Commons; the loss of the Grey family over the Canada crisis weakened any Whig credentials the government might have; above all, the Prime Minister was publicly isolated on the great issues of the ballot and the Corn Laws. Cumulatively, he seemed no longer capable of sustaining the juggling act that had kept the Ministry in being. Just as it appeared profitable to argue about the date on which a government with Tory values was re-established after 1834, so it was possible to suggest that Melbourne had lost power long before the official demise of his administration in the autumn of 1841. For perhaps two years before that, Melbourne held power without exercising it. If evidence were wanting for this view, observers need only point to the Eastern Crisis of the summer of 1840. Because Melbourne could no longer hold the ring between warring Ministers, and because the Cabinet had largely lost whatever sense of common purpose it had ever had, the country only narrowly escaped a major war with France, for which it was neither militarily nor financially prepared. The history of the crisis dramatically underlines the extent to which Melbourne's grasp on events had slipped. Again, everyone talked of resigning. Foreign ambassadors dealt directly with individual Ministers. Each player in the game took initiatives except Melbourne. It was a shambles.

In essence, the problem was a simple one. For much of the 1830s, England and France had worked profitably in alliance. Now, the French patronage of Mehemet Ali's attempts to detach Egypt and Syria from the Turkish Empire, thereby threatening major British interests, seemed to betoken a dramatic change of front. The question was therefore to gauge the extent to which France had decided to cut loose from alliance obligations, in search of a new hegemony in Europe, and to frame an appropriate response. Mehemet Ali's adventurism was bound to be potentially dangerous. The fact, however, that it nearly led Britain into war was a measure of Melbourne's inability any longer to give the government coherence.

In theory, the problem should have been easily contained. The background could hardly have been more propitious. In 1830, Grey's assumption of power had been complemented by a revolution in France that established the Orleanist régime of Louis Philippe. Foxites had for two generations regarded the Orléans family as holding similar values to themselves. Generously, they were dubbed 'French Whigs'. In alliance, between 1830 and 1834, England

and France had guaranteed liberal victories in conflicts in Belgium, Spain, and Portugal. The spectacle of Anglo-French co-operation contrasted pleasantly with Melbourne's memories of the Napoleonic years, when a profound rivalry between the two powers had harmed liberal and constitutional prospects all over Europe. With these reflections in mind, 'he did not think it unnatural to congratulate the world . . . that an earnest had been received for the continuance of peace and union between this country and France'.[90] Even after experiencing the traumas of the 1840 crisis, he still maintained that 'the best security for general Peace is a close alliance and perfect good understanding between England and France', though admitting that it might be 'difficult, Lord Melbourne had almost said impossible to maintain'.[91] The alternative of a Franco-Russian alliance, of the sort that had operated for much of the 1820s, offered little hope for constitutionalists.[92] All things being equal, Melbourne retained enough of his youthful, Whig prejudices to prefer a Europe of parliaments to a Europe of despots.

Given these prejudices, Louis Philippe's ambassadors in London found it a comfortable berth. Melbourne was amused by Talleyrand, whom he had met in Paris on his first visit, working closely with him in the exchanging of intelligence about the movements of Radicals and agitators.[93] His successor, François Sébastiani, reported home that 'les affaires étoient faciles avec les Torys; elles deviendront agréables avec les Wighs',[94] and that 'l'alliance entre la France et l'Angleterre assure le pays du monde. L'ébranler, l'affaiblir, c'est tout mettre en question.'[95] A matter of months before the 1840 crisis developed, a new ambassador, François Guizot, the anglophile biographer of Cromwell, described his situation in the most glowing terms:

J'ai trouvé Lord Melbourne plein de bienveillance pour la France et très persuadé que l'intime alliance de deux pays leur importe également à l'un et l'autre, soit pour leurs intérêts essentiels, soit comme gage de la paix de l'Europe, leur premier intérêt commun. Il s'est expliqué à ce sujet avec ce mélange de laisser-aller et de gravité, d'insouciance et d'autorité qui indique une conviction libre et personnelle plutôt qu'une intention préméditée, et qui donne ailleurs à la conversation et aux manières de Lord Melbourne un agrément particulier.[96]

Whiggery and Orleanism had protected and esteemed each other since the 1780s, and this long association made for comfortable diplomacy.

All this was reinforced by Melbourne's liking for France and the French. He never shared the rampant, and often uncritical, francophilia of the Hollands or, to a lesser extent, Russell. Unlike them, he had never made a Grand Tour as a young man, and he had only visited France twice, in 1815 and 1825. On both occasions, the journey was undertaken to escape the vicissitudes of marriage rather than to enjoy France.[97] Nevertheless, he hailed Paris as 'the Capital of Pleasures, you should spend four thousand pounds, it is not social not to'.[98] To Victoria, he admitted that, in all the things that mattered in life, 'the French are the first nation in the world; we ought to be eternally grateful to them'.[99] Melbourne took pleasure in the affectation that he spoke French badly, claiming that he could never remember the words for the days of the week, and that hesitant attempts to express himself left him feeling 'quite in prison and in chains'. It was, he thought, 'such a tight language'.[100] In fact, Victoria noted more than once that her Prime Minister could speak the language 'very well'. Indeed, when he returned from Paris in 1815, the Duke of Devonshire remarked that 'Lamb is as French as possible and speaks English with an idiom'.[101] Melbourne was less travelled than many others who had enjoyed a Whiggish upbringing, but, like them, he had a preference for France.

In the particular circumstances of the 1830s, prejudice was reinforced by friendship. Louis Philippe's daughter, Louise, married to Victoria's uncle, Leopold, King of the Belgians, recalled that Melbourne and the whole Lamb family had 'always been *most kind* to me and to all mine'.[102] As exiles in England, the Orléans family had dined at Brocket many times.[103] Melbourne claimed to have known one son of Louis Philippe, the Comte de Beaujolais, 'very well', and the other, the Duc de Montpensier, a little.[104] He had dined with Louis Philippe in Paris in 1815, when the future king had referred to him as one of 'his particular friends'.[105] Very reasonably, on forming his first administration, Melbourne asked the English ambassador in Paris to assure the French king that he retained 'a lively recollection of the kindness with which His Majesty had invariably honoured me and others of my family'.[106] French-speaking élites in Europe shared values that crossed national frontiers. Melbourne talked more easily with an Orleanist than with an English Radical. Understandably therefore, when the crisis of 1840 had passed, Melbourne concluded that, 'There has been something ridiculous in this from the beginning.'[107]

In the Prime Minister's view, there was every reason to think that war would be an absurdity. His Navy Minister told him frankly that there were simply too few ships. If a fleet were dispatched to the Levant, the Channel could only be defended by converting steamers and packet boats into improvised warships.[108] Militarily, Melbourne feared that the country was about to 'suffer disasters'.[109] At the same time, he was being bullied by Prince Albert with the thought that a war would dangerously upset Victoria, then in the middle of her first pregnancy.[110] Most important of all, he could understand that a great power like France would seek an influence beyond her borders, and that she was bound to chafe under the restrictions that had been placed on her ambitions by nearly every treaty since 1815. For too long, the French had been invited to watch 'important affairs undertaken to be settled without their concurrence'.[111] Just as the British would resent being told by the international community that movement into Asia would not be tolerated, so the French responded badly to the same reaction to their attempts to penetrate Africa. Properly ensconced in Algeria, it was understandable that the French should take an interest in Egypt.[112] As a result, 'Palmerston's meddling' in the politics of the Middle East often meant that Melbourne 'could not sleep of nights for thinking on these matters'.[113]

Melbourne was prepared to admit that 'the Main-Spring' of much of French policy was a jealousy of English commercial success,[114] and that 'the establishment and consolidation of a strong, active and aggressive Mussulman Power in Egypt is decidedly against us',[115] but he was not convinced that the disadvantage of such a development was worth a war. If Mehemet Ali secured control of Egypt it 'will do'.[116] Even if he extended his régime into Palestine and Syria, it was understandable, if unfortunate.[117] To Palmerston, all this amounted to irresponsible defeatism, but there was a logic in Melbourne's thinking that went beyond military concerns or worries about Victoria's health. Quite simply, to fight France was to depend upon an Austrian alliance, and, in spite of his brother's ambassadorial reports from Vienna, Melbourne was clear that Austria, like Russia, was fundamentally illiberal:

She fears all revolutionary Governments and she considers ours as the most revolutionary Government in Europe. She may perhaps not fear us so much as she does France, because danger from us is neither so possible nor so immediate, but depend upon it she hates us more than she does France.[118]

Metternich was not to be trusted.[119] In his heart, Melbourne subscribed to the Foxite orthodoxy being peddled at Holland House. Post-1815 Europe was divided between parliamentarians and autocrats. France was endlessly tiresome, but, in Manichean terms, was on the side of the angels. Austria and Russia never would be.

This diagnosis was freely reported to the French ambassador. Sébastiani reported home, in January 1840, that

J'ai eu une longue conversation aujourdhui . . . avec Lord Melbourne: il est tout à fait partisan de l'alliance avec notre Roi; il me répétoit souvent, 'indiquez moi un moyen de rapprochement des propositions anglaises et françaises' . . . il juge comme nous les intentions de la Russie, et il m'a dit en parlant du Cabinet de Vienna, 'on ne peut pas y compter car il finit toujours par être le partisan le plus dévoué de la Russie.[120]

For all these reasons, Melbourne spent the crisis urging Palmerston, over and over again, to seek an accommodation with Paris. In doing so, there would be neither 'humiliation nor a disadvantage'.[121] He told the new French ambassador, Guizot: 'il est clair qu'en Orient nous sommes voués vous et nous aux mêmes craintes, aux mêmes désirs, aux mêmes desseins.'[122] At no time during the crisis could the French government have been in much doubt that Melbourne's personal preferences were firmly for that Anglo-French understanding that had proved so profitable for much of the 1830s.

In Melbourne's view, the crisis had little to do with the complexities of the Middle East. Difficult though they were, they were susceptible to resolution. Rather, the problem lay in Paris with the coming to power of Adolphe Thiers. He was a man Melbourne had learnt 'to dread'.[123] He was thought unstable rather than malevolent, but the result was that, 'one never knows what he will do next'.[124] Endlessly taunted by a jingoistic press that accused him of bowing before 'cette aristocratic impitoyable' which governed England, Thiers, to prove his patriotic credentials, might rush headlong into bellicose language.[125] Melbourne, as has been noted, detested the growing power of journalists, and was impressed by it. He asked Palmerston to beg the *Morning Chronicle* to stop printing personal attacks on Louis Philippe.[126] Nothing should be done to unbalance Thiers further. In blaming Thiers for provoking an unnecessary crisis, Melbourne was backed up by successive French ambassadors in London. Sébastiani lamented to the French king's sister that, 'La politique du Roi et ses intérêts sont donc livrés à la capricieuse volonté de Monsieur Thiers et de ses journaux: la guerre est desormais à peu près inévitable . . . le système fondé avec tant de peine et maintenu pendant dix ans avec tant de difficultés vient de s'écrouler aux cris les plus insensés.'[127] His successor, Guizot, agreed.[128] It seemed to Melbourne that Louis Philippe had been overwhelmed by popular views that were not his own: 'The King has let his ministers slip through his fingers.'[129] Melbourne reported him 'apologizing for the Vivacity of Thiers and saying that allowance must be made for him as an Author and Journalist and therefore accustomed to putting things strongly'.[130]

In Melbourne's opinion, therefore, the crisis was to be resolved, not by war or by Palmerston's intricate diplomacy, but by helping the French king to re-establish his authority over Thiers and the French press. Louis Philippe had fought for the French Republic in 1792. He would not abandon the English alliance and liberalism because, 'he has a great deal of Jemappes left about him still'.[131] In the last resort, Thiers would be brought to heel.[132] Melbourne was not surprised, therefore, in October 1840, when Guizot left London with the 'design of supplanting Thiers'.[133] When this *coup* was achieved, the crisis was immediately over. Reflecting on this, one of Melbourne's colleagues observed that, 'Some Dynasty and some Govt there must be in France, and none will suit us so well as L. Philippe's and the Govt of Guizot.'[134] The crisis had started in Paris and it ended there. It had less to do with Mehemet Ali than with Adolphe Thiers.

If all these factors were in place, why then was there a real possibility of war in the summer months of 1840. Louis Philippe had no wish for one and nor did his ambassadors in London. One French politician had to be reined in, a difficult task but one that was eventually accomplished. Above all, Melbourne himself was clear that the French alliance remained of value, and that any suggestion of war would therefore be 'ridiculous'. The fact that a major crisis erupted can only be explained in terms of the weakness and fragility of Melbourne's government. It had so lost all sense of cohesion that any difficulty could quickly escalate into a profound problem. Melbourne absolutely failed to control the situation. Individual Ministers like Palmerston and Holland either took initiatives without consulting their colleagues or in defiance of them. Resignation threats filled the air. The Prime Minister, in spite of having clear views on the question in hand, could not, or would not, impose his authority. In sum, the Eastern question of 1840 exposed a government that had lost the will to govern.

One symptom of this malaise was that the anti-French party in the Cabinet saw Melbourne as their enemy, and so did the pro-French party. The ambiguity and indecisiveness in Melbourne's position could hardly be better stated. According to Sydney Smith and other francophiles, 'Melbourne gives up all foreign affairs to Palmerston swearing at it all. Lord Grey would never have suffered any Minister for Foreign Affairs to have sent such a despatch as Palmerston's note to Guizot . . . Pray don't go to war with France; that *must* be wrong.'[135] Similarly, Russell, whom Guizot frequently identified as the strong man in the government, begged Melbourne to rectify a situation in which Palmerston enjoyed 'the entire want of control or contradiction', brutally adding that 'for that you are more to blame than he is'.[136] The denizens of Holland House lectured Melbourne on how to handle Louis Philippe, and on how to preserve the French alliance.[137] Frequently, they convinced themselves that they had won over Melbourne to their views, and always they found themselves half-deceived. Urged to silence with assurances that all would be as they wished, francophiles then saw Melbourne failing to check Palmerston's strides towards war.[138] Friends of the Anglo-French alliance in London and Paris saw Palmerston as out of control.[139] Melbourne complained to the Queen about him,[140] even remonstrated with him in a tepid way,[141] but was widely seen as unable to control his brother-in-law. Palmerston's Foreign Office was visibly even more a law unto itself than it had ever been.

At the same time, Palmerston was convinced that Melbourne was completely in the pocket of the Holland House set, with whom he dined regularly. The Foreign Secretary officially complained about Holland's habit of using dinner parties to run lines of foreign policy that differed from his own:

I think that when a Cabinet *has* agreed to a system of measures they ought to give that system fair play, and not to raise impediments to its execution in the detail of the measures by which it is to be effected, and that individual members of the Cabinet ought not, as Lord Holland does every day of the week, to speak openly to all who come near them about the policy and measures which the Cabinet of which they are members is embarked in, just as a member of Opposition would speak of the policy of an administration which he was labouring to turn out.[142]

He accused the Hollands of indulging in an 'underhand intrigue', and berated Melbourne for doing nothing to stop it.[143] Emily Lamb, now Lady Palmerston, added her voice to the chorus of discontent, accusing her brother of 'shilly shally', and of failure to support her husband. When fortuitously dining at Holland House herself, she disrupted the whole evening by denouncing 'the Cabal going on there'.[144] It was grimly obvious that the Cabinet was at war with itself.

Both sides were fully prepared to promote their own views with threats of resignation. In July 1840, both Holland and Clarendon offered to resign in protest at 'the infatuation of Lord Palmerston's views'.[145] At the same time, Palmerston tried to take the same course, complaining of neglect and lack of status.[146] In September, it was Russell's turn to belabour the Prime Minister with letters of resignation, in which all the government's troubles were attributed to the fact that 'one member of the Cabinet [Palmerston] is to conduct matters simply as he pleases'.[147] Any one of these threats, if actually carried into practice, could have destroyed the government. Little wonder that Melbourne held Cabinets as infrequently as possible. When they were held, majority decisions were always accompanied by formal memoranda from the dissenting minority.[148] Francophile and francophobe felt that the direction of policy was in the hands of the other. The Prime Minister, suspected by both sides, was thought to be led by the nose by either Palmerston or Holland. His own views seemed to have little bearing on the situation. Quite where authority lay within the government was no longer obvious.

The defence of Melbourne's behaviour would lie in the claim that, in this crisis as in all previous ones, he had to play the role of umpire or referee. His personal views had to be subordinated to the larger task of keeping the government in being. Russell only communicated with Palmerston through Melbourne and vice versa. He became a kind of entrepot, or staging-post, for their views. He toned down phrases, and tried to explain the one to the other. In the event, no one did resign, and the government survived. This in itself was an achievement of sorts, but the price paid for this had been high. Sébastiani noted that 'dans une question étrangère il n'ose pas mettre son veto'.[149] Melbourne literally did not dare to hold a Cabinet on the subject, because 'It'll make a great row if we have one.'[150] When he was forced to call one, on 27 September, the Prime Minister took refuge in sleep, and 'would not take the lead or say a word'.[151] Summoning it at all had left him 'at his wit's end'.[152] No agreed position was reached at these rare meetings, and, as Guizot reported, 'ces petits incidens (sic) vous peignent l'état intérieur du Cabinet, état plein d'embarras et d'hesitation'.[153] The Polish patriot, Czartoryski, dismissed English policy as 'paralysé'.[154] Just as Melbourne avoided Cabinets, so he gave thanks that the crisis had come on during the parliamentary recess. He had no wish for Cabinet divisions to be played out in yet another forum. Only one speech was made on the crisis, and that of such an anodyne character that no one was much the wiser about Melbourne's own views.[155]

With government having no collective voice, individuals felt free to act. Everyone seemed to be taking diplomatic initiatives except Melbourne. Palmerston fired off memoranda, sometimes with, often without, the approbation of his colleagues. Guizot busied himself with projects in both Paris and London.[156] In these, he was aided and abetted by the Hollands, who were happy to pass on government secrets after dinner.[157] Russell was so full of energy and ideas, that ambassadors identified him as 'le premier homme du cabinet'.[158] Melbourne only survived because 'il avait lord john pour appui'.[159] Even the King of the Belgians, related to both Victoria and Louis Philippe, intervened effectively in favour of peace,[160] and so, too, did the Duke of Wellington. The only one not to be writing memoranda, making speeches, threatening resignation, was Melbourne. Instead, he swayed unsteadily at the centre of things, bowing to strong winds from whichever direction they came. Government by departments, with a Prime Minister adjudicating in disputes, had collapsed. There was no government line in the 1840 crisis, and many thought that, thereafter, Melbourne's hold on power was purely nominal.

Officially, Melbourne's administration came to an end because he lost an election in June 1841 and resigned in the following August. In fact, its demise was not so quick or so clean. For some years, cancerous problems had slowly eaten into the government's coherence. It was difficult for a collective view to be formed on issues left over from the Grey government. It was impossible to agree a united front on new issues like the Corn Laws and the ballot. Too often, the Prime Minister found himself holding views on which he was singular. By 1840, Melbourne had lost control of Russell and Palmerston. They never resigned, like Howick and Durham, but they achieved the same freedom of action by simply acting on their own initiative. Melbourne's ability to work with all men on most issues was an invaluable talent in 1834–5. It was less prized five or six years later, when sharply focused issues demanded clear responses. The Prime Minister's agnosticism on virtually everything was no longer to be regarded. With colleagues such as these, Melbourne scarcely had need of political opponents. Tory and Radical could disturb his sleep. Irishmen could add to the cacophony. None of these, however, could ultimately threaten him. Melbourne's government was killed from within. The electorate, in 1841, merely confirmed that it had been dead for some time.

PART III

Women and Private Life, 1828–1841

To understand fully Melbourne's performance as Home Secretary and Prime Minister it is vital to keep in mind the vicissitudes of his private life, for they informed everything he did. His marriage had left terrible scars. He had survived the experience by cauterizing his feelings. Avoiding emotional or intellectual commitment of any sort became his preferred option. He was horribly afraid of taking anything or anyone too seriously, lest such involvement should lead to the experiences of his marriage being repeated. An armour of amused and philosophical detachment was his everyday wear. It is just possible that the young Victoria unconsciously breached his emotional defences. Some contemporaries suspected that he was genuinely fond of her. If this was so, she enjoyed something of a monopoly. After his wife's death, in January 1828, Melbourne was alone. He had friends, houses in which to dine, and a family that worried and fretted about him as they had always done, but these advantages left him increasingly unsatisfied. He looked for diversion rather than commitment, and this was as true in politics as in private life. Losing office left him with time hanging heavily on his hands. When amusements palled, an increasing sourness took over, with letters being written that unreasonably complained of neglect and depression. In a profound sense, the shadows cast over his life by an extraordinary marriage never lifted. Caroline Lamb's death in no sense permitted a freeing of his emotions.

Melbourne had always enjoyed the company of women, and continued to do so after 1828. It was not, however, the physical side of such relationships that was of great importance. Unlike his father, brothers, and virtually every other Whig male, Melbourne seemingly took no mistresses before 1828, apart from the incident in 1802 which he recorded in his draft autobiography. This was abstinence on an almost heroic scale. Even after 1828, he denied that his relationships with Lady Branden and Mrs Norton had ever been physically consummated, even though the world at large thought otherwise. In the case of Mrs Norton, it is quite possible that he was telling the truth. Rather, he liked the company of women who amused him and talked intelligently.

Emotional responses were cold or non-existent. Not surprisingly, women frequently accused Melbourne of being selfish, even despotic in his behaviour. His reply to such charges is enlightening: 'Why when people interfere with one's self and one's own interest is at stake it is time to act a little decisively and the doing so is no violation of the philosophical liberty which I practise and advocate.'[1] He was always self-regarding, always defensive. After 1828, his emotional life followed an almost predictable pattern.

First and foremost, his private life was not to be regulated by the codes which the generality followed. Moral values were for him to discover, and not for society to impose. In this thinking, he was a Lamb and a Whig. He could be shocked by the news that Palmerston had raped a woman, claiming that 'he had *never* attempted any woman against her will',[2] but it was no reason to sever connections with a political colleague or veto him as a prospective brother-in-law. Similarly, if a man had conducted an *affaire* with his wife's sister, this was probably 'bad', but it was no bar to his being given public office.[3] Predictably, throughout his ministerial career, Melbourne's private life was a matter of enormous interest and conjecture, and his reputation was not high. Cabinet Ministers discussed his 'profligacy' and his 'amours' while out riding in the Park.[4] In October 1833, a story that the Home Secretary had absconded to Europe with someone else's wife won immediate credence because it was 'thought Ld M might bear a little more immorality'.[5] Members of his household remembered that their employer preferred women who were a little 'wild',[6] and Melbourne himself openly lectured early Victorian society in words that more properly fitted the 1780s and 1790s. To his former secretary, George Anson, he complained: 'that Women after having lived a very vicious and wicked life, and then turning good, invariably turn stupid at the same time—he thought there was some truth in the remark that very good people were always very dull and stupid.'[7]

Secondly, Melbourne sought the company of women of determined, even masculine character. He had noted this quality with approval in both his mother and his sister, and had not resented their attempts to regulate his life.[8] Similarly, Byron observed that Melbourne's wife was not feminine,[9] sometimes referring to her as Carolus rather than Caroline. The same trait would be noted in Mrs Norton. Lord Malmesbury found her 'very agreeable and amusing, but her beauty, her manners and her conversation are all of the most masculine character—and the latter is often coarser than even a man should be'.[10] An American visitor agreed: 'Her conversation is so pleasant and powerful without being masculine; or rather it is masculine without being mannish, there is the grace and ease of the woman.'[11] Almost certainly Melbourne was attracted to women of forthright and outgoing character because they represented no risk of becoming dependent upon him. The burden of coping with Caroline Lamb for so long had exhausted his capacity to accept the emotional dependence of others.

In particular, no relationship should be bothersome or lead to scandal. Having suffered public obloquy for so long as the husband of Caroline Lamb, he had no stomach left for further public scrutiny. He had developed the lowest possible view of the willingness of society to turn on the wounded, and to identify and persecute victims. As Victoria noted in her diary, in January 1839: 'Talked of dogs, and Lord Alfred said, Hounds had been known to eat one another; and that if one dog, or deer, was hurt, all the others of its own kind would come and attack it; "that's very much the same with mankind", said Lord M., "if anyone gets into a scrape; and with *women*".'[12] He was no longer sure that an individual, even one protected by the walls of Whig exclusiveness, could stand up to sustained attacks of this kind. He told Howick, 'In general persons sit down sadly under any thing like disgrace, or descend from bad to worse in utter recklessness and despair. A disposition to emerge and to struggle upwards again is amongst the rarest and most unusual.'[13] Scandal and the threat of scandal made him physically ill.[14] Mrs Norton reflected, 'I suppose it is in human—at least in man's—nature always to resent being in this sort of scrape.'[15]

When trouble came, women could expect little sympathy or understanding. Melbourne would advise them to go back to their husbands, to accept the loss of their children, to hide, or to go abroad. So cold was his behaviour that Victoria would accuse him of being 'inconsistent, despising and abusing women, and yet always making too much of them'.[16] He was '*always* abusing the ladies and yet always running after them'.[17] His brother, Frederick, thought this judgement too harsh, preferring to think that, in his relations with women, 'Wm is rather like Mr. Weller senior'.[18] Like that venerable Dickensian character, one brush with womankind had been a searing experience, which had produced nothing but caution and distrust. Melbourne wanted and liked the company of women, but only on his terms. They were to amuse him and to provide diversion. They were a hedge against loneliness. He had no responsibility for them in either an emotional or moral sense, because he was no longer capable of that. On one occasion, Melbourne described a certain peer as 'a very strong and a very moral man, whose wife has now been dead near a year. I cannot conceive a more dangerous customer.'[19] If the word moral were removed from this assessment, Melbourne was effectively describing himself.

Lastly, the most sinister aspect of Melbourne's insistence that his conduct should not be governed by the general rules of morality was a long-standing interest in flagellation. In his autobiography, he recorded his memories of beatings at Eton. He had been a member of Dr Langford's House, who was known as 'a rigid disciplinarian'.[20] In his first week in the school, he watched a beating, and felt 'the certainty and rigour of a discipline so different from any thing, which I had ever witnessed'. It filled him 'with the greatest awe and alarm'.[21] He himself escaped with 'no more than three sound floggings which I recollect, were judiciously timed and of no inconsiderable service'.[22] The topic was rehearsed in conversations with Victoria. When the Queen observed that beating schoolboys was 'degrading', Melbourne disagreed, arguing that his experiences at Eton 'had always an amazing effect on him', and that his tutor had not 'flogged me enough, it would have been better if he had flogged me more'.[23] Mrs Norton also disliked the idea of using violence in the upbringing of children, but she was happy to indulge Melbourne's predilections.[24] Writing from Rome in 1839, she observed: 'I saw in a shop of curiosities and pictures the other day, a small black cabinet inlaid with ivory etchings, of birds, and in the centre (to my astonishment) your favourite subject of a woman whipping a child, (or a nymph whipping bacchus, or some such thing) . . . I had half a mind to buy it for you.'[25]

Flagellation was not only argued for as a pedagogical device, however. Women, too, should be beaten. Jokingly, the point was made over dinner at Windsor. In February 1838, Victoria recorded in a diary a conversation about a French woman, 'who was separated from her husband and excited pity as he was known or supposed to have beat her. Upon this, Lord Melbourne said, "Why it is almost worthwhile for a woman to be beat, considering the exceeding pity she excites", which made us laugh.'[26] The matter went beyond humour, however. Mistresses would be regaled with cuttings and pictures on the subject of children or women being beaten, and their comments invited. Caroline Lamb, during the bitter proceedings surrounding the 1825 separation, accused her husband of having beaten her. This assertion can be neither proved or disproved, but other evidence makes the claim plausible. Susan Churchill was one of the children curiously 'adopted' by the Lambs in a manner that became a feature of the marriage.[27] Gratefully, she named her own children William and Caroline, but, in letters to Melbourne she both remembers beatings, and assures him that her own children are being treated in the same manner:

A propos of children I have not forgotten your *practical lessons* upon whipping and follow up the system with great success upon Caroline at least, for William is too young, don't you think so? He is only 10 months. I remember as though it was yesterday the *execution*, then being thrown into a corner of a large couch there was at Brocket you used then to leave the room and I remember your coming back one day and saying 'well cocky does it smart still?' at which of course I could not help laughing instead of crying . . . Does the Queen whip the royal princess I should like to know.[28]

It is impossible to know how far sexual fantasy was enacted, but Melbourne's keen interest in flagellation is a fact that cannot be discounted in any discussion of his emotional responses. It forms part of a recurring pattern.

Melbourne met Elizabeth Branden shortly after arriving in Dublin in 1827, a matter of months before the death of his wife.[29] It was his only extra-marital liaison, and this is itself of interest given the values of the society in which he moved. Lady Branden came from an old Irish family named Latouche, and, in 1815, had married a cousin who laboured under the combined disadvantages of gout, debt, and advanced years. Her relationship with Melbourne developed rapidly and passionately:

I love you as much as ever . . . I never recollect my passions so strong as they are at present. I am generally in a state of great excitement and instability and I feel I want something to subdue me . . . and seeing you so little as I have done and being so near you, and from indifference and coldness which I can never be certain is not assumed (and this very idea . . . excites me more still if possible) drives me almost to madness.[30]

Using his position in the Irish administration, Melbourne was happy to promote Lady Branden's relations, not least her complaisant, clergyman husband. He was offered prosperous livings, and was rumoured to be expecting a bishopric.[31] Accommodating husbands hoping for preferment become standard characters in the dramas of Melbourne's personal life. Vindictive husbands denied their expectations are just as usual. In May 1828, Lord Branden initiated an action for damages against Melbourne for what was then known as criminal conversation with his wife. Intriguingly, Melbourne's future friend and executor, Henry Brougham, agreed to act as Branden's Counsel.[32] It was widely known that the action had been brought only after attempts to blackmail Melbourne into elevating Branden to a bishopric had failed.[33]

The case was dismissed at a preliminary stage because crucial witnesses failed to appear in court. In this respect, Melbourne escaped embarrassment with only a few ruffled feathers, but the experience had shaken him badly. His reaction to it is instructive because it sets a pattern for his relationships with women that would be often repeated. He had been initially attracted by Lady Branden's vivacious and amusing personality, and, when challenged, briefly breathed defiance at a suddenly outraged husband, collecting information about possible witnesses and briefing lawyers. He told Lady Branden: 'If Lord B. proceeds as I suppose he will, I am determined to defend myself by all the means in my power and I expect your assistance and cooperation . . . Pray send me the names both Christian and the sur-name, of the Footman, the Page and the two Maids.'[34] The idea that his private life should become a matter for legal, and then public, scrutiny, was taken as an impertinence. The only proper response was vigorous resistance.

This kind of bluster, however, quickly evaporated. Melbourne's instinct was to distance himself as much as possible from any unpleasantness, handing the conduct of the business over to go-betweens. It was as though he were avoiding an unfortunate smell. In this instance the agent employed was the same Michael Bruce who had been Lady Caroline's reputed lover in Paris in 1815. Behind the public show of injured innocence, Melbourne was only too happy to buy Branden's silence, and was relieved when Bruce reported that this had been done:

Our friend Lord B. has had a fit of delicacy which in him was truly ridiculous. He did not wish the money to be paid to him, or to affix his signature to any receipt. This is straining at gnats after swallowing a camel. To obviate all difficulties I went myself to Snow's Bank and presented your draft and got from them two one thousand pounds (sic) notes, which I have this instant paid into Farquhar's Bank.[35]

Two thousand pounds was a not inconsiderable sum, but it was not the end of the matter. In December 1831, Branden, through Bruce, was again demanding money, complaining of the heavy wrongs that had been heaped upon him.[36] In his will, Branden left only one shilling to his 'très infame et vicieuse épouse dont l'infidelité à mon regard est le moindre des crimes'.[37] He also enjoined his daughter never to marry any man unless 'firmiment résolu de l'aimer, de l'honorer, et de le soigner'.[38]

If Melbourne preferred to shun any contact with difficult husbands, the same tactic was employed with the women, who, as he saw it, had brought him into such disagreeable situations. He was happy to admit to Lady Branden that their months together had been 'the last sun-shine, which would gleam upon my life',[39] but, as soon as the scandal broke, he insisted that they should no longer meet: 'Your letters give me great pain and do me great injustice. I have never deceived or misled you . . . you are wrong in supposing that it is on my own account that I wished you to go to France . . . Now can you also suppose that I am not anxious to see you, but you must feel how impossible it is, that I should do so at the present moment.'[40] Lady Branden was advised to go back to her husband if it would avoid trouble.[41] She was not to offer her husband any excuse for vexation by putting him 'to extraordinary expense, nor to any expense that you can help. Nothing annoys a Man so much.'[42] She was not to send Melbourne violets. Most severe of all was Melbourne's insistence that his mistress should not take any measures to secure the custody of her daughter, Lily, or even to see her:

I am a good deal annoyed . . . I tell you, that I wish you to take no steps at present for seeing your child, and you tell me that you are employed in nothing but in concerting measures for that purpose . . . You have already most unnecessarily and by imprudence raised appearances both against yourself and me.[43]

There was nothing of comfort in the code of practice that Melbourne recommended.

Distancing himself from irritation led Melbourne to prefer physical separation from the human embodiments of embarrassment. Lady Branden went into hiding, using such pseudonyms as 'Mrs Beauchamp' and 'Mrs St John'. In April 1829, Melbourne wrote to say that she might 'now find Dieppe very agreeable'.[44] By July of the same year, Elizabeth Branden was established in Paris, and no longer a source of speculation or much interest. As far as Melbourne was concerned, the incident had been closed without unduly damaging his social or political expectations. Throughout the troubled months of 1828 and 1829, he had generously supplied Lady Branden with money, but had offered no other kind of consolation.[45] Indeed, he went out of his way to make the point that there could be nothing more:

I thought I had already spoken to you distinctly and decisively. The contents and tone of your letter compel me to do so again. I will be your friend, your sincere friend, as long as either of us live, but, come what may, I will not form a permanent connection with you. I have at present no intention of ever marrying again.[46]

Not surprisingly, the Latouche family thought that Melbourne had fallen someway below chivalric standards of behaviour. Lady Branden's sister thought 'it quite inhuman of Ld M. to consider himself *so much* and *you so little*, at least such his conduct *appears to me*'.[47] The criticism is well founded. Melbourne regarded an emotional crisis as an unlooked-for irritation for which he personally bore little or no responsibility. His response was to sever personal contact with all those who were involved in the disagreeable turn of events, and to buy his way out of them. Women could expect financial assistance, but not emotional support or assurance. Almost certainly, his experience of marriage had made it impossible for him to act on any other terms.

There is no record of Melbourne and Lady Branden meeting again after her departure for France and Switzerland. However, she was paid an annuity by Melbourne, first through the banker Charles de Constant, and, after his death, through the Banque Lafitte.[48] At a distance, he was now prepared to assist her in the protracted battle for the custody of her daughter Lily, which ended successfully.[49] In return, Lady Branden was happy to act as guardian to the orphan girl, Susan Churchill, when Melbourne dispatched her to Switzerland in search of a husband.[50] If this arrangement was a slightly odd tying-up of loose ends in Melbourne's private life, stranger still was the ongoing correspondence on the subject of flagellation. Until at least December 1832, letters continue to pass between Lady Branden and her former lover, in which this is the principle subject under discussion. Early in their friendship, he had suggested that Lily should be regularly beaten,[51] and their common interest in this matter was not apparently diminished by their separating to minimize scandal. In August 1830, Melbourne wrote to admit that, in regarding a particular woman, 'I never think of her without wishing . . . that I had the power to order her a brisk application of birch upon that large and extensive field of derrière, which is so well calculated to receive it.'[52] Lady Branden's comments were invited, in 1830, on coloured drawings showing the beating of children, or on illustrations cut out of a piece of French erotica called *Les Dames Galantes*.[53]

The Branden scandal, which dogged Melbourne's career just at the moment when he was about to obtain high office as Home Secretary, very much set a pattern for the future. Elizabeth Branden was a woman of spirit and intellect, married to an unsuccessful husband, who seemed happy to trade his wife's favours for preferment in his career. In short, the lady seemed to offer Melbourne diversion without complication. When difficulties arose, in spite of these promising beginnings, Melbourne turned away. Never emotionally involved, he had no further use for an amusement that had gone sour. Money would be offered, but nothing more. Throughout his life, unpleasantness had been something to avoid rather than confront. The sordid character of his marriage had virtually sent him into hiding. Now, free of that encumbrance, he sent others into exile. His conduct was selfish, even pitiless, but it was governed by rules that he had devised in circumstances of extreme, emotional adversity.

Once it became clear that the Branden escapade had come near to public scandal, the Lamb family once again thought themselves justified in directing William's life. His need for a single source of emotional support, a *maîtresse en titre*, was recognized, and suitable candidates were paraded before him. Emily Lamb hoped that he would marry Olivia de Roos, others Emily Boyle.[54] Both were intelligent and high-spirited, but neither succeeded in capturing Melbourne's attention. A more likely possibility was Emily Eden, the sister of Lord Minto, who became a confidante and companion from 1832 to 1835. Intellectual by nature, she also had wit and a spiritedly insouciant view of politics, all qualities that Melbourne admired:

I write . . . to beg you will not let my politics affect you. They are full of sound and fury, signifying nothing. The only way in which politics ever amused me was by taking them in a regular female . . . unjust prejudiced way and then they delight me— but I am quite aware I am unjust all the time—and I take it it makes politics the safety valve for all my prejudices . . . it cannot signify a straw what I say about public affairs.[55]

Once again, there was a masculine strain in women who Melbourne admired. Emily Eden aspired to be 'an active revolutionary agent', and to stand her trial 'like a hero'.[56] She was introduced to Melbourne in January 1832, once again through the agency of Emily Lamb.[57] They remained friends for three years.

In 1835, however, Emily Eden agreed to go out to India to act as hostess for a bachelor brother, who was taking up an official position in the sub-continent. For her, parting from Melbourne was painful:

I almost once thought of asking you to come and bid us Goodbye this evg. but I had rather you should not. There is no use in it, and I am unhappy enough as it is. You said you would give me some little book which you have read and marked. I do not care what it is. Only let your name be written in it. And if you ever would write to me, you would be doing an act of great kindness. For so many years I have been used to listen to your confidences good and bad that I cannot bear to lose them entirely— and besides I have a vague hope that you will miss me as a listener.[58]

Melbourne was more phlegmatic. He bade no adieux, sent one book and failed to write. He told Victoria that he had not been in communication with Miss Eden for five years, admitting that this was 'rather a long silence towards a friend'.[59] No trouble would be taken with women who disappeared from view, just as little quarter would be given to any woman who caused embarrassment. In self-justification, Melbourne told a story against himself: 'My mother always told me I was very selfish, man and boy, and I believe she was right. I always find some excuse for not doing what I am anxious to avoid.'[60] Women were a necessary part of his life, but their company was only allowed on terms.

Melbourne's family was right to try to find him some emotional anchorage. No sooner had Lady Branden been dispatched to Europe than the cycle was repeated, in a friendship that was forged with Caroline Norton. This time, the scandal would be more public and more costly. It would threaten Melbourne's health and throw even more doubt on his suitability for high office. To have the Prime Minister of England named in court, in 1836, as an adulterer was a spectacle that delighted Europe. At the same time that he was wrestling with the problems of Ireland, Canada, a tiresome House of Lords and Henry Brougham, Melbourne was also fending off the consequences of a legal action against him. It was small wonder that his credentials to be the main adviser and amanuensis to the 18-year-old Victoria, after 1837, were questioned.

Caroline Norton had all the qualifications that Melbourne had always admired in women. First and foremost, she and her two sisters were universally admired for their beauty. At a party in 1831, she was described as 'too

splendidly, magnificently, furiously beautiful. Cleopatra sailing on the Nile
. . . I never saw anything so tormentingly beautiful. One is attracted by her
consummate beauty, one is repelled by her odious manner . . . Mr. Norton
rather fidgeting around her.'[61] Sydney Smith, in rather unclerical language,
called her 'a superb lump of flesh',[62] and the editor of *The Times* ventured the
thought that her 'fleshy attractions are supposed to be as agreeable to Lord
M. as the last patent-easy-chair'.[63] Like Caroline Lamb, Mrs Norton would
provide novelists with lively copy. She has been identified as the model for
characters in a number of novels, most famously as Meredith's *Diana of the
Crossways*.[64] Inevitably, Melbourne himself is dragged into the same literary
representations, and surely no Prime Minister was more used by the novelist.

     To beauty was added wit. Mrs Norton was the granddaughter of the play-
wright Richard Brinsley Sheridan, and Queen Victoria was not alone in recognizing that, 'in no family was talent so hereditary as in the Sheridans'.[65]
Mrs Norton's conversation was sparkling and spicy, her spirits never seemed
to flag, and she could sing comic songs. It must have been a great relief for
a Home Secretary struggling with the terrible disorders of 1831 to receive letters like the following:

After dinner Georgia's sopha is wheeled out on the green, together with a large arm
chair and table for me, and a dumb waiter for the wine and biscuits. The pet lamb
is tied to a stone urn in the centre; the parrot is put in the sun; and a beagle puppy
which had the good luck to be trod on in early infancy and therefore made a pet of,
is laid down on the grass between us . . . I write, as much as I can, and the intervals
are filled up with Georgia's calls to me for assistance in the management of the
menagerie. The parrot takes a shivering fit, the lamb entangles *all* its feet in the cord
intended merely to tether it, and the puppy eats a cambric pocket handkerchief a day.
Today, my feelings so far got the better of me that I said I wished the one pet *roasted*
and the other *hanged*—which set Seymour into one of his father's laughs and occupied
us till tea-time. After tea I am allowed a quiet hour while the young couple caress one
another.[66]

Few people could be more diverting than Caroline Norton, and Melbourne
always thirsted for diversion.

     The last element in this beguiling compound was a certain masculine
coarseness and imperiousness. She called Melbourne her 'old boy', and sometimes promised him that she would 'never speak to you in the imperative
mood again'.[67] There was no bar put on Melbourne's flirtatious language,
though she pretended disapproval of his 'observations on the verb to kiss'.[68]
Emily Lamb noted with concern that the Sheridan sisters were happy 'to
swear and say all sorts of odd things to make the men laugh', and put it down
to the 'odd blood' of that family.[69] Other friends of Melbourne were more

censorious. Lord Holland thought Mrs Norton's behaviour 'dangerous and indecent',[70] while Emily Eden found her 'tiresome society, never natural for one moment, and affecting to be so much more wicked than there is the slightest call for'.[71] Some women had always been protective of Melbourne's good name and well-being. Many saw Caroline Norton as a threat to both. Even Melbourne thought the Sheridans 'clever, but all a little vulgar',[72] but it was a combination of qualities that had rarely repelled him.

Predictably, Mrs Norton's ungovernable behaviour led to whisperings and then condemnation. By 1834, her conversation could genuinely shock. In 1834, Emily Eden, after meeting her socially, confessed that she was 'without the remotest idea whether she was in jest or earnest in all the wonderful anecdotes she tells of "my husband" and "my lovers". I have really seen enough of life not to be *astonished*, but sometimes I want to look up quite aghast . . . I cannot say she does any credit to Lord M. or the very long list of other Lords who she says are also her lovers . . . I suppose she is very amusing to people who have not much principle.'[73] In 1835 Mrs Norton helped her brother to elope with an heiress, whose incensed father retaliated by shooting the young bride's favourite horse.[74] Shortly after, she 'amazed' the *corps diplomatique* at an official reception by kicking Melbourne's hat over his head.[75] For the Prime Minister to be put into such situations led one of his colleagues to reflect: 'what Man in love was ever prudent, but to be . . . 54 is rather an advanced age for an ungovernable passion.'[76]

Melbourne had met Caroline Norton for the first time in or soon after December 1830, when she approached him with the request that her husband should be appointed a stipendiary magistrate in London. Thereafter, the Home Secretary became a regular visitor to Mrs Norton's house in Storey's Gate, situated conveniently near the Palace of Westminster.[77] Like Lord Branden, George Norton was without preferment and without much ability. Like Lord Branden, he was happy to allow his wife's association with Melbourne, as long as there was a good chance that it would advance his career. As a feckless younger son, he was much in need of a patron. According to one Whig lady, he governed his marriage exclusively by the rules of the market place: 'We are all very excited about Norton—that is, all but me . . . I hear the great thing said against him is that he swallows the lovers or not according to their rank and position. Lord Melbourne yes, Captain Trelawney no.'[78] It was clear to everyone that the association with Norton was compromising. Even when quiet, he was so idle that Melbourne had to remonstrate with him, ironically enquiring if he could perhaps be at his desk by midday.[79] If crossed, Norton could be dangerous. His elder brother, Lord Grantley, and his former guardian, Lord Wynford, were leading figures among the Ultra Tories in the Lords, and had no love for

Melbourne. Allowing such men any weapon, even a blunt one like Norton, would prove unwise.

By the time that Melbourne was constructing his first administration in the summer of 1834, he and Mrs Norton had become very involved with each other. Early on, she claimed that she 'wonderfully benefitted' from their friendship,[80] and now described herself as 'in greater thraldom than ever'.[81] In return, Melbourne called her his 'Fornarina', and claimed a monopoly of her company and affections. Reassuring letters were necessary:

Dearest Lord do not be angry with me if I say that it is selfish to be discontented with me . . . you talk of my romping and flirting—and forgetting everything else—I have not forgotten anything. I am sure your name is always in my life, and there is hardly anything they can say, do, or look, that does not bring me back some of your opinions or expressions . . . I *cannot* be with you always, and therefore I amuse myself as I can, or rather amuse others . . . I can assure you I would much rather sit by your sofa in South St. than be Queen of the Revels here. You don't believe me yet it is true.[82]

The liaison was so vivid and so public, that, in April 1835, Disraeli could plausibly claim that Melbourne was using Mrs Norton as a political intermediary in negotiations with Tories.[83] This story was almost certainly untrue, but its countenance by many people is of itself of interest.

The friendship was public because Melbourne took no steps to hide it. Indeed, Mrs Norton was exhibited proudly to guests, who were specifically asked to meet her. In December 1835, Melbourne asked a certain Mr Wortley 'to dinner to meet Mrs. Norton . . . a more jolly party, or anything less like a Prime Minister, I never saw. There was nothing improper said or done, *of course*, but they appeared better friends than I should have liked if I had been Norton.'[84] Emily Lamb's concern about her brother's position now hardened into anxiety. She well knew that, in private, the Nortons lived 'like Cat and Dog'. She was aware that Grantley and Wynford were 'two plotters', and that George Norton would follow any instructions they issued.[85] So much Tory capital could be made out of the situation, that the Lamb family watched its development with helplessness and fatalism.

The blow fell in May 1836, when Norton issued a writ against Melbourne, claiming that he had committed adultery with his wife, and claiming damages of £10,000. Exposed to public scrutiny, Melbourne's reaction was exactly what it had been in the Branden case. He could not operate outside self-obsession. He saw himself as the victim of both the Nortons. Quite unnecessarily, they were about to involve him in unpleasantness. As he complained to Holland, 'The fact is He is a stupid Brute and She had not temper nor dissimulation enough to enable her to manage him.'[86] It was, in short, everyone's fault but his own. As in the Branden case, Melbourne immediately tried to distance himself from the trial and everyone involved in it. Mrs Norton was brutally advised 'to act wisely and prudently',[87] most obviously by not leaving her husband; 'I have always told you that a woman should never part from her husband whilst she can remain with him.'[88] This advice was tendered only four days after the dispatch of another letter admitting that Norton was so thuggish that no one could be expected to live with him.[89]

Melbourne was simply angry that he had been embroiled in difficulties again. He told Mrs Norton that, 'You describe me very truly when you say that I am always more annoyed that there is a row than sorry for the persons engaged in it.'[90] There was good reason for her to believe the self-absorbed sentences in Melbourne's letters rather than his protestations of good faith:

I daresay you think me unfeeling; but I declare that since I first heard I was proceeded against I have suffered more intensely than I ever did in my life. I had neither sleep nor appetite, and I attributed the whole of my illness (at least the severity of it) to the uneasiness of my mind. Now what is this uneasiness for? Not for my own character, because, as you justly say, the imputation upon me is as nothing. It is not for the political consequences to myself . . . The real and principal object of my anxiety and solicitude is you, and the situation in which you have been so unjustly placed by the circumstances which have taken place.[91]

The whole business made him ill. In April and May 1836, Melbourne bombarded his doctor with details of disturbing symptoms; sluggish bowels, lack of appetite, 'a feeling of strangulation'. Even a glass of claret, 'which I used to like so much, tastes quite nauseous to me'.[92] The remedy was to cut himself off from all the sources of irritation. The pattern established in the Branden case began to reassert itself.

Mrs Norton was therefore right to be apprehensive. Even before the trial started, she told him that her 'heart sinks and chills at seeing how little I am to you'.[93] When she broke the news of Norton's legal action to Melbourne, she remembered with dread 'the expression of your eye . . . the *shrinking* from me and my burdensome and embarassing [sic] distress'.[94] With some spirit, she wished Melbourne luck in his attempts to clear himself 'from the imputation of having loved me'.[95] Significantly, their letters protested their innocence of any crime,[96] but Caroline Norton could not bring herself to believe that that fact would prompt Melbourne to stand by her. Throughout his life, he had found means to avoid trouble rather than confront it. Now holding the office of Prime Minister, his tendency to bolt was confirmed. As Greville recorded in his diary: 'John Bull fancies himself vastly moral, and the Court is mighty prudish, and between them our off-hand Premier will find himself in a ticklish position.'[97]

In the event, the trial was a nine-day wonder, although its opening was greeted with intense anticipation. Since the private life of the Prime Minister was to be put on show, the case 'excited more interest than any trial of the sort ever did before'.[98] The crowds of onlookers were so great that it proved impossible to approach within fifty yards of the courtroom, and *The Morning Chronicle* reported that 'five and in some case, we believe, even ten guineas having been given for a seat'.[99] Extraordinary revelations about corruption in high places was expected. It was rumoured that letters would be produced, 'showing that Lord Melbourne had prostituted Government patronage . . . and it was even added that in one he had apologized for not being able to go to her, as he was compelled to attend "that tiresome old fool at Windsor".'[100] Rarely had Whig moral values been held up to such scrutiny and possible chastisement.

As matters turned out, the trial proved a damp squib. From the beginning, Norton's Counsel doubted of success. He asked his client 'if it was true that he had ever walked with Mrs. Norton to Lord Melbourne's house, and then left her there. Upon Mr. Norton's saying that it was so, Follett told him there was an end of his action.'[101] Melbourne's Counsel, Sir John Cope, was correspondingly optimistic. He saw only 'circumstantial evidence' being offered by his opponents, and, more intriguingly, he took comfort from the fact that the jury, with one exception, was entirely composed of merchants.[102] The prosecution questioned the servants at Storey's Gate about bolted doors, soiled linen, and Melbourne's preference for entering and leaving the house by a back entrance, but this evidence was tainted by the fact that these same servants had been dismissed for drunkenness, pregnancies, and other misdemeanours. There was a half-hearted attempt to suggest that Melbourne might be the true father of one of Mrs Norton's children, because, on one occasion, he had patted the child on the head, while remarking that 'it is not much like Norton'.[103] Lastly, three notes were produced setting the times of meetings, but these were of such an innocuous character that they were greeted with laughter.[104] The defence called no witnesses, choosing rather to disparage the evidence brought on Norton's behalf, and to hint darkly that Melbourne's good name was at risk only as a result of political conspiracy. The jury found for Melbourne, without bothering to leave their box for further discussion. The trial had taken on the nature of farce, and it was memorably used as such when Dickens described the case of Bardell v. Pickwick in *The Pickwick Papers*.

Melbourne should have been delighted with this verdict. He drew strength from it politically, the French ambassador observing that, 'cette affaire tourne au profit de l'affermissement de son Ministère, qui est, soyez en sur, long temps chargé du gouvernement d'Angleterre'.[105] The *Morning Chronicle* expressed a popular view in denouncing 'the Tory conspiracy which sought the destruction of a rival party by the blow aimed at the Prime Minister, through the side of an innocent woman'.[106] The Lamb family naturally took William's part,[107] and Cabinet colleagues saw the whole business as 'got up for party purposes'.[108] Lord Wynford took the unusual step of asking a newspaper to state that the trial had not been his 'concern'.[109] George Norton himself bleated that he had been bullied into initiating the action,[110] and told his own lawyers that he believed his wife to be completely above reproach.[111] Palmerston, much experienced in matters of this kind, was sure that it was basically 'a political Engine', for 'If there was nobody to be dealt with but Norton, it would be plain sailing, and one could tell to a Farthing what would suffice to make the thing up.'[112] The insufficiency of money to settle the case proved its political nature. The French were amused that Tory grandees should have attempted such a tactic, because in their party 'la morale est beaucoup plus relachés et qui ont besoin de plus d'indulgence'.[113]

Melbourne won sympathy and friends in all quarters. Rakes of all political persuasions were outraged that their private lives should be opened up to popular view. Wellington and Wellesley forgot their differences with the Prime Minister, and hastened to congratulate him on escaping a low and foul conspiracy.[114] The latter was moved to add a quotation from the *Odyssey* to describe Norton: 'May anyone else who acts in this way die similarly.'[115] More importantly still, William IV was all kindness. Blessed with an army of illegitimate children by Mrs Jordan, he assured Melbourne's nephew that he rejoiced at the verdict, for, if his Prime Minister had been found unfit for office, then he would not be 'fit to be king'.[116] As he reminded one of Melbourne's Ministers, 'We have all had our faults in this way.'[117] In party and personal terms, Melbourne emerged from the Norton trial as a conqueror. All those who had reason to dislike the Ultra Tories had even more reason to do so now. Their attempt to use the feeble George Norton to batter the Ministry had been exposed as small-minded nonsense. Melbourne should have felt a justified jubilation.

In fact, his reaction was very different. It had been an awful experience. He described the affair as 'a cursed scrape', which had been 'as well got through, as it could be'.[118] Misery came in all forms. Legal costs charged by the firm of Vizard and Leman came to the huge sum of £627 9s. 6d.[119] Worse, his health had suffered severely. Melbourne was ill throughout the months of April–June 1836, and, although it must have been some consolation that 'les beaux yeux de Madame Norton ne dissoudront pas le Cabinet',[120] the whole business had reduced him to 'a state of severe mental depression'.[121] Insomnia and bad colds left him weak and complaining.[122] He protested to his lawyers that he had never committed adultery with Mrs Norton,[123] and these statements were rehearsed again and again in the coming years, ending in a death-bed affirmation.[124] No man ever wanted to be more accepted as innocent. Close friends were aware of how near he had come to the flames. Lord Holland received Melbourne's claim that no sexual impropriety had occurred with the Italian expression, 'Forse era ver ma non pero credible' [Perhaps it was true but it is not very credible].[125] Hobhouse was prepared to give him the benefit of the doubt, but went on to reflect that 'it is passing strange that he should have been so much for six years alone with a very beautiful woman without . . .'.[126] The absence of mistresses in Melbourne's life during the long, difficult years of marriage, and a decided preference for women to provide companionship rather than physical satisfaction, should allow some credence to his repeated protestations. However, perhaps the worldly-wise words of his brother Frederick come closest to defining events:

Quel triomphe The verdict was clearly right . . . the whole thing seems to . . . leave the lady in a position in which with a little protection she may do very well. I know them all for Canaille, but we must help her as well we can. Don't let Wm think himself invulnerable for having got off again this time. No man's luck can go further.[127]

Once the ordeal of the trial had passed, Melbourne reverted to a familiar pattern of behaviour. A woman had discomforted him. The only possible response was to disengage. Mrs Norton would be offered money and sympathy. Indeed she would be urged to separate herself from Norton, who was a 'gnome' and 'perfectly earthly and bestial'.[128] But all real contact with Melbourne, too, was expressly forbidden.[129] He attempted to soften the blow by telling her that there was 'nobody who can fill your place',[130] but the interdict was enforced. Effectively, Caroline Norton was abandoned in every sense except the financial. Her innocence recorded in court was no defence in a society which ostracized women with no lover or husband to protect them. Wretchedly, she complained that she was treated 'as if I had been yr. mistress these five years'.[131] In particular, she lost the custody of her children, one of whom had his name legally changed from William to Charles.[132] When she fought back tenaciously, Melbourne offered no help whatever. When a Bill came before the Lords, which would offer women greater access to their children, he failed to stay for the vote. For this, he was rebuked by Victoria, but no concession was offered:

Lord M. said: 'I don't know—I don't think you should give a woman too much right' . . . I repeated it was very cruel; 'There are some instances of great injustice', he said, but he is for the man, and that there should not be 'two conflicting powers'; that a man *ought* to have the right in a family.[133]

Caroline Norton's successful campaign to modify the law owed nothing to Melbourne. In his view, scandal and the fear of renewed scandal terminated all possibility of intimacy.

Predictably, Mrs Norton's letters to Melbourne in 1836–7 represent an altogether more convincing indictment of his behaviour than had ever been presented in court. They catalogued 'great cruelty and great rudeness'.[134] Significantly, she was happy to identify patterns in Melbourne's attitudes, and to find parallels between herself and other women who had come close to him. Her mistake was to think that, 'I came far before and beyond yr. other women'.[135] Her accusation that he was driving her 'mad' could only exhume memories of his marriage.[136] Equally, she admitted to having 'a full recollection of Lady Brandon [sic] and the small space her supposed discomforts occupied in yr. mind. I wish I had never known that *experience by proxy*.'[137] She and Lady Branden had been victims of 'the same thing', which she described as 'the wind up and breaking off of an acquaintance which might have once seemed worth a sacrifice but which time has made you less anxious about'.[138] Three women seemed to have been destroyed by Melbourne's coldness:

You need not have taken so very majestic a tone with me because you are now safe from all risk, and sitting in triumph at South St. . . . What have I ever done to you that *you* should grind me too? Have you *always* so preserved the inequality of age and understanding between us, that you should talk to me like God delivering the tablets of law to Moses? . . . Do not talk so proudly to *me*, who *thro' you* am destroyed, who *by you* should have been comforted, and was not . . . *God* knows it would be a lesson to many a woman if any one *could* read your letters from the first to the last—from the days you flattered me till the days you rose to fling stones at your own clay idol and break it; to prove to it that it was unworthy your worship.[139]

In retrospect, Caroline Norton was clear that Melbourne had never been '*attached* to me', and that, as a result, she had never been able to offer him real 'service or comfort'.[140] Protesting that her love had been so profound that her life had been divided into 'the *days I saw* you and the *days I did not*',[141] she now acknowledged that Melbourne had felt very differently. By way of explanation, she came to the same conclusion that others had expressed. Quite simply, Melbourne was no longer capable of emotional commitment. In March 1837, Caroline Norton significantly accused her former friend of skipping around London, 'with the buoyancy of a boy, and the carelessness of a greyhound:—(the only dog besides yourself who cannot attach himself to *any one person*, but to the cushion where he habitually rests and the house where he is accustomed to be fed). Fie on such love say I!'[142] By temperament, by experience of marriage, or by both, Melbourne could no longer take emotional risks. He wanted to be diverted rather than loved, and was therefore outraged when even this minimal demand on others involved him in public scandal. Caroline Norton's letters make clear the extent to which Melbourne, under a veneer of wit and learning, had grown cold.

Melbourne always described himself as 'a monogamist', and, as one companion was removed from his life, another took her place. Only one month after the trial ended, Caroline Norton had identified her successor as Lady Stanhope:

I leave to you and Lady Stanhope the satisfaction, such as it is, of duping and baffling one very easily duped . . . I think if yr. preference for La[d]y Stanhope was so very decided it is a pity you made such a useless wreck of [m]y life—when you *had* a woman whose husband is quite contented it must be so—a liaison which suits yr. sister and your people much better than I.[143]

Such jealousy merely amused Melbourne: 'as to her hating you and you her, almost all women, as far as I can see, hate one another, and do each other as much harm as they can, nor ever by any chance give each other a good word.'[144] Melbourne had first met Lady Stanhope in 1817 or 1818, as 'the friend' of his brother, Frederick.[145] Mrs Norton had no doubts that she was or had been the mistress of both the brothers,[146] although there is no other evidence to support this view. What is clear is that Lady Stanhope had all the traits of character which Melbourne found attractive in women. Queen Victoria called her 'a very amusing, clever, agreeable woman'.[147] Her tongue was so sharp that she frequently 'gave people a chill in Society'.[148] In conversation, she could be 'high'.[149] She was unpredictable in temperament, and, because, like Caroline Norton, she had Ultra Tory relations, she was politically dangerous. Victoria numbered her among Melbourne's 'bad friends',[150] and he himself admitted that she had 'no judgement, or management, and could do nothing right unless she was told, and always did what she shouldn't, as most women do'.[151]

From 1836 until 1841, Lord Stanhope fought Melbourne's proposals in the House of Lords, while his wife and daughter were endlessly in the Prime Minister's company. Invitations to Holland House and Windsor Castle were secured at Melbourne's request. It was an arrangement that entailed 'the complete exclusion of Politics from social life'.[152] Cabinet colleagues, discussing the Irish Poor Law with the Prime Minister, 'immediately retired' when Lady Stanhope's arrival was announced.[153] In the last years of his tenure of office, she and her daughter, Wilhelmina, also 'rather hard',[154] were always on hand, exciting jealousy and criticism in women as different as Victoria and Lady Holland, who also felt that they had claims on Melbourne's time and attention. Contemporaries never speculated that the relationship ran as far as adultery. Rather they were amused by the capacity of a high-spirited and dominating woman to lead Melbourne into the realms of gossip across party lines. In his friendship with Lady Stanhope, Melbourne was treading a path he had taken many times before. After the disgrace of Caroline Norton, he merely shifted allegiances.

When Henry Brougham approached the task of administering Melbourne's will, he did so without enthusiasm. As he remarked to his fellow executor, Edward Ellice: 'I dare say we shall find more debts than we reckon upon. What a sad pillage! *Women of course*.'[155] As Lord Branden's legal adviser, and as Caroline Norton's amanuensis in her campaign to allow women rights of custody over their children, Brougham had some justification for being apprehensive. In fact, both Lady Branden and Mrs Norton were left legacies, for which the latter recorded thanks of a kind:

I was simply glad, (let those sneer at it who please), that with such a husband and such a destiny of never-ending troubles, the family of the man in whose name I had suffered so much were willing to prove, not for my sake, but for his, that his kindness to me outlived him.[156]

In return, none of the women who had suffered injury ever gave Melbourne up. Lady Holland forgave the Lambs for the domestic disturbances of 1810, and Holland House became Melbourne's second home in widowerhood. Lady Stanhope was a permanent source of comfort and diversion after 1833 or so. Emily Eden fussed about him, observing that 'there is nobody I know whose illness has excited more universal interest'.[157] She reappeared as a visitor to Brocket in the 1840s, a fact which irritated Mrs Norton, who denounced 'the great Triumphal entry into Brocket' of 'that great gaunt woman'.[158] Quite clearly, Melbourne could excite a level of sympathy and concern that overrode memories of indifference and calculating coldness.

Above all, Mrs Norton resumed their friendship after 1840. Favours were exchanged. Caroline Norton used her contacts in the literary world to allow Melbourne to meet such luminaries as Thackeray.[159] She resumed the practice of calling him her 'Dearest Old Boy'. In return, she felt free to ask for help in securing appointments and for money, for which 'she was constantly plaguing him'.[160] Such was the tenacity of Mrs Norton that the Lamb family once again felt justified in protecting William from the unfortunate consequences of his own actions. Emily Lamb and her son, William Cowper, who was now one of Melbourne's secretaries, tried to ensure that they were the intermediaries for all contact between William Lamb and Mrs Norton. William Cowper would help with the drafting and passage of her Bill[161] to ease the situation of divorced and separated women, but he and his mother would have no truck with Mrs Norton's more exaggerated claims. Nor would they countenance any clumsy attempts at blackmail. In 1845–6, they faced down, on Melbourne's behalf, a threat to publish her correspondence with Melbourne. Not surprisingly, Caroline Norton was often moved to complain that 'Your uncle [was] a most careless and supine friend', and that his family, 'who should be foremost to support me are the first to criticize'.[162] She disliked the spectacle of the Lamb family closing ranks to protect their own. She had been 'falsely and grossly wronged' on their behalf, and her reward was to be lectured 'about a later male friendship in the sands at Ryde'.[163]

Even so, in Melbourne's last months, she saw him often,[164] and was genuinely saddened by witnessing his loss of powers:

I observe that nothing amuses Ld M, now, but light stories . . . how bitter and melancholy it is to me sometimes to see that grand intellect (to read and converse with which in my young days, I used to read and study hard books) altered into being so difficult to raise an interest in *anything*.[165]

There was nothing now in their friendship that could alarm the most determined 'Decorumist'.[166] In spite of the extraordinary misadventures which had befallen them, accusation and counter-accusation, the connection was never quite broken, and it continued to give pleasure and comfort to both parties. In this respect, it was a pattern followed by nearly all Melbourne's female friends. Only Lady Branden, living in paid exile in France and Switzerland, drifted out of his life completely. Melbourne's behaviour came nowhere near gallantry. It was often self-absorbed and self-regarding. It was, however, nearly always forgiven.

After his wife's death, Melbourne was free of embarrassment, but was also confronted by an emotional isolation which he found intolerable. As has been noted, he described himself as a 'monogamist', by which he meant that there would always be the need for a single, assured point of emotional support. Such assistance had to be of a particular kind. First and foremost, it was to amuse and divert. A friendship was as much intellectual flirtation as anything else. As a result, he liked women who made no demands on him, but were rather independently minded people of determined, even masculine, forcefulness. Such friends were not to embarrass or trouble him, and they were not to expect deep, emotional responses. It is quite possible that none of these friendships found a physical expression. If trouble came, women must expect to be rejected in all senses but the financial.

Melbourne had a remarkable capacity to shift his confidences from one friend to another at the slightest hint of danger. His instinct was once again to retreat, to take refuge in illness, and, above all, to invoke the assistance of brothers, sisters, and nephews as a kind of praetorian guard. When friendships ruptured, he almost always saw himself as the victim of the situation, rather than a contributory factor in it. In spite of this, William Lamb was affectionately remembered, even by those who claimed recompense for injury. As a young man, Lamb had been characterized by his family as someone with no will of his own, someone who was manipulated, rather than manipulating. This reputation seemed to exonerate him to some extent in the eyes of contemporaries, even in the opinion of those like Mrs Norton, who felt themselves profoundly hurt by his behaviour.

There is much in Melbourne's private life after 1828 that is unedifying. The question arises of whether this cold reluctance to love and be loved, to trust and be trusted, had always been in his character or not. Certainly, he had always been diffident in emotional matters, having none of the libidinous appetites of his natural father, his legal father, or his brothers. Caroline Lamb claimed that she had been neglected, and that William had never been able to show affection for their unfortunate son. From an early age, William's personal life was regulated by an anxious mother and sister. Yet, such evidence is not wholly convincing. There was spontaneity and an outgoing generosity in the young William Lamb, as well as a certain hesitance. He gave every indication of entering into marriage joyfully, of his own volition, and with real love for his future wife. He had had positive feelings in politics and public life. Contemporaries could use the adjective 'ardent' to describe his attitudes to both.

If this is so, then the iciness of Melbourne's later, emotional life must largely be seen as the consequence of living a most extraordinary marriage for over twenty years. He had loved and trusted Caroline Lamb, and the result had been such public humiliation and misery, that he had been forced into terrible introspection. He determined never to love or trust anyone again. The risks involved in doing so were simply too great. His interest in flagellation may have been prompted by a desire to revenge himself on womankind. Certainly, women were to be taken on as friends only on terms. He much prized their company, but he wanted nothing more. He always firmly discountenanced any suggestion that he might remarry. For an amusing, powerful and good-looking man to invite women into friendships, and then to set up barriers and demarcations, could be characterized as cruel and wounding. It was behaviour that seemed to offer more than it could in fact deliver. It was of this that Caroline Norton complained, in advising Melbourne, in 1844, not to 'fly in the face of Heaven who built up your own face into the picture of honesty and generosity thereby (alas!) creating much mistaken trust, and vain expectation, in the hearts of all those whose ill-jud(g)ing eyes have gazed on your countenance'.[167]

12

Victoria, 1837–1841

In June 1837, William IV died. He was succeeded by his niece, Victoria, who was just 18 years old. Not only was she young in years, she was also young in experience. Neither George IV nor William IV had allowed her to see much of the world, or to be trained for kingship. Worse, she had had few emotional points of reference. Her father, Edward, Duke of Kent, had died when she was a mere girl. Her mother was pretentious, ambitious, and increasingly resented. Trust and affection were therefore directed towards her governess, the Baroness Lehzen. For such a girl, spirited, enquiring but unknowing, to come upon the world suddenly as an anointed queen must have been an astonishing experience. The light was dazzling. She was badly in need of a guide and mentor, who could translate the world of politics and social regulation into language that was readily comprehensible. He appeared in the person of Melbourne, 58 years old, and someone who had taken most of the knocks that life could give. For a man with such a reputation to undertake the political education of a young queen naturally gave rise to gossip and questioning. On the face of it, hardly anyone could have had a less attractive curriculum vitae for the task in hand. Yet, the friendship between monarch and minister was quickly recognized as the central fact in politics:

No minister in this country, since the days of Protector Somerset, ever was placed in such a situation . . . He has a young and inexperienced infant in his hands, whose whole conduct and opinions must necessarily be in complete subservience to his views. I do him the justice to believe that he has some feeling for his situation . . . but in the nature of things, this power must be absolute, at least at court.[1]

The Tory diarist, J. W. Croker, tartly observed: 'Wolsey and Walpole were in strait waistcoats compared to him.'[2]

If William IV's doubts about Whigs had permanently clouded Melbourne's political prospects, Victoria's uncritical approval immediately added enormous strength to his government. Victoria may or may not have been Whiggish in sympathy, but she was a Melbournite to the death. No doubt

Melbourne welcomed this, but just as important was the discovery of an emotional contentment that he had not felt since the early days of his marriage. He felt an unguarded affection for Victoria, and was warmed and flattered by her close attention to everything he said, and by her willingness to have all her views and prejudices moulded and shaped by him. There is no doubt that, in spite of the vicissitudes of politics, the years 1837–40 were among the happiest of his life. While it is not very profitable to speculate on the depth or precise nature of his emotional commitment to Victoria, there can be no doubt that he felt for her profoundly. His affection was reciprocated, as far as an 18-year-old girl could admire and be fascinated by a man forty years her senior. For many years, neither queen nor minister had been able to find a safe, emotional anchorage. Briefly, they found it in each other. It was not the love that brings contemporaries together. Rather it was the affection that unites people who had known great loneliness.

In such a relationship, Melbourne took great risks. For over twenty years, he had survived by presenting the world with an impenetrable armour of cynicism and non-involvement. Difficulties were always pushed away as the responsibility of others. Now, these defences were abandoned in response to the needs of a young woman, who made the demands of a daughter. His reward was for a time astonishing happiness, but he had also opened himself once again to rebuff and rejection. It came, with terrible suddenness, in 1840, when Victoria met, loved and married Albert of Saxe-Coburg-Gotha, without consulting Melbourne or asking his advice. Her transfer of affection was total and immediate. She was too young to understand the devastation that these events would wreak on Melbourne, or the bitterness that would be engendered. In the last eight years of his life, he returned to the emotional solitude in which he had camped before he had met Victoria, but his isolation was made worse by the knowledge that he had known a type of happiness that would never be repeated. In illness and old age, he could only watch Victoria drawing ever further away from him. Only she and Caroline Lamb had ever engaged his affections. Knowingly or unknowingly, both she and Caroline Lamb inflicted an enduring pain.

Contemporaries were astonished at the speed with which the bond between Queen and Minister was formed. They had not known each other at all before 1837, and yet they behaved from the start as though they had trusted each other for years. William IV died on 20 June 1837. A Privy Council meeting was called almost immediately, where it was noted that the Queen's speech had been drafted by Melbourne,[3] and that 'she has put herself' into his hands.[4] The French ambassador immediately reported to Paris that a dramatic change had taken place: 'Enfin le Roi Guillaume s'est reposé dans les bras de l'éternité . . . Il est peu regretté même des siens . . . Le Ministère toléré par Guillaume sera sincèrement appuyé par la Reine.'[5] The government was now assured of 'un long avenir'.[6] When Melbourne asked the Queen formally for instructions, her reply could not have been more explicit: 'Je ne suis pas en état de vous donner des ordres mais faites pour le mieux: vous etes interessé (sic) à ce que les affaires aillent bien et vous en etes responsable. Ma confiance en vous est entiere [sic].'[7] Entries in Victoria's journals over the next few weeks detailed her total willingness to follow Melbourne in everything. Rarely can a monarch have reached a decision of such importance with such speed. On 2 July, she recorded her decision to leave politics to his direction: 'He is indeed a most truly honest, straightforward, and noble-minded man and I esteem myself *most* fortunate to have such a man at the head of the Government; a man in whom I can safely place confidence. There are not *many* like him in this world of deceit.'[8]

More important still, Melbourne was within weeks accepted as Victoria's closest personal friend. The entry for 18 July reads, 'I talked with him about *very* important and even to *me* painful things',[9] and that for 8 August, 'Talked over many things which were of great and painful interest to me; things gone by, and past, I mean. Lord Melbourne is so kind, so feeling, and entered quite into my feelings.'[10] Very quickly, any distinction between public and private topics in conversation dissolved. One merged with the other. On 19 October 1837, for example. Victoria recorded that, 'we talked a great deal about Spain and Portugal, and about *other* matters *de l'intérieur*.'[11] It was reassuring to Victoria that Melbourne should like the Baroness Lehzen, and should have shared her suspicions of the tiresome manœuvres of her mother, the Duchess of Kent. Eighteen months after the Norton trial, Victoria indulged in a judgement that would have given many contemporaries pause. She now considered Melbourne to be 'so truly excellent, and moral, and has such a strong feeling against immorality and wickedness; and he is *so* truly kind to me'.[12] Few members of the Lamb family had ever received an encomium in this vein. It was provoked by the gratitude of a young girl, in at last finding an adult who took trouble about her, and who seemed worthy of trust. For different reasons, her father and mother had never been able to fulfil this responsibility. Melbourne was eagerly and speedily accepted in their place.

The closeness of Queen and Minister was immediately noticed. Whigs such as Lady Granville found the situation reassuring, even charming: 'I feel so much interested about that little wonderful Queen, and admire all I hear of hers and Lord Melbourne's relative positions. What a strong anxious tie it is that binds him to her service, so unlike anything else of the sort one ever heard or read of.'[13] Tories, on the other hand, saw the relationship as sinister. According to the *Quarterly Review*, Victoria was 'under the *tutelage* of Lord

Melbourne, and, in fact, no more than an executrix, with him, of the sad legacies imposed on her and on us by the early improvidence and ultimate necessities of William IV'. She was in a kind of 'thraldom'.[14] In 1837, an absurd rumour went the rounds to the effect that Melbourne was actually intent on marrying the Queen.[15] Crowds not infrequently shouted 'Mrs. Melbourne' at Victoria when she appeared in public.[16] For Melbourne himself, Victoria's obvious need of him was a rejuvenating experience. Politics now had at least one firm purpose. The Queen must be protected from the consequences of her own inexperience, and, as far as possible, from the company of politicians she disliked. In July 1837, the sharp eyes of the Princess Lieven noted a great change in the Prime Minister:

I have seen the Queen with her Prime Minister. When he is with her he looks loving, contented, a little pleased with himself; respectful, at his ease, as if accustomed to take first place in the circle, and dreamy and gay—all mixed up together.[17]

A routine of quiet domesticity was established between monarch and minister. Melbourne took to living almost permanently at Windsor or in St James's Palace. He never lived in Downing Street, and was infrequently seen at his own house in South Street. Women like Lady Holland, who had been in the habit of entertaining him with an almost proprietorial air, now complained that he had abandoned them. Routine quickly established itself. There was a formal interview at one in the afternoon when business was discussed for anything up to three or four hours. Once matters of state had been dealt with, there followed a little exercise, usually horse-riding, and then dinner, at which Melbourne had his own chair at the Queen's right hand. According to Tory satirists, Melbourne was as much Victoria's entertainer as her prime minister: 'There is a little riding in the middle of the day, a little eating afterwards, just a quarter of an hour's claret and chat, and then some music, or a quadrille; or, if the court be at St. James's, a journey to the theatre or opera house . . . Vive la bagatelle! . . . . Lord Melbourne is a feeble and effeminate creature, fit only to loll in a palace, to scribble in an album, or to criticize birthday odes, or diplomatic despatches.'[18] Victoria herself observed that Melbourne often 'made me die with laughing'.[19] On days when they could not meet, two or three letters might be exchanged. The Queen observed in her journal that to record every letter sent 'would take up too much time'.[20] If Melbourne was companion and secretary to Victoria as well as minister, there was point in it. He remembered how difficult it had been to communicate with William IV through the prismatic defences of his secretary, Sir Herbert Taylor. There were to be no more such intermediaries. His continual attendance on the Queen was both pleasure and constitutional convenience.[21]

Although the spectacle of monarch and minister so much in each other's company naturally fed speculation, Melbourne took great care that every-thing should be done with propriety. In fact, some visitors to Windsor found its society 'dreadfully dull', and resolved never to 'go through dining there again'.[22] Melbourne's nephew, William Cowper, was employed to find com-pany for the Queen, but his suggestions were vetted for their appropriateness by the Prime Minister.[23] Predictably, his own relations were much in evi-dence. His sister and her children, his Lyttelton cousins and the Stanhopes were habitués of Windsor evenings, and all of them were pumped with ques-tions from Victoria about Melbourne's antecedents, early history and tastes. So remorseless were these enquiries, that Victoria's journals offer some of the best evidence for an account of Melbourne's youth and childhood. Victoria became an honorary member of the Lamb family. She had some objection to Melbourne falling asleep in company, and to his snoring while doing so, but this was a small matter. She regretted his indifference to music, but could find no other fault.[24] As for Melbourne, politics now had a purpose. As Greville observed: 'Melbourne seems to hold office for no other purpose but that of dining at Buckingham Palace.'[25] It was worth putting up with tire-some colleagues and fractious opponents, if the reward was association with someone who admired him and showed affection. As a cousin noted, he was unassailable 'while her present Majesty lives, unless he contrives to displace himself by dint of consommés, truffles, pears, ices, and anchovies, which he does his best to revolutionize his stomach with every day'.[26]

At the beginning of their friendship, the strongest bond between Victoria and Melbourne was undoubtedly their joint determination to thwart the ambitions of the Duchess of Kent and her protégé, Sir John Conroy. In this enterprise, they saw themselves as fellow conspirators. Victoria had never enjoyed good relations with her mother, and bitterly resented any attempt by her to capitalize on her own high expectations. In particular, there was to be no question of Conroy becoming her private secretary. William IV had brusquely dealt with his sister-in-law's importunity, and Melbourne, with Victoria's full approval, determined to do the same. Patronage applications from the Duchess were sharply denied.[27] When she asked for an official res-idence in Richmond Park, she was offered a smaller residence in Kew, which was 'inadequately furnished'.[28] There were to be no new carpets or curtains in Kensington Palace.[29] French diplomats, in amused paragraphs, reported the unremitting warfare between Kensington and Windsor, Duchess and King.[30] William IV was grateful that Melbourne was apparently quite happy to be a target for 'the Anger and Indignation of a weak foolish Woman'. He was also relieved that his niece and heir held aloof from 'the Kensington Cabal'.[31]

After Victoria's accession, hostilities continued. Melbourne took care to ensure that the women chosen to serve in the Queen's Bedchamber should be 'independent of those who belong to the Duchess of Kent'.[32] With Victoria's approval, he declined to pay her mother's debts, objecting 'to the Queen's being subjected to any expense or charge'.[33] Whenever the Baroness Lehzen challenged the Duchess, she could count on Melbourne as an ally. So far from peace-making, Melbourne enlisted in the war, thereby prolonging it in a manner which did nothing for the image of the monarchy, and which Victoria herself later came to regret.[34] It was clear to everyone that there were two parties at Court. To Lady Holland, Melbourne characterized the situation as a rehearsal of the politics of the early 1760s, when another royal mother and her protégé allegedly attempted to dominate a young monarch: 'The part played by Lord Bute and the Princess Dowager is exactly that which has been taken by the Duchess of Kent and Conroy. The former succeeded through their influence with the King. The latter were baffled by the sense and firmness of the Queen.'[35] The squabbling was unseemly, but a lack of affection between generations was not an unknown feature of Hanoverian monarchy.

For a Prime Minister to be so entangled in divisions within the Royal Family carried dangers. Holland recalled that the great Whig families had sensibly held aloof from such arguments. He feared that 'these Court dissensions harrass [sic] Lord Melbourne and engross his Mind too much . . . I should avoid, as I have throughout life . . . any interference with the concerns of Royal personages.'[36] No doubt, Melbourne's reputation for statesmanship would have been enhanced if he had attempted to reconcile the factions, instead of conducting prejudiced conversations with Victoria, who joyfully recorded them in her journal: 'Talked of my dislike of Mama, Lord M. said that she was a liar and a hypocrite. "I never saw so foolish a woman", said M. Which is very true and we both laughed.'[37] On the other hand, Melbourne genuinely believed that the Duchess was without judgement and Conroy without scruple. The young Queen had to be protected from both. Bickering tarnished the monarchy, but to allow the Duchess any real influence in politics would be still more debilitating. On this point, Melbourne's constitutional concerns dovetailed with Victoria's emotional priorities. Keeping the Duchess and Conroy on the margins of politics and society was a task that both could relish. It was a bond that united them in a common purpose.

A relationship so quickly formed and so publicly enjoyed between a man of 58 and a girl of 18 inevitably became a matter of speculation. It was based on the meeting of mutual need. Emotionally, in 1837, Victoria was a kind of orphan. A dead father and an unlovable mother had left her without resources. In Melbourne she found an alternative. She claimed to 'love him like a Father'.[38] To her, he had the fascination of being a much-lived man who was informed about everything, and who had known everyone of consequence over two generations. She pestered him for stories and encouraged him to reminisce. There were tales of Fox and Byron, Pitt and the Duchess of Devonshire. In addition, as a relation by illegitimacy and as a minister, Melbourne was able to talk of George IV and William IV, uncles of whom Victoria knew little. Further, gossip was mixed with instruction. Melbourne directed the Queen's reading in literature, history, and philosophy, drawing on his own wide experience in these areas. He seemed omnicompetent. He could lecture on Racine and Dr Johnson. He could be amusing about Nell Gwynne, describing her as 'very celebrated in one capacity or another'.[39] The long years spent hiding in the library at Brocket now paid dividends. Victoria found the whole performance awe-inspiring: 'he knows about everybody and everything; *who* they are, and *what* they did; and he imparts his knowledge in such a kind and agreeable manner; it does me a *world* of good; and his conversations always improve one greatly.'[40]

Almost certainly, Melbourne was the first adult to flatter Victoria by taking her seriously. To be so complimented by a man of great intelligence and urbanity was a beguiling prospect. She demanded his attention and company, and became jealous of rivals like Lady Holland: 'I was sure she didn't care for him *half* as *much* as I did, which made him laugh. I'm certain *no one cares* for him *more* or is *fonder* of him, than I am; for I owe so much to him.'[41] The Queen's intellectual and emotional dependence on Melbourne was noted by Cabinet Ministers, and it must have played some part in their continuing acceptance of him as leader. Lord Hatherton, for example, observed that Victoria 'could not bear that he should be out of her sight . . . if Melbourne even left the room, her eyes followed him, and . . . she sighed when he was gone!'[42] For a girl to become queen, knowing nothing of the task in particular or of the world in general, it was not unreasonable to identify kindness and hang on to it. Later, Victoria had doubts about the wisdom of her behaviour. Writing in her journal in December 1842, she made the following entry: 'Talked afterwards over former days . . . my unbounded affection and admiration of Ld. Melbourne which I said to Albert I hardly knew from what it arose, excepting the fact that I clung to someone, and having very warm feelings. Albert thinks I worked myself up to what really became at last, quite foolish.'[43] For a brief term of years, Melbourne's concern and protective affection became the focal point of Victoria's emotional life.

For his part, Melbourne, one year after the calamity of the Norton trial, found himself invited to mould the thinking of an intelligent and passionate young woman, who hung upon his every word. He could instruct her in the same way that, in the early months of his marriage, he had tried to instruct Caroline Lamb. As Victoria became possessive of his company, so Melbourne became protective of her good name. London society was amused that a man with Melbourne's reputation should now be so concerned with propriety. His friend, Lady Holland, as a divorced woman, could not be presented at Court. Victoria was not to waltz. Her Maids of Honour were not to walk on the terrace at Windsor Castle unless chaperoned.[44] When a novel was to be dedicated to the young Queen, Melbourne thought it prudent to read it through himself, to ensure that there was nothing 'objectionable'.[45] Ever jealous of the Queen's reputation, he made honest attempts not to involve her personality with the Whig party, or to derive narrow, political advantage from their association. In this endeavour he was not wholly successful, as will be seen below, but it was always his stated purpose not 'to mix himself and the Government with Your Majesty's personal popularity'.[46]

Melbourne deeply respected his new charge. Holland noted that he was 'struck with her sagacity and yet more with her calm and deliberate determination', even though her 'girlish enjoyment of novelty and curiosity' was in need of direction.[47] Her views were to be treated with 'unbounded consideration and respect'.[48] A high-spiritedness, which Melbourne had always admired in women, made her the real mistress of the situation. He frankly told the French ambassador that 'aucun obstacle ne l'opposait à ce que la Reine ne le réalisoit si elle en avoit envie: il est certain que la consitution ni aucune loi ne s'y opposent'.[49] Victoria was Melbourne's pupil, but a pupil of the most challenging kind. She listened absorbedly to everything that he said, but never lost the capacity to form her own views or to insist on being heard. As a result, it was reported to Paris that Melbourne 'aime autant qu'il respecte la Reine'.[50]

Significantly, however, Melbourne's involvement went beyond that of an amused tutor of a lively and responsive pupil. For over twenty years, he had suffered the humbling humiliations of a disastrous marriage, the effect of which had been to cauterize the springs of his emotions. After Caroline Lamb's death, he cared deeply for no one. Lady Branden and Mrs Norton, Lady Stanhope and Emily Eden, had provided diverting company but nothing more, and even then had sometimes entangled him in scrapes. Now, with Victoria, he had stumbled across someone for whom he was compelled to take an emotional risk. The defensive deployment of ironic detachment no longer met the case. Within three months of Victoria's accession, the diarist Charles Greville noted the depth of Melbourne's emotional investment, and proceeded to pen some of the most perceptive remarks ever written about him:

I have no doubt he is passionately fond of her as he might be of his daughter if he had one, and the more because he is a man with a capacity for loving without having anything in the world to love. It is become his province to educate, instruct, and form the most interesting mind and character in the world.[51]

Melbourne, the 'loving' man, whose own children were now all dead, and whose friendships with women too often ended in scandal, now seemed to have found safe anchorage.

So close was the friendship between Queen and Prime Minister, that in spite of all Melbourne's best efforts, it rapidly became a point of controversy in party politics. Victoria was not perceived to be above party, and this had grave implications in a constitutional monarchy, where a monarch's ability to work with men of all political persuasions was an essential part of the process. Instead, 'the Clubs say that the Queen has turned up trumps for Melbourne and the Whigs and if they added and *for the country* I think their joke would have the merit of truth.'[52] It was an open question whether Victoria could ever have been described as pro-Whig, but she was incontrovertibly pro-Melbourne. When talking of his government and herself, she was happy to use the word 'we'.[53] Equally, Tories pitied her obsession with Melbourne, and called her 'that poor little chit'.[54] In fact, Melbourne endlessly instructed the Queen to be open-minded both about Peel and Wellington as individuals, and about the possibility of accepting them in government.[55] Little of this advice was known to the world at large. Rather, it seemed that Victoria had become the leader of one party in the state, or that Melbourne had expropriated the monarchy. Tories cried foul, and increasingly grew less interested in making a distinction between attacking the government and attacking the Queen. By 1839, Victoria had become so unpopular as a result of her supposed, political partiality, that she was hissed by Tories at the Ascot race-meeting.

Two events in 1839 underline the extent to which doubts about the Queen's politics had become constitutionally damaging. The first of these concerned Lady Flora Hastings, one of Victoria's ladies-in-waiting. Early in the year, a swelling stomach gave rise to a rumour, which Lady Tavistock retailed to the Queen, that Lady Flora had become pregnant. Victoria ordered her to be examined by her own doctor, Sir James Clark, but this appraisal proved inconclusive. In fact, the unfortunate young woman was suffering from a tumour, which killed her in July 1839. This episode should not have developed beyond the limits of personal and family tragedy, but, such was the ambiguous nature of the Queen's relations with leading politicians, that it became high politics. As the French ambassador reported home, 'L'affaire de Lady Flora Hastings s'envenima et donne beaucoup de tourments à la Reine.'[56] The Hastings family was Tory, and they decided to claim that Lady Flora had been the victim of a conspiracy to destroy her reputation, hatched by 'the baneful influence which surrounds the throne'.[57] Willingly or unwillingly Victoria presided over a Court that was 'as depraved and licentious as that of Marie Antoinette'.[58] Further, Hastings took trouble to ensure that the whole *affaire* would be given the widest publicity, publishing correspondence and commissioning articles and cartoons. His behaviour led Victoria to 'wish to have hanged the Editor and the whole Hastings family for their Infamy'.[59] Typically, Melbourne dismissed the whole business as 'all Politicks',[60] but damage had been done. The impartiality of the executive was called into question. Queen and Ministry were attacked together. If the monarchy had become a party matter, on the model of France, it risked losing the confidence, even the allegiance, of those who disliked Whigs. The Flora Hastings *affaire* should have warned Victoria of real danger.

More serious still, in these same months, there occurred a full-scale constitutional crisis, which gravely exposed the Queen's role in politics. On 6 May, the government's majority on a Bill to suspend the Jamaican Assembly fell to five votes.[61] Next day, Melbourne informed Victoria that he would probably have to resign. She was appalled:

It was some minutes before I could muster up courage to go in,—and when I did, I really thought my heart would break; he was standing near the window; I took that kind, dear hand of his, and sobbed, and grasped his hand in both of mine, and looked at him and sobbed out, 'You will not forsake me' . . . he gave me such a look of kindness, pity and affection, and could hardly utter for tears, 'Oh! no', in such a touching voice.[62]

Melbourne responsibly advised her to send for Wellington and Peel. A Tory government of some complexion seemed unavoidable. Significantly, however, he also agreed that Victoria should ask her new Ministers that none of her Household officers should be dismissed, particularly the Ladies of the Bedchamber.[63] In allowing this request, Melbourne played some part in setting up the whole Bedchamber Crisis, but he did this unwittingly. It is very unlikely that he saw this tactic as a device to scupper plans for a Tory administration. On 10 May, he informed Grey that, sadly, there was no chance of survival: 'I do not think that we have the least chance having declared our resignation upon the grounds of want of confidence and want of power. If we go on, we shall only fail more compleatly [sic] and deliver the Queen more compleatly . . . into their hands.'[64] His Cabinet colleagues largely agreed.[65]

A crisis developed when Victoria formally requested that the personnel of the Bedchamber should not be changed, and when Peel insisted that no government could allow the monarch to continue to be surrounded by its political opponents. Understandably, Victoria turned again to Melbourne for guidance, but, in doing so, was, as Greville noted in his diary, already treading on doubtful, constitutional ground:

As it was, the Queen was in communication with Sir Robert Peel on one side, and Lord Melbourne on the other, at the same time; and through them with both their Cabinets; the unanimous resolutions of the former being conveyed to, and her answer being composed by, the latter. The Cabinet of Lord Melbourne discussed the proposals of that of Sir Robert Peel, and they dictated to the Queen the reply in which she refused to consent to the advice tendered to her by the man who was *at that moment* her Minister, and it was this reply which compelled him to resign the office with which she had entrusted him.[66]

Melbourne had, in theory, announced his intention to resign, but was still offering the monarch counsel. Peel, theoretically commissioned to form a new administration, saw his suggestions rejected on the advice of his predecessor. Not surprisingly, Peel and his friends found the situation insupportable and terminated their efforts to re-enter office. When news of this decision reached Victoria, she sent the following note to Melbourne: 'As the negotiation with the Tories is quite at an end, the Queen hopes Lord Melbourne will not object to dining with her on *Sunday*.'[67]

The Bedchamber Crisis seriously impaired the reputation of the monarchy. Victoria was publicly seen to be a Melbourne partisan. As such, it was doubted whether she could properly perform her allotted, constitutional role of being above party. Tory England had some justification in thinking that she was not their queen. For a monarch to be so closely identified with one party, to the disadvantage of the other, inevitably led to her prerogative powers being called into question. In an embarrassed speech, Melbourne attempted to explain the situation away to an audience of sceptical peers. He asserted that Court ladies should not be subjected 'to the changes and vicissitudes of political parties', and that he had withdrawn his resignation, because he would 'not abandon my Sovereign in a situation of difficulty and distress, and especially when a demand is made upon her Majesty, with which I think she ought not to comply'.[68] It was absurd that the monarch's social life should be disrupted every time a government changed, and it was insulting to suggest that a king or queen was so lacking in determination, that all their views would be moulded by their personal servants.[69] Unfortunately, the Bedchamber Crisis convinced many contemporaries that this was precisely what was happening. When Melbourne announced that he could not be sure of a continuing majority in the House of Commons, every constitutional precedent gave Peel the right to attempt to form a government. He had been thwarted, not by votes in Parliament, but by royal intransigence, backed up by the whisperings of defeated Ministers behind the arras. It discredited monarchy, and brought its powers into question.

In fact, Melbourne had repeatedly urged Victoria to look on Peel or Wellington as future ministers, reminding her that her duty was to work with all parties. Within living memory, monarchs had been able to operate exclusions by personal whim, but, after the Reform Bill, politics had now to be played by other rules. Almost certainly, Melbourne was led into the difficulties of May 1839, not by a stubborn determination to cling to power, but by his protective affection for Victoria. He offered her the appropriate advice, but, when she baulked at accepting Peel and the Tories, he could not bring himself to abandon her. The price to be paid was high. Constitutional procedures had been bruised, and Victoria's political reputation tarnished. In March 1840, Lord Holland observed that 'the Whig or Melbourne party joined with the Court is by far the strongest of any one in the country'.[70] It is of interest that he should see 'Whig' and 'Melbourne' as denoting slightly different things, that the government, by this date, was nothing more than an expression of Melbourne's personality, and that it had somehow merged with Court politics. Victoria was a Melbournite. Amid all the difficulties he faced in 1839–40, the support of the monarch must have been one of his trump cards. Unfortunately, however, for a Queen to be the confidante of only one politician was not acceptable in a constitutional monarchy. Within two years of her accession, Victoria had become deeply unpopular. The emotional interdependence of Queen and Minister was poisoning politics.

Even within a friendship of this intensity, however, there was one reserved topic. Victoria never consulted Melbourne on the subject of her marriage, and it was a reticence that he noted. One of his Tory opponents observed with great pleasure, as early as September 1837, that, on this significant issue, Melbourne was cut out of all influence: 'I hear Melbourne says, in all his numerous conversations with the Queen, he never has been able to extract an opinion in what quarter or where she has a predilection. This he stated with great surprise.'[71] The reason was obvious. Victoria was much in need of emotional security, but she was strictly monogamous in searching for it. Loving and trusting a husband would inevitably mark the end of Melbourne's pre-eminence. When Albert of Saxe-Coburg-Gotha began to be talked of as a possible Prince Consort, Grey had no doubt that: 'this event will probably make a material change in Ld. Melbourne's position; and not, I am afraid, in making it more easy.'[72] As though recognizing this fact, Melbourne, in his long conversations with Victoria, always encouraged her to put off the idea of marriage until she was older. Such advice could have stemmed from genuine concern for a girl, who was not yet 21, but it could also have been prompted by fear of a rival.

When Victoria agreed to marry Prince Albert at the end of 1839, it was a decision in which her Prime Minister had no part:

The Queen settled everything about her marriage herself, and without consulting Melbourne at all on the subject, not even communicating to him her intentions. The reports were already rife, while he was in ignorance; and at last he spoke to her, told her that he could not be ignorant of the reports, nor could she; that he did not presume to enquire what her intentions were, but that it was his duty to tell her, that if she had any, it was necessary that her Ministers should be apprised of them. She said she had nothing to tell him, and about a fortnight afterwards she informed him that the whole thing was settled . . . If she has already shaken off her dependence on Melbourne, and begins to fly with her own wings, what will she not do when she is older.[73]

In fact, Victoria had been entirely secretive about the whole arrangement, as though tacitly acknowledging that Melbourne's affection for her would inevitably prevent him from giving disinterested advice. When the engagement was announced, Melbourne, in public, was dutifully pleased. He told Victoria's uncle, King Leopold of the Belgians, that he was 'much assured of a good and happy result'.[74] To Victoria herself, he pleasantly commented: 'you will be much more comfortable; for a woman can't stand alone for long in whatever situation she is.'[75] He was therefore 'glad' to see her provided for.

Public statements such as these, however, barely disguised the bitterness and resentment he felt. As early as July 1839, he had expressed his distaste for any 'connection' with the Coburg family.[76] They seemed intent on dominating Europe by providing an army of bridegrooms. They were humourless, moralistic, and, possibly, had a German distaste for parliaments. Albert himself seemed to personify most of these qualities, and Melbourne was right to suspect that he would not be sympathetic to Whiggish ways of living. It was much more likely that the serious-minded Peel, good husband and professional politician, would be more to his taste. As a result, it was not always easy to bridle his tongue in the interests of diplomacy. When Victoria, for instance, reported that Albert was not interested in fashionable women, Melbourne sarcastically observed that 'that will come later'.[77] No one was in the slightest doubt, and Melbourne least of all, that Victoria's marriage might materially undermine his own political and emotional well-being.

He was right to be concerned. From the beginning, it was clear that Albert intended to cut a figure in politics, and that he would exercise enormous influence over a wife who adored him. In the winter of 1839/40, he caused a minor political crisis by claiming precedence over the Queen's surviving uncles. He found it hard to accept that the rules of precedence were established by Parliament. Melbourne smoothed the matter over by persuading Royal Dukes to give way, but the episode revealed how determined and how dangerous Albert would be. Victoria's unqualified backing made him invincible.[78] He made little secret of finding Whigs frivolous, irreligious, and unserious in their approach to politics. Inevitably, his views would quickly lead Victoria to re-evaluate the qualities of her erstwhile friends, and even to doubt her trust in Melbourne. Albert's arrival on the scene, wholly occupying the Queen's emotions, represented a major caesura in politics.

Entries in Victoria's journal make it clear how acutely conscious she herself was of her changed situation. On 1 October 1842, she re-read what she had written on 22 March 1839. Then she had trembled at the thought of being forced to give Melbourne up. Now, she wondered at how shallow her feelings had been:

Reading this again, I cannot forbear remarking what an artificial sort of happiness *mine* was *then*, and what a blessing it is I have now in my beloved Husband *real* and solid happiness, which no Politics, no worldly reverses can change . . . kind and excellent as Ld. M. is, and kind as he was to [me], it was but in Society that I had amusement.[79]

Three years later, her memory had hardened still more: 'In 1841, I grieved and lamented at the loss of Ld. Melbourne, as that of a friend, whom I had looked to (particularly *before* I married) for advice for almost everything.'[80] There would be no repetition of the Bedchamber Crisis. Under Albert's tutelage, Victoria would come to see Peel and the Tories with new eyes. Melbourne's primacy in politics based on royal approval could now be challenged. The loosening of his ties with the Queen was a central fact in the unravelling of his administration.

There was, however, more at stake than the loss of political power. In personal terms, Victoria's marriage was for Melbourne a catastrophe. After his resignation from office, a friendship which had developed so quickly cooled just as rapidly. There continued to be meetings with the Queen, but they became more and more infrequent. Initially, it appeared that nothing had changed. In August 1841, Victoria condescended to visit Brocket, and Emily Lamb rejoiced to see 'Wm with his grey hair floating in the wind and the Queen on his arm as he walked her round the lawn'. Thirty-six people sat down to dinner, and in the centre of the table were three pieces of silver presented to Melbourne by Victoria and Albert, to mark the occasion of their marriage.[81] It seemed that Melbourne was still esteemed,[82] and foreign rulers continued to write to him as a man of consequence.[83] In fact, however, this much-publicized visit was rather valedictory than offering any prospect of continued intimacy. If a visiting dignitary was to be dined at Windsor or in Buckingham Palace, Melbourne might well be invited,[84] but such meetings could not disguise the fact that a psychological separation had swiftly taken place.

Frederick Lamb was inclined to think that Victoria was simply bowing to the constitutional demands of the situation: 'I apprehend there must be a total separation of his relations with the Q. when out, or it wd. expose him to great désagrémens [sic].'[85] Now that Peel was Prime Minister, Victoria simply could not, with propriety, maintain her old relations with his political opponent. It was politely pointed out to Melbourne for example that he could hardly dine at Windsor immediately after making a speech in the Lords attacking the Queen's Prime Minister.[86] But this argument was more convenient than convincing. Such considerations had not prevented Victoria tenaciously clinging to Melbourne in 1839, in defiance of Peel and popular opinion. It was therefore obvious that circumstances had changed. Quite simply, Victoria, a woman of passionate loyalties, had suddenly transferred her trust from Melbourne to her new husband. Suggestions that she should not be disloyal to Peel by entertaining Melbourne now appeared much more attractive. Melbourne could do nothing to stop himself being brusquely frozen out of the Queen's confidence and affection. Peel, Prince Albert, Leopold of Belgium, and his representative in London, Baron Stockmar, all agreed that this should be so. Victoria was now happy to follow their direction. It was an ostracism that Melbourne found bitter to accept and harder to forgive.

First, slowly but determinedly, the former prime minister's influence at Court was snuffed out. Presuming on the friendship of 1837–40, Melbourne continued to offer unsolicited advice to the Queen on a wide range of issues. As an honoured guest at the christening of the future Edward VII,[87] he bombarded the royal parents with views about education in general and about suitable reading lists for princes in particular.[88] More controversially, he offered opinions on foreign policy and recommendations for preferment and patronage. Until at least the autumn of 1842, Melbourne and Victoria continued a correspondence which discussed affairs of state as a matter of course. Occasionally, Victoria encouraged his desire to continue as a royal amanuensis by referring state papers to him and inviting comment.[89] None of this could be pleasing to Peel and his colleagues. For a monarch to seek counsel outside the circle of her official government carried the risk that the formulation of policy would become blurred, and that rumours would start about the nature of royal backing for the Peel administration. It was behaviour that ran counter to advice that Melbourne had himself offered the Queen. On leaving office, he urged her to behave in such a way as 'to secure to Your

Majesty the affection, attachment, approbation and support of all parties'.[90] It was doubtful if his own conduct materially assisted this process.

A fierce, and increasingly insensitive, determination to remain a force in politics led Melbourne to offer advice whenever it was solicited, and sometimes when it was not. Just as Victoria had been lectured on the character and limitations of Sir Robert Peel, so Peel received instructions on the successful handling of the Queen:

The Queen is not conceited; she is aware there are many things she cannot understand, and she likes to have them explained to her elementarily, not at length and in detail, but shortly and clearly; neither does she like long audiences, and I never stayed with her a long time.[91]

Peel expressed polite thanks for Melbourne's concern, but he can hardly have welcomed his predecessor's lingering on the stage. Melbourne seemed to have difficulty in finding an exit line. Just as Grey's shadow fell across the early years of his own term of office, so Melbourne's darkened Peel's. It was clear that he had no intention of slipping quietly away into an honoured retirement. He would have to be forced to step aside.

The campaign was conducted through the medium of George Anson, once Melbourne's secretary, and now Private Secretary and Treasurer to Prince Albert. In September 1841, Stockmar asked Anson to put it frankly to his former employer that his continuing correspondence with the Queen 'is productive of the greatest possible danger, and especially to Lord Melbourne; he thought no Government could stand such undermining influence'.[92] In November, Stockmar wrote directly to Melbourne, begging him 'to let a certain correspondence die a natural death'. He expressed great 'disappointment' that Melbourne 'had volunteered the promise, to write from time to time', and retailed a story, circulating in London drawing-rooms, that Peel had declared his intention of resigning if this occult influence continued. All in all, Melbourne was engaged in a 'hazardous enterprise'. Stockmar's letter concluded with both an appeal and an admonition:

I beg to remind you of a conversation I had with you on the same subject in South Street the 25th of last month. Though you did not avow it then in direct words, I could read from your countenance and manner, that you assented in your head and heart to all I have said.[93]

These words fell on deaf ears. In December, Anson had to report that although the correspondence was not carried on 'in its pristine vigour', Melbourne 'has taken no notice of the Baron's remonstrance to him, and we are in the dark in what manner, if at all, he means to deal with it'.[94]

At the same time that Stockmar was attempting to frogmarch Melbourne out of the Queen's life, Prince Albert himself opened up a second front, again using Anson as a channel of communication. In February 1841, he deeply resented the former prime minister taking the side of the Baroness Lehzen, when Albert insisted that no business or opinion should reach Victoria through the lips of her old governess. The Baroness had been Melbourne's staunch ally in his battles with the Duchess of Kent, and he boldly told Anson that he had not only 'never found the Baroness in my way', but also that 'the P. wd. be quite unjustified in making a stand upon such ground'.[95] Taking sides against a Prince Consort was playing politics of a highly dangerous kind. It seemed that he wished to separate the Queen from her husband in politics, bringing squabbles within the royal circle into the exposed area of public debate. Melbourne much resented any attempt by Albert to become a political figure, brutally telling Anson that 'the Prince is indolent, and it would be better if he was more so, for in his position we want no activity'.[96] Not surprisingly, Anson was frequently required to pass on complaints from the Prince about Melbourne's continued meddling.[97] He remained, however, absolutely impervious to the criticism that his conduct might compromise the Queen with her new administration or with her new husband. His letters to Victoria had less and less impact, but they continued to be written. Only the onset of a stroke in the autumn of 1842 resolved the problem. Until then, Melbourne fought tenaciously to hold on to Victoria's good opinion. There was to be no gracious departure from politics. He was removed by illness and the determination of Victoria's new idols that he should be superseded. For a full year after retiring from office, however, he remained a major irritant in official and Court politics.

Sadder still was the dissolution of friendship and affection. By 1843, Victoria recorded in her journal her sudden surprise in finding Melbourne an old man. She abruptly recognized the psychological distance that separates generations:

Ld. Melbourne looked very nervous, and there is a strained altered look in his face, which it pains me to see. He is growing very thin, and uses his left hand with difficulty. But he talked on all subjects very well and quite like his old self. He said, 'I am very weak. I am so crippled', but I assured him he looked very well and only begged he would take great care of himself. 'Well, I will try', he answered.[98]

He was no longer her friend and the purveyor of wise counsel, but an old man who fussed about his health. No doubt this realization helped her to put the years 1837–40 into unsentimental perspective. In January 1843, she wrote, 'Good Lord Melbourne was here from Saturday till this morning, looking very well, and I *almost* fancied happy old times were returned; but alas! the dream is past.'[99] For a time, she always remembered his birthday, and for this act of recollection he was almost childishly grateful.[100] In 1847, however, the day passed unnoticed, and it was little consolation to be told by Anson that the Queen had asked him to remind her of it in future.[101] Only a very few years earlier, she would not have required any such prompting. From her perspective, friendship with Melbourne had become nothing more than the warm remembrance of a period that had been emotionally and politically dismissed.

For Melbourne, by contrast, being parted from Victoria was a matter of immediate and ongoing pain. The occasion of his leaving office was described as that 'melancholy day'. He hoped that he would be able hereafter to look back upon it 'with less grief and bitterness of feeling, than it must be regarded at present'.[102] Almost certainly, this aspiration was never fulfilled. In turning down the offer of both the Garter and an earldom, he was more than happy to accept some lithographs as a personal present from the Queen.[103] This action underlined the extent to which the holding of office had become a personal matter between him and Victoria. Working with her had been 'the proudest as well as the happiest part of his life'.[104] Even in 1844, he still regretted and missed 'the time when he had daily confidential communication with your Majesty'.[105] He anxiously looked out for letters and presents, as evidence that their friendship still held firm. There was a terrible sense of personal loss. Meeting the Queen could now leave him in tears. In 1843, he and Victoria found themselves as guests at Chatsworth, but the encounter was only productive of embarrassment:

Lord Melbourne was so much broken in health that he was nearly in a state of second childhood. I believe he had not met Her Majesty since he ceased to be her Minister. Her manner to him was kind; still, he bitterly felt the change in the situation, and, it was sad to see him with tears frequently in his eyes.[106]

With royal invitations becoming more and more infrequent, driving past Buckingham Palace was an agonizing experience. Through windows, Melbourne claimed to be able to distinguish familiar pictures and pieces of furniture, or even the lighting of candles.[107] He was now outside a building which had only recently been a second home. He very much feared that he was now beyond Victoria's affection as well.

So searing was the pain of separation that George Anson began to wonder if it had not turned the mind of his old friend and patron. Frederick Lamb reported to his sister Emily that, 'Anson asked about Wms. hysterical emotions which were what struck him most. I, observing what he wd. have spoken of, answered that such was frequently the case when there was a mention of the Queen which always moved him greatly.'[108] It was entirely understandable that Melbourne's family and friends should be concerned. There was something unbalanced about his dogged refusal to release Victoria to the

influence of her new Ministers and of her husband. Illness, not argument,
finally forced him to let go. For the only time since Caroline Lamb's death
Melbourne had allowed himself to feel a deep affection, which had apparently been reciprocated. Love for Caroline Ponsonby degenerated into a
mockery of a marriage. Affection for Victoria was cut off as soon as a more
appropriate focal point for her emotions appeared on the scene. If Greville
was right to describe Melbourne as 'a loving man', then this attribute never
brought him happiness. He was in safer waters when he sought amusement
with a Lady Branden or a Mrs Norton.

The epilogue to the story of this extraordinary relationship could only be
sombre. Victoria was saddened to hear of Melbourne's death, and was particularly distressed by the type of death it was. She observed in her journal
that, 'it was a dreadful end, though more for those who witnessed it, for he
was hardly conscious . . . it was one of the most dreadful struggles imagin-
able. It grieves me deeply to think of poor dear Ld. Melbourne having such
a sad end.'[109] However, her principal concern was immediately to badger
Melbourne's family and executors to return any of her letters that might be
found among his papers.[110] Enormous care was taken that none should be
kept back. Having received a first batch of letters, Victoria noticed that the
correspondence for 1837 and 1838 was still missing, and asked that it be
found and returned.[111] When all had been returned, she thanked Frederick
Lamb for his efforts, and said frankly that it was 'a great satisfaction to her
to know them in safety'.[112] Others willingly helped in this campaign to gain
control of the past. Lord John Russell destroyed letters from Melbourne, 'in
which the Queen is mentioned', because they 'ought not to be kept'.[113] It
seemed that Melbourne had become an embarrassment. His passing allowed
the discomfort he had caused to be quietly locked away.

　　Steadily, too, Victoria's opinions about her former mentor hardened.
Three days after his death, her judgement was already unsentimental: 'Our
poor old friend Melbourne died on the 24th. I sincerely regret him for he was
truly attached to me, and tho' not a good or firm minister he was a noble,
kind-hearted generous being.'[114] By 1890, Victoria was happy to record 'a
most affte. remembrance' of Melbourne, while thinking him 'weak as a
Minister'.[115] As he lay dying, she acknowledged his kindness at a particular
moment in her life, but the passing of that phase in her emotional development left no regrets:

I regret so not to have seen him this year . . . He has had 2 fits in the last 3 days. I
can never forget his great kindness and I may say his affection towards me for 4 years
. . . I shall ever gratefully remember this, but I am sure I do not wish those times
back.[116]

With great honesty, Victoria recorded gratitude for a friendship which in youth she had badly needed. Abruptly and finally that need had been met in marriage. Thereafter, the figure of Melbourne, suddenly old and ill, was an embarrassment. His clinging ways and tearful evocations of the past only underlined the fact that both he and the Queen had been involved in what Prince Albert would describe as a great deal of silliness.

13

The Last Years, 1841–1848

MELBOURNE always feared the loss of office. As his government faced one crisis after another, each of them threatening a final dissolution, he grew adept at rationalizing a determination to stay in power. Duty to friends and duty to country were invoked as justifications, as was the urgent need of a young queen for stable government. He frankly admitted that he 'preferred being charged with tenacity of office, than with a readiness to abandon the government'.[1] Yet, power and the manipulation of men and events gave him little pleasure. As has been noted, he had little personal engagement with most of the great issues of his prime ministership. What he looked for in politics was not influence, but occupation. A busy political day, amusedly watching others running after honours and recognition, filled hours that would otherwise hang heavily. His sister, Emily, understood this point only too well. Writing in 1834, she observed that, 'In some respects office is useful to Wm. It employs his mind and makes him get up early, before he was in office I was often more anxious about him than I am now. He used to lye in bed till 12 o'clock and had got so fat and full and red.'[2] From 1827 to 1841, politics had given Melbourne's vigorous and restless intellect a focus. While always approaching debate with such philosophical detachment that many contemporaries accused him of a lack of seriousness, he nevertheless had a deep, personal need of the political game.

On resigning as Prime Minister, he publicly expressed relief and a studied calm. He enjoyed receiving expressions of thanks for his years of service, and assured his sister that he was determined to enjoy 'the fun of opposition'.[3] It was not a convincing performance. Colleagues were shown another face. On 1 September 1841, Lord Campbell called on his leader unannounced—between twelve and one:

I found him shaving. This was his levée. I said I came to offer my congratulations on his release from the cares of office, and that I hoped he was happy. 'Oh, very happy.' He smiled, but 'in such sort . . .'.

In truth, he will feel it more than any of us. He not only loses the occupation and excitement of office, but his whole existence is changed. With him it is as if a man were to have a wife and children, with whom he had lived affectionately and happily, torn from him when he falls from power . . . I know not what is to become of him. The trees at Brocket will be very funereal.[4]

The event had long been dreaded. Eighteen months before the blow fell, Melbourne had been reading the journal of a former friend, John Dudley. He reflected on 'his evident happiness *in* office, and his misery *out*': a kind of presage to Melbourne, who, I think, read it with that feeling. He added, 'But I suppose that any man who kept a journal, if he put down every feeling of dissatisfaction and unhappiness that occurred to him would appear a very miserable fellow.'[5] Long preparation for the inevitable was of little assistance in the end. There were moments of frank despair. He shamelessly confessed to Hatherton that he 'could not bear the idea of parting with his position'.[6]

Loss of office cruelly exposed Melbourne in both political and emotional terms. As Caroline Norton well knew, 'He has never been well since his son died: and after all it *is* a desolate life,—tho' I know you all laugh, because he has a careless manner generally.'[7] Whatever he had felt for Caroline Lamb had died with her in 1828. His involvement with Lady Branden and Caroline Norton had never been as deep. His favourite brother, George, had died in 1834. Two years later, his son, Augustus, also passed away. Father and son had never been close. Augustus always addressed his father as 'Mr. Lamb'.[8] Melbourne found it tiresome to be endlessly required to look out for nurses and keepers, because 'That sort of Person . . . is generally a great annoyance in a house.'[9] Probably unfairly, Emily Lamb accused her brother of giving himself 'no trouble' about his son.[10] When Augustus died, none of the Lamb family was inclined to mourn. Frederick thought that 'One can not but feel it to be a good thing',[11] while Mrs George Lamb observed that 'Ld. M. seems pretty well. He was a good deal affected at the time, but you know it cannot be looked upon as a misfortune.'[12] An autopsy revealed a brain so unusually 'dense', that it could 'resist the knife in an uncommon manner'.[13] From the point of view of the Lamb family, Augustus had been unlovable, but his passing nevertheless removed one more person for whom Melbourne might have felt affection.

After his wife's death, Melbourne reverted to a bachelor existence without strong attachments, either to people or places. Significantly, he was without feelings for his surroundings. He increasingly disliked having to visit Melbourne Hall in Derbyshire, which was more often than not leased or lent to the George Lambs. In London, he inherited Melbourne House from his father in 1828, but almost immediately leased it to the French Ambassador.[14] Two years later, he sold it to Lord Dover, finding it 'too large and expensive'.[15] The sale of the family home gave other members of the family twinges of regret, but not Melbourne.[16] Indeed, he was quite happy to be invited back as a dinner-guest of the Dovers. His hostess worried that he might have found the experience painful, but instead found him 'very good-natured about it'.[17] On becoming Prime Minister, Melbourne never lived in Downing Street, ostensibly because it kept him 'out of the way of the bore'.[18] As far as he can be said to have had a London house, it was a modest property in South Street. Most of his official letters carried this address. Even Brocket was not so precious that it could not be leased to others. As his sister-in-law worriedly noted, 'he seems determined to leave himself no house'.[19] It seemed that few people and no building held any attachment for him. He had become a solitary.

Bachelors and the widowed are natural diners-out. Melbourne sought diversion in company, not in the masculine ambience of a club, but in the society of the salon, which was in every way more varied. For the whole period of office-holding, Holland House became his preferred watering-hole. He repeatedly dined and slept there. His long friendship with the Hollands had survived many difficulties, and had matured into genuine acceptance. The food could be a little problematical, but the company was the best in London. An entry in Holland's journal for 16 January 1832 sets the mood:

Remarkable only for a dinner singularly agreable [sic]. Scarce any politicks were talked and Melbourne, Jeffray [sic] and Sydney Smith in their different ways were very particularly agreable . . . I scarcely ever heard more wit, learning, and good sense in any society, and the remaining part of the Evening did not fall off when Talleyrand came and closed it with some anecdotes, both political and literary, in which his conversation abounds.[20]

It was a forum in which he could more than hold his own. At such dinners, his 'excellent scholarship and universal information remarkably display themselves'.[21] He could startle the company by claiming to have the whole of *Henry V* 'by heart', and his fellow guests noted that literary disputes always excited him more than politics.[22]

Of course, like almost everyone else, he complained of Lady Holland's imperious manner, and teased her husband for being under his wife's thumb. He once jokingly reported to Russell that, 'Lady Holland is out of town, which greatly promotes peace of mind',[23] but he was well aware that the Hollands were to be numbered among his oldest and closest friends. Their personal and political history had been interwoven for over thirty years. He was happy to do them favours. It was pleasant being Prime Minister, if it allowed him to grant Lady Holland the special privilege of having her 'Garden Chair' wheeled around Kensington Gardens.[24] Lord Holland's death, in October 1840, was a terrible loss for Melbourne. For the next five years, Lady Holland was one of the few people whom the retired politician was always pleased to see. Her death, late in 1845, closing social possibilities and putting an end to so many pleasant associations, left him bereft. As he explained to Victoria;

Lady Holland's death will be a great loss to many and Ld. Melbourne is not only ready but anxious to admit that it will be so to him. The advantage of her house was that she asked almost every body and that it offered an opportunity of seeing persons whom one wished to see and whom one had no chance of seeing any where else. Lord Melbourne always found her a very certain friend.[25]

Between 1841 and 1845, Melbourne lost the society of Windsor, Buckingham Palace, and Holland House. He never found satisfactory substitutes.

As Melbourne lived increasingly with his own thoughts, he developed a wide range of mannerisms and eccentricities that his family and friends noted and tolerated. Victoria objected to Melbourne snoring in church, but was otherwise happy to accept William Cowper's account of his uncle's oddities:

Lord Melbourne is very absent when in company, often, and talks to himself every now and then, loud enough to be heard, but never loud enough to be understood. I am now, from habit, quite accustomed to it, but at first I turned round sometimes, thinking he was talking to me. Mr. Cowper says he does not think his uncle is aware of it; he says he is much less absent than he used to be.[26]

Others could be disconcerted by Melbourne's strangeness of manner and his increasingly unkempt style of living. The dandy of 1800 no longer took much trouble with appearances. Lord Clarendon, calling on a point of business in 1840, found the Prime Minister 'in bed—everything in the room in a great litter, the bed *dirty*, and books pamphlets, papers, boots and shoes all tumbling indiscriminately about'.[27] His wife was even more put out at an official dinner, when Melbourne turned to her and asked if she loved her neighbour as herself.[28] Stories abounded on the subject of Melbourne's growing eccentricities. On one occasion, he was found in the lobby of Brooks's Club saying to himself, 'I will be hanged if I will do it for you, my Lord.'[29] Increasingly isolated by the world, Melbourne in turn made increasingly little attempt to keep on terms with it. By 1847, even his brother Frederick found him 'so odd a fish', that it was impossible to predict his mood or opinions from one day to the next.[30] Eccentrics are commonly those who have been, or feel themselves to have been marginalized by society. They are treated with amusement and affection, but never taken seriously. This completes the process of estrangement. It was a process Melbourne experienced at first hand.

Not the least pronounced of his eccentricities was a growing preoccupation with money. Increasingly, he was worried by fears of debt and poverty. In fact, after his father's death, he was always a relatively wealthy man. The first

Viscount Melbourne's will had been 'much what was expected'.[31] Apart from small legacies, everything had gone to William. His sister-in-law calculated that, although there were debts charged to the estate of £113,000, William could still look forward to a clear income of £13,000 a year. There were only two indications that his father had been influenced by his knowledge of his heir's illegitimacy. He first stipulated that, in the event of remarrying, William should not settle more than £1,000 a year on his new wife, and secondly, and more seriously, much of the Lamb property was entailed. William could enjoy the income, but could not sell or raise capital against the estate. It was to pass intact to Emily's children. In view of all this, the Lamb family found it hard to understand why William should be 'in the greatest state of indecision looks very gloomy and talks openly to nobody'.[32] He had every reason to look forward to an assured future.

Estimates of his income remain fairly constant thereafter. In 1835, he himself thought that his total income of £21,000 a year fell to £11,000, once annual obligations and charges had been met. His expenditure was thought to be £10,000, which left him with a small but comfortable margin. While in office, he hoped to save at least £6,000 a year.[33] In 1847, the situation had not changed very much. Agricultural rents from estates in Derbyshire, Nottinghamshire, Leicestershire, and Hertfordshire accounted for £15,585; canal shares for £46; colliery investments for £1,776; and timber sales for £769. Together, they provided him with an income of £18,176.[34] At his death, Henry Brougham, his executor, thought that his late friend's income had been £19,000 a year, of which £13,000 was disposable income.[35] Melbourne was therefore a wealthy man. He had no dependants and only a small establishment to maintain. His concerns about money were not wholly rational. Instead, they reflected an unease about handling money and a carelessness in doing so. In 1841, he found 'upwards of £20,000 laying idle' at his Banker's, which surprised and delighted him.[36] Two years later, while bemoaning his inability to be too generous to a favourite nephew on the occasion of his marriage, Melbourne, according to his brother, 'seems to me to have been like a child, is astonished at having a balance at his Bankers that he could not contain himself about it'.[37] Even with an annuity due to Lady Branden of £1,000 a year, and an astonishing outlay of £800 a year on doctors, Melbourne was very comfortably placed.

He refused to be reassured. In a manner that was almost unbalanced, he bombarded Victoria with begging letters. In December 1847, he told her that he had 'for a long time found himself much straitened in his pecuniary circumstances', and that 'he dreads before long that he shall be obliged to add another to the list of failures and bankruptcies of which there have lately been so many'.[38] Two months later, he formally requested a state pension.[39]

Victoria responded by offering Melbourne a personal loan of £20,000, even though George Anson thought the whole transaction 'improper'. He was clear that Melbourne 'broods over imaginary (to a great extent) difficulties'.[40] Odder still was the fact that, in addressing the Queen, Melbourne came very close to threatening a kind of blackmail: 'Lord Melbourne is not surprised that Your Majesty should be a little anxious about your letters. They have all been kept together . . . Lord Melbourne felt certain that Your Majesty would be anxious to assist Lord Melbourne in any difficulties.'[41] Linking the future of their correspondence with the question of his supposed poverty had an unfortunate character. It is possible that, at the end of his life, an unfounded preoccupation with the fear of poverty had, to some extent, overbalanced his mind.

The same eccentricity was in evidence when Melbourne came to execute his will. It was drawn up on 30 January 1843, and was to be 'a plain and simple affair'.[42] The contents of the document were unexceptional. The Melbourne properties were to pass, as his father had intended, first to Frederick, who was childless, and then to Emily. One servant named Joseph Scorey was to receive £500, but no other individuals were mentioned. The oddity came in Melbourne's choice of executors. The first named were Lord John Russell and Henry Brougham.[43] Russell was an obvious choice as a long-standing personal and political friend. By 1848, however, he had been supplanted by Edward Ellice, a man with whom Melbourne had not been friendly at all, and who had, on a number of occasions, attempted to embarrass his administration. It seemed that he was chosen as an act of spiteful revenge on Russell, who had successfully taken over Melbourne's role as the leader of Whiggery, and who, on issues like the Corn Laws, now found himself at odds with his old friend. The choice of Brougham was justly described by Victoria as 'strange'.[44] He had taken the part of both Caroline Lamb and Lord Branden against Melbourne. He had championed the cause of Mrs Norton after 1836. He had been so difficult on so many occasions that Melbourne had refused to give him government office. Yet, he now insisted that he would not have troubled Brougham, 'if I knew of another Man upon whose integrity, judgment, temper, prudence and discretion I could place an equal trust'.[45] The decision to employ Brougham poignantly underlined Melbourne's isolation. He had quarrelled with many of his old friends, and many more had died. Those who survived too often, he complained, neglected him.

When Brougham came to report to Melbourne's brother-in-law, Palmerston, he could only marvel at an extraordinary financial history. Although enjoying a large private income, and although he had drawn over £50,000 in official salaries, Melbourne had made only £12,000 worth of purchases in capital ventures.[46] He had apparently spent up to the limits of his income, showing little or no concern for the future. The Melbourne estate was not diminished by his tenure, but it was barely augmented. It was hard to understand on what a man with so few liabilities could have disgorged such considerable sums of money. Annuities to female friends were significant, but could not account for the phenomenon. Melbourne had not been providential in looking to the financial future, and nor did he have an over-pious appreciation of what was owed to the rest of his family. He took little trouble about his income, and uncertainty bred fear. In matters of personal finance, Melbourne lived for the day. He could have no confidence in the fact of his well-being because he took no trouble to plan or give structure to his affairs.

Inevitably, he was very dependent on the goodwill of servants. In 1839, he told Victoria that he employed no less than sixteen in London alone, all of whom exercised a kind of mastery over him. Victoria noted that, 'all his servants drink, he believes. I wondered they didn't cheat him; "They *do* cheat", he replied. Did he scold much? "No, I don't speak to them much," he replied, "nothing I hate so much as speaking to servants." '[47] One of his grooms was particularly skilful at thieving, but there was no question of dismissing him for he was 'the best groom for loading a gun a-shooting in England'.[48] His establishment in London was presided over by a housekeeper, 'a plain Yorkshire woman', who was with Melbourne for over thirty years, in spite of a rather ambiguous reference. She was 'particularly clever as a still-room woman, and about confectionary, but not quite as good as to attending how the house is cleaned. She has rather a temper he thinks. I said one never could find a *servant* who was *all* what one liked; "or anything else", Lord Melbourne said.'[49] Servants went unsupervised as part of a life-style that was in many other respects also unregulated.

There was delegation, too, in the management of estates. In collections of Melbourne's personal papers, the letters of agents are numerous and prominent. Melbourne was interested in the development of his properties, but clearly relied heavily on the opinion of Thomas Dawson at Brocket, Thomas Barber in Nottinghamshire, and Thomas Fox at Melbourne Hall.[50] According to Victoria's journal, Melbourne displayed an affected indifference to these men and their work: 'of Lord M's Bailiff Dawson, who Lord M quite forgot was not still his gardener, and laughed much on being reminded by me that he was his Bailiff.'[51] In fact, he took them very seriously, not only as managers of estates, to whom everything could be delegated, but also as agents in many other projects. They were to recommend an estate manager for Lord Stanhope; they were to mobilize the Melbourne interest at election time; and, most importantly, they were to represent the opinion of the common man.[52] He was happy to dine with these men and to listen to their views. When Melbourne was asked to account for the poor showing of the Whigs in the 1837 election, he answered by rehearsing the opinion of his Hertfordshire agent:

My steward here, who is a clever fellow and a Dissenter tells me that the real reason we suffered in public opinion is from the cry against O'Connell, and the notion of England being governed by Irishmen and Roman Catholics. He thinks this nonsense himself, but says that the impression is strong, general and impossible to counteract.[53]

Melbourne had no intention of enfranchising opinion at this level, but he recognized it as an increasing force in politics, and was pleased to have supper in its commonsensical company.

Melbourne's liking for the society of individuals from the lower orders was again considered among his eccentricities by contemporaries, who were inclined to discuss it as a misplaced *nostalgie de la boue*. In particular, the figure of Thomas Young baffled them. Melbourne, for much of the 1830s, described him as 'my weather gauge, through him I am able to look down below; which is for me more important than all I can learn from the fine gentlemen clerks about me'.[54] Known as 'Ubiquity Young',[55] this man acted as Melbourne's Sam Weller, always running errands, always making paths smooth, always ready with down-to-earth opinions. He was born in Nairne and was the son of a small farmer. Before meeting his future patron, he had made a certain amount of money trading in India and as purser on the Duke of Devonshire's yacht. None of this experience particularly qualified him to become Melbourne's amanuensis, but such was his position by 1830. He had the invaluable talent of making himself agreeable. One Whig recalled that, 'I never saw greater dexterity than he shews in accommodating himself to his company. You never quit him without having a better opinion of yourself than before.'[56] Until at least 1837, he acted as Melbourne's secretary, when that post was taken over by the more respectable figures of George Anson and William Cowper.[57]

Controversially, Young was given an extended brief. As has been noted above, he was used as an intermediary in negotiations with Radicals during the fraught years of 1830–4, talking to Place and persuading Hobhouse to join the government.[58] He was also asked to influence the editors of newspapers, and he thought himself 'entitled to praises and thanks for the services which I have been enabled to render the Whig Ministry through the Press'.[59] Certainly, Melbourne thought so highly of his services that he believed the Whigs should find 'something good and permanent for him,'[60] admitting his own 'implicit confidence' in his judgement. Allegedly, it was Young's opinion that pushed Melbourne into accepting the office of Prime Minister in 1834.[61]

Little wonder, then, that he should badger Grey repeatedly on his secretary's behalf.[62]

Young continued to be of service to Melbourne long after he had ceased to serve as his secretary. Like Dawson and the other estate managers, Young tested the mood of popular opinion, and reported it in letters that were read out to the Queen.[63] In September 1838, she recorded a conversation in her journal, of which Young was the topic:

I asked Lord M. how long Mr. Young had been his Private Secretary; from 30 to 34, when Lord M. had the power to give him his present situation; and he is ready to assist him now, whenever Lord M. sends to him. Lord M. said how necessary it was that these Private Secretaries should be discreet; for Lord M. said, they have unbounded confidence; see everything, copy everything.[64]

In these remarks, there is the faint suggestion of something sinister, namely that Young now knew so much about Melbourne's affairs, that he exercised an influence over them. As has been observed, the decision of Young to publish letters deeply disturbed Melbourne's last months. Certainly, the fact that Melbourne put himself so much into the hands of a man of such lowly social origins was controversial, and excited speculation. Mrs Norton warned Melbourne to be more circumspect: 'Don't on any account trust *Young* about this affair. Norton has drawn him into it, and he is a very mischievous man—more I think, than you are aware.'[65] In October 1840, Frederick Lamb, reflecting on the fact that Young had just helped in extricating his brother from another scrape, whose nature can only be guessed at, observed that, 'T. Young is one of his weaknesses and they are inexcusable.'[66] When Young died, he was worth £30,000. Clearly, he had been greatly rewarded for the important, if shadowy, role he had played in Melbourne's life. It is perhaps a measure of how isolated Melbourne felt himself in official politics, that he should put real store by the views of such men as Dawson and Young. It was certainly an unusual and distinctive habit in the circles in which Melbourne moved.

Retirement from office and the absence of any alternative occupation gave him the time to become a confirmed valetudinarian. He had always worried about his health, and, indeed, had a history of taking refuge in illness from difficulties in personal and political life. Genuine ill-health mingled with a pronounced hypochondria. By 1843, Melbourne was spending the huge sum of £800 a year on doctors.[67] As early as 1832, he was laid low by the recurrence of what his brother, George, called 'his awkward complaint', which seems to have turned on a malfunctioning bladder or prostate.[68] Two years later, the problem returned in a manner that seriously alarmed his sister, who thought it aggravated by his liking to drink 'two or three bottles of wine a day'.[69] For much of his prime ministership, his letters to his family and close friends chronicled a sad history of illness, which manifested itself in fevers, sleeplessness, and recalcitrant bowels. They, in turn, fretted over Melbourne's refusal to take exercise, or to counter the effects of overworking with a sensible diet and regular hours. Instead, he put on weight and ridiculed those who could rise without effort at five in the morning.[70]

By April 1839, Melbourne admitted to Victoria that he thought his constitution to be 'worn out'.[71] By this date, he weighed between thirteen and a half and fourteen stones.[72] His brother now seriously began to think that he could no longer sustain the demands of office without risking serious illness:

I do not like your acct. of Wm, it vexes me very much. I know how ill and how low He gets. I don't like Holland's physicking. He never could bear it from a boy. The remedy for over eating is eating less, physicking only makes things worse. What can I do for him. I could only sit and be melancholy to see him low. Oh dear oh dear it makes me very unhappy. He never will be out of office now and while in it nothing can be done for him, and if out he would probably do nothing of what I should recommend. We each follow our destiny and there is no help for it.[73]

In Frederick Lamb's opinion, William, instead of spending the summer of 1840 immersed in the Eastern Crisis, would have done better to seek rest and refreshment in Carlsbad. His brother's health seemed to be going from 'bad to worse'.[74]

Significantly perhaps, it was not the holding of office that brought on a crisis in Melbourne's health, but retirement. In October 1842, he suffered 'a slight paralytic stroke'. As his sister-in-law explained to Emily Lamb, William's speech was unimpaired, 'but the use of one side is encumbered . . . he will recover. It is only such a dreadful thing for the future.'[75] His recovery was 'gradual and constant but very slow and distressing'.[76] In fact, the left-hand side of his body was to be permanently weakened, and his features had changed in a manner that alarmed Mrs George Lamb: 'his face much better, tho' still a good deal altered. It still makes the most dreadful impression on me, whenever I go into the room, almost more now that he tries to laugh, than when he was low and almost in a stupor . . . I cannot describe the effect of seeing that powerful mind, and beautiful countenance thus affected.'[77] By the end of the year, he was walking again unassisted and had a revived interest in politics and social gossip, but there was no doubt that he had been in a real sense diminished by the illness. Now, Mrs Lamb noticed that 'he pauses before he speaks, and stares, and seems to collect his thoughts'.[78]

In this, as in every other crisis in his life, the Lamb family closed ranks. Everyone seemed anxious to be part of a conspiracy that denied the possibility of a stroke. Melbourne himself admitted that he had 'never had so hard a knock',[79] and that his left hand and leg were so crippled that attending Parliament was out of the question,[80] but he insisted that 'this d—d gout had been at the bottom of it'.[81] Mrs George Lamb reported that the rest of the family took a similar view:

There is no denying that it has been that *sort* of attack though the family were anxious it should not be said, which prevented my saying more to you. But it seems now thought that it proceeds from a deranged stomach which is not so bad or so likely to return as from other causes . . . Lady Palmerston has been with Ld. M., and thinks he looks well, she said she was sorry to hear he had been ill, and he said, oh there was not much the matter, not so much as they thought, and as a proof of how it has been exaggerated, he wrote a long letter to Ld. Palmerston upon the Boundary question.[82]

Dissimulation on this scale no doubt helped morale, but it barely disguised the harsh reality of the situation. The paralysis limited his movements and made him unsteady. Early in 1843, he suffered a fall 'which shook him so much'. After it, 'he does not talk more, and is unwilling to go out . . . the surgeon says he will never recover his arm—the muscles all crushed—and it was the paralized [sic] side'.[83] No doubt as a by-product of his illness, he began to suffer problems in connection with blood circulation. For this he underwent 'frictions with hot saltwater, which naturally tended to diminish his chilliness'.[84] No euphemism or family treaty could effectively mask the fact that, after 1842, his expectations in life would have to be severely curtailed.

Illness and the loss of office inevitably took Melbourne away from the centre of London society and politics to its margins. Indeed, he increasingly found it difficult to visit London at all. Brocket was the only place for attentive nursing and convalescence. As a result, friends were now required to travel to Hertfordshire in order to visit him. Living in the countryside threatened Melbourne with terminal boredom. For a man who had once been so personally fastidious, it was bad enough to watch his own body decay, but for a gregarious man also to be denied company was a terrible, additional burden. Since 1828, Melbourne had been accustomed to living among the most diverting company that London could offer. To find himself outside its warm conviviality was loathsome. As a result, Melbourne was a difficult patient, acting, according to Mrs George Lamb, 'quite like a spoilt child'.[85] Intensely lonely, Melbourne 'often sinks for hours into gloomy silence and reverie'.[86] Chance visitors like William Leigh Hatherton were greeted warmly. He found Melbourne, 'in his dressing gown and slippers, without a cravat, and entirely en deshabille', and inclined to talk for hours.[87] He made increasing demands on the goodwill of his friends, and pronounced himself 'mortified' when they inevitably failed to meet all of them.[88] He complained bitterly of an intolerable isolation. To one visitor he observed: 'I am glad you have come. I have sat here watching that timepiece and heard it strike four times without seeing the face of a human being; and, had it struck the fifth, I feel I could not have borne it.'[89]

It became a necessary, psychological prop for him to believe the unbelievable. He continued to insist that he was the leader of Whiggery, and that he would be the natural choice for Prime Minister when that party returned to office. This became a pathetic stance to adopt, when it was obvious to everyone that he was 'quite unfit for it'.[90] The fantasizing had a grim quality to it. At a Windsor dinner party in 1844, he held forth to his startled fellow-guests about the likelihood of his returning to politics:

It was very strange, and everybody looked amazed. He has been a very curious man all his life, and he is as strange as ever now, in the sort of make-believe with which he tries to delude himself and others. Whilst all indicates the decay of his powers, and his own consciousness of it, he assumes an air and language as if he was the same man, and ready to act his old part on any stage and at any time. His friends are, I think vexed and pained, and think it, as it is, a rather melancholy spectacle.[91]

Too often he was in 'a very nervous, lachrymose state',[92] and there was 'on his face a perpetual consciousness of his glory obscured'.[93] Even the closest of his friends found this refusal to face facts very difficult to manage.

When, in December 1845, there finally came a real prospect of a Whig return to government, Melbourne's feelings were treated with the greatest consideration by his former colleagues. They all behaved as though he would obviously have been Prime Minister again, if only his health had been a little stronger. Anson observed that 'in his present state of health he could not have incurred any fatigue without great risk'.[94] Lord John Russell, who in fact had the Queen's commission to form a government, patiently wrote to Melbourne with the same message, attempting to sugar the pill by telling him that his nephew, William Cowper, had been nominated for a place at the Treasury.[95] Melbourne had to admit that he had been treated 'kindly'.[96] He was consulted about appointments and flatteringly listened to. At the end, it appeared that the decision not to resume office had been his and his alone. He did not feel 'excluded'.[97] Such a view bore little relationship with the reality of the situation, but it allowed him to retain a certain personal pride and dignity.

The truth, however, lay elsewhere. His stroke had so diminished his powers, that all talk of a serious role in politics was but an unnecessary disturbance of the air. Diarists recorded his decline. In December 1843, Greville noted that Melbourne 'had been at the Queen's party at Chatsworth, which excited him, and was bad for him. At first he attempted to talk in his old strain; but it was evidently an effort, he soon relapsed into silence . . . I have no doubt he chafes and frets under the consciousness of his decay.'[98] In moments of personal honesty, Melbourne acknowledged his decline, and almost accepted it. In April 1844, he told Victoria,

Your Majesty is quite right in saying that Lord Melbourne has still some health left, if he will but take care of it . . . At the same time, the change from strength to weakness and the evident progress of decadence is a very hard and disagreeable trial. Lord Melbourne has been reading Cicero on old age, a very pretty treatise, but he does not find much consolation after it . . . It is certainly, as your Majesty says, wrong to be impatient and to repine at everything, but still it is difficult not to do so.[99]

In 1846, he expressed a great longing to see Victoria but feared 'the weight of the full dress uniform'.[100] Wriggle how he might, there was no escaping the fact that the events of 1841–2 had brought an abrupt end to his active life.

The diminishing of his powers was all too public. In 1842, before his stroke, he spoke in Lords debates twelve times. After his illness, he spoke only twice more, in 1844 and 1846. On each occasion, it was a ceremonial speech, seconding an address to the monarch congratulating her on the safe birth of a child. Even his insistence on attending the Lords worried his family that he might not be 'the worse for it'.[101] His brother, Frederick, knew the risk that such journeys involved, but accepted the inevitable:

I suspect that some of his ladies have been pressing him to come up, and I know him to have confided to them that he finds his life here very dull. If he is ordered to give up the House of Lords He may not improbably give up London along with it, and in that case what can be done to amuse him. He will not move, and here I believe him to be unamusable and I take a state of apathy and ennui to be a great drawback to his perfect recovery.[102]

When he appeared at debates, dragging a crippled leg and speaking to old friends in a voice so broken that it was 'if he had been going to burst into tears',[103] it merely convinced his erstwhile colleagues that his claims to leadership were at an end, and that they should look elsewhere.

In the months immediately following his resignation, Melbourne could entertain the hope of continuing to influence politics. He was consulted by Russell on old problems like the correct way of handling O'Connell,[104] and by Palmerston and others on new problems like Peel's Income Tax proposals.[105] There was also work to be done in tidying-up loose ends from his own administration, and in justifying its record. He was tenacious in defending his own reputation. In February 1842, he ironically congratulated Peel on admitting that the affairs of the country, as he had inherited them, 'were not quite in such a desperate condition as they were then represented by the noble Lords opposite'. He refused to concede that he had bequeathed to his successor 'immense financial difficulties . . . He did not mean to deny that there were difficulties, but he did assert that they were not immense.'[106] Inevitably, however, the notes inviting his opinion on the management of affairs became more and more infrequent. Inevitably, too, discussions of the politics of the 1830s lost relevance. Melbourne quickly became a figure on the margin of public life.

He gave his last vote in the House of Lords in May 1848, on a Bill to give full civil rights to Jews, but his effective political life had ended six years earlier. He had no choice but to watch Lord John Russell gradually confirming his position as the new leader of Whiggery. It was a spectacle that Melbourne resented, though, in theory, he should have been pleased. Russell was a protégé of Holland House, and, during the 1830s, had been one of Melbourne's most trusted and most helpful colleagues in office. In these respects, he was Melbourne's natural heir. Unfortunately, Melbourne could not accept his own eclipse, and, just as Grey had harried his friends after resigning in 1834, so Melbourne now attempted the same thing. He accused Russell of not showing 'as much courage as he expected of him'.[107] He refused social invitations, declaring that he did not 'feel myself strong enough for John Russell dinners'.[108] In these last years, Melbourne was uncongenial company, complaining of neglect and lost authority. Former friends like Russell and Lansdowne were pushed away and alienated. Mobilizing a very long memory, Melbourne embroiled himself in trivial, but bitterly felt, exchanges with Sydney Smith and others over incidents that had happened many years before.[109] It was an unedifying performance. But then, as his family well knew, Melbourne found it hard to live with illness and the recollection of once having been powerful.

The issue which confirmed Russell's ascendancy and Melbourne's political demise was the Corn Law question. As has been noted above, Melbourne had never been in favour of either abolishing or modifying these Laws, whereas Russell had become increasingly convinced of their harmful nature. For Melbourne, the misery and dislocations that attended the development of industrial society were unfortunate but inevitable. Government could do little or nothing to mitigate their effects. To pretend otherwise was to raise dangerous expectations that could not possibly be fulfilled. As he told the Lords, in February 1842, 'I believe that the difficulties and the destitution of the manufacturing population are inseparable from, belonging to, and inherent in that condition of industry and of capital engaged in manufactures which exist in this country.'[110] Although, as he lectured Victoria, 'the reality is very bad', he could 'not perceive any measure, which it is in the power of the Government to take for the relief of the suffering'.[111] Groups with interests that were harmed by the fluctuations of trade cycles should look to their own resources, not to Government, for relief'.[112] As Home Secretary, he had firmly told JPs and Lords-Lieutenant to manage their own affairs without governmental assistance, and his views had not changed, even though he himself might be a victim of disturbance:

Melbourne itself is a large manufacturing and political village, it is twenty-five miles from Leicester, seventeen from Nottingham, eight from Derby . . . an inflammable neighbourhood—Perhaps however they may leave me quite alone, and if they do not, I must manage as well as I can.[113]

This philosophical response was assisted by his suspicion that the Corn Law agitation was wholly artificial, and kept alive only by the frantic efforts of the Anti-Corn Law League.[114]

In the months between his resignation and his stroke, he spoke often about the Corn Laws. It was clearly the issue on which he most wished to continue to make a mark. Having delayed discussion of it for so long while prime minister, he still had hopes of influencing the debate yet further. In rather confused speeches, he told the Lords that, although he 'was a warm friend to the principles of free trade', he yet saw merit in protecting agriculture and the society which depended on it.[115] He now argued, not that such protection was necessary to ensure that England would be self-sufficient in food production, but that the removal of all controls would lead to markets being flooded with foreign imports. Prices would sink and agricultural society would be fatally disrupted.[116] He could envisage supporting a sliding-scale of duties, but that would be the limit of his concessions on the subject.[117] Public statements in the Lords and at dinner tables suggested that Melbourne had shifted a little in his views over a decade of debate. His basic objections to change remained, but the arguments brought against it were not necessarily the same, and nor were they consistently weighted.

Contemporaries, however, were left in no doubt that 'Melbourne seemed to be more frightened at the prospect of foreign corn than anybody'.[118] Mrs George Lamb noted that the question of the Corn Laws was one of the few that could still rouse her brother-in-law to angry commitment: 'Ld. M. is as much as ever against a total repeal of the Corn Laws and thinks it wicked and dishonest. He goes quite into a passion about it.'[119] At the heart of his arguments was a profound suspicion of the new industrial landscape that was taking shape around him. He never lost a preference for agricultural society. Parishes and counties benignly governed by landowners was a model of stable society which he cherished. Historically, it had proved its worth in the wars of his childhood, and it had protected England from the revolutions that had devastated Europe in his adult life. The Corn Laws, quite apart from economic arguments in their favour, were the symbol that that order of society was prized. Melbourne detested the notion that the values of industrial England should be equally regarded. He knew little or nothing of it from experience. Its leaders never appeared at Holland House dinners. It was a dark, mysterious and threatening energy. Past stability had rested on an agricultural base. Melbourne could not see guarantees of comparable balance in any alternative.

When the crisis came on, in 1845–6, provoked by famine in Ireland, Melbourne refused to accept it. For him, the whole incident had been fabricated. On 2 December 1845, he wrote to Victoria as follows:

Lord Melbourne is not surprised that different accounts are received by the Government of the state of the potatoes. Lord Melbourne is convinced that the fears taken are much exaggerated and the appearance of a dearth of corn still more so. Lord Melbourne is very clear that the Government have to come to a determination not to alter the Corn Laws at present, and he hopes that they will persevere in it.[120]

Eleven days later, Russell was told the same thing. Reports of dearth had been grossly 'exaggerated', and he was to 'Remember this in whatever you determine'.[121] In January 1846, Melbourne's frustration and indignation boiled over at a dinner party at Windsor, stunning his fellow guests. Greville eagerly recorded the incident;

There has been a curious scene with Melbourne at Windsor . . . It was at dinner, when Melbourne was sitting next to the Queen. Some allusion was made to passing events and to the expected measure [Corn Law repeal], when Melbourne suddenly broke out, 'Ma'am it is a damned dishonest act.' The Queen laughed and tried to quiet him, but he repeated, 'I say again it is a very dishonest act,' and then he continued a tirade against abolition of Corn Laws, the people not knowing how to look, and the Queen only laughing.[122]

Another version of the affair had Melbourne describing repeal as 'd—d treachery to the Farmers'.[123] So infamous was this dinner party, that Greville was still trying to establish an authorized account of it two years later, by cross-questioning Melbourne's sister-in-law. According to her, Melbourne had ultimately been silenced by the Queen herself.[124] His performance had had a petulance and intemperance that even old age barely excused.

When Peel determined that he would sponsor the abolition of the Corn Laws, the majority of Whigs agreed to support him. It was a decision against which Melbourne 'bounced and complained'.[125] In the end, he cast a proxy vote for repeal in the House of Lords.[126] Emily Lamb thought that he had acted 'out of regard for the Q'.[127] Melbourne himself declared that, if his friends 'as a party resolved to eat any dirt Peel may make, I will not refuse my mouthful'.[128] It was in one sense a generous act. To support repeal after being its main opponent for so long was a humiliating reversal of position.

Criticism of his behaviour was predictable. For him to accept it rather than embarrass either Victoria or Russell was courageous. Even so, no one was deceived about his isolation within the Whig ranks. To have voted against his friends would, in a real sense, have been more humiliating, exposing the fact of his marginalization in politics. Quite simply, as Prime Minister, Melbourne had been able to control the issue. It was ungainly to try to continue to do so. Outbursts provoked by the keen appreciation of his impotence merely silenced dinner parties.

The Corn Law crisis destroyed what remained of his friendship with Lord John Russell. It had been cooling ever since 1841, but it was still costly for Melbourne. For much of the 1830s, Russell and Lansdowne had been his two closest associates in politics. Russell himself had regarded Melbourne with a certain reverence and affection. He was only too aware that supplanting him in the leadership of Whiggery was a delicate business, and he took trouble to coax Melbourne into an acceptance of both his new situation and the probable necessity of revising the extent of agricultural protection.[129] The two issues seemed to have become linked in Melbourne's mind. When, for example, in 1842, he insisted that it was impolitic to panic in the face of one bad harvest, because it was 'an event so casual, so uncertain, so much the creature of chance and accident',[130] Russell patiently begged to differ:

I am glad to find that you are not pledged to the present corn law. But I wish you would also engage to consider the subject somewhat further.

I do not see why the exaggeration of the distress should prevent your taking into view the actual suffering. In a popular government no question is ever carried by the mere calm reasoning of wise men. . . . Neither do men separate entirely political expediency from the accidents of harvests and trade in peace, victory and war. Such is the nature of government, and no dislike of yours can alter human nature in this respect.

Your esoteric doctrine has the effect of hurting yourself, for tho' you may find it very easy to change your course, it is not done without a diminution of your character for foresight and practical wisdom.[131]

When repeal was passed in 1846, the two men formally voted on the same side, but all intimacy, all civility even, had gone. Melbourne described Russell's leadership as 'hasty and reckless . . . erroneous and mischievous'.[132] Equally sharply, Russell told his former leader that rejection of the Bill could only lead to 'violent agitation'.[133] It was a parting of ways. It came at a time when Melbourne could ill-afford such losses. For far too long he claimed an influence in politics that, by the nature of things, could not possibly be his.

Illness, the loss and death of friends, together with a marginalization in politics exposed Melbourne's isolation and vulnerability. This had in fact been his condition since 1828, but it had been successfully masked by his playing the game of politics, and by the company of such as Mrs Norton. For one reason or another, all those diversions were now denied him. Mrs George Lamb reported, in 1842, that Melbourne had lost interest in the present and had no hope of the future. Quite simply, 'the past is his only amusement'.[134] He felt deeply what she called 'the not being able to mix himself up with politics and all that goes on'.[135] In this situation, he returned to the point from which he had started out. The Lamb family had always been on hand to arrange William's life and to bring him safely out of crises. Now, he surrendered to its authority almost completely. His brother George had died in 1834, but all the others were alive, and all of them were anxious once again to offer protection and sympathy. Their concern had always been the one focus of support in his life that could be absolutely guaranteed.

George Lamb's widow, Caroline, was at Brocket for much of the period 1842–8, acting as nurse and companion, reading to Melbourne and trying, with increasing desperation, to engage his attention.[136] She found him a difficult patient: 'he is rather a difficult person to manage, for he won't tell me how he feels, does not like to talk of his health, and one can't make out if he likes to be alone or not.'[137] In fact, Mrs Lamb, while well-meaning and complaisant, was not as intellectually gifted as her husband's other relations. Melbourne acknowledged her kindnesses, but found it hard to tolerate her company for any length of time. Other members of the family, in drawing up a rota of attendance, were aware of this. Frederick reminded his sister, Emily: 'A fortnight in town will do for Adine and me and after that we can undertake the rest of the summer, but you must not suppose that Caroline can replace you or me with Wm unless for a few days therefore take yr measures accordingly.'[138] There was no escaping the fact that Melbourne appreciated Mrs Lamb more for the memory of a beloved brother than for any quality of her own.

Inevitably, it was with his brother and sister that intimacy grew even deeper. Frederick's successful career in diplomacy had come to an end in 1841. Two years earlier, he had been created Baron Beauvale. Late in life, he had married a young woman from the Austrian aristocracy, Adine von Maltzahn. Melbourne was devoted to both of them, and they became the principal supports of his final years. As Lady Holland gratefully observed, the Beauvales made the care of Melbourne a first priority in their lives: 'The Beauvales are inestimable to him. They square all their motions to his advantage and comfort. There never was a greater change in a man's character made by matrimony than has been effected in Lord B's.'[139] Inevitably, Frederick spoke in the same idiom as his brother, 'dealing pretty much in persiflage like Lord Melbourne.'[140] The brothers employed the accents and cadencies of the late eighteenth-century. They had been formed by the same values, many of which were now being discounted by the generation coming to prominence in the 1840s. Without complaint, Frederick formally became his brother's keeper, and watched 'over him as a Mother does her first baby'.[141]

Adine Beauvale willingly cooperated in her husband's attempts to ease Melbourne's life. She was compassionate, intelligent, and undemanding. Her new brother-in-law liked and admired her from the beginning. As a companion at Brocket, she was prized, and she became the one who was most constantly in attendance. She, in turn, became much 'attached' to him, and it distressed her to witness the fading of his interest in all the things that had once given him pleasure.[142] It was a matter of regret to her that Melbourne was often 'thoughtful and low'.[143] Very quickly, she became indispensable, sending bulletins on his health to the Queen or Lady Holland, and trying to persuade friends to come down from London to amuse him. She took frank pleasure in her efforts: 'it fills one with happiness to be able to try at least to vary and enliven his sad confinement, and he is alive to all topics of amusement which are presented to him . . . I have nothing more to say about Lord Melbourne, and therefore I end my letter knowing you care but for that.'[144]

Standing solidly beside her brothers was Emily, still trying to fulfil the matriarchal responsibilities that her mother had bequeathed her. Though she was more conservatively inclined than William, the two had never undergone any kind of estrangement. He had liked and respected her first husband, Lord Cowper, and had felt his death keenly.[145] When, two years later, Emily married her long-standing lover, Palmerston, Melbourne gave the union his full blessing. In politics, he found Palmerston often belligerent and intimidating, but the two men each appreciated that they came from the same milieu. Intellectual and moral perspectives were the same. They could joke in common. Palmerston was quite happy to spend time in Hertfordshire 'to keep Melbourne Company',[146] providing an invaluable link with politics and an informed source of gossip. Palmerston's estate at Panshanger was conveniently situated for almost daily visits to Brocket. As for Emily herself, in her attacking, energetic approach to life, she was described as 'still quite juvenile'.[147] She happily took her turn in nursing her brother, reading to him and reporting his latest epigram.[148] She also continued to try to regulate and 'alter' his life, as she had always done, even in the detail of determining the moment when he should go to bed.[149] It was a deep affection fussily expressed. Melbourne had occasionally struggled against its imperiousness in the past, but he rarely did so now.

The family cohort closing ranks around Melbourne was completed by William and Fanny Cowper, Emily's children by her first marriage. Their company was always welcomed. As Mrs Lamb observed: 'how amusing of

Ld. Melbourne with the 3rd generation. What a youthful mind he retains.'[150] Fanny was spirited, intelligent and approved of, but it was William who was his uncle's particular favourite. He had served him as a personal secretary, and was increasingly treated as an adopted son. On Melbourne's behalf, he had negotiated with the press and with the Hastings family, advised on the scale of mourning that was appropriate to mark the death of Victoria's cousin, and had run errands of all kinds. Now, he was his uncle's 'dear Will'.[151] He lent him money, and offered advice about women and marriage, though his qualifications for doing so might have been questioned:

My dear William, I think you are quite right not to engage further in these affairs without the certainty of an adequate provision; and I am glad that you find a consolation in St. Paul's epistle to the Corinthians. But you must not run about flirting with girls and persuading them that you intend to marry, unless you have the intention. St. Paul would not approve of this. Indeed, would he like to think his epistles made the instruments of flirtation?[152]

In return, the nephew took his turn in the watching and the reading aloud, regulating contact with Mrs Norton, and keeping friends informed of his uncle's condition.[153]

Few men, therefore, were so blessed in his family relationships than Melbourne. For the whole of his life the support of brothers and sister never faltered. In old age, their care was exemplary, and they were assisted by a much-loved niece and nephew. Melbourne was never actually alone. Yet, being surrounded by so much kindness was, for Melbourne, a mitigation of his condition, not a cure. He sensed an isolation which no family affection could ultimately overcome. He lost friends like Russell by showing an almost calculated intemperance. Others were treated with indifference. It seemed that he increasingly withdrew into himself, losing contact with other people, uncaring about their opinions and increasingly unable to talk freely. It was Adine Beauvale's greatest regret that, however much kindness the family showered on William Lamb, 'he don't open his heart to others'.[154]

From 1845 onwards, Melbourne's decline into illness and decrepitude was precipitous. The crippling effects of his stroke, and gout, became progressively worse, and made any long-term of residence in London impossible. Deafness soured the life of someone for whom conversation had been vitally important.[155] In his last three years, Melbourne's most constant companion was a Miss Cuyler, who appears to have combined the roles of nurse and amanuensis.[156] She was 'a most strange but active' woman, who, although sometimes treating her patient 'as you do a troublesome child', was yet 'very serviceable'.[157] Lady Palmerston chronicled the steady deterioration in her brother's health. The stroke in 1842, and the fall which almost immediately followed it;[158] the onset of jaundice early in 1848;[159] and then the final slippage towards death. In October 1848, Melbourne suffered another stroke and fainting fits.[160] Over the next six weeks, as his sister recorded, his condition worsened. On 25 October, he was 'poorly'.[161] On the evening of 11 November, there was 'an Epileptic fit which frightened us all dreadfully'.[162] After this, the patient was 'entirely feeding on slops'.[163] On 21 November, he suffered four more fits, after which all speech became virtually impossible. At this point, all hope of recovery was abandoned, and the Lamb family could only contemplate 'a sad scene of misery'.[164] Three days later the end mercifully came: 'fits came on which were dreadful to see . . . at last he was quite quiet and calm and went out like a candle with only a sigh a short time before six.'[165]

Two days after her brother's death, Emily Palmerston attempted a résumé of his final illness for the instruction of her cousin, Mrs Huskisson:

Poor dear William is now in heaven and one must not grieve too much that he is removed from this Earth, and from all the wrong anxiety and pain and trouble from which he has suffered these last six years of bad health and more particularly since last April when he had a slight attack of the same kind as the first and his Stomach completely failed in addition to all the former distress.

Epileptic fits he had the last few days which were very painful to see, but I trust and believe to himself free of pain—as pressures on the brain destroy sensation.

Tho' conscious to a certain degree up the last day or two and knowing those around him, his mind was quite composed and peaceful and I believe he felt no anxiety or painful thoughts now, tho' he had no doubt long contemplated his own death, and his mind was quite prepared for the awful change. At last, thank God his end was peaceful and he only breathed one sigh.[166]

On 1 December, he was buried in the family vault in Hatfield Church. It was a low-key affair. Outside the group of family mourners, there was his local doctor, Mr Thomas, his London solicitor, Mr Cookney, his housekeeper, his steward and 'several other of the upper servants'.[167] It was the most anonymous of endings for someone who had once been Prime Minister. No representative of the Queen is mentioned in press reports. There was no talk of St Paul's or the Abbey.

Among Melbourne's personal papers the letters of condolence sent to members of his family after his death are carefully preserved. They came from an extraordinary range of people. Louis Philippe wrote on behalf of his family.[168] Mrs Norton was inevitably driven to remember her time with Melbourne, and she did so without recrimination: 'The old days come back again—as I sit here alone—old days when I was young, and very proud of his liking me.'[169] For Lady Morgan and others, his death was a real water-shed, severing an important link with the world of Pitt and Fox.[170] Melbourne's eighteenth-century values in private life, salonard wit, and dandified appearance had an antique quality in the world of railways and Chartism. With the exception of a brief dispute between Russell and Frederick Lamb about the returning of letters,[171] Melbourne's death involved no one in undue trouble or disturbance. The sense of loss was real, and so too was the indignation expressed at the unflattering obituaries put out by some newspapers, notoriously by *The Times*. Editors seemed too grudging, too unwilling to acknowledge 'an absence of prejudice and the great readiness with which he listened to very opposite views'.[172] Contemporaries seemed too ready to value Melbourne below Peel, Russell, or Grey.

Even his friends found it unusually difficult to make a final assessment. Lord Dacre, a friend from childhood, thought that Melbourne was a man who, to a quite exceptional degree, obscured his real views and feelings with 'his apparent alienation of manner'.[173] He seemed incapable of admitting that he cared for anything or anyone. Many people, and certainly most politicians have a public face and a private character. In Melbourne's case, the chasm between the two was huge. Very few men and women were allowed to breach the polished surface which he presented to the world. The problem was perfectly set out by the Radical journalist, Albany Fonblanque:

Lord Melbourne's, indeed, is a character not to be hit off in a few generalities; it is very difficult to draw. We doubt whether anyone knows it who has not mistaken it more than once . . . Absurdly misrepresented as a Sybarite, his mind is of a turn and temper for the driest studies. By superficial observers he has been taken for a trifler, for no better reason than because he trifles so well; but who in the next breath reasons more acutely, who philosophizes more deeply, who brings readier and ampler knowledge to bear on any question that arises?[174]

At one level, his carelessness of manner, which turned aside anything of seriousness into epigram, underpinned a reputation for being 'a lounger'.[175] Disraeli and other opponents brilliantly confirmed this image in the popular mind. For them, he was possibly benign, avuncular in his dealings with a young and inexperienced Queen, but at bottom profoundly superficial. He could be dismissed as someone who hated to take any decision in private or public life, and who was happy to delegate difficulty to others. It was typical of the man that, if this kind of image was unfair, he made no effort whatever to correct it.

In his poem, *St Stephen's* Bulwer Lytton attempted to present a more rounded picture. A Hertfordshire neighbour, and possibly a lover of Caroline Lamb, Lytton knew Melbourne well, and suspected him of having depths of character of an almost uncharted kind:

In stalwart contrast, large of heart and frame,
Destined for power, in youth more bent on fame,
Sincere, yet deeming half the world a sham,
Mark the rude handsome manliness of Lamb!
None then foresaw his rise; e'en now but few
Guess right the man so many thought they knew;
Gossip accords him attributes like these—
A sage good humour based on a love of ease,
A mind that most things undisturb'dly weigh'd,
Nor deem'd the metal worth the clink it made.
Such was the man, *in part*, to outward show;
Another man lay coil'd from sight below—
As mystics tell us that this fleshly form
Enfolds a subtler which escapes the worm,
And is the true one which the Maker's breath
Quicken'd from dust, and privileged from death.
His was a restless, anxious intellect;
Eager for truth, and pining to detect;
Each ray of light that mind can cast on soul,
Chequering its course, or shining from its goal,
Each metaphysic doubt—each doctrine dim—
Plato or Pusey—had delight for him.
His mirth, though genial, came by fits and starts—
The man was mournful in his heart of hearts.
Oft would he sit and wander forth alone;
Sad—why? I know not; was it ever known?
Tears came with ease to these ingenuous eyes—
A verse, if noble, bade them nobly rise.
Hear him discourse, you'd think he scarcely felt
No heart more facile to arouse or melt;
High as a knight's in some Castilian lay
And tender as a sailor's in a play.
This was the Being with his human life
At variance—noiseless, for he veil'd the strife;
The Being serious, gentle, shy, sincere
The life St. Stephen's, and a Court career;
Train'd first in salons gay with roué wits,
And light with morals the reverse of Pitt's.
As England's chief, let others judge his claim,
And strike just balance between praise and blame;
I from the Minister draw forth the man,
Such as I saw before his power began,
And glancing o'er the noblest of our time,
Who won the heights it wears out life to climb,

On that steep table-land which, viewed afar,
Appears so proud a neighbour of the star,
And, reach'd, presents dead levels in its rise
More dimm'd than valleys are by vapoury skies,
I mark not one concealing from mankind
A larger nature or a lovelier mind,
Or leaving safer from his own gay laugh
That faith in good which is the soul's best half.[176]

The accounts of Disraeli and Lytton, so contrasting in their emphasis, so contradictory in their conclusions, are yet both true. Intelligent, well-read, and ultimately wise, Melbourne denied all these qualities in his manner, and refused to employ them seriously in politics. He cared little for any of the great issues of his time, seeing virtue only in prevarication and delay. He took pleasure in manipulating the ambitions of others, and in watching them scramble for honours and titles that meant nothing to him. As he was well aware, only exceptional circumstances in politics could have wafted him to the prime ministership and kept him there for so long. On the other hand, Melbourne had once been an earnest disciple of Fox and his Scots tutors, recognized as a coming man in his generation. The question therefore becomes one of deciding why these talents had to be obscured by mannerisms, and by a wish to hold life at arm's length. The answer perhaps lies in two overriding factors.

First, throughout his life, Melbourne lacked a confidence in decision-making. Even in matters of the most profound, personal interest, he followed the directions of others. His mother, his sister, much-loved brothers, and, for a time, mistresses could order his affairs without challenge. He had a passivity in the face of events and difficulties that was remarked on again and again. If problems arose, he was likely to escape from them in illness or secluded reading. For much of his life before taking up politics seriously at the age of 48, the library at Brocket had fed a highly intelligent mind, but also acted as a kind of refuge. Even as Prime Minister, Melbourne felt an enduring lack of confidence in himself and his views. He spoke little in the Lords, and his chairing of a Cabinet frequently took the form of refereeing the views of others. In the politics of the 1830s, this diffidence had merits, but it was ultimately a defensive mechanism. Melbourne chose to make light of what he lacked the confidence to determine.

Second, and most importantly, he never recovered from a traumatic marriage. It was a twenty-two year exercise in public humiliation, which he never had the courage to terminate. Understandably, he resolved that no one should be allowed to cause such hurt again, certainly not a Lady Branden or a Mrs Norton. It was a resolution that held until he was confronted by the young Victoria, who became a surrogate daughter. Their association brought three years of great happiness, until her sudden transfer of affection to Prince Albert left him without further emotional resource. In twice offering affection, Melbourne, as he saw it, had been mocked by Caroline Lamb and rejected by Victoria. The bitter edge to his last years must have, to some extent, been produced by these experiences. He must seriously have wondered, despite the kindnesses of family and friends, if he himself was lovable. Cynicism and a diffident manner became a man who, as Greville observed, was a loving man with nothing in the world to love.

Notes

Chapter 1

1. Royal Archives, Windsor Castle; The Journal of Queen Victoria, 30 Jan. 1840.
2. G. Anson to ?, 7 May 1843; Royal Archives, Y55 fo. 11.
3. A. Hayward, *Eminent Statesmen and Writers* (London 1880), i. 329.
4. *Morning Chronicle*, 27 Nov. 1848.
5. H. Dunckley, *Lord Melbourne* (London 1890), 53.
6. E. A. Smith, *Whig Principles and Party Politics* (Manchester 1975), 4.
7. QVJ, 1 Sept. 1838.
8. Ibid. 29 Aug. 1838.
9. Ibid. 1 Sept. 1838.
10. BL Add. MSS 69972.
11. Cecil, 11. See also QVJ, 2 Sept. 1838.
12. Anon., *The Memoirs of Harriette Wilson* (London 1825), i. 2. See also E. Steele, *The Memoirs of Sophia Baddeley* (London 1787).
13. P. O'Leary, *Sir James Mackintosh* (Aberdeen 1989), 132.
14. K. Bourne, *Palmerston* (London 1982), 185.
15. QVJ, 9 June 1838.
16. Ibid. 31 Dec. 1838.
17. W. Lamb, *Epilogue to the Comedy of the Fashionable Friends* (London 1801).
18. W. Cowper, *The Nation*, 15 (1884), 49–50.
19. BL Add. MSS 51723, fo. 166; Lady Bessborough to Lady Holland, 23 June [1803].
20. William Lamb's Autobiography; Herts. PRO, Panshanger MSS, D/ELb F12.
21. QVJ, 3 Nov. 1837.
22. Ibid. 30 Dec. 1838.
23. H. Reeve, *A Journal of the Reigns of King George IV, King William IV and Queen Victoria by the late Charles Greville* (London 1888), vi. 247.
24. BL Add. MSS 56560, fo. 88; the diary of J. C. Hobhouse, 2 March 1839.
25. BL Add. MSS 51725, fo. 181; Egremont to Holland, 12 April 1835.
26. Lord J. Townshend to Lady Melbourne, n.d.; Hatfield House MSS, unfol.
27. Diary of Lady Palmerston, 7 Nov. 1840; Hatfield House MSS.
28. BL Add. MSS 45551, fo. 189; F. Lamb to E. Lamb, 7 Nov. 1837.
29. Lady C. Lamb to Lady Bessborough, 1807; Lord Bessborough, *Lady Bessborough and Her Family* (London 1940), 166.
30. Lady Palmerston to Lord Leconfield, 1 Nov. 1867; Petworth, Egremont MSS, 704. See also, same to same 13 Nov. 1867 and 25 Feb. [1868].
31. QVJ, 27 March 1838.
32. Lady C. Lamb to Lady Bessborough, n.d.; West Sussex RO, Bessborough MSS, fo. 161.
33. Dunckley, *Lord Melbourne*, 237.
34. Ibid.

35. Melbourne to G. Wyndham, 28 Jan. 1839; Petworth, Egremont MSS, 684. See also G. Wyndham to Melbourne, 27 Jan. 1839; ibid.
36. Diary of Frances, Lady Shelley, 17 April 1818; R. Edgcumbe, *The Diary of Frances, Lady Shelley* (London 1913), i. 6.
37. QVJ, 1 Jan. 1838.
38. In the late 18th cent., Melbourne House stood on the site of what is now the Albany.
39. T. Moore to J. Atkinson, [autumn 1806]; W. S. Dowden, *The Letters of Thomas Moore* (Oxford 1964), i. 107.
40. Cecil, 13.
41. QVJ, 9 Oct. 1838.
42. Ibid. 22 Dec. 1837.
43. Cecil, 39.
44. W. Lamb to Lady Morpeth, 4 April 1818; Castle Howard, Carlisle MSS, J18/44/145.
45. Diary of Lady Palmerston, 6 April 1840 and 6 April 1842; Hatfield House MSS.
46. Cecil, 20.
47. QVJ, 23 Nov. 1839.
48. Ibid. 14 June 1838.
49. Ibid. 14 Sept. 1838.
50. Ibid. 25 Sept. 1838.
51. Cecil, 50.
52. QVJ, 18 Dec. 1839.
53. Miss E. Eden to Miss Villiers, 21 Sept. 1828; V. Dickinson, *Miss Eden's Letters* (London 1919), 167.
54. QVJ, 15 May 1838.
55. E. Lamb to F. Lamb, 14 March [1818]; Herts. RO, Panshanger MSS, D/ELb F75.
56. Lady Granville to Lady Morpeth, 28 Aug. 1819; F. Leveson Gower, *The Letters of Harriet, Countess Granville* (London 1894), i. 143.
57. Greville, vii. 35.
58. Ibid.
59. Ibid.
60. Ibid. i. 141.
61. Ibid. vi. 124.
62. BL Add. MSS 45552, fo. 38; F. Lamb to E. Lamb, 29 Jan. [1839].
63. QVJ, 4 and 6 June 1838, 19 Aug. 1838.
64. Lady H. Cavendish to Lady G. Morpeth, 12 Dec. 1807; Sir G. Leveson Gower, *The Letters of Lady Harriet Cavendish* (London 1940), 268–9. See also D. M. Stuart, *Dearest Bess* (London 1914).
65. Journal of Henry Edward Fox, 20 Dec. 1821; Lord Ilchester, *The Journal of Henry Edward Fox* (London 1923), 93.
66. G. Lamb, *The Poems of Caius Valerius Catullus* (London 1821), Preface xxxiii.
67. Sir John to Lady Mackintosh, 1817; O'Leary, *Sir James Mackintosh*, 128.
68. BL Add. MSS 51725, fo. 157; Lord Egremont to Lord Holland, 21 July 1834.

69. Mrs G. Lamb to F. Lamb 20 Jan. [1834]; Herts. RO, Panshanger MSS D/ELb F81. Mrs G. Lamb to Lady Carlisle, [1834]; Castle Howard MSS, J18/44/144.

70. Mrs Norton to Melbourne, 25 Aug. [1831]; J. Hoge and C. Olney, *The Letters of Caroline Norton to Lord Melbourne* (Ohio 1974), 57.

71. Cecil, 282.

72. Ibid. 146.

73. Lord Melbourne to Lord Hatherton, 28 Aug. 1838; Staffs. RO, D260/M/F/5/27/12, fo. 171.

74. Mrs G. Lamb to Lady Morpeth, n.d.; Castle Howard MSS, J18/44/140.

75. *Parliamentary History*, 3rd Series, liv. 31, 12 May 1840.

76. Cecil, 119 and 149.

77. Lady Bessborough to G. Leveson Gower, 29 Jan. 1796; Lady Granville, *Lord Granville Leveson Gower* (London 1916), i. 119–20.

78. Commonplace Book; Herts. RO, Panshanger MSS, D/ELb F28.

79. Lord Broughton, *Recollections of a Long Life* (London 1909), i. 194.

80. D. Howell-Thomas, *Lord Melbourne's Susan* (Woking 1928), 52.

81. Lord Broughton, *Recollections*, i. 325.

82. QVJ, 2 Jan. 1839.

83. Herts. RO, Panshanger MSS, D/ELb F94.

84. Lady H. Cavendish to Lady G. Morpeth, [1802]; Sir G. Leveson Gower, *The Letters of Lady Harriet Cavendish*, 23.

85. Ziegler, 47.

86. Ibid.

87. Lady H. Cavendish to Lady G. Morpeth, 15 Jan. 1803; Sir G. Leveson Gower, *The Letters of Lady Harriet Cavendish*, 44.

88. Lady S. Napier to Lady S. O'Brien, 25 March 1783; Lady Ilchester and Lord Stavordale, *The Letters of Sarah Lennox* (London 1901), ii. 36.

89. QVJ, 28 Aug. 1838.

90. Ibid. 12 Jan. 1838.

91. Mrs Arbuthnot's Journal, 24 March 1822; F. Bamford, *The Journal of Mrs. Arbuthnot* (London 1950), i. 154.

92. Melbourne to Lord J. Russell, 21 Jan. 1837; Southampton Univ. Lib.; Melbourne MSS MEL/RU/297.

93. QVJ, 29 April 1838.

94. Ibid. 26 Dec. 1838.

95. Lady Melbourne to Prince of Wales, 4 Feb. 1811; Herts. RO; Panshanger MSS, D/ELb F8.

96. BL Add. MSS 45548, fo. 109; Prince of Wales to Lady Melbourne, 30 Nov. 1803.

97. BL Add. MSS 45546, fo. 1; Melbourne to Lady Melbourne, 26 Feb. 1812.

98. W. Lamb's Autobiography; Herts. RO, Panshanger MSS, D/ELb F12.

99. First Viscount Melbourne to Prince of Wales, 26 Feb. 1812; A. Aspinall, *The Letters of George IV* (Cambridge 1938), i. 27.

100. QVJ, 14 Jan. 1839.

101. Ibid. 29 April 1838.

102. Ibid. 24 June 1838.
103. Ibid. 27 Aug. 1838.
104. Ibid.
105. Ibid. 17 July 1838.
106. Ibid. 10 May 1839.
107. Ibid. 1 Nov. 1838.
108. *Parl. Hist.* xx. 495, 6 June 1811. W. Lamb's Autobiography; Herts. RO, Panshanger MSS, D/ELb F12.
109. T. Grenville to Lord Grenville, 8 June 1811; Hist. MSS Comm. *Fortescue* X, 149.
110. QVJ, 2 Sept. 1838.
111. Lady Cowper to F. Lamb, 15 Feb. [1821]; T. Lever, *The Letters of Lady Palmerston* (London 1957), 70.
112. Lady Cowper to F. Lamb, 8 Feb. 1821; Lady Airlie, *Lady Palmerston and Her Times* (London 1922), i. 84.
113. Ibid. 22 June 1821; ibid. i. 91.
114. W. Lamb to F. Lamb, 29 July 1820; Herts. RO, Panshanger MSS, D/ELb F78.
115. Ibid. 18 Dec. 1820; ibid.
116. W. Lamb to W. Wilberforce, 2 Aug. 1820; Bodleian Library, Melbourne MSS, (microfilm), Box 39/122.
117. Ibid.

Chapter 2

1. Greville, 29 Nov. 1848, vi. 249.
2. W. Cowper, 'Melbourne', *The Nation*, 15 (1884), 54.
3. Melbourne to Lord John Russell, 10 Oct. 1839; Melbourne MSS, Box 14/67.
4. Melbourne to Lord Minto, 29 Oct. 1839; Nat. Lib. of Scotland; Minto MSS, 12/25 fo. 94.
5. Melbourne to Duncannon, 24 Nov. 1834; W. Sussex RO; Bessborough MSS, 182 unfol.
6. Melbourne to Sir J. Campbell, 1 Oct. 1838; Melbourne MSS, Box 92/30.
7. Melbourne to T. Attwood, 1 Oct. 1839; ibid. Box 23/76.
8. *Parl. Hist.* xlix. 371–3; 16 July 1839.
9. Melbourne to Lord John Russell, 26 Sept. 1838; Melbourne MSS, Box 13/75.
10. Commonplace Book, n.d.; Herts. RO, Panshanger MSS, D/ELb F28.
11. Lord John Russell to Melbourne, 9 Oct. 1835; Southampton Univ. Lib.; Melbourne MSS, MEL/RU/11/1.
12. Lord Hatherton's Diary, 7 July 1835; Staffs. RO; D260/M/F/15/26/9.
13. QVJ, 28 Jan. 1839.
14. Ibid. 6 Feb. 1838.
15. Ibid. 27 April 1838. Melbourne informed Victoria that, as a young man, he had had one or two nasty falls in the hunting field, and had been accidentally shot, in 1836, at a shooting party at Holkham. His game books were meticulously kept up. From 12 Oct. 1808 to Dec. 1823, he accounted for 4,499 head of game 'viz 613 Pheasants—1339 Patridges—35 Woodcocks—1 Ferroce [sic]—8 Landrails—3 Squirrels—54 Wild Ducks—5 Teal—1 Dawn Bird—74 Snipes—

3 Herons—571 Hares—1282 Rabbits.' There are no entries after 1823. Herts. RO, Panshanger MSS; Game Book, D/ELb F52.

16. W. Lamb to Lady C. Lamb, 26 Sept. 1807; W. Sussex RO; Bessborough MSS, 182 unfol.

17. W. Lamb to F. Lamb, 23 Feb. 1821; Herts. RO; Panshanger MSS, D/ELb F78.

18. B. Disraeli to S. Disraeli, [Feb. 1839]; W. Monypenny and G. Buckle, *The Life of Benjamin Disraeli* (London 1920), ii. 55.

19. *Parl. Hist.* lxiv. 1278–9; 11 July 1842.

20. BL Add. MSS 51560, fo. 32; Melbourne to Lady Holland, 1 Nov. 1836.

21. *Parl. Hist.* xiii. 1156, 29 June 1832. In spite of remarks such as these, one of Melbourne's earliest biographers claimed that he had played a large part in certain aspects of the regulation of industrial society. W. Torrens, *Memoirs of Lord Melbourne* (London 1890), 271.

22. Melbourne to Lord John Russell, 6 Oct. 1835; Southampton Univ. Lib., Melbourne MSS, MEL/RU/182.

23. Melbourne to E. Ellice, 28 May 1838; Nat. Lib. of Scotland, Ellice MSS, fo. 70.

24. QVJ, 26 July 1838.

25. Ibid. 4 April 1838.

26. Ibid. 6 April 1838.

27. Melbourne to Victoria, 30 Oct. 1841; Windsor, Royal Archives, A4/32.

28. Melbourne to W. Cowper, 29 Oct. 1840; Southampton Univ. Lib., Melbourne MSS, MEL/CO/26.

29. Lady Palmerston to Col. Wyndham, 19 Dec. 1848; W. Sussex RO, Petworth MSS, 703.

30. Melbourne to B. Wall, 8 Sept. 1839; Melbourne MSS, Box 39/7.

31. Melbourne to Lady Holland, 26 Dec. 1840; ibid. Box 27/178.

32. Melbourne to Lord Grey, 15 June 1832; Durham Univ. Lib., Grey MSS, fo. 72.

33. *Parl. Hist.* xxxv. 968; 8 Aug. 1836.

34. Melbourne to William IV, 17 July 1835; Melbourne MSS, Box 112/11.

35. *Parl. Hist.* xxvii. 1333–4, 21 May 1835. See also ibid. xxix. 71–6, 30 June 1835.

36. W. Lamb to Lady C. Lamb, 11 April 1827; W. Sussex RO; Bessborough MSS, 182 unfol. Caroline Lamb was of a different opinion. See Lady C. Lamb to J. Lancaster, 1817; Univ. of Michigan, Ann Arbor; Diedrich Coll.

37. Melbourne to Sir J. Abercromby, 16 Oct. 1835; Nat. Lib. of Scotland, Abercromby MSS, fo. 26.

38. QVJ, 6 Dec. 1837.

39. Cecil, 211.

40. Ibid. 212.

41. QVJ, 7 April 1839.

42. Ibid. 20 Aug. 1838.

43. BL Add. MSS 56561, fo. 37; Diary of J. Hobhouse, 21 June 1839.

44. QVJ, 10 Feb. 1839.

45. Cecil, 284.

46. Melbourne to Lord J. Russell, 27 Nov. 1838; Melbourne MSS, Box 13/99.

47. Cecil, 238.

48. Cecil, 284.
49. Melbourne to Lord J. Russell, 7 Feb. 1839; L. C. Sanders, *Lord Melbourne's Papers* (London 1889), 395.
50. QVJ, 7 April 1839.
51. Melbourne to Lord John Russell, 24 Oct. 1837; Southampton Univ. Lib.; Melbourne MSS, MEL/RU/415. See also BL Add. MSS 51558, fo. 158; Melbourne to Holland, 30 Sept. 1837.
52. Cecil, 150.
53. Melbourne to Victoria, 27 May 1837; Windsor, Royal Archives, A1/7.
54. QVJ, 29 May 1838.
55. Melbourne to F. Fox, 8 March 1842; Melbourne Hall MSS, 235/2/10.
56. Melbourne to Lord John Russell, 1 Dec. 1838; Melbourne MSS, Box 39/102.
57. *Parl. Hist.* xxxv. 29; 28 Jan. 1817.
58. Ibid. xxv. 272; 21 July 1834.
59. Melbourne to Althorp, 30 Dec. 1832; Melbourne MSS, Box 15/92. See also Melbourne to P. Bouverie, 25 Nov. 1831; ibid. Box 20/12.
60. *Parl. Hist.* xliii. 3; 21 May 1838. See also ibid. xxxvii. 847; 7 April 1837.
61. BL Add. MSS 51588, fo. 152; Melbourne to Holland, 22 Sept. 1837.
62. Cecil, 237.
63. Melbourne to F. Fox, 9 June 1841; Melbourne Hall MSS, 235/2/i. See also ibid. 10 Feb. 1846; Box 235/3/29.
64. BL Add. MSS 51872, fos. 1131–2; Holland's Political Journal, June 1839.
65. *Le National*, 19 Jan. 1840.
66. Melbourne to E. Baines, 20 Dec. 1839; Melbourne MSS, Box 19/13. See also *Parl. Hist.* lii. 541 f.; 24 Jan. 1840.
67. *Parl. Hist.* l. 522; 23 Aug. 1839.
68. Ibid. xlvii. 1163; 31 May 1839.
69. Lord John Russell to Melbourne, 6 Nov. 1839; Southampton Univ. Lib., Melbourne MSS, MEL/RU/110.
70. QVJ, 1 May 1839.
71. Melbourne to Lord J. Russell, 8 Nov. 1839; Melbourne MSS, Box 14/80.
72. BL Add. MSS 56562, fo. 27; Diary of J. Hobhouse, 9 Jan. 1840.
73. Melbourne to Victoria, 22 June 1843; Lord Esher, *The Letters of Queen Victoria* (London 1908), i. 483.
74. Melbourne to Revd W. Deive, 25 Sept. 1840; Melbourne MSS, Box 23/82.
75. Cecil, 287.
76. Ibid. 150.
77. Melbourne to W. Cowper, 9 Nov. 1840; Ziegler, 217.
78. QVJ, 23 Sept. 1839.
79. Cecil, 304.
80. Ibid. 332.
81. QVJ, 30 Dec. 1838.
82. Ibid. 14 Sept. 1839.
83. Ibid. 22 Sept. 1838.
84. Ibid. 19 April 1838.

85. Monypenny and Buckle, *Life of Disraeli*, ii. 32.
86. Greville, ii. 234; 1 Jan. 1832.
87. Lord G. W. E. Russell, *Collections and Recollections* (London 1903), 81.
88. Greville, iii. 331; 16 Dec. 1835.
89. H. and M. Swartz, *Disraeli's Reminiscences* (London 1975), 110.
90. H. Fortescue to W. Watson, 21 Sept. 1840; R. Brent, *Liberal Anglican Politics* (Oxford 1987), 121.
91. Commonplace Book; Herts. RO, Panshanger MSS, D/ELb F26.
92. Greville, iii. 142; 25 Sept. 1834.
93. Melbourne to Bishop of Salisbury, 12 Jan. 1835; Bod. Lib., MS Eng. Lett. c137 f1.
94. Journal of Lord Hatherton, 12 July 1836; Staffs. RO; Hatherton MSS, D260/M/F/5/26/12.
95. Ibid. 24 Feb. 1836; ibid.
96. Lady Holland to Lord W. Russell, 24 July 1835; G. Blakiston, *Lord William Russell and his Wife* (London 1972), 337.
97. *Parl. Hist.* liii. 640–1, 7 April 1840.
98. Melbourne to Sir J. Easthope, 13 Oct. 1845; Torrens, *Memoirs of Lord Melbourne*, 541.
99. Melbourne to Victoria, 21 May 1841; Windsor, Royal Archives, A3/160.
100. Melbourne to Howick, 21 Jan. 1837; Durham Univ. Lib., Grey MSS, unfol.
101. *Parl. Hist.* xxv. 1057, 8 Aug. 1834.
102. Melbourne to W. Cowper, 9 Aug. 1841; Southampton Univ. Lib., Melbourne MSS, MEL/CO/42.
103. *Parl. Hist.* xxxiv. 882, 27 June 1836.
104. Melbourne to Lord Egremont, 18 July 1841; W. Sussex RO; Petworth MSS, 1665.
105. Melbourne to W. Cowper, 30 Oct. 1840; Southampton Univ. Lib., Melbourne MSS, MEL/CO/33.
106. Greville, iii. 132; 5 Sept. 1834.
107. Lord G. W. E. Russell, *Collections and Recollections*, 64.
108. BL Add. MSS 56561, fo. 69; Diary of J. Hobhouse, 10 Aug. 1839.
109. Melbourne to Archbishop of Canterbury, 23 May 1835; PRO, Russell MSS, 30/22/1E/XC/10466 fo. 148.
110. Melbourne to Holland, 29 Aug. 1840; Bod. Lib., MS Eng. Hist. c1033 f 79.
111. BL Add. MSS 34590, fo. 105; Melbourne to Bishop Butler, 6 April 1836.
112. H. Fortescue to W. Watson, 21 Sept. 1840; Brent, *Liberal Anglican Politics*, 120.
113. Melbourne to Lord Lansdowne, 2 March 1837; Torrens, *Memoirs of Lord Melbourne*, 432.
114. Cecil, 245.
115. Melbourne to Lord John Russell, 13 Aug. 1837; Southampton Univ. Lib., Melbourne MSS, MEL/RU/387.
116. BL Add. MSS 51560, fo. 72; Melbourne to Lady Holland, 2 Sept. 1840.
117. *Parl. Hist.* xx. 247–8; 1 Aug. 1833.
118. Ibid. xxxix. 343–4; 28 Nov. 1837.

119. Melbourne to Lord J. Russell, 23 April 1840; Melbourne MSS, Box 14/116.
120. Melbourne to J. Hobhouse, 26 Sept. 1839; India Office, Broughton MSS, Eur F213/7, fo. 231.
121. W. Lamb. to Lady Melbourne, 27 March 1800; Herts. RO, Panshanger MSS, D/ELb F5.
122. Melbourne to T. Barber, 18 June 1829; Notts. RO, Barber MSS, D.D.2B.8/5.
123. *Parl. Hist.* xxix. 526–9, 14 July 1835 and ibid. xxv. 842, 1 Aug. 1834.
124. Melbourne to Lord John Russell, 15 Dec. 1836; Southampton Univ. Lib., Melbourne MSS, MEL/RU/281.
125. Melbourne to E. B. Pusey, 3 March 1836; Melbourne MSS, Box 79/31.
126. Melbourne to P. Shuttleworth, 11 Nov. 1840; Bod. Lib., MS Eng. Hist. c/033 fo. 96.
127. Melbourne to Victoria, 17 Jan. 1842; Windsor, Royal Archives, A4 fo. 47.
128. Melbourne to W. Cowper, 30 Oct. 1840; Southampton Univ. Lib., Melbourne MSS, MEL/CO/33.
129. BL Add. MSS 51559 fo. 69; Melbourne to Lord Holland, 30 Aug. 1840.
130. Melbourne to Victoria, 17 Jan. 1842; Windsor, Royal Archives, A4 fo. 47.
131. Sanders, *Lord Melbourne's Papers*, 504.
132. *Parl. Hist.* xxxix. 1401, 21 Dec. 1837.
133. Melbourne to William IV, 15 Feb. 1836; Sanders, *Lord Melbourne's Papers*, 499.
134. *Parl. Hist.* xxxvii. 1020; 11 April 1837.
135. Melbourne to R. Hampden, 13 Feb. 1836; Oriel Coll., Hampden MSS, DC 1 13 fo. 28.
136. Ibid. 9 June 1836; ibid. fo. 34.
137. Ibid. 7 June 1836; ibid. fo. 33.
138. Ibid. 10 Feb. 1836; ibid. fo. 26.
139. Melbourne to Howick, 11 Feb. 1836; Durham Univ. Lib., Grey MSS, unfol.
140. Diary of Lord Holland, Sept. 1836; A. D. Kriegel, *The Holland House Diaries* (London 1977), 343.
141. Melbourne to R. Hampden, 3 March 1836; Oriel Coll. Hampden MSS, DC 1 13 fo. 30.

Chapter 3

1. QVJ, 11 Oct. 1837.
2. Ibid. 14 Jan. 1838.
3. Ibid. 29 May 1838.
4. Ibid. 22 Sept. 1838.
5. Ibid. 27 Sept. 1838.
6. Ibid. 27 Jan. 1839.
7. Autobiography; Herts. RO, Panshanger MSS, D/ELb F12
8. QVJ, 1 Oct. 1838.
9. Ibid. 23 Sept. 1838.
10. Autobiography; Herts. RO, Panshanger MSS, D/ELb F12.
11. Ibid.
12. Ibid.

13. QVJ, 9 Feb. 1838.
14. Ibid. 23 Sept. 1838.
15. Ibid. 29 May 1838.
16. Ibid. 28 Oct. 1838.
17. Cecil, 24–5.
18. Autobiography; Herts. RO; Panshanger MSS, D/ELb F12.
19. G. Bishop to W. Lamb, n.d.; ibid; F25.
20. Autobiography; ibid. F12. See also QVJ, 6 June 1838, and D. Marshall, *Lord Melbourne* (London 1977), 8–9.
21. Autobiography; Herts. RO; Panshanger MSS, D/ELb F12.
22. Ibid. I am most grateful to Penny Hatfield for supplying school lists and other information from the Eton College Archives.
23. Ibid.
24. Melbourne to Sir H. Halford, 26 Feb. 1835; Leics. RO; Halford MSS, DG24/904/4. I owe this reference to the kindness of John Walsh.
25. Autobiography; Herts. RO; Panshanger MSS, D/ELb F12.
26. Melbourne to Lord Denman, 22 Oct. 1838; Melbourne MSS, Box 23/55.
27. The speech chosen was taken from *The History of England* by David Hume (London 1782), vol. vi, ch. 4, 403–6.
28. QVJ, 26 Sept. 1839.
29. He was always anxious for 'the success of Eton and for the maintenance of the particular character of the school'; Add. MSS 37312, fo. 229; Melbourne to Lord Wellesley, 2 April 1840.
30. Autobiography; Herts. RO, Panshanger MSS, D/ELb F12.
31. *Verses by the Honourable W. L-B, written in 1797*; A. F. Steuart, *The Diary of a Lady in Waiting* (London 1908), ii. 90–1.
32. QVJ, 30 Jan. 1840.
33. W. Lamb to Lady Melbourne, 24 Jan. 1800; Herts. RO, Panshanger MSS, D/ELb F5.
34. Autobiography; Herts. RO, Panshanger MSS, D/ELb F12.
35. Ibid.
36. Ibid.
37. Ibid.
38. QVJ, 20 March 1839.
39. Autobiography; Herts. RO, Panshanger MSS, D/ELb F12.
40. QVJ, 20 March 1839.
41. Lord Lauderdale to J. Millar, 11 June 1799; Torrens, *Memoirs of Lord Melbourne*, 25.
42. Autobiography; Herts. RO, Panshanger MSS, D/ELb F12.
43. Ibid.
44. Ibid.
45. W. Lamb to Lady Melbourne, 29 April 1800; Herts. RO, Panshanger MSS, D/ELb F5.
46. F. Lamb to Lady Melbourne, [1800]; ibid.
47. Ibid.

48. Ibid.
49. W. Adam to Melbourne, 14 Jan. 1836; Melbourne MSS, Box 18/17. See also Melbourne to W. Adam, 20 Jan. 1836; ibid. Box 18/18.
50. W. Lamb to Lady Melbourne, 6 Jan. 1800; Herts. RO, Panshanger MSS, D/ELb F5.
51. Autobiography; ibid. F12.
52. W. Lamb to Lady Melbourne, 9 Feb. 1800; ibid. F5.
53. Melbourne to Lord John Russell, 12 Sept. 1837; Southampton Univ. Lib., Melbourne MSS, MEL/RU/399.
54. Autobiography; Herts. RO, Panshanger MSS, D/ELb F12.
55. Notebooks; Melbourne MSS, Boxes 120 and 121.
56. W. Lamb, *Essay on the Progressive Improvement of Mankind* (London 1860), 15.
57. Lecture Notes, Dec. 1799; Melbourne MSS, Box 120/1–11.
58. Ibid.
59. Ibid.
60. The Foxite secession lasted from 1797 to 1801.
61. Cecil, 143–4.
62. H. Ellis to Melbourne, 21 Feb. 1834; Melbourne MSS, Box 24/69.
63. Journal of Lord Hatherton, 16 April 1837; Staffs. RO, Hatherton MSS, D260/M/F/5/26/12. Lord John Russell was the other man so complimented.
64. QVJ, 19 April 1839.
65. Ibid. 29 Aug. 1839.
66. Ibid. 30 Dec. 1838.
67. Epistle to the Editors of the Anti Jacobin; *Morning Chronicle*, 17 Jan. 1798.
68. L. Melville, *Beau Brummell* (London 1924), 296–7.
69. Autobiography; Herts. RO, Panshanger MSS, D/ELb F12.
70. Ibid.
71. BL Add. MSS 51560, fo. 109; Melbourne to Lady Holland, 14 Feb. 1842.
72. Anon., *Extracts from the Diary of the late Dr. Robert Lee* (London 1897), 26. See also Melbourne to Lord Clarendon, 9 April 1841; Bod. Lib., Clarendon MSS, c469 unfol.
73. Lamb, *Essay on the Progressive Improvement of Mankind*, 13.
74. Lecture Notes, Dec. 1799; Melbourne MSS, Box 120/1–11.
75. Cecil, 26.
76. Lecture Notes, Dec. 1799; Melbourne MSS, Box 120/1–11.
77. W. Lamb to Lady Melbourne, 6 March [1800]; Herts. RO, Panshanger MSS, D/ELb F5.
78. Ibid. 27 March 1800; ibid.
79. Autobiography; Herts. RO, Panshanger MSS, D/ELb F12.
80. W. Lamb to Lady Melbourne, 24 Jan. 1800; ibid. F5.
81. Ibid. [14 Jan. 1800]; ibid.
82. Autobiography; Herts. RO, Panshanger MSS, D/ELb F12.
83. Melville, *Beau Brummell*, 296–7. QVJ, 16 May 1838.
84. Torrens, *Memoirs of Lord Melbourne*, 35.
85. Autobiography; Herts. RO, Panshanger MSS, D/ELb F12.

86. Mrs G. Lamb to Lady Morpeth, [1804]; Castle Howard MSS, J18/44/137.

87. QVJ, 29 Oct. 1838.

88. Lady Holland's Journal, 13 Feb. 1799; Lord Ilchester, *The Journal of Elizabeth, Lady Holland* (London 1908), i. 225.

89. Ibid. 24 Feb. 1799; ibid.

90. Ibid. 1800; ibid. ii. 100.

91. BL Add. MSS 51560, fo. 3; W. Lamb to Lady Holland, 18 Dec. 1801.

92. Lady Holland to Lady Melbourne, 22 Sept. 1802; Hatfield House MSS.

93. L. C. Sanders, *Lord Melbourne's Papers* (London 1889), 91.

94. Ibid.

95. M. Lewis to Sir W. Scott, 5 March 1799; L. Peck, *A Life of Matthew G. Lewis* (Harvard 1961), 49.

96. Ibid.

97. Autobiography; Herts. RO, Panshanger MSS, D/ELb F12.

98. W. Lamb to Lady Melbourne, 1800; Peck, *Life of Lewis*, 49.

99. Ibid.

100. Lady C. Lamb to Lord Hartington, 21 July [1810]; Chatsworth MSS, Papers of the 5th Duke of Devonshire, fo. 1982.

101. BL Add. MSS 45548, fo. 104; M. G. Lewis to Lady Melbourne, 16 Oct. 1802.

102. Journal of H. E. Fox, Jan. 1818; Lord Ilchester, *The Journal of Henry Edward Fox* (London 1923), 31.

103. A. Blake to J. St. Aubyn, 23 April 1819; Peck, *Life of Lewis*, 270.

104. Cecil, 21.

105. QVJ, 15 Sept. 1839.

106. Ibid. 28 Oct. 1838.

107. Ibid. 5 Sept. 1839.

108. Ibid. 5 Oct. 1839.

Chapter 4

1. Representations of the Lamb marriage have been identified in the following novels; T. Lister, *Granby*; B. Disraeli, *Vivian Grey* and *Venetia*; Mrs Humphry Ward, *The Marriage of William Ash*; Bulwer Lytton, *De Lindsey*; Lady Lytton, *Cheveley or The Man of Honour*. See E. Jenkins, *Lady Caroline Lamb* (London 1932), 276.

2. Commonplace Book; Herts. RO, Panshanger MSS, D/ELb F28.

3. Lecture Notes, *c*.1799; Melbourne MSS, Box 120/6.

4. For over a decade, she conducted an *affaire* with Lord Granville Leveson Gower, who subsequently married her niece.

5. Cecil, 52.

6. Ibid. 36.

7. D. Marshall, *Lord Melbourne* (London 1975), 14.

8. Lady C. Lamb to Lady Morpeth, n.d.; Castle Howard MSS, J18/35.

9. Lady H. Cavendish to Lady G. Morpeth, [1802]; Sir G. Leveson Gower, *The Letters of Lady Harriet Cavendish* (London 1940), 23.

10. W. Lamb to C. Ponsonby, [May 1805]; West Sussex RO, Bessborough MSS, 182, unfol.

11. Lady Bessborough to G. Leveson Gower, [8 May] 1805; Lady Granville, *Lord Granville Leveson Gower* (London 1916), ii. 67.

12. Duncannon to C. Ponsonby, [1805]; West Sussex RO, Bessborough MSS, 26 unfol.

13. W. Lamb to C. Ponsonby, [May 1805]; ibid. 182 unfol.

14. Lady Melbourne to F. Fox, 27 May 1805; Melbourne Hall MSS, 234/5/23.

15. W. Lamb to C. Ponsonby, [May 1805]; West Sussex RO, Bessborough MSS, 182 unfol.

16. QVJ, 30 Dec. 1838.

17. Lady Bessborough to G. Leveson Gower, 2 [May 1805]; Lady Granville, *Lord Granville Leveson Gower*, ii. 67. See also ibid. [6 May 1805]; ibid.

18. Marriage Certificate, 3 June 1805; West Sussex RO, Bessborough MSS, 161 unfol.

19. QVJ, 21 Dec. 1839.

20. Lady Bessborough to G. Leveson Gower, [7 June] 1805; Lady Granville, *Lord Granville Leveson Gower*, ii. 75–6.

21. According to the family account given to Queen Victoria, Caroline 'wouldn't go with her husband, and after 2 hours of histericks [sic], Lord Melbourne, then Mr. Lamb, was obliged to carry her downstairs into the carriage by force, and cut his hand by doing so'. QVJ, 29 Oct. 1838.

22. W. Lamb to Lady Spencer, 5 June 1805; W. Sussex RO, Bessborough MSS, 182 unfol. Lady Bessborough to G. Leveson Gower, [9 June] 1805; Lady Granville, *Lord Granville Leveson Gower*, ii. 85.

23. QVJ, 3 Aug. 1839.

24. Lady C. Lamb to ?, n.d.; V. and A. Museum, Forster Bequest, fo. 2.

25. Lady C. Lamb, *Ada Reis* (London 1823), i. 33.

26. QVJ, 20 Nov. 1838.

27. Ibid. 29 Oct. 1838.

28. Egremont to Lady Melbourne, n.d.; Hatfield House MSS.

29. Lady Bessborough to G. Leveson Gower, 12 June [1805]; Lady Granville, *Lord Granville Leveson Gower*, ii. 81.

30. Lady C. Lamb to Lady Morpeth, n.d.; Castle Howard MSS, J18/35.

31. Ibid. [1805]; ibid.

32. Lady C. Lamb to Lady Spencer, 9 Dec. 1805; West Sussex RO, Bessborough MSS, 161 unfol.

33. Mrs G. Lamb to Lady Morpeth, n.d.; Castle Howard MSS, J18/44/139.

34. Ibid. n.d.; ibid. J18/44/137. There are a number of similar letters in this volume.

35. Lady C. Lamb to Lady Morpeth, [1805]; ibid. J18/35.

36. Mrs G. Lamb to Lady Morpeth, [1805]; ibid. J18/44/137.

37. Lady C. Lamb to Lady Morpeth, [1806]; ibid. J18/35.

38. Ibid.

39. Lady Bessborough to W. Ponsonby, 30 Jan. 1809; Lord Bessborough, *Lady Bessborough and Her Family Circle* (London 1940), 182.

40. Sir G. Leveson Gower, *The Letters of Lady Harriet Cavendish*, 137.

41. Lady H. Cavendish to Lady G. Morpeth, [Jan.] 1806; ibid. 150.
42. Ibid. [Oct.] 1805; ibid. 125.
43. Ibid. 21 Oct. 1805; ibid. 122.
44. Lady C. Lamb to Lady Morpeth, n.d.; Castle Howard MSS, J18/35.
45. Lady H. Cavendish to Lady Morpeth, 12 Nov. 1807; Sir G. Leveson Gower, *The Letters of Lady Harriet Cavendish*, 242–3.
46. Lady C. Lamb to Lady Morpeth, 13 Oct. 1807; Castle Howard MSS, J18/35.
47. Cecil, 81.
48. Lady H. Cavendish to Lady Morpeth, 13 Nov. 1806; Sir G. Leveson Gower, *The Letters of Lady Harriet Cavendish*, 162.
49. Lady C. Lamb to Lady Morpeth, [1 Aug. 1807]; Castle Howard MSS, J18/35.
50. Byron to J. Murray, 31 Aug. 1820; L. Marchand, *Byron's Letters and Journals* (London 1973–81), vii. 169.
51. Mrs G. Lamb to Lady Morpeth, n.d.; Castle Howard MSS, J18/44/137.
52. W. Lamb to Duke of Devonshire, 22 Sept. 1821; Chatsworth MSS, Papers of the 6th Duke of Devonshire, fo. 577. See also Devonshire to Dowager Duchess of Devonshire, 30 Dec. 1821; ibid. 586.
53. Lady C. Lamb to Lady Morpeth, [July 1805]; Castle Howard MSS, J18/35.
54. Ibid.
55. Chatsworth MSS; Papers of the 5th Duke of Devonshire, fo. 1814.
56. D. M. Stuart, *Dearest Bess* (London 1914), 167–8.
57. Lady C. Lamb to Duke of Devonshire, [19 May 1822]; Chatsworth MSS, Papers of the 6th Duke of Devonshire, fo. 966.
58. Ibid. 12 July 1823; ibid. fo. 817.
59. Ibid. 3 Aug. 1810; ibid. fo. 1983.
60. G. Lamb to Duke of Devonshire, 12 April 1824; ibid., fo. 949.
61. Lady C. Lamb to Lady Morpeth, n.d.; Castle Howard MSS, J18/35.
62. Marriage Settlement, 22 May 1805; Melbourne Hall MSS, X94/1/5.
63. Mrs G. Lamb to Lady Morpeth, n.d.; Castle Howard MSS, J18/44/140.
64. Ibid. 15 Aug.; ibid. J18/44/139.
65. BL Add. MSS 39949, fo. 17; W. Huskisson to Mrs Huskisson, 14 Jan. 1819.
66. Ibid. fo. 45; ibid. 27 Jan. 1819. See also ibid., fo. 74; ibid. 28 July 1819.
67. W. Lamb to F. Fox, 21 Feb. 1824; Melbourne Hall MSS, 234/7.
68. BL Add. MSS, 45548, fo. 161; W. Lamb to F. Lamb, 26 Dec. 1825.
69. Princess Lieven to Metternich, 3 April 1823; P. Quennell, *The Private Letters of Princess Lieven to Prince Metternich* (London 1937), 251.
70. Dunckley, *Lord Melbourne*, 109–10.
71. BL Add. MSS 51560, fo. 7; W. Lamb to Lady Holland, 29 Aug. 1807.
72. Mrs G. Lamb to Lady Morpeth, [1807]; Castle Howard MSS, J18/44/137.
73. Cecil, 55.
74. Mrs G. Lamb to Lady Morpeth, n.d.; Castle Howard MSS, J18/44/137.
75. Ibid. n.d.; ibid.
76. Lady C. Lamb to Lady Morpeth, [1811]; ibid. J18/35.
77. Ibid. 30 Sept. 1808; ibid.
78. Ibid.

79. BL Spencer MSS, F40; Lady C. Lamb to Lady Spencer, 23 Jan. 1814.
80. BL Add. MSS 51560, fo. 131; Lady C. Lamb to Lady Holland, 31 May 1810.
81. Lady Cowper to F. Lamb, 13 March 1821; Lever, *The Letters of Lady Palmerston*, 75–6.
82. Lady C. Lamb to Lady Morpeth, 13 Oct. 1807; Castle Howard MSS, J18/35.
83. Mrs G. Lamb to Lady Morpeth, n.d.; ibid. J18/44/137.
84. W. Lamb to A. Lamb, 25 June 1825; Herts. RO, Panshanger MSS, D/ELb F69.
85. Ibid. 21 Oct. 1825; ibid.
86. A. Lamb to Lady C. Lamb, 31 Aug. 1827; West Sussex RO, Bessborough MSS, 161 unfol.
87. W. Lamb to Sir G. Blanc, 12 Oct. 1817; Anon., *Extracts from the Diary of the late Dr. Robert Lee*, 13.
88. BL Add. MSS, 45550, fo. 187; Lady Cowper to F. Lamb, 14 Aug. [1825].
89. Ibid.
90. Lady H. Cavendish to Lady G. Morpeth, 11 Nov. 1806; Sir G. Leveson Gower, *The Letters of Lady Harriet Cavendish*, 159.
91. Stuart, *Dearest Bess*, 155.
92. Lady H. Cavendish to Lady G. Morpeth, 12 Nov. 1807; Sir G. Leveson Gower, *The Letters of Lady Harriet Cavendish*, 242–3.
93. BL Add. MSS, 51560, fo. 131; Lady C. Lamb to Lady Holland, [31 May 1810].
94. Lady C. Lamb to W. Lamb, 4 Sept. [1809]; Herts. RO, Panshanger MSS, D/ELb F32.
95. Ibid. [27 May 1809]; ibid.
96. Lady C. Lamb to Lady Morpeth, n.d.; Castle Howard MSS, J18/35.
97. Lady C. Lamb to Lady Bessborough, 15 Jan. 1807; Lord Bessborough, *Lady Bessborough and Her Family Circle*, 156.
98. Lady H. Cavendish to Lady G. Morpeth, 28 Oct. 1807; Sir G. Leveson Gower, *The Letters of Lady Harriet Cavendish*, 223.
99. Lady C. Lamb to Lord Hartington, 2 Oct. [1810]; Chatsworth MSS, Papers of the 5th Duke of Devonshire, fo. 1990.
100. BL Add. MSS, 45546, fo. 21; Lady C. Lamb to Lady Melbourne, 1810.
101. Ibid. 51560, fo. 153; Lady C. Lamb to Lady Holland, [2 Jan. 1811].
102. Ibid. fo. 151.
103. Ibid. fo. 155; ibid. [7 Jan. 1811].
104. Ibid. fo. 182; ibid. [May 1811].
105. Lady Granville to Lady G. Morpeth, 18 Sept. 1811; F. Leveson Gower, *The Letters of Harriet, Lady Granville*, i. 20.
106. Lady C. Lamb to Lady Morpeth, n.d.; Castle Howard MSS, J18/35.
107. BL Add. MSS, 51558, fo. 7; Lady C. Lamb to Lord Holland, 27 June 1811.
108. Lady C. Lamb to Lady Morpeth, n.d.; Castle Howard MSS, J18/35.
109. Ibid.
110. BL Add. MSS, 51560, fo. 184; Lady C. Lamb to Lady Holland, [5 June 1811].
111. Marchand, *Byron's Letters and Journals*, ii. 169.
112. BL Add. MSS 54088, unfol.; Lady C. Lamb to H. Colbourne, [c. 1824].

113. Lady Byron to Lady Noel, 27 March 1816; Bod. Lib., Byron–Lovelace MSS 30, fos. 62–3.
114. Lady H. Cavendish to Duke of Devonshire, 10 May 1812; Chatsworth MSS, Papers of the 6th Duke of Devonshire, fo. 58.
115. Cecil, 88.
116. Poem by Caroline Lamb; Bod. Lib., Bruce MSS, unfol.
117. Diary of J. Hobhouse, 9 Feb. 1816; T. A. J. Burnett, *The Rise and Fall of a Regency Dandy* (Oxford 1981).
118. Byron to J. Hobhouse, 26 Dec. 1812; Marchand, *Byron's Letters and Journals*, xi. 182.
119. Byron to Lady Melbourne, 26 June 1814; ibid. iv. 133.
120. Ibid. 16 May 1814; ibid. iv. 116.
121. Byron to A. Milbanke, 9 Oct. 1814; ibid. iv. 204.
122. Byron to A. Leigh, 14 Sept. 1816; ibid. v. 93.
123. Ibid. 7 April [1813]; iii. 37.
124. Byron to J. Hobhouse, 6 April 1819; ibid. vi. 107.
125. Byron to T. Moore, 16 March 1818; ibid. vi. 23.
126. Journal of Mrs Arbuthnot, 13 July 1824; F. Bamford, *The Journal of Mrs. Arbuthnot* (London 1950), i. 327. See also ibid. i. 173.
127. Lady C. Lamb to Lady Byron, n.d.; Bod. Lib., Lovelace–Byron MSS, 78 fos. 164–5. Between 1813 and 1818, Lady Melbourne is one of Byron's major correspondents.
128. BL Add. MSS 45546, fo. 37; Lady C. Lamb to Lady Melbourne, 14 Oct. 1812.
129. Lady Williams Wynn to Mrs H. Williams Wynn [1814]; R. Leighton, *The Correspondence of Charlotte Grenville* (London 1920), 183.
130. BL Add. MSS 45547, fo. 43; Lady Melbourne to Byron, 29 Sept. 1812.
131. Lady Williams Wynn to Mrs H. Williams Wynn, [1814]; Leighton, *Correspondence of Charlotte Grenville*, 183.
132. QVJ, 1 April 1838.
133. Ibid. 6 April 1838.
134. Ibid. 1 April 1838.
135. Essay, 30 Nov. 1816; Herts. RO, Panshanger MSS, D/ELb F54.
136. Miss A. Milbanke to Lady Melbourne, [16 March 1812]; Bod. Lib., Lovelace–Byron MSS, 29 fo. 64.
137. Ibid. 78 fo. 138.
138. Lady Byron to Mrs G. Lamb, [1843]; ibid. fo. 85.
139. Melbourne to Lady Byron, 6 March 1830; ibid. 92 fos. 116–17.
140. Melbourne to Richmond, 21 Dec. 1832; West Sussex RO, Richmond MSS, 1513 fos. 183–4.
141. Lady C. Lamb, *Ada Reis* (London 1823), introd. 8.
142. Ibid. i. 26.
143. Ibid. 28.
144. Ibid. ii. 96.
145. Lady Holland to H. Fox, 21 March 1823; Lord Ilchester, *Elizabeth, Lady Holland to Her Son, 1821–45* (London 1946), 17.

146. W. Lamb to J. Murray, 20 Dec. 1822; S. Smiles, *A Publisher and His Friends* (London 1891), ii. 144.
147. BL Add. MSS 54088, unfol.; Lady C. Lamb to H. Colbourne, n.d.
148. BL Spencer MSS F40; Lady C. Lamb to Lady Spencer, 13 Dec. 1813.
149. BL Add. MSS 45911, fo. 56; Lady C. Lamb to Lady Melbourne, [20 Oct. 1812].
150. BL Add. MSS 51560, fo. 201; Lady C. Lamb to Lady Holland, [July 1813].
151. Mrs G. Lamb to Lady Morpeth, 22 Nov. 1813; Castle Howard MSS, J18/44/137.
152. BL Add. MSS 51739 fos. 178–9; Lord Holland to C. Fox, 23 Oct. 1813.
153. Mrs G. Lamb to Lady Morpeth, 22 Nov. 1813; Castle Howard MSS, J18/44/137.
154. BL Add. MSS 45546, fo. 42; Lady C. Lamb to Lady Melbourne, Oct. 1812.
155. QVJ, 31 Aug. 1838.
156. BL Add. MSS 45546, fo. 85; Lady C. Lamb to Lady Melbourne, July 1815.
157. BL Add. MSS 45546, fo. 138; F. Lamb to Lady Melbourne, 7 Aug. 1815.
158. Cecil, 105.
159. Jenkins, *Lady Caroline Lamb*, 165.
160. Lady Granville to Lady Morpeth, [1815]; F. Leveson Gower, *The Letters of Harriet, Lady Granville*, i. 74.
161. Lady C. Lamb to M. Bruce, [1815]; Bod. Lib., Bruce MSS, unfol.
162. Mrs G. Lamb to Lady Morpeth, 9 Aug. [*c*.1815]; Castle Howard MSS, J18/44/139.
163. QVJ, 14 June 1838.
164. H. Colbourne to Lady C. Lamb, [1816]; Vict. and Alb. Mus., Forster MSS, fo. 10.
165. Lady C. Lamb, *Glenarvon* (London 1816), i. 146.
166. Ibid. i. 147.
167. Ibid. 134.
168. Ibid. 151–2.
169. Ibid. ii. 139.
170. Ibid. i. 279.
171. Ibid. ii. 160.
172. Byron to T. Guiccioli, 7 Feb. 1820; Marchand, *Byron's Letters and Journals*, vii. 37.
173. Byron to J. Murray 2 April 1817; ibid. v. 204.
174. Byron to S. Rogers, 29 July 1816; ibid. 86.
175. Lady Holland to Mrs Creevey, 21 May 1816; Sir H. Maxwell, *The Creevey Papers* (London 1904), i. 254–5.
176. Lady C. Lamb to Lady Londonderry, 14 Jan. 1817; Kent RO, Camden MSS, U840 c 154.
177. Lady Melbourne to A. Milbanke, 29 June 1816; Bod. Lib., Lovelace–Byron MSS 92, fo. 97.
178. BL Add. MSS 45550, fo. 16; Lady Cowper to Lady C. Lamb, [1816].
179. Mrs G. Lamb to Lady Byron, 17 May [1816]; Bod. Lib., Lovelace–Byron MSS 78, fos. 24–5.
180. BL Add. MSS 51558, fo. 19; W. Lamb to Lord Holland, 27 May 1816.

181. Ibid.
182. Lady C. Lamb to G. Leveson Gower, [1816]; Lady Granville, *Lord Granville Leveson Gower* (London 1916), ii. 542.
183. Lady C. Lamb to H. Colbourne, [1816]; Vict. and Alb. Mus., Forster MSS, fo. 43.
184. W. Lamb to H. Colbourne, 17 May 1816; ibid. fo. 12.
185. Byron to Lady Melbourne, 5 Feb. 1815; Marchand, *Byron's Letters and Journals*, iv. 266–7.
186. BL Add. MSS 45548, fo. 141; Lady C. Lamb to Lady Melbourne, [April 1816].
187. BL Add. MSS 51558, fo. 21; Lady C. Lamb to Lord Holland, [May 1816].
188. Lord Broughton, *Recollections of a Long Life*, i. 341.
189. Miss E. Eden to Lady Buckinghamshire, 25 Oct. 1816; V. Dickinson, *Miss Eden's Letters* (London 1919), 3.
190. Lady Cowper to F. Lamb, n.d.; Herts. RO, Panshanger MSS, D/ELb F75.
191. Ibid.

Chapter 5

1. Greville, vi. 248.
2. Lady C. Lamb to M. Bruce, [*c.*1817]; Bod. Lib., Bruce MSS, unfol.
3. Lady Caroline reported that she knew 'not how to live and I dare not die', and William 'wishes he was dead'. Lady C. Lamb to M. Bruce, [July 1817]; Bod. Lib., Bruce MSS, unfol. and BL Add. MSS 45546, fo. 119; Lady C. Lamb to Lady Melbourne, 2 April 1817.
4. BL Add. MSS 50142, fo. 8; Lady C. Lamb to Mrs Opie, 22 Jan. 1822.
5. Lady C. Lamb, *Graham Hamilton* (London 1822), ii. 11.
6. Lady C. Lamb to H. Colbourne, [1822]; Vict. and Alb. Mus., Forster MSS, fo. 32.
7. W. Lamb to H. Colbourne, 29 March 1822; ibid. fo. 51.
8. Lady C. Lamb to H. Colbourne, 12 March 1822; ibid. fo. 33.
9. Lady Cowper to F. Lamb, 20 Feb. 1818; Lady Airlie, *Lady Palmerston and Her Times* (London 1922), i. 43.
10. Lady Morpeth to Duke of Devonshire, 5 Aug. [1820]; Chatsworth MSS, Papers of the 6th Duke of Devonshire, 454.
11. Princess Lieven to Prince Metternich, 11 March 1820; Quennell, *The Private Letters of Princess Lieven to Prince Metternich*, 20–1.
12. Byron to J. Hobhouse, 6 April 1819; Marchand, *Byron's Letters and Journals*, vi. 107.
13. Lady Holland to H. Fox, [Aug. 1824]; Lord Ilchester, *Elizabeth, Lady Holland to Her Son*, 29.
14. Mrs G. Lamb to Lady Morpeth, 4 Feb. 1824; Castle Howard MSS, J18/44/139.
15. Cecil, 128. See also BL Add. MSS 45550, fo. 100; Lady Cowper to F. Lamb, 16 March 1821.
16. Lady Cowper to F. Lamb, [18 Sept. 1820]; Lady Airlie, *Lady Palmerston and Her Times*, i. 65.

17. Lady C. Lamb to Lady Morpeth, [*c.*1810]; Castle Howard MSS, J18/35.
18. Lady C. Lamb to Lady Londonderry, 14 Jan. 1817; Kent. RO, Camden MSS, U840 c. 154.
19. Lady C. Lamb to Lady Morpeth, 15 Oct.; Castle Howard MSS, J18/35.
20. Ibid.
21. Lady C. Lamb to H. Colbourne, n.d.; Vict. and Alb. Mus., Forster MSS, fo. 20.
22. Ibid. [1826]; ibid. fo. 49.
23. Melbourne MSS, Box 106/70–83.
24. Details may be found in D. Howell-Thomas, *Lord Melbourne's Susan* (Woking 1928), and in Herts. RO, Panshanger MSS, D/ELb F35.
25. Mrs Norton to Melbourne, 1 Aug. 1831; J. Hoge and C. Olney, *The Letters of Caroline Norton to Lord Melbourne* (Ohio 1974), 29.
26. QVJ, 28 March 1838.
27. Lord Lytton, *Edward Bulwer, Lord Lytton* (London 1883), i. 330.
28. B. Lytton to Miss Wheeler, Anon., *Letters of the late Edward Bulwer, Lord Lytton* (London, 1884), 10.
29. B. Lytton to Lady C. Lamb, n.d.; Herts. RO, Lytton MSS, DE/K c. 28, fo. 29.
30. Lady C. Lamb to B. Lytton, 1826; ibid. c 1, fo. 4.
31. Lord Lytton, *Edward Bulwer, Lord Lytton*, i. 330.
32. Ibid. 333.
33. Mrs G. Lamb to Lady Carlisle, 2 April [1839]; Castle Howard MSS, J18/44/143.
34. Lady Holland to H. Fox, 4 Nov. 1824; Lord Ilchester, *Elizabeth, Lady Holland to Her Son*, 31.
35. F. Lamb to C. Cookney, 4 May 1825; Melbourne Hall MSS, X94/1/5/36.
36. Ibid. 5 May 1825; ibid. X94/1/5/4.
37. The name is variously given as Washington or Wilmington.
38. Lady Byron to Mrs G. Lamb, 19 March 1826; Bod. Lib., Byron–Lovelace MSS, 78, fo. 68.
39. Lady C. Lamb to H. Colbourne, [1826]; Vict. and Alb. Mus., Forster MSS, fo. 58.
40. Lady C. Lamb to W. Fleming, n.d.; ibid. fo. 52. See also Lady C. Lamb to H. Colbourne, ibid. fos. 49 and 53.
41. J. Burn to Melbourne, 20 Aug. 1831; Herts. RO, Panshanger MSS, D/ELb F39. M. Simpson to Melbourne, [1837]; ibid.
42. Lady C. Lamb to Lady Morpeth, n.d.; Castle Howard MSS, J18/35.
43. W. Lamb to Lord Lansdowne, 3 Aug. 1827; Ziegler, 58.
44. Duke of Devonshire to H. Leveson Gower, 10 Oct. 1824; Chatsworth MSS, Papers of the 6th Duke of Devonshire, 1041.
45. BL Add. MSS 45550, fo. 17; E. Lamb to F. Lamb, 22 Jan. 1820.
46. Ibid.
47. Mrs G. Lamb to Lady Morpeth, n.d.; Castle Howard MSS, J18/44/140.
48. P. Marshall, *William Godwin* (Yale 1984), 355 and 374. W. Godwin to Melbourne, 22 Sept. 1834; Melbourne MSS, Box 42/109. Diary of Lady C. Bury, 1819; Lady C. Bury, *The Diary of a Lady in Waiting* (London 1908), ii. 214–15.

49. W. Jerdan, *Autobiography* (London 1852), ii. 286.
50. Mrs G. Lamb to Lady Morpeth, n.d.; Castle Howard MSS, J18/44/139.
51. E. Lamb to F. Lamb, 7 Oct. 1822; Lever, *The Letters of Lady Palmerston*, 111.
52. BL Add. MSS 45549, fo. 217; E. Lamb to Lady Melbourne, [15 July] 1817.
53. BL Add. MSS 45546, fo. 13; Lady C. Lamb to Lady Melbourne, 24 March 1810.
54. BL Add. MSS 45550, fo. 165; E. Lamb to F. Lamb, 24 May [1825].
55. Lady C. Lamb to ?; Herts. RO, Panshanger MSS, D/ELb F62.
56. Poem by Lady C. Lamb; ibid. F64.
57. Cecil, 254.
58. Lady C. Lamb to Lord Hartington, 29 Sept. 1809; Chatsworth MSS, Papers of the 5th Duke of Devonshire, fo. 1954.
59. BL Add. MSS 51560, fo. 137; Lady C. Lamb to Lady Holland, [10 July 1810].
60. Lord Hatherton's Diary, 29 Aug. 1835; Staffs. RO, Hatherton MSS, D260/M/F/5/26/9.
61. QVJ, 12 Sept. 1839.
62. Greville, 29 Nov. 1848, vi. 253–4.
63. Lady C. Bury, *Diary of a Lady in Waiting*, 243.
64. Lady Lytton, *Cheveley or The Man of Honour*, 32, 31, 110, 68.
65. BL Add. MSS 51739, fo. 97; Lord Holland to Caroline Fox, 25 Dec. 1812.
66. Lady C. Lamb to J. Murray, 1817; S. Smiles, *A Publisher and His Friends* (London 1891), i. 380.
67. QVJ, 21 Jan. 1839.
68. Ibid. 14 May 1838.
69. Ibid. 21 Dec. 1838.
70. Ibid. 1 Jan. 1838.
71. Dr Goddard to Melbourne, 19 Oct. 1825; Herts. RO, Panshanger MSS, D/ELb F33.
72. Melbourne to Sir H. Halford, 26 Feb. 1835; Leics. RO, Halford MSS, DG24/904/4. I am indebted to Dr J. Walsh for this reference.
73. Melbourne to Fox Maule, 28 Oct. 1840; Scots. RO, G14/640/20.
74. Lady C. Lamb to Duke of Devonshire, [April 1825]; Chatsworth MSS, Papers of the 6th Duke of Devonshire, fo. 1129.
75. Duke of Devonshire to G. Lamb, 17 April 1825; ibid. fo. 1132.
76. BL Add. MSS 45548, fo. 159; W. Lamb to F. Lamb, 21 May 1825.
77. Ibid.
78. G. Lamb to Devonshire, 15 April 1825; Chatsworth MSS, Papers of the 6th Duke of Devonshire, fo. 1131.
79. C. Cookney to F. Lamb, 21 April 1825; Melbourne Hall MSS, X94/1/5/2.
80. C. Pepys to Fitzwilliam, 30 June 1825; Sheffield City Library, Wentworth Woodhouse MSS, F84/2. See also Melbourne to Fitzwilliam, 22 June and 5 July 1825; ibid. F84/1 and F85/4.
81. Althorp to Devonshire, 13 June 1825; Chatsworth MSS, Papers of the 6th Duke of Devonshire, fo. 1155.
82. Duncannon to Lady Duncannon, n.d.; West Sussex RO, Bessborough MSS

83. BL Add. MSS 45550, fo. 165; E. Lamb to F. Lamb, 24 May 1825.
84. Ibid.
85. Ibid. fo. 176; ibid. 10 June [1825].
86. E. Lamb to F. Lamb, 14 July 1825; Lever, *The Letters of Lady Palmerston*, 137.
87. Ibid. 7 July 1825; ibid.
88. BL Add. MSS 45550, fo. 186; E. Lamb to F. Lamb, 19 July [1825].
89. E. Lamb to F. Lamb, 12 [July 1825]; Lady Airlie, *Lady Palmerston and Her Times*, i. 118–19.
90. C. Cookney to Lord Bessborough, 20 Aug. 1825; Melbourne Hall MSS, X94/1/6/2.
91. W. Lamb to C. Cookney, 26 June 1825; ibid.
92. W. Lamb to F. Lamb, 28 May 1825; Herts. RO, Panshanger MSS, D/ELb F78.
93. E. Lamb to F. Lamb, 7 June [1825]; Lever, *The Letters of Lady Palmerston*, 135–6.
94. BL Add. MSS 45550, fo. 165; E. Lamb to F. Lamb, 24 May 1825.
95. E. Lamb to F. Lamb, 27 Oct. 1825; Lever, *The Letters of Lady Palmerston*, 141.
96. Ibid. 1 Aug. [1825]; ibid. 138.
97. QVJ, 22 Feb. 1838.
98. Lady C. Lamb to Devonshire, [26 Oct. 1825]; Chatsworth MSS, Papers of the 6th Duke of Devonshire, fo. 1217.
99. Lady C. Lamb to W. Lamb, 12 Sept. 1825; Herts. RO, Panshanger MSS, D/ELb F32.
100. A. Ellis to Lady Holland, 13 Nov. 1825; Lady Leconfield and J. Gore, *Three Howard Sisters* (London 1955), 49.
101. BL Add. MSS 51600, fo. 138; E. Lamb to Lady Holland, 23 [Feb. 1826].
102. E. Lamb to F. Lamb, 20 March [1827]; Lever, *The Letters of Lady Palmerston*, 162. See also BL Add. MSS 45551, fos. 21 and 37; E. Lamb to F. Lamb, 3 March and 26 May 1826.
103. W. Lamb to Lady C. Lamb, 21 Aug. 1827; W. Sussex RO, Bessborough MSS, 182.
104. QVJ, 27 April 1838.
105. Lady C. Lamb to B. Lytton, 1826; Herts. RO, Lytton MSS, D/EK c 1 f 4.
106. Jenkins, *Lady Caroline Lamb*, 272.
107. Mrs Hawtre to Lady Morgan, 22 Nov. 1827; Lady Morgan, *Memoirs* (London 1862), ii. 245.
108. Melbourne to Spring Rice, 4 Jan. 1828; Torrens, *Memoirs of Lord Melbourne*, 191.
109. W. Lamb to Lady C. Lamb, 6 Jan. 1828; W. Sussex RO, Bessborough MSS, 182.
110. W. Ponsonby to Lady Morgan, 26 Jan. 1828; Lady Morgan, *Memoirs*, ii. 253.
111. W. Lamb to Lady Branden, 27 Jan. 1828; Herts. RO, Panshanger MSS, D/ELb F43.
112. Ibid. 7 Feb. 1828; ibid.
113. Ibid. 18 Feb. 1828; ibid.
114. BL Add. MSS 45551, fos. 110–11; E. Lamb to F. Lamb, [Jan. 1828].
115. Lady Gower to Lady C. Lascelles, Jan. 1828; Lady Leconfield and J. Gore, *Three Howard Sisters*, 107.

116. Cecil, 141.
117. BL Add. MSS 51725, fo. 169; Egremont to Holland, 6 Oct. 1834.
118. Torrens, *Memoirs of Lord Melbourne*, 446.
119. Commonplace Book; Herts. RO, Panshanger MSS, D/ELb F28.
120. Diary of R. Lee, 30 Aug. 1821; Anon., *Extracts from the Diary of the late Dr. Robert Lee*, 24–5.
121. Lady Clarendon's Journal, 5 Feb. 1840; Sir H. Maxwell, *The Life and Letters of the 4th Earl of Clarendon* (London 1913), i. 182.
122. Melbourne to Russell, 13 Oct. 1839; Melbourne MSS, 14/70.
123. Melbourne to W. Cowper, 19 April 1843; Southampton Univ. Lib., Melbourne MSS, MEL/CO/49.
124. Autobiography; Herts. RO, Panshanger MSS, D/ELb F12.
125. Cecil, 292.
126. J. Clive, *Thomas Babington Macaulay* (London 1973), 498.
127. Cecil, 116–17.
128. BL Add. MSS 45551, fo. 55; E. Lamb to F. Lamb, 21 Aug. 1826.
129. F. Guizot, *An Embassy to the Court of St. James in 1840* (London 1862), 9.
130. F. W. Haydon, *Correspondence and Table Talk of Benjamin Haydon* (London 1876), ii. 371.
131. W. Cowper, *The Nation*, 15 (1884), 50.
132. Ibid. 51.
133. Ibid.
134. Ibid. 52.
135. Lord Houghton, *Fortnightly Review*, 23 (1884), 217.
136. W. Cowper, *The Nation*, 15 (1884), 55.

Chapter 6

1. Lady Holland's Journal, 24 Dec. 1810; Lord Ilchester, *The Journal of Elizabeth, Lady Holland*, ii. 280.
2. QVJ, 1 June 1838.
3. W. Lamb to F. Lamb, 13 April 1826; Herts. RO, Panshanger MSS, D/ELb F78.
4. E. B. de Fonblanque, *The Life and Letters of Albany Fonblanque* (London 1874), 88.
5. Greville, 12 March 1840, iv. 285.
6. Journals; Herts. RO, Panshanger MSS, D/ELb F15, F16.
7.

Date	Seat	Patron
1806	Leominster	Lord Kinnaird
1806–7	Haddington	Lord Lauderdale
1807–12	Portarlington	Purchased for £5,000
1816–19	Peterborough	Lord Fitzwilliam
1819–26	Hertfordshire	—
1827	Newport	The Holmes Family
1827–8	Bletchingley	W. Russell

8. BL Add. MSS 45551, fo. 10; E. Lamb to F. Lamb, 2 Feb. 1826.
9. Ibid. fo. 28; ibid. 16 March 1826.

10. Ibid. fo. 21; ibid. 3 March 1826.
11. Torrens, *Memoirs of Lord Melbourne*, 137.
12. Ibid. 138.
13. Cecil, 79.
14. Lady C. Lamb to Lady Morpeth, [Nov. 1806]; Castle Howard MSS, J18/35.
15. Autobiography; Herts. RO, Panshanger MSS, D/ELb F12.
16. Journal, March 1807; ibid., F15.
17. W. Lamb to Lady C. Lamb, 24 Jan. 1810; W. Sussex RO, Bessborough MSS, 182.
18. *Gentleman's Magazine*, xxxi. 84, Jan. 1849.
19. QVJ, 21 Feb. 1838.
20. R. Thorne, *The House of Commons, 1790–1820* (London 1986), 360.
21. BL Add. MSS 51558, fo. 1; W. Lamb to Holland, Sept. 1806.
22. Lady C. Lamb to Lady Morpeth, 14 Sept. [1806]; Castle Howard MSS, J18/35.
23. Stuart, *Dearest Bess*, 152.
24. Lady T. Lewis, *Extracts from the Journals and Correspondence of Miss Berry* (London 1865), iii. 524.
25. *Parl. Hist.* xv. 384; 12 Feb. 1810.
26. Ibid. ix. 287; 7 April 1807.
27. Journal, April 1807; Herts. RO, Panshanger MSS, D/ELb F15.
28. *Parl. Hist.* xxi. 1012; 27 Feb. 1812.
29. Ibid. xxiii. 23; 15 May 1812.
30. Ibid. xxxiv. 340; 7 May 1816.
31. Ibid. xl. 505; 18 May 1819.
32. Mrs E. Fox to Melbourne, 16 Dec. 1835; Melbourne MSS, Box 25/126.
33. BL Add. MSS 44703, fo. 8; Gladstone, The Melbourne Administration, 30 Jan. 1890.
34. Autobiography; Herts. RO, Panshanger MSS, D/ELb F12.
35. E. A. Smith, *Whig Principles and Party Politics* (Manchester 1975), 331.
36. *Parl. Hist.* lxiv. 56, 17 June 1842.
37. Journal, Dec. 1808; Herts. RO, Panshanger MSS, F16.
38. Ibid.
39. Sanders, *Lord Melbourne's Papers*, 64.
40. *Parl. Hist.* xxi. 909–10, 23 Feb. 1812.
41. T. Grenville to Lord Grenville, 15 Dec. 1815; HMC, Fortescue MSS, x. 408.
42. BL Add. MSS 45548, fo. 139; Prologue to *Ina*.
43. *Parl. Hist.* viii. 37, 19 Dec. 1806.
44. Lady T. Lewis, *Extracts from the Journals and Correspondence of Miss Berry*, ii. 196. See also BL Add. MSS 51560; W. Lamb to Lady Holland, 23 Feb. 1802.
45. *Parl. Hist.* x. 1366, 23 March 1824.
46. Ibid. viii. 1029; 16 April 1823.
47. Cecil, 228.
48. *Parl. Hist.* xxxv. 26, 28 Jan. 1817.
49. W. Lamb to F. Fox, 12 Sept. 1819; Melbourne Hall MSS, X94/234/6/28.
50. *Parl. Hist.* xxxv. 30, 28 Jan. 1817.

51. Ibid. xxxvii. 999, 11 March 1818.
52. Ibid. xxxv. 800, 28 Feb. 1817.
53. Ibid. xli. 554, 30 Nov. 1819.
54. W. Lamb to Earl Fitzwilliam, 3 Oct. 1819; Wentworth Woodhouse Muniments, F49b/74.
55. *Parl. Hist.* xxxvi. 1225, 27 June 1817.
56. Lord Hatherton's Journal, 24 March 1836; Staffs. RO, Hatherton MSS, D260/M/F/5/26/12.
57. Autobiography; Herts. RO, Panshanger MSS, D/ELb F12.
58. Cecil, 303.
59. Dunckley, *Lord Melbourne*, 97.
60. Notes for a speech; Melbourne MSS, Box 120/121.
61. *Parl. Hist.* xv. 714; 27 April 1826.
62. W. Lamb to F. Fox, 25 Feb. 1817 and 15 June 1819; Melbourne Hall MSS, X94/254/6/12 and X94/234/6/25.
63. Notes for a speech, [*c.*1819]; Melbourne MSS, Box 120/121.
64. *Parl. Hist.* xvi. 786, 2 May 1810.
65. Ibid. xxxvi. 789–90, 20 May 1817.
66. Ibid. 790.
67. Ibid. 798.
68. Ibid. xxxviii. 1179, 2 June 1818.
69. BL Add. MSS 38458, fo. 323; W. Lamb to C. Arbuthnot, 19 March 1820.
70. F. Lamb to W. Lamb, 4 March [1816]; Melbourne MSS, Box 106/4.
71. *Parl. Hist.* xviii. 337, 21 Dec. 1810. See also Brougham to Melbourne, 28 April 1810; Melbourne MSS, Box 1/71.
72. W. Lamb to Fitzwilliam, 17 Jan. 1820; Wentworth Woodhouse Muniments, F49b/76.
73. Ibid. See also, W. Lamb to Brougham, 7 Nov. 1838; Univ. Coll. London, Brougham MSS, 43560 a.
74. E. Lamb to F. Lamb, 9 May 1826; Lever, *The Letters of Lady Palmerston*, 149.
75. Commonplace Book, 14 Dec. 1819; Herts. RO, Panshanger MSS, D/ELb F28.
76. Sanders, *Lord Melbourne's Papers*, 96.
77. E. Lamb to F. Lamb, 10 Aug. 1827; Lever, *The Letters of Lady Palmerston*, 173.
78. Lord Hatherton's Journal, 12 June 1840; Staffs. RO, Hatherton MSS, D26/M/F/5/26/18.
79. Journal, April 1807; Herts. RO, Panshanger MSS, D/ELb F15.
80. Ibid. 3 Jan. 1808; ibid.
81. W. Lamb to F. Lamb, 3 Dec. 1827; ibid. F78.
82. BL Add. MSS 45546, fo. 2; W. Lamb to Lady Melbourne, 28 July 1812.
83. The Betting Book of Brooks's Club.
84. W. Lamb to J. W. Ward, 29 Sept. 1822; Anon., *Letters of the Earl of Dudley* (London 1840), 362–3.
85. *Parl. Hist.* xviii. 337, 21 Dec. 1810.
86. Melbourne to Mrs G. Lamb, 24 Dec. 1838; Univ. Coll. London, Brougham MSS, 8064.

87. Torrens, *Memoirs of Lord Melbourne*, 40.
88. Melbourne to Brougham, 19 Sept. 1830; Univ. Coll. London, Brougham MSS, 43480.
89. E. Huskisson to Lady Byron, 16 Feb. 1849; Bod. Lib., Lovelace–Byron MSS, 360.
90. Lady Bessborough to G. Leveson Gower, 24 Feb. [1806]; Lady Granville, *Lord Granville Leveson Gower*, ii. 180.
91. Cecil, 56.
92. Autobiography; Herts. RO, Panshanger MSS, D/ELb F12.
93. Ibid.
94. Melbourne to Victoria, 6 April 1842; Windsor Castle, Royal Archives, A4 fo. 61.
95. H. Brougham to Lord Grey, [23 July 1811]; Thorne, *The House of Commons, 1790–1820*, 361.
96. Mrs G. Lamb to Lady Morpeth, n.d.; Castle Howard MSS, J18/44/140.
97. E. Lamb to F. Lamb, 22 April [1823]; Lever, *The Letters of Lady Palmerston*, 123.
98. Duke of Bedford to Holland, [14 Feb. 1819]; Thorne, *The House of Commons, 1790–1820*, 355.
99. Althorp to Spencer, 17 Oct. 1819; D. Le Marchant, *Memoir of Viscount Althorp* (London 1876), 95.
100. Lady Bessborough to G. Leveson Gower, [1809]; Lady Granville, *Granville Leveson Gower*, ii. 342.
101. BL Add. MSS 45546, fo. 3; W. Lamb to Lady Melbourne, 29 Sept. 1812.
102. D. Giles to Lady Melbourne, 11 Sept. 1811; Hatfield House MSS. See also BL Add. MSS 45548, fo. 126; Lady Melbourne to D. Giles, Sept. 1811.
103. Lady Bessborough to G. Leveson Gower, 29 Sept. [1812]; Lady Granville, *Granville Leveson Gower*, ii. 462.
104. W. Lamb to C. Grey, 3 Nov. 1812; Durham Univ. Lib., Grey MSS.
105. C. Grey to W. Lamb, 12 and 29 Nov. 1812; ibid. See also BL Add. MSS 51558, fo. 11. W. Lamb to Holland, [Oct. 1812].
106. Autobiography; Herts. RO, Panshanger MSS, D/ELb F12.
107. Ibid.
108. Ibid.
109. W. Lamb to Lady Melbourne, 23 Feb. 1814; Southampton Univ. Lib., Melbourne MSS, MEL/ME/1.
110. BL Add. MSS 51558, fo. 13; W. Lamb to Holland, 10 Dec. 1815. This letter hints at a formal separation from Whig politics.
111. Ibid. fo. 15; ibid. 26 March 1816.
112. Mrs G. Lamb to Lady Morpeth, n.d.; Castle Howard MSS, J18/44/139.
113. Journal, 1807; Herts. RO, Panshanger MSS, D/ELb F15.
114. W. Lamb to G. Canning, 21 April 1827; Leeds City Archives, Canning MSS, 80c.
115. *Parl. Hist.* vi. 178–9, 8 Feb. 1822; xii. 71–2, 3 Feb. 1825; and xii. 445, 15 Feb. 1825.
116. Commonplace Book; Herts. RO, Panshanger MSS, D/ELb F28.

117. E. Lamb to F. Lamb, 27 April 1827; Lever, *The Letters of Lady Palmerston*, 165–6.
118. Ibid. 1 May 1827; ibid. 166.
119. BL Add. MSS 45551, fo. 94; E. Lamb to F. Lamb, 16 April 1827.
120. Lord Howick's Journal, 29 Aug. 1839; Durham Univ. Lib., Grey MSS, c 3/4.
121. Melbourne to E. Ellice, 12 Feb. 1833; Nat. Lib. of Scotland, Ellice MSS, 15031, fo. 2.
122. Holland to Carlisle, 6 Aug. [1827]; Castle Howard MSS, LB13.
123. W. Lamb to ?, 30 Oct. 1827; Torrens, *Memoirs of Lord Melbourne*, 181.
124. BL Add. MSS 37305, fo. 97; W. Lamb to Lord Wellesley, 28 April 1827.
125. W. Lamb to F. Lamb, 2 July 1827; Herts. RO, Panshanger MSS, D/ELb F78.
126. BL Add. MSS 47551, fo. 96; E. Lamb to F. Lamb, 15 May 1827.
127. Torrens, *Memoirs of Lord Melbourne*, 155.
128. R. Bennett to D. O'Connell, 9 June [1827]; M. O'Connell, *The Correspondence of Daniel O'Connell* (Dublin 1972–80), iii. 322.
129. D. O'Connell to R. Bennett, 11 June 1827; ibid. iii. 322.
130. Ibid. 26 Sept. 1827; ibid. iii. 344.
131. BL Add. MSS 45551, fo. 104; E. Lamb to F. Lamb, 3 Aug. 1827.
132. W. Lamb to G. Canning, 15 July 1827; Leeds City Archives, Canning MSS, 80c.
133. Cecil, 163.
134. W. Lamb to Anglesey, 18 Dec. 1830; NRA, transcripts of the Anglesey MSS, D 619/29c.
135. BL Add. MSS 37305, fo. 173; W. Lamb to Lansdowne, 19 Sept. 1827.
136. BL Add. MSS 45548, fo. 165; W. Lamb to F. Lamb, 27 Aug. 1827.
137. Lord Anglesey, *The Life and Letters of the First Marquess of Anglesey* (London 1961), 183.
138. W. Lamb to Lord Lansdowne, 3 Aug. 1827; Ziegler, 93.
139. Ibid. 11 Nov. 1827; ibid.
140. Draft speech, March 1829; Melbourne MSS, Box 120/121. See also *Parl. Hist.* xx. 645, 2 March 1829.
141. BL Add. MSS 51558, fo. 27; Anglesey to Melbourne, [June 1828].
142. Melbourne to F. Fox, 7 March 1829; Melbourne Hall MSS, 235/1/46.
143. Melbourne to Anglesey, 10 May 1828; Melbourne MSS, Box 93/27.
144. W. Lamb to Sir R. Peel, 29 March 1828; Lord Mahon, *Memoirs of the Rt. Hon. Sir Robert Peel* (London 1856), i. 25.
145. W. Lamb to Anglesey, 24 March 1828; Lord Anglesey, *The Life and Letters of the First Marquess of Anglesey*, 194–5.
146. Melbourne to Anglesey, 25 Jan. 1831; NRA, Anglesey Transcripts, D619/29c.
147. W. Lamb to Anglesey, 6 March 1828; PRO, Anglesey MSS, D619/31N/27.
148. W. Lamb to Sir R. Peel, 3 May 1828; Lord Mahon, *Memoirs of Sir Robert Peel*, i. 57. See also W. Lamb to Anglesey, 24 April 1828; Melbourne MSS, Box 93/13.
149. W. Lamb to G. Canning, 26 July 1827; Leeds City Archives, Canning MSS, 80c.
150. BL Add. MSS 37305, fo. 236; W. Lamb to Lord Wellesley, 2 Jan. 1828.
151. Melbourne to Anglesey, 29 Dec. 1830; NRA, Anglesey Transcripts, D619/29c.

152. Ibid. 22 Dec. 1830; ibid.
153. Lord J. Russell to Melbourne, 9 Sept. 1837; PRO, Russell MSS, xc10466, fo. 73.
154. Wellington to W. Lamb, 12 Jan. 1828; Melbourne MSS, Box 17/57. See also W. Lamb to Wellington, 14 Jan. 1828; ibid. Box 17/58, and H. Gregory to Sir R. Peel, 3 Feb. 1828; Lord Mahon, *Memoirs of Sir R. Peel*, i. 19.
155. W. Lamb to F. Lamb, 28 Jan. 1828; Herts. RO, Panshanger MSS, D/ELb F78.
156. Sir R. Peel to W. Lamb, May 1828; Lord Mahon, *Memoirs of Sir R. Peel*, i. 104.
157. Lady Dover to Lady C. Lascelles, 20 Jan. 1828; Lady Leconfield and J. Gore, *Three Howard Sisters*, 102.
158. W. Lamb to F. Lamb, 12 Jan. 1828; Herts. RO, Panshanger MSS, D/ELb F78.
159. W. Lamb to Anglesey, 3 June 1828; Melbourne MSS, Box 93/36.
160. In Lady Holland's view, the connection was 'quite personal, not political'. K. Bourne, *Palmerston* (London 1982), 294. Melbourne himself was so nervous about this incident that he risked a major confrontation with Brougham, ten years later, over his account of it. See Melbourne to Brougham, 2 Nov. 1838; Southampton Univ. Lib., Melbourne MSS, MEL/BR/32/1; and Brougham to Melbourne, 3 Nov. 1838; Melbourne MSS, Box 2/55.
161. E. Lamb to F. Lamb, 28 May [1828]; Herts. RO, Panshanger MSS, D/ELb F75.
162. BL Add. MSS 38757, fo. 65; Goderich to Huskisson, 13 Sept. 1828. Greville, ii. 96–7, 16 Dec. 1830. Princess Lieven to A. Benckendorff, 8 July 1830; L. G. Robinson, *Letters of Dorothea, Princess Lieven*, 224–5. Bamford, *The Journal of Mrs Arbuthnot*, 395. L. G. Jones to D. O'Connell, 16 Oct. 1830; O'Connell, *The Correspondence of Daniel O'Connell*, iv. 216.
163. Melbourne to Palmerston, 13 Oct. 1830; Southampton Univ. Lib., Palmerston MSS, GMC/40. See also Ziegler, 117.
164. Melbourne to Palmerston, 8 Oct. 1830; Southampton Univ. Lib., Palmerston MSS, GMC 39.
165. Palmerston to E. Lamb, 25 Nov. 1829; Bourne, *Palmerston*, 306.

Chapter 7

1. W. Lamb to G. Lamb, 15 Aug. 1821; Herts. RO, Panshanger MSS, D/ELb F90.
2. Melbourne to Revd M. Fogarty, 27 Aug. 1831; Melbourne MSS, Box 25/91.
3. W. Lamb to G. Lamb, 3 May 1820; Herts. RO Panshanger MSS, D/ELb F78.
4. Melbourne to Lady Branden, 12 Nov. 1830; ibid. F42.
5. Lord Holland's Diary, 16 Nov. 1831; A. D. Kriegel, *The Holland House Diaries* (London 1977), 79.
6. Grey to Melbourne, 13 Oct. 1813; Melbourne MSS, Box 5/111.
7. E. Lamb to F. Lamb, 17 Aug. 1820; Lever, *The Letters of Lady Palmerston*, 39.
8. Melbourne to Anglesey, 12 Sept. 1832; NRA, Anglesey Transcripts, D619/293.
9. Melbourne MSS, Box 121/11.
10. *Parl. Hist.* xxiv 612, 20 June 1834. See also ibid. xvii. 1017, 7 May 1833.
11. W. Lamb to Fitzwilliam, 17 Jan. 1820; Sheffield City Archives, Wentworth Woodhouse MSS, F496/76.

12. Torrens, *Memoirs of Lord Melbourne*, 53.
13. *Parl. Hist.* xxi. 848; 18 Feb. 1812.
14. *Gentleman's Magazine*, xxxi. 85, Jan. 1849.
15. Lord Mahon to Lady Stanhope, 1 Dec. 1831; Kent RO, Stanhope MSS, c 318/2.
16. Ziegler, 139.
17. Lord Howick's Journal, 29 Aug. 1839; Durham Univ. Archives, Grey MSS, c 3/4.
18. Lord Holland's Diary, 5 Sept. 1831; Kriegel, *The Holland House Diaries*, 47–8. Ibid. [Feb. 1833]; ibid. 206. Grey to Melbourne, 9 Jan. 1833; Durham Univ. Archives, Grey MSS, fo. 99A. Melbourne to Grey, 11 Jan. 1833; ibid. fo. 100.
19. BL Add. MSS 51600, fo. 205; E. Lamb to Lady Holland, n.d.
20. Lady Dover to Lady C. Lascelles, 7 Dec. 1830; Lady Leconfield and J. Gore, *Three Howard Sisters*, 173.
21. Greville, ii. 92–3, 12 Dec. 1830.
22. This chapter draws heavily on important work by R. D. H. Custance, presented in an Oxford D.Phil. thesis, entitled 'The Political Career of William Lamb, Second Viscount Melbourne, to 1841.'
23. Melbourne to Grey, 11 June 1831; Durham Univ. Archives, Grey MSS, fo. 30. See also Melbourne to H. Bouverie, 20 Aug. 1833; Melbourne MSS, Box 80/14.
24. Melbourne to J. Poulett Scrope, 27 Jan. 1831; ibid. Box 35/60. See also J. Philips to Revd J. Corry, 12 Nov. 1831; PRO, HO 43, 41/f24.
25. Melbourne to H. Duncombe, 23 Jan. 1831; Melbourne MSS, Box 86/78.
26. Melbourne to Lord Talbot, 18 Aug. 1832; ibid. Box 89/60.
27. Melbourne to Lord Derby, 16 Jan. 1831; ibid. Box 86/63.
28. Melbourne to Wellington, 26 Nov. 1830; Southampton Univ. Archives, Wellington MSS, 4/1/2/2/22.
29. Melbourne to Richmond, 24 Oct. 1831 and 10 Feb. 1834; W. Sussex RO, Richmond MSS, 636 fo. 92 and 668 fo. 49.
30. Melbourne Memorandum, n.d.; Melbourne MSS, Box 88/15. For an opposite view, see D. Philips and R. D. Storch, 'Whigs and Coppers: The Grey Ministry's National Police Scheme, 1832', *Historical Research*, 67 (1994).
31. Melbourne to Sir T. Gooch, 13 Dec. 1830; Custance 36.
32. Melbourne to Lord Airlie, 11 April 1831; Scots. RO GD16/52/48/1.
33. Melbourne to Sir G. Clerk, 16 April 1831; ibid. GD/8/3332/2.
34. Melbourne to Grey, 31 Oct. 1831; Durham Univ. Archives, Grey MSS, fo. 44.
35. Melbourne to Col. Wodehouse, various dates; Norfolk RO, Wodehouse MSS, LLC/1.
36. Melbourne to W. Hilton, 30 Dec. 1830; Melbourne MSS, Box 87/54.
37. Circular to Magistrates, 5 Dec. 1830; ibid. Box 88/18.
38. Cabinet Minute, 22 Nov. 1830; ibid. Box 5/89.
39. Lord Hatherton's Journal, 4 Dec. 1831; Staffs. RO, Hatherton MSS, D260/M/F/5/26/7. Melbourne to Lord Lyttelton, 11 Nov. 1833; Melbourne MSS, Box 87/121.

40. *Parl. Hist.* vii. 87–8, 16 Sept. 1831.
41. Melbourne to Grey, 29 Oct. 1831; Durham Univ. Archives, Grey MSS, fo. 40.
42. Torrens, *Memoirs of Lord Melbourne*, 278.
43. For a detailed account of Melbourne's response to the Unions, see Custance, ch. 2.
44. *Parl. Hist.* ix. 834, 26 Jan. 1832. Grey to Melbourne, 4 and 16 Nov. 1831; Melbourne MSS, Box 5/94 and 95. William IV to Melbourne, 5 Aug. and 23 Sept. 1831; ibid. Box 108/14. Sir H. Taylor to Melbourne, 28 Oct. 1831; ibid. Box 108/50.
45. J. Philips to G. Pouch, 26 Nov. 1831; PRO, HO 43, 41/f86.
46. Melbourne to Wellington, 10 Nov. 1832; Southampton Univ. Archives, Wellington MSS, 4/1/4/1/26. See also, Melbourne to William IV, 8 Jan. 1833; Melbourne MSS, Box 109/40.
47. Melbourne to Sir H. Taylor, 26 Sept. 1831; L. C. Sanders, *Lord Melbourne's Papers*, 134.
48. Melbourne to William IV, 23 Sept. 1831; Melbourne MSS, Box 108/27.
49. BL Add. MSS 41567, fo. 153; Melbourne to Mr Foster, 26 March 1834.
50. Melbourne to Lord Portman, 12 Dec. 1833; Melbourne MSS, Box 88/84.
51. *Parl. Hist.* xviii. 854–5, 17 June 1833. Melbourne to Grey, 26 Dec. 1830; Durham Univ. Archives, Grey MSS, fo. 12. Melbourne to William IV, 2 April 1834; Melbourne MSS, Box 109/121.
52. Melbourne to Lord Sandon, 15 June 1833; Melbourne MSS, Box 89/24.
53. Melbourne to F. Lamb, 21 Feb. 1834; Herts. RO, Panshanger MSS, D/ELb F78. See also Melbourne to Lord Bute, 24 Oct. 1831; Custance, 118.
54. Melbourne to Lord Lyttelton, 29 March 1834; Melbourne MSS, Box 87/136.
55. Melbourne to William IV, 24 Nov. 1831; ibid. Box 108/64.
56. BL Add. MSS 41567, fo. 143; J. Philips to J. Frampton, 6 March 1834.
57. All the depositions and other evidence may be found among the Melbourne MSS.
58. See BL Add. MSS 41567, fos. 121–157 for the correspondence between Melbourne and the Dorset JP, John Frampton.
59. BL Add. MSS 38080, fo. 60; Melbourne to Lord John Russell, 11 June 1834. See also Melbourne to Lord John Russell, 13 Oct. 1835; Southampton Univ. Lib., Melbourne MSS, MEL/RU/186.
60. Melbourne to Lyttelton, 29 March 1834; Melbourne MSS, Box 87/136.
61. Lord Holland's Diary, 7 Nov. 1831; Kriegel, *The Holland House Diaries*, 74.
62. *Parl. Hist.* xxiii. 95–6, 28 April 1834.
63. *Morning Chronicle*, 29 April 1834.
64. Palmerston to E. Lamb, 5 Nov. 1831; Custance, 71.
65. *Morning Chronicle*, 16 Jan. 1834.
66. Melbourne to Sir F. Burdett, 27 Oct. 1831; Melbourne MSS, Box 20/103. In reply, Burdett assured Melbourne of his wish to avoid any activities, which might be thought 'dangerous'. Sir F. Burdett to Melbourne, 29 Oct. 1831; ibid. Box 20/112.
67. Melbourne to Brougham, 31 Oct. 1831; Univ. Coll. London, Brougham MSS,

20386. See also Lord Hatherton's Diary, 28 Oct. 1831; Staffs. RO, Hatherton MSS, D260/M/F/5/26/7.

68. BL Add. MSS 60482, fo. 96; T. Young to Lord Beauvale, 11 Oct. 1848.

69. Ibid. 35149, fo. 187; Diary of F. Place, 26 Aug. 1832.

70. Born in 1790, Thomas Young, after a career as ship's purser, became Melbourne's personal secretary from, approximately, 1831 to 1835. His reward was the office of Receiver General at the Post Office at a salary of £800 a year. He died in 1864, leaving an estate of £30,000. He seems to have been used by Melbourne as a personal emissary, particularly in matters of a delicate or personal kind. Quite why Melbourne should have so trusted a man of such a background was a matter of considerable speculation.

I am indebted to Dr A. I. M. Duncan for this information.

71. BL Add. MSS 60482, fo. 91; Melbourne to Beauvale, 10 Oct. 1848. See also ibid. fo. 121; Melbourne to T. Young, 14 Oct. 1848.

72. E. Lamb to F. Lamb, May 1832; Bourne, *Palmerston*, 522.

73. Brougham to Melbourne, 1831; Melbourne MSS, Box 1/84.

74. Melbourne to Buckingham, 6 Nov. 1831; ibid. Box 86/22.

75. Melbourne to T. Barber, 10 Nov. 1831; Notts. RO, Barber MSS, D.D.2B 8/14. Melbourne to Newcastle, 12 Nov. 1831; Melbourne MSS, Box 88/29. Melbourne to Newcastle, 15 Oct. 16 Nov. 31 Dec. 1831 and 19 Aug. 1833; Nottingham Univ. Lib., Newcastle MSS, NeC5, 053, 055, 058, 060.

76. One major speech is recorded in 1831, and one in 1832.

77. Melbourne to Anglesey, 26 Feb. 1831; I. Newbould, *Whiggery and Reform, 1830–1841* (London 1990), 60.

78. Melbourne to T. Barber, 14 Dec. 1832; Notts. RO, Barber MSS, D.D.2B 8/22.

79. F. W. Haydon, *The Correspondence and Table Talk of Benjamin Haydon* (London 1853), ii. 421.

80. Sanders, *Lord Melbourne's Papers*, 101.

81. Cecil, 161–2.

82. Greville, iii. 138, 19 Sept. 1834.

83. Custance, 7.

84. Kriegel, *The Holland House Diaries*, xxv–xxvi.

85. Lord Hatherton's Diary, 6 March 1832; Staffs. RO, Hatherton MSS, D260/M/F/5/26/7.

86. F. Lamb to Melbourne, 1831; Melbourne MSS, Box 106/10.

87. D. Le Marchant, *Memoir of Viscount Althorp* (London 1876), 294.

88. Melbourne to Sir J. Abercromby, 28 June 1831; Nat. Lib. of Scot., Abercromby MSS, fo. 1.

89. Greville, ii. 250, 5 Feb. 1832.

90. Ibid. ii. 331, 28 Sept. 1832.

91. Lord Holland to Lord Carlisle, 15 Feb [1832]; Castle Howard MSS LB139. Lord Holland's Diary 2 Jan. and 15 Feb. 1832; Kriegel, *The Holland House Diaries*, 108 and 131. Lord Hatherton's Diary, 27 Feb. 1832; Staffs. RO, Hatherton MSS, D260/M/F/5/26/7.

92. BL Add. MSS 60463, fo. 92; Palmerston to F. Lamb, 8 May 1832.

93. *Parl. Hist.* vii. 1177–86, 4 Oct. 1831, and xii. 45–6, 9 April 1832.
94. Torrens, *Memoirs of Lord Melbourne*, 322.
95. Melbourne to Palmerston, 10 Oct. 1831; Southampton Univ. Lib., Palmerston MSS, GC/ME/12.
96. Newbould, *Whiggery and Reform*, 63.
97. Greville, ii. 283, 1 April 1832.
98. Ibid.
99. Ibid. vi. 250, 28 Nov. 1848.
100. *Quarterly Review*, lxiv. 276, June 1839.
101. Ibid.
102. D. Le Marchant's Diary, July 1833; A. Aspinall, *Three Early Nineteenth Century Diaries* (London 1952), 366.
103. Draft speech, n.d.; Melbourne MSS, Box 120/121.
104. Melbourne to Victoria, 8 Oct. 1841; Windsor, Royal Archives, A4 fo. 21.
105. William IV to Melbourne, 10 June 1832; Melbourne MSS, Box 108/110.
106. Melbourne to Howick, 25 Aug. 1839; Durham Univ. Lib., Grey MSS, unfol.
107. BL Add. MSS 56560, fo. 173; Diary of J. Hobhouse, 28 May 1839.
108. Melbourne to Lord J. Russell, 24 Oct. 1837; Southampton Univ. Lib., Melbourne MSS, MEL/RU/415.
109. Ibid. [1835]; ibid. 135.
110. Melbourne to F. Lamb, 8 Sept. 1832; Melbourne MSS, Box 106/13.
111. Melbourne to Lady Stanhope, 10 Aug. 1832; Kent RO, Stanhope MSS, c229/5.
112. Melbourne to Lord J. Russell, 5 Oct. 1835; Southampton Univ. Lib., Melbourne MSS, MEL/RU/181.
113. Lord J. Russell to Melbourne, 9 Sept. 1837; PRO, Russell MSS, 30/22/2F xc10466, fo. 73. Melbourne to Lord J. Russell, 12 Sept. 1837; ibid. fo. 80.
114. T. Taylor, *The Life of Benjamin Robert Haydon* (London 1853), ii. 345.
115. Custance, 204.
116. Melbourne to Anglesey, 9 Jan. 1832; Melbourne MSS, Box 94/2.
117. Custance, 204.
118. BL Add. MSS 37306, fos. 306–7; Melbourne to Wellesley, 4 Jan. 1834.
119. Melbourne to E. Littleton, 24 Sept. 1833; Melbourne MSS, Box 96/26.
120. Melbourne to Sir J. Abercromby, 23 May 1834; Nat. Lib. Scot., Abercromby MSS, fo. 3.
121. Melbourne to Stanley, 18 Nov. 1832; Liverpool RO, Derby MSS, 920 DER (14) 117/7.
122. BL Add. MSS 38103, fo. 155; Melbourne to Anglesey, 18 Dec. 1830.
123. Ibid. fo. 159.
124. Melbourne to Anglesey, 31 March 1831; Melbourne MSS, Box 93/122. See also A. D. Macintyre, *The Liberator: Daniel O'Connell and the Irish Party, 1830–1867* (London 1965), 45–6.
125. Melbourne to Stanley, 25 Jan. 1831; Liverpool RO, Derby MSS, 920 DER (14) 117/7.
126. Ibid. 10 Jan. 1831; Melbourne MSS, Box 95/31.

127. BL Add. MSS 37306, fo. 72; Melbourne to Wellesley, 8 Sept. 1833. See also Melbourne to Stanley, 19 Jan. 1831; Melbourne MSS, Box 95/56.
128. Melbourne to Ebrington, 9 April 1839; Devon RO, Fortescue MSS, 1262 M/L135.
129. D. O'Connell to Althorp, 17 Aug. 1832; O'Connell, *The Correspondence of Daniel O'Connell*, iv. 439.
130. Melbourne to Anglesey, 29 Dec. 1830; Melbourne MSS, Box 93/64.
131. *Parl. Hist.* xix 965, 19 July 1833.
132. Melbourne to Grey, 11 Oct. 1833; Durham Univ. Lib., Grey MSS, fo. 116.
133. BL Add. MSS 37306, fo. 104; Melbourne to Wellesley, 19 Sept. 1833.
134. Melbourne to Anglesey, 25 Oct. 1831; Lord Anglesey, *One Leg: The Life and Letters of the First Marquess of Anglesey*, 263.
135. BL Add. MSS 37306, fo. 134; Melbourne to Wellesley, 19 Oct. 1833.
136. Anglesey to Melbourne, 25 Feb. 1833; Melbourne MSS, Box 94/66.
137. Melbourne to Stanley, 20 Dec. 1830; Newbould, *Whiggery and Reform*, 134.
138. Melbourne to Anglesey, 26 Feb. 1831 and 22 Dec. 1832; Melbourne MSS, Box 93/112 and Box 94/61.
139. Ibid. 2 April 1833; Box 94/99.
140. Melbourne to Grey, 12 March 1832; Durham Univ. Lib., Grey MSS, fo. 65.
141. *Parl. Hist.* xv. 843, 18 Feb. 1833.
142. Melbourne to Stanley, 20 Dec. 1832; Melbourne MSS, Box 95/113.
143. Melbourne to Lansdowne, 28 Sept. 1832; ibid. Box 8/77.
144. BL Add. MSS 37306, fo. 167; Melbourne to Wellesley, 10 Nov. 1833.
145. *Parl. Hist.* xviii. 1041, 21 June 1833.
146. Melbourne to Stanley, 13 Sept. 1832; Liverpool RO, Derby MSS, 920 DER (14) 117/7.
147. Melbourne to Anglesey, 2 May 1833; Melbourne MSS, Box 94/104. Melbourne to E. Littleton, 29 Aug. 1833; ibid. Box 96/8.
148. Melbourne to Anglesey, 30 July 1832; ibid. Box 94/38. See also, Melbourne to Grey, 31 Aug. 1832; Durham Univ. Lib., Grey MSS, fo. 85.
149. Greville, ii. 330, 28 Sept. 1832.
150. Lord Hatherton's Diary, 12 Jan. 1837; Staffs. RO, Hatherton MSS, D260/M/F/5/26/13.
151. See below, Ch. 8.
152. Lord Hatherton's Diary, 7 July 1835; ibid.
153. Melbourne to Mulgrave, 20 May 1835; Melbourne MSS, Box 99/9.
154. Wellesley to Lady Wellesley, 29 Jan. 1836; Anon., *The Wellesley Papers* (London 1914), ii. 300–1. Wellesley to Holland, 13 Nov. 1839; ibid. ii. 352. Wellesley talked of 'Lord Melbourne's persecution of me', ibid. 353.
155. BL Add. MSS 37311, fo. 254; Melbourne to Wellesley, 19 April 1835.
156. Lord Hatherton's Diary, 18 April 1835; Staffs. RO, Hatherton MSS, D260/M/F/5/26/9. See also, ibid. 19 July 1835.
157. BL Add. MSS 37312, fo. 7; Wellesley to Melbourne, 21 June 1837.
158. G. Anson Memorandum, 9 April 1843; Windsor Royal Archives, Y55 fo. 6.

Chapter 8

1. Charles Greville, quoted in Cecil, 226.
2. Macintyre, *The Liberator*, 131–4.
3. Lord Hatherton's Diary, 15 Jan. and 13 March 1835; Staffs. RO, Hatherton MSS, D260/M/F/5/26/12. Lord Hatherton, *Political Occurrences in June and July 1834* (London 1872).
4. Kriegel, *The Holland House Diaries*, 257.
5. Lord Wharncliffe to J. S. Wortley, 16 July 1834; C. Grosvenor, *The First Lady Wharncliffe and Her Family* (London 1927), 200. See also BL Add. MSS 37311, fo. 153; Brougham to Wellesley, [July 1834].
6. Lord Mahon to Lady Stanhope, 29 May 1834; Kent RO, Stanhope MSS, c 318/2.
7. Melbourne to Duncannon, 18 Jan. 1835; W. Sussex RO, Bessborough MSS, 182.
8. Melbourne to Palmerston, 8 July 1834; Ziegler, 168–9.
9. Lord Hatherton, *Political Occurrences in June and July 1834*, 38.
10. Melbourne to Brougham, 20 Feb. 1835; Univ. Coll. London, Brougham MSS, 43523.
11. Melbourne to Palmerston, 8 July 1834; Southampton Univ. Lib., Palmerston MSS, GC/ME/17.
12. Melbourne to William IV, 10 and 11 July 1834; Melbourne MSS, Box 110/9–10. William IV to Melbourne, 11 July 1834; ibid. Box 110/11.
13. Ibid. See also Sir R. Peel to Lord Lyndhurst, 15 July 1834; Sir T. Martin, *A Life of Lord Lyndhurst* (London 1883), 316–18, and Wellington to William IV, 12 July 1834; Melbourne MSS, Box 110/21.
14. Melbourne to Brougham, 12 July 1834; Univ. Coll. London, Brougham MSS, 43502.
15. Lord W. Russell's Diary, 12 July 1834; G. Blakiston, *Lord William Russell and his Wife* (London 1972), 313.
16. E. Littleton to J. Fazakerley, 11 July 1834; Lord Hatherton, *Political Occurrences in June and July 1834*, 39.
17. F. Lamb to Melbourne, 19 July 1834; Melbourne MSS, Box 106/16.
18. Melbourne to William IV, 15 July 1834; ibid. Box 110/31.
19. Custance, 149.
20. Ibid.
21. *Parl. Hist.* xxv. 22–3, 14 July 1834.
22. Cecil, 224.
23. Ibid. 225.
24. Lord Howick's Diary, 15 July 1834; Ziegler, 173.
25. Kriegel, *The Holland House Diaries*, 300.
26. E. Ellice to Melbourne, [July 1834]; Herts. RO, Panshanger MSS, D/ELb 09.
27. Mrs G. Lamb to Lady Carlisle, [29 May 1834]; Castle Howard MSS, J18/44/141.
28. ? to F. Lamb, 24 July [1834]; Herts. RO, Panshanger MSS, D/ELb F82.

29. E. Eden to Lady Grey, 18 July 1834; Durham Univ. Lib., Grey MSS, unfol.
30. E. Lamb to F. Lamb, 14 June 1834; Lady Airlie, *Lady Palmerston and Her Times*, i. 182.
31. A. Bourke, *The Correspondence of Joseph Jekyll* (London 1894), 327.
32. Cecil, 229.
33. C. Fox to ?, [July] 1834; Lord Ilchester, *Chronicles of Holland House* (London 1937), 170.
34. Sir R. Peel to Sir G. Clerk, 14 July 1834; Scots. RO, GD/8/3347.
35. Grey to Melbourne, 17, 26, and 29 July 1834; Durham Univ. Lib., Grey MSS, fos. 140–2. See also Melbourne to Richmond, 21 July 1834; West Sussex RO, Richmond MSS, 670 fo. 119.
36. *Parl. Hist.* xxv. 467, 25 July 1834.
37. D. Barnes, *Thomas Barnes of the Times* (Cambridge 1944), 78.
38. Aberdeen to Wellington, 31 Aug. 1834; J. Brooke and J. Gandy, *Wellington's Political Correspondence* (London 1975), 652.
39. BL Add. MSS 37307, fo. 98; Melbourne to Wellesley, 30 June 1834.
40. Greville, iii. 111, 15 July 1834.
41. E. Stanley to Richmond, 12 July 1834; West Sussex RO, Richmond MSS, 689 fo. 27.
42. Torrens, *The Memoirs of Lord Melbourne*, 293.
43. Melbourne to Palmerston, 13 Nov. 1834; Southampton Univ. Lib., Palmerston MSS, GC/ME/23. See also BL Add. MSS 43060, fo. 138; Melbourne to William IV, 12 Nov. 1834.
44. Melbourne to Grey, 14 Nov. 1834; Durham Univ. Lib., Grey MSS, fo. 146.
45. Melbourne to Spencer, 14 Nov. 1834; Le Marchant, *Memoir of Viscount Althorp*, 525.
46. Grey to Melbourne, 15 Nov. 1834; Melbourne MSS, Box 5/126.
47. Lord Holland's Diary, 12 Nov. 1834; Kriegel, *The Holland House Diaries*, 271.
48. Greville, iii. 148, 16 Nov. 1834.
49. BL Add. MSS 51870, fo. 783; Lord Holland's Political Journal, 16 Nov. 1834. The *Morning Chronicle*, 15 Nov. 1834.
50. Greville, iii. 151–2, 16 Nov. 1834.
51. Melbourne to William IV, 15 Nov. 1834; Melbourne MSS, Box 110/32.
52. BL Add. MSS 51558, fo. 52; Melbourne to Holland, 25 Nov. 1834.
53. Melbourne to Auckland, 18 Nov. 1834; Trinity Coll. Camb., Cullum MSS, fo. 077.
54. J. Croker to Lord Hertford, 24 Nov. 1834; L. J. Jennings, *The Correspondence and Diaries of J. W. Croker* (London 1885), ii. 242.
55. BL Add. MSS 37307, fo. 290; Melbourne to Wellesley, 15 Nov. 1834. Wellington to Sir R. Peel, 15 Nov. 1834; Lord Mahon, *Memoirs of the Rt. Hon. Sir Robert Peel*, ii. 23.
56. Melbourne to Duncannon, 3 Dec. 1834; W. Sussex RO, Bessborough MSS, 182.
57. Melbourne to Carlisle, 22 Nov. 1834; Castle Howard MSS, J17/1/769.
58. Lord Holland's Diary, 15 Nov. 1834; Kriegel, *The Holland House Diaries*, 274.

59. E. Lamb to Princess Lieven, 18 Nov. 1834; Lord Sudley, *The Lieven–Palmerston Correspondence* (London 1943), 62.
60. BL Add. MSS 51725, fo. 175; Egremont to Holland, 3 Dec. 1834.
61. Melbourne to Grey, 19 Nov. 1834; Sanders, *Lord Melbourne's Papers*, 228.
62. Melbourne to Brougham, 20 Nov. 1834; Univ. Coll. London, Brougham MSS, 43522.
63. Mrs G. Lamb to Lady Carlisle, 26 Nov. [1834]; Castle Howard MSS, J18/44/142. See also other letters on the same topics between the same correspondents in J18/44/141 and J18/44/144.
64. Ibid. [Dec. 1834]; ibid. J18/44/141.
65. Lord Lyttelton to Melbourne, 8 Dec. 1834; Melbourne MSS, Box 29/153.
66. E. Eden to Mrs Lister, 23 Nov. 1834; V. Dickinson, *Miss Eden's Letters*, 247.
67. Lady Brownlow, *The Eve of Victorianism*, 194.
68. *Morning Chronicle*, 5 Dec. 1834.
69. Greville, iii. 175; 6 Dec. 1834.
70. Melbourne to J. Abercromby, 29 Dec. 1834; Abercromby MSS, fo. 10.
71. *Parl. Hist.* xxvi. 79, 24 Feb. 1835.
72. BL Add. MSS 56558, fo. 29; Diary of J. Hobhouse, 5 Sept. 1838.
73. Melbourne to Grey, 23 Jan. 1835; Grey MSS, fo. 151.
74. BL 51558, fo. 64; Melbourne to Holland, 12 Feb. 1835.
75. Melbourne to Grey, 6 Feb. 1835; Grey MSS, fo. 152.
76. Holland to Melbourne, 22 Jan. 1835; Sanders, *Lord Melbourne's Papers*, 232.
77. Holland to Melbourne, 9 Feb. 1835; Melbourne MSS, Box 7, fo. 12.
78. Grey to Melbourne, 1 Feb. 1835; *The Early Correspondence of Lord John Russell*, ii. 84.
79. Melbourne to Grey, 11 Feb. 1935; Sanders, *Lord Melbourne's Papers*, 253.
80. Melbourne to Lansdowne, 29 Dec. 1834; Torrens, *Memoirs of Lord Melbourne*, 329.
81. Melbourne to J. Abercromby, 5 Jan. 1835; Nat. Lib. of Scotland, Abercromby MSS, fo. 14.
82. A. Kriegel, 'The Politics of the Whigs in Opposition, 1834–5', *Journal of British Studies*, 7 (1968).
83. Melbourne to D. O'Connell, 20 Feb. [1835]; Bod. Lib. MS Eng. Lett. c 396, fo. 179.
84. Lord Hatherton's Diary, 5 March 1835; Staffs. RO, Hatherton MSS, D260/M/F/5/26/9.
85. E. Ellice to Durham, 28 March 1835; A. Aspinall, *Lord Brougham and the Whig Party* (London 1972), 295.
86. Melbourne and others to Grey, 11 April 1835; Melbourne MSS, Box 111/14.
87. Melbourne to Palmerston, 12 April 1835; Southampton Univ. Lib., Palmerston MSS, GC/ME/24.
88. Melbourne to Lord J. Russell, 12 April 1835; ibid., Melbourne MSS, MEL/RU/148.
89. Lord Holland's Diary, Kriegel, *The Holland House Diaries*, 286.
90. Melbourne to E. Ellice, 11 April 1835; Nat. Lib. of Scotland, Ellice MSS, 15031 fo. 20.

91. Melbourne to Spencer, [April 1835]; Le Marchant, *Memoir of Viscount Althorp*, 538.
92. Palmerston to Melbourne, 12 April 1835; Melbourne MSS, Box 11/13.
93. Melbourne to Lord J. Russell, 12 Feb. 1835; Southampton Univ. Lib., Melbourne MSS, MEL/RU/143.
94. T. Creevey to Miss Ord, 11 Sept. 1834; Sir H. Maxwell, *The Creevey Papers*, ii. 285.
95. Melbourne to William IV, 13 and 15 April 1835; Melbourne MSS, Box 111/19 and 29.
96. R. Brent, *Liberal Anglican Politics* (Oxford 1987), 111.
97. BL Add. MSS 51754, fos. 43–8; Lord Holland to H. Fox, 24 March 1835.
98. Melbourne to Palmerston, 15 April 1835; Southampton Univ. Lib., Palmerston MSS, GC/ME/27.
99. Lord Hatherton's Diary, 13 April 1835; Staffs. RO, Hatherton MSS, D260/M/F/5/26/9.
100. BL Add. MSS 44703, fo. 7; 'The Melbourne Government', Jan. 1890.
101. B. Newman, *Lord Melbourne* (London 1930), 119.
102. Sébastiani to Mme Adelaide, 2 April 1835; Paris, Bib. Nat. n.a.f. 12219, fo. 13.
103. J. Freshfield to Lord Stanhope, 5 May 1835; Kent RO, Stanhope MSS, U1590/C381/1.
104. Lord Hatherton's Diary, 17 April 1835; Staffs. RO, Hatherton MSS, D260/M/F/5/26/9.
105. Newbould, *Whiggery and Reform, 1830–1841*, 10–11.
106. Melbourne to J. Abercromby, 23 April 1835; Nat. Lib. of Scotland, Abercromby MSS, fo. 21.
107. Melbourne to Ebrington, 4 Nov. 1839; Custance, 192.
108. Lord Hatherton's Diary, 6 May 1837; Staffs. RO, Hatherton MSS, D260/M/F/5/26/9.
109. Melbourne to Sir E. Sugden, 23 Dec. 1835; Melbourne MSS, Box 37/40.
110. William IV to Melbourne, 16 Aug. 1836; Sanders, *Lord Melbourne's Papers*, 369.
111. Melbourne to Sir J. Wrottesley, 23 Jan. 1836; Melbourne MSS, Box 40/27.
112. Melbourne to T. Spring Rice, 30 Aug. 1837; Custance, 183.
113. BL Add. MSS 51560, fo. 30; Melbourne to Lady Holland, 25 Oct. 1836.
114. Melbourne to J. Abercromby, 23 Dec. 1834; Nat. Lib. of Scotland, Abercromby MSS, fos. 7–8.
115. Lord Hatherton's Diary, 25 Nov. 1848; Staffs. RO, Hatherton MSS, D260/M/F/5/26/47.
116. E. Lamb to Palmerston, 5 Sept. 1840; Lever, *Lady Palmerston and Her Times*, ii. 45.
117. QVJ, 4 Nov. 1839.
118. Lord Hatherton's Diary, 30 Aug. 1835; Staffs. RO, Hatherton MSS, D260/M/F/5/26/9.
119. Lady Howick's Diary, 14 July 1838; Custance 351.
120. BL Add. MSS 56558, fo. 4; Diary of J. Hobhouse, 8 July 1835.
121. Howick to E. Ellice, 6 Sept. 1839; Kriegel, *The Holland House Diaries*, xlv.
122. F. Guizot to A. Thiers, 8 May 1840; Paris, Bib. Nat., n.a.f. 20610, fo. 82.
123. BL Add. MSS 51559, fo. 80; Melbourne to Holland, 18 Sept. 1840.
124. Melbourne to Lord J. Russell, 19 Sept. 1840; Melbourne MSS, Box 15/2.

125. F. Lamb to Melbourne, [1840]; Herts. RO, Panshanger MSS, D/ELb F34.
126. Melbourne to Lord J. Russell, 14 Nov. 1838; Melbourne MSS, Box 13/93.
127. Mrs Hardcastle, *Life of John, Lord Campbell* (London 1881), ii. 157.
128. Melbourne to E. Ellice, 14 Sept. 1837; Ziegler 204–5.
129. Lord Holland's Diary, [March 1837]; Kriegel, *The Holland House Diaries*, 359.
130. Melbourne to Lord J. Russell, 29 Oct. 1839; Melbourne MSS, Box 14/75.
131. Melbourne to Howick, 29 Jan. 1839; Durham Univ. Lib., Grey MSS, unfol.
132. *Quarterly Review*, lxvi. 304, Dec. 1839.
133. T. Creevey to Miss Ord, 29 Jan. 1836; Maxwell, *The Creevey Papers*, ii. 308–9.
134. E. B. de Fonblanque, *The Life and Letters of Albany Fonblanque* (London 1874), 89.
135. Palmerston to J. Hobhouse, Nov. 1839; Bourne, *Palmerston*, 591.
136. B. Disraeli, *The Runnymede Letters*, Letter 1.
137. Lord Hatherton's Diary, 18 April 1835; Staffs. RO, Hatherton MSS, D260/M/F/5/26/9.
138. Melbourne to Ebrington, 3 Sept. 1839; Devon RO, Fortescue MSS, 1262M/L193.
139. G. Berkeley, *My Life and Recollections* (London 1866), iii. 346.
140. Melbourne to T. Macaulay, 17 Dec. 1839; Melbourne MSS, Box 30/5.
141. Melbourne to Lord J. Russell, n.d.; ibid. Box 14/35.
142. Cecil 348.
143. Mrs G. Lamb to Lady Carlisle, n.d.; Castle Howard MSS, J18/44/144.
144. BL Add. MSS 56560, fo. 23; Diary of J. Hobhouse, 20 Nov. 1838.
145. QVJ, 1 Feb. 1839. See also Sébastiani to Mme Adelaide, 2 Feb. 1839; Paris, Bib. Nat., n.a.f. 12220, fo. 134.
146. QVJ, 4 Oct. 1838.
147. Melbourne to Glenelg, 3 Feb. 1839; Melbourne MSS, Box 5/77.
148. Lord Hatherton's Diary, 8 July 1839; Staffs. RO, Hatherton MSS, D260/M/F/5/26/9.
149. Sébastiani to Mme Adelaide, 27 Jan. 1840; Paris, Bib. Nat., n.a.f 12220, fo. 201.
150. BL Add. MSS 51558, fos. 92, 94, 108, 192; Melbourne to Holland, 24 May, 26 May, 27 Dec. 1836, 20 Jan. 1837.
151. QVJ, 17 Sept. 1839.
152. Melbourne to Sir H. Halford, 3 Feb. 1837; Leics. RO, Halford MSS, DG24/904/8.
153. Melbourne to Lord J. Russell, 30 June 1838; Southampton Univ. Lib., Melbourne MSS, MEL/RU/509.
154. Baron Stockmar to Victoria, 4 July 1838; Windsor, Royal Archives, Y152 fo. 7.
155. Mrs G. Lamb to Lady Carlisle, 2 Dec. 1838; Castle Howard MSS, J18/44/144.
156. BL Add. MSS 45552, fo. 1; F. Lamb to E. Lamb, 2 Jan. [1838].
157. Ibid., fo. 42; ibid. 2 March [1839].
158. Ibid., fo. 47; ibid. 5 April [1839].
159. BL Add. MSS 45552, fos. 48–9; F. Lamb to E. Lamb, 5 April [1839].
160. Gladstone was highly critical of the 'financial faults' he saw in the Melbourne Government, BL Add. MSS 44703, fo. 32; Jan. 1890. This is somewhat unfair. Though not enjoying the experience, Melbourne could discuss economic policy, and even speak to it; *Parl. Hist.* lii. 505, 23 Jan. 1840 and Scots. RO, Loch MSS

GP2/117/11B; Melbourne to J. Loch, 7 Sept. 1836. See also Ziegler, 333 and Sanders, 403–4.

161. S. J. Reid, *Life and Letters of the First Earl of Durham* (London 1906), ii. 129.
162. Melbourne to Lord J. Russell, 2 Oct. 1838; Melbourne MSS, Box 13/77.
163. Ibid. 31 Aug. 1838; ibid. Box 13/66.
164. Ibid. 22 April 1839; ibid. Box 14/12.
165. Ibid. 8 Sept. 1838; Ann Arbor, Michigan, Russell Papers, unfol.
166. Holland to Egremont, 24 Nov. [1834]; West Sussex RO, Petworth MSS, fo. 84.
167. Melbourne to Sir B. Brodie, 25 July 1838; Melbourne MSS, Box 59/28.
168. Melbourne to Lord Combermere, 12 May 1838; ibid. Box 59/65.
169. Lord Hatherton's Diary, 22 Aug. 1835; Staffs. RO, Hatherton MSS, D260/M/F/5/26/9.
170. Melbourne to Lord Carrington, 2 Feb. 1840; Melbourne MSS, Box 62/39.
171. Lord J. Russell to Melbourne, 20 Sept. 1839; ibid. Box 30/7.
172. Melbourne to B. Lytton, 13 Sept. 1839; Herts. RO, Lytton MSS, D/EK6 fo. 111.
173. BL Add. MSS 56560, fos. 7–8; Diary of J. Hobhouse, 18 Aug. 1838.
174. Melbourne to Lord Minto, 7 Sept. 1840; Nat. Lib. of Scotland, Minto MSS, 12/26 fo. 25.
175. Leopold I to A. Thiers, 23 Aug. 1840; Bib. Nat. n.a.f. 20611, fo. 76.
176. F. Guizot to A. Thiers, 7 Sept. 1840; ibid. 20610, fo. 276.
177. *Parl. Hist.*, xxix. 1346–54, 3 Aug. 1835.
178. Lord Hatherton's Diary, Aug. 1839; Staffs. RO, Hatherton MSS, D260/M/F/5/26/17.
179. Ibid. 25 Nov. 1848; ibid. 47. See also *Gentlemen's Magazine*, xxxi. 86, Jan. 1839.
180. Ibid. n. 178, D20/M/F/5/26/16.
181. *Quarterly Review*, lix. 252, July 1837.
182. Ibid.
183. E. von Stockmar, *Memoirs of Baron Stockmar* (London 1873), i. 389.
184. Lord Hatherton's Diary, 19 July 1836; Staffs. RO, Hatherton MSS, D260/M/F/5/26/12.
185. Ibid. 26 March 1836; ibid.
186. BL Add. MSS 56558, fo. 92; Diary of J. Hobhouse, 23 Feb. 1836.
187. Lord Hatherton's Diary, 21 July 1836; Staffs. RO, Hatherton MSS, D260/M/F/5/26/12. See also ibid. 16 July 1838; ibid. 16.
188. Ibid. 1 Dec. 1848; ibid. 47.
189. *Morning Chronicle*, 27 Nov. 1848.
190. Ibid.

Chapter 9

1. QVJ, 23 July 1841.
2. BL Add. MSS 51754, fo. 71; Lord Holland to H. Fox, 5 May 1835.
3. Sébastiani to Mme Adelaide, 5 Feb. 1836; Bib. Nat., n.a.f. 12219, fo. 84.
4. Melbourne to Minto, 1 Sept. 1836; Nat. Lib. of Scotland, Minto MSS, 12/25 fo. 9.
5. Custance, 177.

6. Von Stockmar, *Memoirs of Baron Stockmar*, ii. 49.
7. Custance, 178.
8. Von Stockmar, *Memoirs of Baron Stockmar*, ii. 49.
9. Melbourne to Lord J. Russell, 18 Aug. 1837; Southampton Univ. Lib., Melbourne MSS, MEL/RU/389. See also ibid. 7 Sept. 1837; ibid. 396.
10. QVJ, 16 Dec. 1838.
11. Ibid. 13 Feb. 1838.
12. Ibid. 7 April 1838.
13. Lord Hatherton's Diary, 14 Aug. 1835; Staffs. RO, Hatherton MSS, D260/M/F/5/26/9.
14. Ibid. 6 Dec. 1835; ibid. 11.
15. Ibid. 2 June 1835; ibid. 12.
16. Sébastiani to Mme Adelaide, 20 June 1835; Bib. Nat. n.a.f. 12219, fo. 25.
17. Ibid. 15 May 1835; ibid., fo. 23.
18. Lord Hatherton's Diary, 16 April 1835; Staffs. RO, Hatherton MSS, D260/M/F/5/26/9.
19. Melbourne to William IV, 17 April 1835; Melbourne MSS, Box 111/41.
20. BL Add. MSS 51558, fo. 67; Melbourne to Holland, 17 April 1835.
21. William IV to Melbourne, 31 May 1835; Melbourne MSS, Box 111/109.
22. Ibid. 31 May 1835; ibid. Box 111/110. See also, ibid. 16 Aug. 1835; ibid. Box 112/42.
23. Melbourne to William IV, 29 June 1835; Melbourne MSS, Box 4/9.
24. Ibid. 2 June 1835; ibid. Box 111/114.
25. Melbourne to Sir H. Taylor, 25 Jan. 1836; ibid. Box 113/18.
26. Sébastiani to Mme Adelaide, 9 July 1835; Bib. Nat., n.a.f. 12219, fo. 31.
27. BL Add. MSS 56558, fo. 5; Diary of J. Hobhouse, 11 July 1835.
28. Kriegel, *The Holland House Diaries*, 348.
29. Ibid. 349.
30. Ibid.
31. Grey to Melbourne, 15 Aug. 1834; Melbourne MSS, Box 5/125.
32. Lady Holland to H. Fox, 29 July 1834; Lord Ilchester, *Elizabeth, Lady Holland to Her Son*, 152.
33. QVJ, 29 Aug. 1839.
34. Melbourne to Palmerston, 28 Aug. 1834; Southampton Univ. Lib., Palmerston MSS, GC/ME/18. See also Melbourne to T. Spring Rice, 29 Oct. 1838; Torrens, *Memoirs of Lord Melbourne*, 463.
35. Lord Hatherton's Diary, 2 July 1836; Staffs. RO, Hatherton MSS, D260/M/F/5/26/12.
36. Kriegel, *The Holland House Diaries*, 331.
37. Melbourne to Grey, 14 April 1835; Durham Univ. Lib., Grey MSS, fo. 160. Grey to Melbourne, 10 May 1839; Melbourne MSS, Box 5/140.
38. Melbourne to Grey, 5 Jan. 1836; Durham Univ. Lib., Grey MSS, fo. 166.
39. Grey to Melbourne, 8 Jan. 1836; Southampton Univ. Lib., Palmerston MSS, GC/ME/517. Palmerston to Melbourne, 12 Jan. 1836; ibid. 518.
40. Sir R. Heron, *Notes* (Grantham 1850), 221.

41. Kriegel, *The Holland House Diaries*, 272. See also Lord Hatherton's Diary, 10 April 1835; Staffs. RO, Hatherton MSS, D260/M/F/5/26/9.

42. Aspinall, *Lord Brougham and the Whig Party*, 296–7.

43. Holland to Melbourne, 17 July 1840; Melbourne MSS, Box 7/27.

44. Lord Hatherton's Diary, 29 Dec. 1835; Staffs. RO, Hatherton MSS, D260/M/F/5/26/11.

45. Smith, *Lord Grey*, 317.

46. E. Lamb to Princess Lieven, 2 June [1835]; Lord Sudley, *The Lieven–Palmerston Correspondence*, 85.

47. E. Eden to Lord Clarendon, 7 Jan. 1834; Maxwell, *The Life and Letters of the 4th Earl of Clarendon*, i. 83.

48. Melbourne to Grey, 5 Jan. 1834; Durham Univ. Lib., Grey MSS, fo. 122.

49. H. Brougham to Lord Wellesley, [April 1835]; Anon., *The Wellesley Papers* (London 1914), ii. 275–6.

50. Howick to Melbourne, 2 June 1836; Melbourne MSS, Box 7/53. Melbourne to Howick, 1 and 17 June 1836; Durham Univ. Lib., Grey MSS, unfol.

51. BL Add. MSS 56561, fo. 119; Diary of J. Hobhouse, 25 Aug. 1839.

52. Howick Memorandum, n.d.; Durham Univ. Lib., Grey MSS, unfol. Howick to Melbourne, 30 Jan. 1839; Melbourne MSS, Box 8/29.

53. *Brighton Guardian*, 5 Sept. 1839. Quoted in J. C. Clark, 'From Business to Politics, The Ellice Family, 1760–1860' (Oxford D.Phil.), 216.

54. Howick to Melbourne, 24 Aug. 1839; Melbourne MSS, Box 8/43. See also, ibid. 21 Aug. 1839; ibid. 8/42. Diary of Lord Howick, 24 Aug. 1839; Durham Univ. Lib., Grey MSS, c 3/4.

55. BL Add. MSS 49479, fo. 216; Grey to Sir J. Gordon, 3 Sept. 1839.

56. QVJ, 29 Aug. 1839. See also, Melbourne to Lord J. Russell, 28 Aug. 1839; Southampton Univ. Lib., Melbourne MSS, MEL/RU/545.

57. Kriegel, *The Holland House Diaries*, 410.

58. QVJ, 4 Jan. 1838. See also, Smith, *Lord Grey*, 321.

59. QVJ, 29 Aug. 1839.

60. BL Add. MSS 45552, fo. 54; F. Lamb to E. Lamb, 19 May [1839]. See also ibid., fo. 60; ibid. 20 June [1839].

61. Melbourne to Lord J. Russell, 16 Sept. 1839; Melbourne MSS, Box 115/163.

62. I. D. C. Newbould, 'Whiggery and the Dilemma of Reform', *Bulletin of the Institute of Historical Research*, 63 (1980).

63. Melbourne to B. Lytton, 12 Dec. 1834; Herts. RO, Lytton MSS, D/EKc6 fo. 106.

64. Melbourne to J. Parkes, 22 Sept. 1836; Univ. Coll. London, Parkes MSS, fo. 16.

65. Newbould, *Bulletin of the Institute of Historical Research*, 63 (1980), 234.

66. BL Add. MSS 51872, fos. 1150–1; Lord Holland's Journal, June 1839.

67. F. Lamb to Melbourne, Oct. 1837; Melbourne MSS, Box 106/26.

68. Kriegel, *The Holland House Diaries*, 376. BL Add. MSS 56560, fo. 141; Diary of J. Hobhouse, 7 May 1839.

69. J. Hume to Melbourne, 25 May 1839; Melbourne MSS, Box 28/30.

70. Melbourne to J. Hume, 25 May 1839; ibid. Box 28/33.
71. Lord Stanley to Melbourne, 13 May 1839; ibid. Box 36/124.
72. Greville, iv. 220, 1 June 1839.
73. QVJ, 2 June 1839. Mrs G. Lamb to Lady Carlisle, 23 April [1839]; Castle Howard MSS, J18/44/103.
74. J. A. Roebuck to A. Purdie, 11 June 1839; R. Leader, *Life and Letters of John Arthur Roebuck* (London 1897), 123.
75. BL Add. MSS 35151, fo. 337; Mrs Grote to F. Place, 2 May 1841.
76. Melbourne to Lord J. Russell, 9 Jan. 1836; Southampton Univ. Lib., Melbourne MSS, ME/RU/210.
77. Ibid. 8 Oct. 1843; ibid. 550.
78. Ibid. 7 Feb. 1835; ibid. 142. See also Lord J. Russell to Melbourne, 17 Feb. and 14 Dec. 1835; ibid. 4 and 15.
79. Melbourne to E. Ellice, 1 April 1837; Nat. Lib. of Scotland, Ellice MSS, fo. 46.
80. Mrs G. Lamb to Lady Carlisle, n.d.; Castle Howard MSS, J18/44/144.
81. Melbourne to H. Brougham, 14 Feb. 1835; Melbourne MSS, Box 2/26.
82. Lord Hatherton's Diary, 15 April 1835; Staffs. RO, Hatherton MSS, D260/M/F/5/26/9.
83. Brougham to Melbourne, n.d.; Southampton Univ. Lib., Melbourne MSS, MEL/BR/20. E. Ellice to Melbourne, 23 Sept. [1835]; Herts. RO, Panshanger MSS, D/ELb 09. Brougham to Melbourne, 15 Feb. 1835; Melbourne MSS, Box 2/27.
84. Brougham to Melbourne, 22 July 1835; ibid. Box 2/24.
85. Brougham to Melbourne, n.d.; ibid. Box 2/29.
86. BL Add. MSS 45552, fo. 28; F. Lamb to E. Lamb, 26 April [1838]. E. Lamb to Princess Lieven, 13 Feb. [1838]; Lord Sudley, *The Lieven–Palmerston Correspondence*, 145.
87. Greville, iv. 33, 14 Dec. 1837.
88. *Parl. Hist.* xl. 686, 2 Feb. 1838.
89. Melbourne to Duncannon, 24 Nov. 1834; W. Sussex RO, Bessborough MSS, 182.
90. Lord Hatherton's Diary, July 1839; Staffs. RO, Hatherton MSS, D260/M/F/5/26/17.
91. Ibid. 1 Dec. 1835; ibid. 11.
92. Mrs G. Lamb to Lady Morpeth, n.d.; Castle Howard MSS, J18/44/139.
93. QVJ, 21 Oct. 1839.
94. Brougham had been the lover of Mrs George Lamb, and an intimate of the family thereafter.
95. Melbourne to Brougham, 19 Feb. 1847; Univ. Coll. London, Brougham MSS, 43564.
96. Melbourne to Russell, 26 Oct. 1838; Melbourne MSS, Box 13/86.
97. BL Add. MSS 56560, fo. 6; Diary of J. Hobhouse, 16 Aug. 1838.
98. Melbourne to E. Ellice, 27 Oct. 1837; Nat. Lib. of Scotland, Ellice MSS, 15031, fo. 34.
99. QVJ, 7 March 1838.

100. Melbourne to E. Ellice, 14 Dec. 1835; Nat. Lib. of Scotland, Ellice MSS, 15031, fo. 28.

101. Melbourne to Lord J. Russell, 11 Dec. 1838; Melbourne MSS, Box 13/110. See also, ibid. 21 Oct. 1838; Sanders, *Lord Melbourne's Papers*, 434–5.

102. Ibid. 7 July 1837; Southampton Univ. Lib., Melbourne MSS, MEL/RU/367.

103. Melbourne to E. Ellice, 29 Oct. 1838; Nat. Lib. of Scotland, Ellice MSS, 15031, fo. 96.

104. Newbould, *Whiggery and Reform, 1830–1841*, 218.

105. For a discussion of the Canadian crisis, see Newbould, *Whiggery and Reform, 1830–1841*.

106. Melbourne to Victoria, 10 Aug. 1838; Windsor, Royal Archives, A1 fo. 182.

107. *Parl. Hist.* xliv 1092, 9 Aug. 1838. See also, ibid. 1127–31; 10 Aug. 1838.

108. Holland to Melbourne, 20 Oct. 1838; Melbourne MSS, Box 7/16.

109. Melbourne to Poulett Thomson, 30 Oct. 1830; Sanders, *Lord Melbourne's Papers*, 436–7.

110. Sébastiani to Mme Adelaide, 18 Oct. 1838; Bib. Nat. n.a.f. 12220, fo. 95.

111. Melbourne to Richmond, 11 Dec. 1838; West Sussex RO, Richmond MSS, 1595, fo. 921.

112. Melbourne to Lord Mulgrave, 21 Oct. 1837; Custance, 237.

113. A. Thiers to F. Sébastiani, 28 Feb. 1836; Bib. Nat., n.a.f. 20607, fos. 11–12.

114. QVJ, 19 Aug. 1838.

115. Melbourne to Sir H. Taylor, 31 Oct. 1836; Melbourne MSS, Box 113/154.

116. Melbourne to Lord J. Russell, 5 Sept. 1838; ibid. Box 13/71.

117. Ibid. 6 Oct. 1835; Southampton Univ. Lib., Melbourne MSS, MEL/RU/182.

118. Melbourne to E. Littleton, 18 Oct. 1839; Melbourne MSS, Box 96/48. See also *Parl. Hist.* xxxviii. 304–11, 28 April 1837.

119. Melbourne to Lord Dacre, 9 Dec. 1835; Southampton Univ. Lib., Palmerston MSS, GC/ME/59.

120. Kriegel, *The Holland House Diaries*, 330.

121. *Parl. Hist.* xxvii. 1002, 18 April 1835 and ibid. xli. 315, 1 March 1838. See also Melbourne to Lord Ebrington, 10 Nov. 1835; Devon RO, Fortescue MSS, 1262M/FC91.

122. Lord Hatherton's Diary, 6 April and 12 Aug. 1835; Staffs. RO, Hatherton MSS, D260/M/F/5/26/9.

123. *Parl. Hist.* xxxii. 1123, 18 April 1836.

124. Ibid. liii. 1163, 4 May 1840.

125. Melbourne to Lord J. Russell, 11 March 1838; Custance, 255.

126. Ibid. 4 Sept. 1837; PRO, Russell MSS, 30/22/2F XC10466.

127. Lord Hatherton's Diary, July 1835; Staffs. RO, Hatherton MSS, D260/M/F/5/26/9. For a full discussion of Irish Church questions, see M. Condon, 'The Irish Church and the Reform Ministries', *Journal of British Studies*, iii. no. 2, 1964.

128. Melbourne to Lord Lansdowne, 29 Oct. 1835; Ziegler, 208.

129. F. Sébastiani to Mme Adelaide, 22 July 1835; Bib. Nat. n.a.f. 12219, fo. 35.

130. Notes for a speech, Aug. 1835; Melbourne MSS, Box 103/30.

131. *Parl. Hist.* xxx. 717–27, 20 Aug. 1835.
132. Melbourne to Lord J. Russell, 1 Feb. 1838; Southampton Univ. Lib., Melbourne MSS, MEL/RU/442.
133. Macintyre, *The Liberator*, esp. ch. 5.
134. For his personal and public views on O'Connell, see Anon., *A Heavy Blow and Great Discouragement of Protestantism* (London 1838). Anon., *A Letter to Lord Melbourne by a Conservative Whig* (London 1836). Melbourne to Lord J. Russell, 22 Oct. 1835; PRO, Russell MSS, 30/22/1E XC10466, fo. 223. Ibid. 26 Sept. 1838; Melbourne MSS, Box 13/75. Melbourne to William IV, 7 Oct. 1834; ibid. Box 110/80.
135. BL Add. MSS 51558, fo. 60; Melbourne to Holland, 21 Jan. 1835.
136. Melbourne to Lord Mulgrave, 16 Oct. 1835; Custance, 236.
137. Ibid. 19 Oct. 1835; Melbourne MSS, Box 99/72.
138. Ibid. 23 Oct. 1835; ibid. 76.
139. Melbourne to Lord J. Russell, 23 Aug. 1834; Melbourne MSS, Box 13/23.
140. Melbourne to Lord Clarendon, 23 Jan. 1844; Bod. Lib., Clarendon MSS, c 469.
141. Macintyre, *The Liberator*, 128.
142. Ibid. 193 and 255.
143. D. O'Connell to P. Fitzpatrick, 17 Nov. 1834; O'Connell, *The Correspondence of D. O'Connell*, v. 201.
144. Ibid. 14 May 1839; ibid. vi. 244.
145. Lord Wellesley to Melbourne, 15 May 1835; Melbourne MSS, Box 98/46.
146. Melbourne to Brougham, 13 Oct. 1835; Ziegler, 214.
147. Lord J. Russell to Melbourne, 13 Aug. 1839; PRO, Russell MSS, 30/22/2F XC10466, fo. 9.
148. BL Add. MSS 44703, fo. 5; W. E. Gladstone, 'The Melbourne Government', 1890.
149. QVJ, 23 Sept. 1839.
150. Ibid. 10 April 1839.
151. Sir J. Graham to Lord Stanley, 26 Sept. 1834; J. T. Ward, *Sir James Graham* (London 1967), 141.
152. Melbourne to E. Ellice, 19 Sept. 1834; Nat. Lib. of Scotland, Ellice MSS, 15031, fo. 6.
153. It is significant that Melbourne showed no interest in the developments in party organization, notably in the registration of voters, that were so important in the politics of the 1830s.
154. QVJ, 10 April and 16 June 1839.
155. Melbourne to Lord J. Russell, 28 Sept. 1837; R. Russell, *The Early Correspondence of Lord John Russell* (London 1913), ii. 204.
156. F. Guizot to A. Thiers, 24 March 1840; Bib. Nat. n.a.f. 20610, fo. 35.
157. Cecil, 336.
158. Ibid. 328.
159. Ibid. 316–17.
160. BL Add. MSS 51601, fo. 171; E. Lamb to Lady Holland, [15 Nov. 1837].
161. BL Add. MSS 45552, fo. 14; F. Lamb to E. Lamb, 23 Feb. 1838.
162. QVJ, 16 Aug. 1838.

163. Victoria to Melbourne, 8 May 1839; Lord Esher, *The Letters of Queen Victoria* (London 1908), i. 158–9.

164. F. Guizot to A. Thiers, 9 June 1840; Bib. Nat. n.a.f. 20610, fo. 118.

165. F. Sébastiani to Mme Adelaide, 3 Aug. 1835; ibid. 12219, fos. 43–4.

166. Disraeli, *The Runnymede Letters*, Letter xv, March 1836.

167. Lord Londonderry to Lord Buckingham, 28 Jan. 1838; Lord Buckingham and Chandos, *Memoirs of the Courts and Cabinets of William IV and Victoria* (London 1861), ii. 310–11.

168. *Parl. Hist.* xxv. 1305 f., 18 Aug. 1836; and l. 522, 23 Aug. 1839.

169. Melbourne to Lord J. Russell, 3 Sept. 1836; Ziegler, 245. See also, Lord Hatherton's Diary, 28 and 31 Aug. 1835; Staffs. RO, Hatherton MSS, D260/M/F/5/26/9.

170. *Parl. Hist.* xxx. 340, 12 Aug. 1835.

171. Ibid.

172. Ibid. 1295, 3 Sept. 1835.

173. Melbourne to Hatherton, 12 Jan. 1836; Staffs. RO, Hatherton MSS, D260/M/F/5/27/12, fo. 5. Melbourne to E. Ellice, 12 Jan. 1836; Nat. Lib. of Scotland, Ellice MSS, fo. 34.

174. BL Add. MSS 51871, fos. 991–2; Lord Holland's Diary, 1836.

175. F. Sébastiani to Mme Adelaide, 19 May 1836; Bib. Nat. n.a.f. 12219, fo. 100.

176. Melbourne to Lord J. Russell, 18 April 1836; PRO, Russell MSS, 30/22/2B XC10466, fo. 65.

177. Melbourne to Sir J. Abercromby, 16 Oct. 1835; Nat. Lib. of Scotland, Abercromby MSS, fo. 26.

178. Wellington to Lord Lyndhurst, 15 Oct. 1836; Trinity Coll., Cambridge, Lyndhurst MSS, fo. 44.

179. Melbourne to Richmond, Feb. 1835; West Sussex RO, Richmond MSS, 1578, fo. 364.

180. Melbourne to Lord Mulgrave, 23 Sept. 1836; Custance, 155.

181. Melbourne to Lord Dacre, 9 Dec. 1835; Southampton Univ. Lib., Palmerston MSS, GC/ME/59.

182. Melbourne to Sir J. Abercromby, 25 Feb. 1837; Nat. Lib. of Scotland, Abercromby MSS, fo. 35.

183. Melbourne to Lord Stanhope, 21 July 1839; Kent RO, Stanhope MSS, c 471/19.

184. Lord Stanley to Melbourne, 5 June 1835; Melbourne MSS, Box 36/119. Lord Hatherton's Diary, 17 Aug. 1835; Staffs. RO, Hatherton MSS, D260/M/F/5/26/9.

185. Melbourne to Lord Minto, 22 Aug. 1838; Nat. Lib. of Scotland, Minto MSS, 12/25 fo. 43. Wellington to Melbourne, 2 March 1839; Melbourne MSS, Box 17/96.

186. Wellington Memorandum, 18 Aug. 1840; Southampton Univ. Lib., Wellington MSS, 2/70/99. Melbourne to Lord J. Russell, 19 and 22 Aug. 1840; Melbourne MSS, Box 14/144 and 148. Melbourne to Lord Minto, 19 Aug. 1840; Nat. Lib. of Scotland, Minto MSS, 12/6 fo. 9.

187. F. Guizot to A. Thiers, 18 Aug. 1840; Bib. Nat. n.a.f. 20610, fo. 225.
188. A. Thiers to Comte de St. Aulaire, 23 Aug. 1840; ibid. 20614, fo. 227.
189. QVJ, 23 Dec. 1837. Wellington to Melbourne, 4 Jan. 1838; Southampton Univ. Lib., Wellington MSS, 2/48/154. QVJ, 19 Jan. 1838.
190. Diary of J. Allen, 28 March 1838; Kriegel, *The Holland House Diaries*, 385.
191. BL Add. MSS 40310, fo. 222; Wellington to Peel, 22 Feb. 1838.
192. F. Sébastiani to Mme Adelaide, 5 March 1838; Bib. Nat. n.a.f. 1220, fo. 26.
193. Diary of E. Lamb, 3 Feb. 1837; Hatfield House MSS
194. Diary of Lord Hatherton, 3 Aug. 1835; Staffs. RO, Hatherton MSS, D260/M/F/5/26/9.
195. Newbould, *Whiggery and Reform, 1830–41*, esp. ch. 8.
196. F. Sébastiani to Mme Adelaide, 2 Sept. 1835; Bib. Nat. n.a.f. 12219, fo. 55.
197. Ibid. 6 Oct. 1837; ibid. fo. 189. See also ibid. 18 Sept. 1835 and 23 Oct. 1837; ibid. fos. 59 and 193.
198. Lord Wallace, *Three Letters addressed to the Right Hon. Lord Viscount Melbourne and the Right Hon. Sir Robert Peel* (London 1835), 17.
199. Melbourne to Lord Stanley, 30 Jan. 1836; Custance, 258.
200. Melbourne to E. Ellice, 14 Sept. 1834; Nat. Lib. of Scotland, Ellice MSS, fos. 48–9.
201. Melbourne to J. Abercromby, 26 Sept. 1835; ibid. Abercromby MSS, fo. 23.

Chapter 10

1. Cecil, 237.
2. E. J. Whately, *The Life and Correspondence of Richard Whately* (London 1875), 466–7.
3. Howick to Grey, 14 Feb. 1839; Ziegler, 276.
4. Ibid. 305.
5. QVJ, 29 Jan. 1839.
6. Melbourne to E. Ellice, 29 Oct. 1838; Nat. Lib. of Scotland, Ellice MSS, fo. 97.
7. BL Add. MSS 45562, fo. 139; F. Lamb to E. Lamb, 12 Sept. [1841].
8. Melbourne to Sir J. Abercromby, 27 Dec. 1837; Sanders, *Lord Melbourne's Papers*, 370.
9. Melbourne to Lord Mulgrave, 12 Dec. 1834; Newbould, *Whiggery and Reform, 1830–1841*, 31.
10. Melbourne to H. Tufnell, 22 Oct. 1839; Melbourne MSS, Box 52/105.
11. Lord J. Russell to Melbourne, 12 June 1839; PRO, Russell MSS, 30/22/3C XC10466, fo. 342.
12. *Parl. Hist.* xliii. 1174–5, 2 July 1838.
13. F. Sébastiani to Mme Adelaide, 29 Jan. 1839; Bib. Nat., n.a.f. 12220, fo. 132.
14. Melbourne to Hatherton, 12 Jan. 1841; Staffs. RO, Hatherton MSS, D260/M/F/5/27/14, fo. 76.
15. BL Add. MSS 56560, fo. 55; Diary of J. Hobhouse, 23 Jan. 1839.
16. Melbourne to Lord J. Russell, 29 Jan. 1839; Sanders, *Lord Melbourne's Papers*, 390.
17. Melbourne to Ebrington, 27 Jan. 1839; Devon RO, Fortescue MSS, 1262M/L17.

18. *Parl. Hist.* xlv. 564, 18 Feb. 1839.
19. Melbourne to Ebrington, 27 Jan. 1839; Devon RO, Fortescue MSS, 1262M/L17.
20. BL Add. MSS 51560, fo. 69; Melbourne to Lady Holland, 28 Dec. 1839.
21. QVJ, 15 July 1841.
22. Melbourne to Lord J. Russell, 20 Jan. 1839; Melbourne MSS, Box 13/124.
23. E. Lamb to Mrs Wyndham, [1841]; W. Sussex RO, Petworth MSS, 1665.
24. *Parl. Hist.* xlvi. 611, 14 March 1839.
25. Melbourne to Lord J. Russell, 29 Dec. 1838; Melbourne MSS, Box 13/117. See also, ibid. 5 and 19 Jan. 1839; ibid. fos. 118 and 123. *Parl. Hist.* xlv. 27–8, 5 Feb. 1839.
26. E. Ellice to Lord Durham, 13 Feb. 1839; J. C. Clark, 'From Business to Politics' (Oxford D.Phil.), 376.
27. Melbourne to Lord Ebrington, 19 Jan. 1839; Devon RO, Fortescue MSS, 1262M/L16.
28. BL Add. MSS 56562, fo. 25; Diary of J. Hobhouse, 8 Jan. 1840.
29. Melbourne to Duke of Bedford, 23 July 1841; Woburn MSS, unfol.
30. Althorp to Melbourne, 3 Feb. 1839; Melbourne MSS, Box 15/118.
31. Duke of Roxburghe to Melbourne, 14 May 1841; ibid. Box 34/107. Melbourne to Duke of Hamilton, 31 Jan. 1839; ibid. Box 27/27.
32. C. J. Tower to R. Alston, 13 June 1841; ibid. Box 18/43.
33. Melbourne to Duke of Bedford, n.d.; Woburn MSS, unfol.
34. Lord Hatherton's Diary, 3 and 11 May 1841; Staffs. RO, Hatherton MSS, D260/M/F/5/26/19.
35. *Parl. Hist.* lii. 1311, 23 March 1840.
36. Ibid. liv. 1040, 11 June 1840.
37. Ibid. lvii. 69, 3 May 1841. See also, Cecil, 352–3.
38. Lord Hatherton's Diary, June 1840; Staffs. RO, Hatherton MSS, D260/M/F/5/26/18.
39. Greville, iv. 374, 9 Jan. 1841.
40. Lord Hatherton's Diary, 6 May 1841; Staffs. RO, Hatherton MSS, D260/M/F/5/26/19.
41. Custance, 195.
42. Melbourne to Lord J. Russell, 14 May 1841; Melbourne MSS, Box 15/37.
43. Greville, v. 22, 9 July 1841.
44. Lord Malmesbury's Diary, 20 April 1841; Lord Malmesbury, *Memoirs of an Ex-Minister* (London 1884), i. 131.
45. Lady Lyttelton to Lord Lyttelton, 23 March 1841; H. Wyndham, *The Correspondence of Sarah Spencer, Lady Lyttelton* (London 1912), 309.
46. Melbourne to Victoria, 14 Sept. 1841; Windsor, Royal Archives, A4 fo. 9.
47. Greville, v. 222, 29 Dec. 1843.
48. Melbourne to Victoria, 9 Dec. 1845; Lord Esher, *The Letters of Queen Victoria*, ii. 52.
49. Victoria to King Leopold, 6 Jan. 1846; Windsor, Royal Archives, Y92 fo. 38.
50. E. Eden to Lady Grey, 13 Jan. 1846; Durham Univ. Lib., Grey MSS, unfol.

51. Melbourne to Duke of Bedford, 5 Nov. 1847; Woburn MSS, unfol.
52. Melbourne to Lord J. Russell, 3 Jan. 1837; Southampton Univ. Lib., Melbourne MSS, MEL/RU/284.
53. Ibid.
54. Melbourne to Richmond, 23 Dec. 1836; West Sussex RO, Richmond MSS, 1874, fo. 880.
55. Ibid.
56. Melbourne to Lord J. Russell, 13 Aug. 1837; Southampton Univ. Lib., Melbourne MSS, ME/RU/387.
57. *Parl. Hist.* xlviii. 819, 25 June 1839.
58. Melbourne to F. Lamb, 7 Oct. 1837; Herts. RO, Panshanger MSS, D/ELb F78.
59. Melbourne to Lord J. Russell, 5 Jan. 1839; Melbourne MSS, Box 13/114.
60. Melbourne to Lord Tavistock, 6 Nov. 1838; Woburn MSS, unfol.
61. Melbourne to Mr Buckland, 16 Feb. 1838; Melbourne MSS, Box 20/69. Melbourne to Leith Petitioners, 23 Feb. 1838; ibid. Box 38/30.
62. Melbourne to Lord J. Russell, 15 Sept. 1837; Russell, *The Early Correspondence of Lord John Russell*, ii. 202–3. See also Melbourne to Poulett Thompson, 11 Jan. 1837; Sanders, *Lord Melbourne's Papers*, 315; and Lord Hatherton's Diary, 27 Nov. 1836; Staffs. RO, Hatherton MSS, D260/M/F/5/26/12.
63. Lord J. Russell to Melbourne, 11 Aug. 1837; Southampton Univ. Lib., Melbourne MSS, MEL/RU/381.
64. QVJ, 18 May 1839.
65. BL Add. MSS 56561, fo. 15; Diary of J. Hobhouse, 6 June 1839.
66. Melbourne to Lord Ebrington, 3 Sept. 1839; Devon RO, Fortescue MSS, 1262M/L193.
67. BL Add. MSS 56569, fo. 21; Diary of J. Hobhouse, 14 Feb. 1838.
68. Melbourne to E. Ellice, 17 Nov. 1836; Nat. Lib. of Scotland, Ellice MSS, fo. 42.
69. *Parl. Hist.* lv. 512, 7 July 1840.
70. Ibid. xl. 882, 8 Feb. 1838.
71. Melbourne to J. Hobhouse, 28 Aug. 1838; India Office, Broughton MSS, MSS. EUR F213/6, fo. 450.
72. Melbourne to Lord John Russell, 29 May 1840; Melbourne MSS, Box 14/122.
73. Melbourne to Poulett Thompson, 11 Feb. 1840; ibid., Box 15/159.
74. Melbourne to Durham, 7 Jan. and 19 Aug. 1838; ibid., Box 4/21 and 45. Melbourne to Lord J. Russell, 19 and 23 Dec. 1838; ibid., Box 13/112 and 114. Melbourne to Lord Hatherton, 21 Dec. 1838; Staffs. RO, Hatherton MSS, D260/M/F/27/12, fo. 183.
75. Melbourne to Durham, 22 July 1837; Reid, *Life and Letters of the First Earl of Durham*, ii. 137.
76. Whately, *The Life and Correspondence of Richard Whately*, 467.
77. Mrs G. Lamb to Lady Morpeth, n.d.; Castle Howard MSS, J18/44/141.
78. Lecture notes, [1799]; Melbourne MSS, Box 126/7.
79. Melbourne to Lord J. Russell, 3 Sept. 1838; ibid., Box 13/69. See also, *Parl. Hist.* xli. 461–2, 6 March 1838.
80. Melbourne to Lord J. Russell, 3 Sept. 1838; Melbourne MSS, Box 13/69.

81. Melbourne to Victoria, 19 Feb. 1838; Windsor, Royal Archives, A1 fo. 104.
82. Melbourne to Palmerston, 12 Sept. 1840; Melbourne MSS, Box 12/50.
83. Melbourne to Lord J. Russell, 3 Sept. 1838; Sanders, *Lord Melbourne's Papers*, 376–7. See also, Melbourne to Lord Minto, 2 Sept. 1838; Nat. Lib. of Scotland, Minto MSS, 12/25 fo. 58.
84. *Parl. Hist.* xl. 687, 2 Feb. 1838.
85. Melbourne to Victoria, 27 and 30 Dec. 1832, and 13 and 20 Jan. 1838; Windsor, Royal Archives, A1 fos. 73, 75, 83, 87.
86. Lord Howick to Melbourne, 29 Dec. 1837; Sanders, *Lord Melbourne's Papers*, 423–4.
87. Melbourne to Lord J. Russell, 31 Dec. 1837; Southampton Univ. Lib., Melbourne MSS, MEL/RU/432.
88. Melbourne to Lord Durham, 28 July 1838; Melbourne MSS, Box 4/44.
89. Melbourne to Lord Howick, 2 Jan. 1839; Durham Univ. Lib., Grey MSS, unfol.
90. *Parl. Hist.* xxxi. 320, 12 Feb. 1836.
91. Melbourne to Victoria, 10 Oct. 1841; Windsor, Royal Archives, A4 fo. 22.
92. Melbourne to Grey, 9 Jan. 1836; Durham Univ. Lib., Grey MSS, fo. 169.
93. Melbourne to Talleyrand, 26 Jan. 1831; PRO, Home Office MSS, 43 39/fo. 389.
94. F. Sébastiani to Mme Adelaide, 26 April 1835; Bib. Nat., n.a.f. 12219, fo. 20.
95. Ibid. 3 Oct. 1837; ibid. fo. 176.
96. F. Guizot to A. Thiers, 10 March 1840; ibid. 20610, fo. 25. See also ibid. 1 June 1840; ibid. fos. 107–9. Guizot, *An Embassy to the Court of St. James in 1840*.
97. QVJ, 25 Sept. 1839.
98. Cecil, 323.
99. QVJ, 12 May 1839.
100. Ibid. 9 April, 28 Sept. and 17 Oct. 1838.
101. Ibid. 5 May 1839. Duke of Devonshire to Lady Spencer, n.d.; Chatsworth MSS, 6th Duke's MSS, fo. 123.
102. Louise of Belgium to Victoria, 9 Sept. 1838; Windsor, Royal Archives, Y6 fo. 13.
103. Ibid.
104. QVJ, 15 and 18 Sept. 1838.
105. Lady Bessborough to W. Ponsonby, 20 Nov. [1815]; Lord Bessborough, *Lady Bessborough and Her Family Circle*, 256.
106. Melbourne to Lord Granville, 19 July 1834; Melbourne MSS, Box 26/76.
107. Melbourne to Lord J. Russell, 18 July 1841; Bourne, *Palmerston*, 620.
108. Lord Minto to Melbourne, 23 Aug. 1840; Sanders, *Lord Melbourne's Papers*, 464–7. Ibid. 4 Oct. 1840; Nat. Lib. of Scotland, Minto MSS, 12/26 fo. 29.
109. Melbourne to Lord J. Russell, 26 Aug. 1840; Melbourne MSS, Box 14/149.
110. Prince Albert to Melbourne, 9 Oct. 1840; Southampton Univ. Lib., Palmerston MSS, RC/J/3.
111. Melbourne to Palmerston, 20 Oct. 1840; ibid. GC/ME/443.
112. Ibid. 11 March 1840; ibid. GC/ME/360.
113. BL Add. MSS 56558, fo. 101; Diary of J. Hobhouse, 9 March 1836.
114. BL Add. MSS 51558, fo. 153; Melbourne to Holland, 22 Sept. 1837.

115. Ibid. 51559 fo. 68; ibid. 30 Aug. 1840.
116. Melbourne to Lord J. Russell, 9 Oct. 1840; Melbourne MSS, Box 15/8.
117. Melbourne to Palmerston, 16 June 1836; Southampton Univ. Lib., Palmerston MSS, GC/ME/104.
118. Ibid. 29 April 1837; ibid. GC/ME/162.
119. Ibid. 15 Dec. 1840; ibid. GC/ME/467.
120. F. Sébastiani to Mme Adelaide, 27 Jan. 1840; Bib. Nat. n.a.f. 12220, f 201.
121. Melbourne to Palmerston, 10 Oct. 1840; Southampton Univ. Lib., Palmerston MSS, GC/ME/436. See also ibid. 12 Oct. 1840; ibid. 438.
122. F. Guizot to A. Thiers, 10 March 1840; Bib. Nat. n.a.f. 20610, fos. 25–6.
123. BL Add. MSS 51559, fo. 18; Melbourne to Holland, 28 Dec. 1838. He reminded Russell that, in 1836, Thiers had ordered French troops to the Spanish frontier without consulting the King. Melbourne to Lord J. Russell, 23 Oct. 1840; Sanders, *Lord Melbourne's Papers*, 485–6.
124. QVJ, 14 Jan. 1839.
125. *Le National*, 13 Jan. 1840. The same newspaper hoped that Thiers would earn 'la jalousie et même le haine de cette oligarchie qui pensionna le cardinal Dubois et Talleyrand, et qui assassina si lâchement Napoleon'; 1 March 1840.
126. Melbourne to Palmerston, 12 Sept. 1836; Southampton Univ. Lib., Palmerston MSS, GC/ME/123. He asked Joseph Parkes to try to moderate the tone of the Radical press; Melbourne to J. Parkes, 22 Sept. 1836; Univ. Coll. London, Parkes MSS, fo. 16.
127. F. Sébastiani to Mme Adelaide, 15 Aug. 1840; Bib. Nat., n.a.f. 12220, fo. 214.
128. QVJ, 8 March 1840.
129. Ibid. 18 Aug. 1840.
130. Melbourne to Lord J. Russell, 19 Sept. 1840; Melbourne MSS, Box 15/1.
131. Melbourne to Palmerston, 25 Aug. 1839; Southampton Univ. Lib., Palmerston MSS, GC/ME/412.
132. Melbourne to Lord Clarendon, 17 Sept. 1840; Bod. Lib., Clarendon MSS, c 469.
133. Melbourne to Lord J. Russell, 23 Oct. 1840; Sanders, *Lord Melbourne's Papers*, 485–6.
134. Lord Clarendon to Melbourne, 27 Oct. 1840; Melbourne MSS, Box 3/12.
135. S. Smith to Lady Grey, 29 Nov. 1840; Mrs Austin, *Memoir and Letters of the Rev. Sydney Smith* (London 1855), 438.
136. Lord J. Russell to Melbourne, 29 Sept. 1840; Southampton Univ. Lib., Melbourne MSS, MEL/RU/124. Palmerston's most recent biographer asserts that Melbourne only once tried to stand up to his Foreign Secretary, but was then faced down. Bourne, *Palmerston*, 581–2.
137. Lord John Russell to Melbourne, 21 Sept. 1840; G. Gooch, *The Later Correspondence of Lord John Russell* (London 1925), i. 18. BL Add. MSS 51559, fo. 62; Holland to Melbourne, [July 1840]. Holland to E. Ellice, 20 July 1840; Nat. Lib. of Scotland, Ellice MSS, fo. 193.
138. Kriegel, *The Holland House Diaries*, 411.
139. M. de Sages to M. de Pontris, 27 July 1840; Bib. Nat., n.a.f. 20615, f. 158.
140. QVJ, 3 Sept. 1840.

141. Melbourne to Palmerston, 7 June and 14 Sept. 1840; Southampton Univ. Lib., Palmerston MSS, GC/ME/389 and 418.

142. Palmerston to Melbourne, 16 Sept. 1840; Sanders, *Lord Melbourne's Papers*, 475–6.

143. Palmerston to Melbourne, 25 Oct. 1840; Melbourne MSS, Box 13/5.

144. BL Add. MSS 45553, fo. 22; Lady Palmerston to Palmerston, 1 Dec. 1840. Diary of Lady Palmerston, 21 Sept. 1840; Hatfield House MSS.

145. Kriegel, *The Holland House Diaries*, 418.

146. Palmerston to Melbourne, 5 and 6 July 1840; Southampton Univ. Lib., Palmerston MSS, GC/ME/535 and 537. See also Melbourne to Palmerston, 6 and 7 July 1840; ibid. 394 and 395.

147. Lord J. Russell to Melbourne, 19 Sept. 1840; PRO, Russell MSS, 30/22/3E XC10495, fo. 16. See also, ibid. 15 and 27 Sept. 1840, and 2 Oct. 1841; ibid. fos. 33, 131 and 161. Melbourne to Lord J. Russell, 16 and 26 Sept. 1840; Melbourne MSS, Box 14/155 and Box 15/2.

148. As in the fraught Cabinet meetings in the first week of July, 1840.

149. F. Sébastiani to Mme Adelaide, 27 Jan. 1840; Bib. Nat., n.a.f. 12220, fo. 203. For a detailed discussion of Melbourne's handling of the matter, see Custance, 320–350. Melbourne to Palmerston, 19 Sept. 1840; Southampton Univ. Lib., Palmerston MSS, GC/ME/423.

150. QVJ, 13 Sept. 1840.

151. Greville, iv. 322 and 331, 26 Sept. 1840.

152. Ibid.

153. F. Guizot to A. Thiers, 2 Oct. 1840; Bib. Nat. n.a.f. 20610, fo. 327.

154. A. Czartoryski to A. Thiers, 1 Aug. 1840; ibid. 20609, fo. 75.

155. *Parl. Hist.* lv. 1114, 30 July 1840. See also, Melbourne to Lord J. Russell, 26 Aug. 1840.

156. F. Guizot to A. Thiers, 29 July 1840; Bib. Nat., n.a.f. 20610, fo. 207. A. Thiers to F. Guizot, 16 and 21 July 1840; ibid. 20613, fos. 137 and 148.

157. Melbourne to Lord J. Russell, 28 Dec. 1840; Melbourne MSS, Box 15/22.

158. F. Guizot to A. Thiers, 9 Sept. 1840; Bib. Nat., n.a.f. 20610, fo. 283. Lord J. Russell to Melbourne, 9 Oct. 1840; Ann Arbor, Russell MSS.

159. F. Guizot to A. Thiers, 9 Sept. 1840; Bib., n.a.f. 20610, f. 283.

160. Leopold I to Melbourne, 4 July 1840; Melbourne MSS, Box 117/87. Lord Clarendon to Lord J. Russell, 1 Nov. 1840; Gooch, *The Later Correspondence of Lord John Russell*, i. 29–30.

Chapter 11

1. Melbourne to Lady Branden, 12 Sept. 1829; Herts. RO, Panshanger MSS, D/ELb F41.

2. Ziegler, 270.

3. Melbourne to Lord J. Russell, 9 April 1838; Southampton Univ. Lib., Melbourne MSS, MEL/RU/475.

4. Lord Hatherton's Diary, 31 July 1835; Staffs. RO, Hatherton MSS, D260/M/F/5/26/9.

5. Emily Eden to Lady Grey, 14 Oct. 1833; Durham Univ., Grey MSS.
6. Anon., *Extracts from the Diary of the late Dr. R. Lee*, 28.
7. G. Anson Memorandum, 7 May 1843; Windsor, Royal Archives, Y55 fo. 11.
8. See Ch. 1.
9. Byron to Lady Melbourne, 25 Feb. [1813]; Marchand, *Byron's Letters and Journals*, iii. 21.
10. Diary of Lord Malmesbury, 11 Oct. 1848; Lord Malmesbury, *Memoirs of an Ex-Minister*, i. 234.
11. Ziegler, 228.
12. QVJ, 27 Jan. 1839.
13. Melbourne to Lord Howick, 26 Sept. 1835; Durham Univ. Grey MSS.
14. Melbourne to Mrs Norton, 9 June 1836; Torrens, *Memoirs of Lord Melbourne*, 409.
15. BL Add. MSS 42767, fo. 43; Mrs Norton to R. Sheridan, [June 1836].
16. QVJ, 28 Aug. 1839.
17. Ibid. 5 Dec. 1839.
18. BL Add. MSS 45552, fo. 114; F. Lamb to E. Lamb, 22 Dec. [1840].
19. Ibid. 51560, fo. 34; Melbourne to Lady Holland, 31 Dec. 1836.
20. Autobiography; Herts. RO, Panshanger MSS, D/ELb F12.
21. Ibid.
22. Ibid.
23. QVJ, 15 Oct. 1838.
24. Mrs Norton to Lord Melbourne, 25 Aug. [1830]; Hoge and Olney, *The Letters of Caroline Norton to Lord Melbourne*, 156.
25. Ibid. 19 Dec. [1839]; ibid. 157. See also BL Add. MSS 51560, fo. 103; Melbourne to Lady Holland, 6 Oct. 1842.
26. QVJ, 9 Feb. 1838.
27. See Ch. 5.
28. Susan Churchill to Lord Melbourne, 5 April 1842; Herts. RO, Panshanger MSS, D/ELb F35. See also ibid. 30 April and 14 June 1842; ibid.
29. For details of the Branden case, see Cecil, 168–9 and Ziegler, ch. 7.
30. Lady Branden to Melbourne, n.d.; Herts. RO, Panshanger MSS, D/ELb F36.
31. Bamford, *The Journal of Mrs Arbuthnot*, ii. 311.
32. Torrens, *Memoirs of Lord Melbourne*, 211.
33. T. Creevey to Miss Ord, 17 June 1828; Maxwell, *The Creevey Papers*, ii. 160.
34. Melbourne to Lady Branden, 5 Nov. 1828; Herts. RO, Panshanger MSS, D/ELb F43. See also Melbourne to T. Barber, 7 Oct. 1829; Notts. RO, Barber MSS, D.D. 2B 8/6.
35. M. Bruce to Melbourne, 12 Nov. 1829; Ziegler, 108. See also, J. Dickinson to Lady Branden, 7 July 1828; Herts. RO, Panshanger MSS, D/ELb F44.
36. Lord Branden to M. Bruce, 11 Dec. 1831; Melbourne MSS, Box 106/55.
37. Lord Branden's will, n.d.; ibid. Box 106/61.
38. Ibid.
39. Melbourne to Lady Branden, 28 Jan. 1828; Herts. RO, Panshanger MSS, D/ELb F43.
40. Ibid. 24 June 1828; ibid.

41. Ibid. 28 Jan. 1828; ibid.
42. Ibid. 28 Feb. 1828; ibid.
43. Ibid. 17 May 1829; ibid. F41.
44. Ibid. 22 April 1829; ibid. See also, ibid. 8 Dec. 1828; ibid. F43.
45. Ibid. 19 June 1828; ibid. F43. 'I think myself bound and am happy to supply you with any money you may want.'
46. Ibid. 12 April 1829; ibid. F41.
47. Mrs H. Hatton to Lady Branden, 1829; ibid. F44. This bundle contains many important letters from Lady Branden's family and solicitors.
48. Howell-Thomas, *Lord Melbourne's Susan*, 78.
49. Lady Branden to Melbourne, 6 July 1832; Melbourne MSS, Box 106/63. H. Tevor to Melbourne, 10 Oct. 1832; ibid. 66. Memorandum by S. Lushington, 31 July 1832; ibid. 64A.
50. See above, Ch. 5.
51. Melbourne to Lady Branden, 9 July 1828; Herts. RO, Panshanger MSS, D/ELb F43.
52. Ibid. 30 Aug. 1830; ibid. F42.
53. Ibid. 8 March and 30 Dec. 1830; ibid.
54. QVJ, 10 April and 14 Oct. 1839. Mrs G. Lamb to Lady Carlisle, 1 Oct [1839?]; Castle Howard MSS, J18/44/144. Ibid. n.d.; ibid. 141.
55. E. Eden to Lady Grey, [26 Jan. 1828]; Durham Univ. Lib., Grey MSS.
56. Ibid. 25 Jan. 1828; ibid.
57. E. Eden to Mrs T. Lister, [Jan.] 1832; Dickinson, *Miss Eden's Letters*, 215–16.
58. E. Eden to Melbourne, [1835]; Herts. RO, Panshanger MSS, D/ELb F37.
59. Melbourne to Victoria, 14 Dec. 1840; Windsor, Royal Archives, A3 fo. 114.
60. E. Eden to ?, [Oct. 1835]; E. Eden, *Letters from India* (London 1872), i. 5.
61. Mrs F. Sullivan to Mr Sullivan, 7 March 1831; G. Lyster, *A Family Chronicle* (London 1908), 69.
62. C. Olney, 'Caroline Norton and Lord Melbourne', *Victorian Studies*, 8 (1965), 258.
63. T. Barnes to B. Disraeli, 17 Jan. 1836; Barnes, *Thomas Barnes of The Times*, 91.
64. Olney, *Victorian Studies*, 8 (1965), 256.
65. QVJ, 22 March 1839.
66. Mrs Norton to Melbourne, 11 July 1831; Hoge and Olney, *The Letters of Caroline Norton to Lord Melbourne*, 25.
67. Ibid. 7 Aug. 1831, 40.
68. Ibid. 16 Aug. [1831], 49.
69. E. Lamb to F. Lamb, 1827; ibid. 3.
70. Ibid. 4.
71. E. Eden to Lord Clarendon, 7 Jan. 1834; Maxwell, *The Life and Letters of the 4th Earl of Clarendon*, i. 82.
72. QVJ, 14 Aug. 1839.
73. E. Eden to Lady Grey, 4 Jan. 1834; Durham Univ. Lib., Grey MSS.
74. Diary of Lord Malmesbury, 16/17 May 1835; Lord Malmesbury, *Memoirs of an Ex-Minister*, i. 66–7.

75. Ibid.
76. Diary of Lord Hatherton, 13 May 1836; Staffs. RO, Hatherton MSS, D260/M/F/5/26/12.
77. Hoge and Olney, *The Letters of Caroline Norton to Lord Melbourne*, 6.
78. Lady Granville to Lady Carlisle, 22 April 1836; Leveson Gower, *The Letters of Harriet, Lady Granville*, ii. 202.
79. Melbourne to Mrs Norton, 19 July 1831; Torrens, *Memoirs of Lord Melbourne*, 273.
80. Mrs Norton to Melbourne, 26 Aug. [1831]; Hoge and Olney, *The Letters of Caroline Norton to Lord Melbourne*, 60.
81. E. Eden to Lady Campbell, 23 July 1834; Dickinson, *Miss Eden's Letters*, 240–1.
82. Mrs Norton to Melbourne, 29 Sept. [1832]; Brit. Mus. microfilm, Berg MSS, 593.
83. B. Disraeli to I. Disraeli, [April] and 17 April 1835; Monypenny and Buckle, *The Life of Benjamin Disraeli*, i. 278–9.
84. J. Wortley to Lady Wharncliffe, 8 Dec. 1835; Grosvenor, *The First Lady Wharncliffe and Her Family*, ii. 271.
85. BL Add. MSS 51601, fo. 110; E. Lamb to Lady Holland, [4 April 1836].
86. BL Add. MSS 51558, fo. 86; Melbourne to Holland, 6 April 1836.
87. Melbourne to Mrs Norton, 19 April 1836; Hoge and Olney, *The Letters of Caroline Norton to Lord Melbourne*, 63.
88. Ibid. 10 April 1836; ibid. 63.
89. Ibid. 6 April 1836; J. G. Perkins, *The Life of Mrs Norton* (London 1909), 83. In this letter, Norton's behaviour is called 'unaccountable', and it is agreed that he was not to be humoured: 'Open breaches of this kind are always to be lamented, but you have the consolation that you have done your utmost to stave this extremity off as long as possible.'
90. Melbourne to Mrs Norton, 8 April 1836; ibid. 85.
91. Ibid. [April 1836]; Hoge and Olney, *The Letters of Caroline Norton to Lord Melbourne*, 74.
92. Melbourne to Sir H. Halford, 23, 25, and 29 May 1836; Leics. RO, Halford MSS, DG24/904/7.
93. Mrs Norton to Lord Melbourne, [April 1836]; Hoge and Olney, *The Letters of Caroline Norton to Lord Melbourne*, 73.
94. Ibid. [late April 1836]; 75.
95. Ibid.
96. Melbourne to Mrs Norton, 23 April 1836; Torrens, *Memoirs of Lord Melbourne*, 409.
97. Greville, iii. 356, 11 May 1836.
98. Lord Hatherton's Diary, 22 June 1836; Staffs. RO, Hatherton MSS, D260/M/F/5/26/12.
99. *Morning Chronicle*, 23 June 1836.
100. Lord Hatherton's Diary, 22 June 1836; Staffs. RO, Hatherton MSS, D260/M/F/5/26/12.
101. T. Creevey to Miss Ord, 13 May 1836; Maxwell, *The Creevey Papers*, ii. 311.
102. BL Add. MSS 51558, fo. 95; Sir J. Cope to Melbourne, [22 June 1836].
103. *Morning Chronicle*, 23 June 1836.

104. The contents of the three notes from Melbourne were (1) 'I will call about half past four.' (2) 'How are you? I shall not be able to come today. I shall tomorrow.' (3) 'No house today. I will call after the levee. If you wish it later let me know. I will then explain about going to Vauxhall.'
    A. Acland, *Caroline Norton* (London 1948), 90.
105. F. Sébastiani to A. Thiers, 25 June 1836; Bib. Nat., n.a.f. 20606, fo. 210.
106. *Morning Chronicle*, 25 June 1836.
107. BL Add. MSS 51601, fo. 124; E. Lamb to Lady Holland, [24 June 1836].
108. Ibid. 56558, fo. 156; Diary of J. Hobhouse, 23 June 1836.
109. *Morning Chronicle*, 29 June 1836.
110. Mrs Norton to Melbourne, [April 1836]; Hoge and Olney, *The Letters of Caroline Norton to Lord Melbourne*, 70.
111. Perkins, *The Life of Mrs Norton*, 121.
112. BL Add. MSS 60465, fo. 56; Lord Palmerston to F. Lamb, 10 May 1836.
113. F. Sébastiani to Mme Adelaide, 9 June 1836; Bib. Nat., n.a.f. 12219, fo. 111.
114. Kriegel, *The Holland House Diaries*, 345.
115. Lord Wellesley to Melbourne, 27 June 1836; Melbourne MSS, Box 39/74.
116. BL Add. MSS 51559, fo. 85; W. Cowper to Lady Holland, [June 1836].
117. Lord Hatherton's Diary, 12 May 1836; Staffs. RO, Hatherton MSS, D260/M/F/5/26/12.
118. Melbourne to Sir J. Abercromby, 23 June 1836; Nat. Lib. of Scotland, Abercromby MSS, fo. 31.
119. Melbourne Hall MSS, Box 233, Bundle 8/2.
120. F. Sébastiani to A. Thiers, 24 May 1836; Bib. Nat., n.a.f. 20606, fo. 200.
121. Lord Hatherton's Diary, 8 May 1836; Staffs. RO, Hatherton MSS, D260/M/F/5/26/12.
122. Mrs Hardcastle, *The Life of John, Lord Campbell*, ii. 84. After winning the case for his client, Campbell was so fêted that he felt 'like the Duke of Wellington after the Battle of Waterloo'; ibid. ii. 90.
123. Ibid. ii. 83.
124. Greville, vi. 259, 9 Dec. 1848.
125. Kriegel, *The Holland House Diaries*, 345 n.
126. BL Add. MSS 56558, fo. 156; Diary of J. Hobhouse, 23 June 1836.
127. BL Add. MSS 45551, fo. 150; F. Lamb to E. Lamb, 28 [June] 1836.
128. Melbourne to Mrs Norton, [July] 1836; Perkins, *The Life of Mrs Norton*, 105–6.
129. Mrs Norton to Melbourne, [June] 1836; Hoge and Olney, *The Letters of Caroline Norton to Lord Melbourne*, 82.
130. Melbourne to Mrs Norton, 24 July [1836]; Perkins, *The Life of Mrs Norton*, 107.
131. Mrs Norton to Melbourne, [1836]; Hoge and Olney, *The Letters of Caroline Norton to Lord Melbourne*, 107.
132. Ibid.
133. QVJ, 19 July 1839.
134. Mrs Norton to Lady C. Stanhope, n.d.; Kent RO, Stanhope MSS, c 502/19.
135. Mrs Norton to Lord Melbourne, [March 1837]; Hoge and Olney, *The Letters of Caroline Norton to Lord Melbourne*, 120.

136. Ibid. 121.
137. Ibid. 120.
138. Ibid. 1 July 1836; ibid. 93.
139. Ibid. [8 July 1836]; ibid. 96–7.
140. Ibid. [21 June 1836]; ibid. 89.
141. Ibid.
142. Ibid. 17 March [1837]; ibid. 115.
143. Mrs Norton to Melbourne, [July 1836]; Olney, *Victorian Studies*, 8 (1965), 261.
144. Melbourne to Mrs Norton, 3 Feb. 1837; Herts. RO, Panshanger MSS, D/ELb F49.
145. QVJ, 15 April 1839.
146. Mrs Norton to Melbourne, Feb. 1839; Hoge and Olney, *The Letters of Caroline Norton to Lord Melbourne*, 148.
147. QVJ, 15 March 1838.
148. Ibid. 27 April 1838.
149. Ibid. 19 May 1838.
150. Ibid. 13 Jan. 1840.
151. Ibid. 15 April 1839.
152. Lord Hatherton's Diary, 10 March 1837; Staffs. RO, Hatherton MSS, D260/M/F/26/14.
153. Ibid. 1 Aug. 1833; ibid. 9.
154. QVJ, 18 July 1838; Wilhelmina is an unusual name for a girl, and it might be tempting to speculate that William Lamb might have been her natural father. In fact, the name almost certainly owes more to Lord Stanhope's interest in German politics and literature.
155. H. Brougham to E. Ellice, [c.1849]; Ziegler, 360–1.
156. Perkins, *The Life of Mrs Norton*, 213.
157. E. Eden to Lady Grey, [Nov. 1842]; Durham Univ. Lib., Grey MSS.
158. Mrs Norton to W. Cowper, n.d.; BL, Berg MSS, micro. 593.
159. Perkins, *The Life of Mrs Norton*, 196–7. See also Cecil, 361–5.
160. Lord Hatherton's Diary, May 1840; Staffs. RO, Hatherton MSS, D260/M/F/5/26/17.
161. Mrs Norton to W. Cowper, n.d.; BL, Berg MSS, micro. 593. See also Diary of Lady Palmerston, 10 April 1839; Hatfield House MSS.
162. Mrs Norton to W. Cowper, 12 May 1846; BL, Berg MSS, micro. 593.
163. Ibid. [c.1840]; ibid.
164. Diary of Lady Palmerston, 26 July 1848; Hatfield House MSS.
165. Mrs Norton to W. Cowper, n.d.; BL, Berg MSS, micro. 593.
166. W. Brookfield to Mrs Brookfield, 26 March 1847; *Mrs Brookfield and Her Circle* (London 1905), i. 209–10.
167. Mrs Norton to Melbourne, 6 Dec. [1844]; Hoge and Olney, *The Letters of Caroline Norton to Lord Melbourne*, 168.

Chapter 12

1. Lord Aberdeen, quoted in Ziegler 263–4.
2. Ibid. 264.
3. Melbourne MSS, Box 115/110 and 110a.
4. *The Journal of Lady Charlotte Guest*, 19 June 1837; 48.
5. F. Sébastiani to Mme Adelaide, 20 June 1837; Bib. Nat., n.a.f. 12219, fo. 151.
6. Ibid. 21 June 1837; ibid. fos. 151–2.
7. Ibid. 23 June 1837; ibid. fo. 155.
8. QVJ, 2 July 1837.
9. Ibid. 18 July 1837. The day before she had written that Melbourne 'is my friend. I know it.'
10. Ibid. 8 August 1837.
11. Ibid. 19 Oct. 1837.
12. Ibid. 12 Dec. 1837.
13. Lady Granville to Lady Carlisle, 4 Aug. 1837; Leveson Gower, *The Letters of Harriet, Lady Granville*, ii. 238–9.
14. *Quarterly Review*, lix. 245; July 1837.
15. Lady Grey to T. Creevey, 10 Oct. 1837; Maxwell, *The Creevey Papers*, ii. 327.
16. C. Oman, *The Gascoyne Heiress* (London 1968), 300.
17. Cecil, 277.
18. *Fraser's Magazine*, xix. 188, 191, Feb. 1839. See also, Cecil, 268–9.
19. QVJ, 23 Dec. 1837.
20. Ibid. 13 Nov. 1837.
21. Melbourne to Lord J. Russell, 17 Dec. 1837; Southampton Univ. Lib., Melbourne MSS, MEL/RU/426. See also, ibid. 12 June 1837; ibid. 341. He wished 'to revert to the ancient practice of the Sovereign having no private secretary and transacting business only with the ministers'.
22. Mrs G. Lamb to Lady Carlisle, n.d.; Castle Howard MSS, J18/44/144.
23. Melbourne to W. Cowper, 23 Sept. 1839; Southampton Univ. Lib., Melbourne MSS, MEL/CO/26.
24. QVJ, 23 Sept. 1838.
25. Greville, iv. 136, 12 Sept. 1837.
26. Lady Lyttelton to C. Lyttelton, 25 Oct. 1838; Wyndham, *The Correspondence of Sarah Spencer, Lady Lyttelton*, 284–5.
27. Melbourne to Duchess of Kent, 17 March 1837; Melbourne MSS, Box 116/33.
28. Ibid. June 1835; Ibid. Box 115/1. See also, Duchess of Kent to Melbourne, 3 July 1835; ibid. 3.
29. Sir H. Taylor to Melbourne, 23 April 1836; ibid. Box 115/62.
30. F. Sébastiani to Mme Adelaide, 3 and 17 June 1837; Bib. Nat., n.a.f. 12219, fos. 143 and 147.
31. William IV to Melbourne, 24 and 26 May 1837; Melbourne MSS, Box 115/90 and 93.
32. Melbourne to Lord Tavistock, 22 June 1837; Woburn MSS.
33. Melbourne to E. Ellice, 16 Feb. 1838; Nat. Lib. of Scotland, Ellice MSS, fo. 60.

34. QVJ, 24 Jan. 1847.
35. BL Add. MSS 51560, fo. 91; Melbourne to Lady Holland, 18 March 1842.
36. Kriegel, *The Holland House Diaries*, 395–6.
37. Cecil, 290.
38. QVJ, 4 Sept. 1838.
39. Ibid.
40. Cecil, 293.
41. S. Keppel, *Sovereign Lady* (London 1974), 328.
42. Lord Hatherton's Diary, 30 Sept. 1838; Staffs. RO, Hatherton MSS, D260/M/F/26/15.
43. QVJ, 17 Dec. 1842.
44. Cecil, 286.
45. Melbourne to Victoria, 12 Aug. 1837; Windsor Archives, A1 fo. 25.
46. Ibid. 6 Oct. 1837; ibid. fo. 36.
47. Kriegel, *The Holland House Diaries*, 372.
48. Greville, iv. 22, 30 Aug. 1837.
49. F. Sébastiani to Mme Adelaide, 26 Aug. 1843; Bib. Nat., n.a.f. 12220, fo. 230.
50. Ibid. 10 Oct. 1837; ibid. 12219, fo. 196.
51. Greville, iv. 136, 12 Sept. 1837.
52. Lord Holland to Duke of Grafton, 19 Sept. 1837; Suffolk RO, Grafton MSS
53. QVJ, 25 May 1838.
54. Palmerston to Melbourne, 14 Oct. 1837; Melbourne MSS, Box 11/63.
55. Ziegler, ch. 21.
56. F. Sébastiani to Mme Adelaide, 16 April 1839; Bib. Nat. n.a.f. 12220, fos. 156–7.
57. Lord Hastings to Melbourne, 26 Feb. 1839; Melbourne MSS, Box 115/116.
58. Ibid. 3 March 1839; ibid. 141.
59. QVJ, 16 April 1839.
60. Ibid.
61. See Ziegler, ch. 21, for details of this crisis.
62. QVJ, 7 May 1839.
63. Ibid.
64. Melbourne to Grey, 10 May 1839; Durham Univ. Lib., Grey MSS, fo. 174.
65. T. Spring Rice to Melbourne, 9 May 1839; Melbourne MSS, Box 10/22.
66. Greville, iv. 217, 12 May 1839.
67. Cecil, 321.
68. *Parl. Hist.* xlvii. 1010 and 1015, 14 May 1839.
69. Melbourne to W. Cowper, 13 May 1839; Southampton Univ. Lib., Melbourne MSS, MEL/CO/22.
70. BL Add. MSS 51757, fos. 183–4; Lord Holland to H. Fox, 20 March 1840.
71. Lord Londonderry to Duke of Buckingham, 1 Sept. 1837; Lord Buckingham and Chandos, *Memoirs of the Courts and Cabinets of William IV and Victoria*, ii. 288.
72. BL Add. MSS 49479, fo. 220; Grey to Sir J. Gordon, 19 Oct. 1839.
73. Greville, iv. 256–7, 27 Nov. 1839.
74. Melbourne to Leopold of Belgium, 8 Dec. 1839; Melbourne MSS, Box 117/12.
75. Cecil, 335.

76. QVJ, 13 July 1839.
77. Cecil, 339–40.
78. BL Add. MSS 51559, fos. 43–51; Melbourne to Holland and vice versa, Dec. 1839. See also, Clarendon to Melbourne, 1 Feb. 1840; Melbourne MSS, Box 3/10.
79. QVJ, 1 Oct. 1842.
80. Ibid. 6 Dec. 1845.
81. BL Add. MSS 39949, fo. 191; E. Lamb to Mrs Huskisson, [Aug. 1841].
82. Ibid. fo. 198; 28 Aug. 1841.
83. Leopold of Belgium to Melbourne, 3 Sept. 1841; Herts. RO, Panshanger MSS, D/ELb F39.
84. BL Add. MSS 51613, fo. 127; Lady Beauvale to Lady Holland, [Sept.] 1844.
85. Ibid. 45552, fo. 135; F. Lamb to E. Lamb, [1841].
86. Memorandum by G. Anson, 29 Aug. 1841; Windsor, Royal Archives Y54 fo. 84. See also, ibid. fo. 66.
87. Melbourne to Victoria, 22 Dec. 1841; Windsor, Royal Archives, A4 fo. 42.
88. Ibid. 20 Oct. 1842; ibid. fo. 84.
89. Ibid. 13, 17, 26 Oct., 22 Dec. 1841, 7 March 1842; ibid. fos. 24, 27, 29, 42, 57.
90. Ibid. 3 Sept. 1841; ibid. fo. 1.
91. Greville, v. 39–40, 4 Sept. 1841.
92. Anson Memorandum, 21 Sept. 1841; Lord Esher, *The Letters of Queen Victoria*, i. 330–1.
93. Baron Stockmar to Melbourne, 23 Nov. 1841; Melbourne MSS, Box 117/98.
94. Anson Memorandum, 26 Sept. 1841; Lord Esher, *The Letters of Queen Victoria*, i. 368.
95. Anson Memorandum, 17 Feb. 1841; Windsor, Royal Archives, Y54 fo. 16.
96. Anson Memorandum, 19 Feb. 1841; ibid. fo. 17.
97. G. Anson to Melbourne, 3 Sept. 1841; Melbourne MSS, Box 117/102.
98. QVJ, 26 July 1843.
99. Victoria to Leopold of Belgium, 4 Jan. 1843; Lord Esher, *The Letters of Queen Victoria*, i. 451.
100. Melbourne to Victoria, 19 March 1845; Windsor, Royal Archives, A4 fo. 135.
101. G. Anson to Melbourne, April 1847; Herts. RO, Panshanger MSS, D/ELb F38.
102. Melbourne to Victoria, 30 Aug. 1841; Windsor, Royal Archives, A3 fo. 205.
103. Melbourne to Victoria, 9 Oct. 1844; Lord Esher, *The Letters of Queen Victoria*, ii. 24.
104. Cecil, 359.
105. Melbourne to Victoria, 9 Oct. 1844; *The Letters of Queen Victoria*, ii. 24.
106. F. Leveson Gower, *Bygone Years* (London 1905), 47.
107. Melbourne to Victoria, 20 April 1842; Windsor, Royal Archives, A4 fo. 63.
108. BL Add. MSS 45552, fo. 155; F. Lamb to E. Lamb [*c*.1842].
109. QVJ, 15 Feb. 1849.
110. F. Lamb to E. Ellice, [1848]; Nat. Lib. of Scot., Minto MSS, 12/25 fo. 143.
111. F. Lamb to Victoria, 29 Nov. 1848; Windsor, Royal Archives, A4/159.
112. Victoria to F. Lamb, 5 Dec. 1848; Melbourne MSS, Box 115/178.
113. Lord J. Russell to F. Lamb, 29 Jan. 1831; ibid. Box 106/147.

114. Victoria to Leopold of Belgium, 27 Nov. 1848; Lord Esher, *The Letters of Queen Victoria*, ii. 204.
115. Victoria to Sir H. Ponsonby, 9 Jan. 1890; Windsor, Royal Archives, L16 fo. 32.
116. QVJ, 20 Nov. 1848. See also, Victoria to Leopold of Belgium, 21 Nov. 1848; Lord Esher, *The Letters of Queen Victoria*, ii. 203.

Chapter 13

1. Custance, 186. He told Lord John Russell: 'I have only two scruples about resigning, one lest we should bring about a state of things in which it is difficult to form a government and the other lest our friends should be discontented with us.' Melbourne to Lord J. Russell, 1 April 1837; Southampton Univ. Lib., Melbourne MSS, MEL/RU/320.
2. E. Lamb to F. Lamb, 8 Feb. 1834; Herts. RO, Panshanger MSS, D/ELb F76.
3. Torrens, *Memoirs of Lord Melbourne*, 525. Diary of Lady Palmerston, 2 Sept. 1841; Hatfield House MSS.
4. Lord Campbell to Sir G. Campbell, 1 Sept. 1841; Mrs Hardcastle, *Life of John, Lord Campbell*, ii. 159.
5. Diary of Lord Hatherton, 20 Jan. 1840; Staffs. RO, Hatherton MSS, D260/M/F/5/26/17.
6. Ibid. 25 Nov. 1848; ibid. 47.
7. BL Add. MSS 42767, fo. 97; Mrs Norton to R. Sheridan, 4 Jan. 1839.
8. A. Lamb to Lady C. Lamb, 31 Aug. 1827; Lord Bessborough, *Lady Bessborough and Her Family Circle*, 289–90.
9. BL Add. MSS 45548, fo. 165; W. Lamb and F. Lamb, 27 Aug. 1827.
10. Ibid. 45551, fo. 77; E. Lamb to F. Lamb, 12 Feb. 1827.
11. Ibid. fo. 157; F. Lamb to E. Lamb, 10 [Dec. 1836].
12. Mrs G. Lamb to Lady Morpeth, [1836]; Castle Howard MSS, J18/44/140.
13. Autopsy Report by Sir H. Halford, 26 Nov. 1836; Herts. RO, Panshanger MSS, D/ELb F72.
14. Melbourne to Duke of Devonshire, 5 Nov. 1829; Chatsworth MSS, Papers of the 6th Duke, fo. 1851.
15. QVJ, 28 Jan. 1838. It is now the Scottish Office.
16. Mrs G. Lamb to Lady Carlisle, 15 April [1830]; Castle Howard MSS, J18/44/144.
17. Lady Dover to Lady C. Lascelles, Dec. 1831; Lady Leconfield and J. Gore, *Three Howard Sisters* (London 1955), 230.
18. Taylor, *Life of Benjamin Robert Haydon*, ii. 362.
19. Mrs G. Lamb to Lady Carlisle, 27 Aug. [1830]; Castle Howard MSS, J18/44/144.
20. Kriegel, *The Holland House Diaries*, 115.
21. Greville, iii. 134, 7 Sept. 1834.
22. Ibid.
23. Melbourne to Lord John Russell, 18 Aug. 1837; Southampton Univ. Lib., Melbourne MSS, MEL/RU/389.
24. BL Add. MSS 51560, fo. 46; Melbourne to Lady Holland, 2 Aug. 1837.

25. Melbourne to Victoria, 2 Dec. 1845; Windsor, Royal Archives, A4 fo. 141.
26. QVJ, 27 Dec. 1837.
27. Lady Clarendon's Journal, 1 Feb. 1840; Maxwell, *The Life and Letters of the 4th Earl of Clarendon*, i. 179.
28. Ibid. 30 March 1840; i. 207.
29. Cecil, 324.
30. BL Add. MSS 45552, fo. 199; F. Lamb to E. Lamb, [1847].
31. Mrs G. Lamb to Lady Morpeth, [1828]; Castle Howard MSS, J18/44/139.
32. Ibid. 6 Aug. 1828; Castle Howard MSS, J18/44/140.
33. Lord Hatherton's Diary, 18 April 1835; Staffs. RO, Hatherton MSS, D260/M/F/5/26/9.
34. Herts. RO, Panshanger MSS, D/ELb E15.
35. H. Brougham to Palmerston, n.d.; Nat. Lib. of Scotland, Minto MSS, 12/25 fo. 132.
36. G. Anson Memorandum, 2 Jan. 1841; Windsor, Royal Archives, Y54 fo. 12.
37. BL Add. MSS 45552, fo. 165; F. Lamb to E. Lamb, [c.1843].
38. Melbourne to Victoria, 30 Dec. 1847; Lord Esher, *The Letters of Queen Victoria*, ii. 140.
39. Prince Albert's Diary, 11 Feb. 1848; Windsor, Royal Archives, Y204 fo. 181.
40. G. Anson to F. Lamb, 8 Feb. 1848; ibid. A4 fo. 174.
41. Melbourne to Victoria, 27 Jan. 1848; ibid. fo. 172. See also fo. 175.
42. Melbourne to Brougham, 30 Jan. 1843; Univ. Coll. London, Brougham MSS, 43562.
43. Melbourne to Lord Minto, 30 Jan. 1843; Nat. Lib of Scotland, Minto MSS, 12/25 fo. 118.
44. QVJ, 2 Dec. 1848.
45. Melbourne to Brougham, 30 Jan. 1843; Univ. Coll. London, Brougham MSS, 43562.
46. H. Brougham to Palmerston, n.d.; Nat. Lib. of Scotland, Minto MSS, 12/25 fo. 132.
47. QVJ, 25 Sept. 1839.
48. Ibid.
49. Ibid. 27 March 1838.
50. Melbourne MSS, Box 106/102–112 for letters from Thomas Dawson.
51. QVJ, 24 Oct. 1839.
52. Melbourne to Thomas Barber, 4 Jan. 1825; 28 Nov. 1826; 27 May 1828; 1 July 1830; 25 April 1831 and 31 July 1831; Notts. RO, Barber MSS, D.D. 2B 8/1, 2, 3, 8/9, 11, 13.
53. Melbourne to Lord J. Russell, 24 Aug. 1837; Southampton Univ. Lib., Melbourne MSS, MEL/RU/392.
54. Cecil, 178–9.
55. Greville, iii. 129, 4 Sept. 1834.
56. Diary of Denis Le Marchant, 18 Aug. 1831; Aspinall, *Three Early Nineteenth Century Diaries*, 118.
57. QVJ, 21 Nov. 1837 and 22 Jan. 1838.

58. BL Add. MSS 56556, fo. 52; Diary of J. Hobhouse, 31 Jan. 1832.
59. T. Young to H. Brougham, 19 Sept. 1834; Univ. Coll. London, Brougham MSS, 43571.
60. Melbourne to H. Brougham, 23 Aug. 1834; ibid. 43505.
61. Greville, iii. 129, 4 Sept. 1834.
62. Melbourne to Grey, 24 April 1832 and 20 March 1834; Durham Univ. Lib., Grey MSS, fos. 70 and 130.
63. QVJ, 1 Oct. 1837.
64. Ibid. 2 Sept. 1838.
65. Mrs Norton to Melbourne, [April 1836]; Hoge and Olney, *The Letters of Caroline Norton to Lord Melbourne*, 72.
66. F. Lamb to H. Brougham, 8 Oct. 1840; Univ. Coll. London, Brougham MSS, 31377.
67. BL Add. MSS 45552, fo. 165; F. Lamb to E. Lamb, [*c.*1843].
68. G. Lamb to F. Lamb, 26 Aug. 1832; Herts. RO, Panshanger MSS, D/ELb F80. See also Melbourne to F. Lamb, 8 Sept. 1832; Melbourne MSS, Box 106/13.
69. E. Lamb to F. Lamb, 8 Feb. 1834; Herts. RO, Panshanger MSS, D/ELb F76.
70. Melbourne to Palmerston, 25 Aug. 1839; Southampton Univ. Lib., Palmerston MSS, GC/ME/313.
71. QVJ, 28 April 1839.
72. Ibid. 22 Oct. 1838.
73. BL Add. MSS 45552, fos. 90–1; F. Lamb to G. Lamb, 15 Dec. [1839].
74. Ibid. fo. 113; ibid. 22 Dec. [1840].
75. Ibid. fo. 157; Lady Beauvale to E. Lamb, 23 Oct. [1842].
76. Diary of E. Lamb, 23 Oct. 1842; Hatfield House MSS
77. Mrs G. Lamb to Lady Carlisle, [1842]; Castle Howard MSS, J18/44/142.
78. Ibid.
79. Melbourne to Lord J. Russell, 18 Dec. 1842; Melbourne MSS, Box 15/63.
80. Ibid. 8 Jan. 1843; ibid. 65.
81. Mrs G. Lamb to Lady Carlisle, [1842]; Castle Howard MSS, J18/44/142.
82. Ibid. [28 Oct. 1842]; ibid. J18/44/143.
83. Ibid. [1843]; ibid. J18/44/145.
84. BL Add. MSS 51613, fo. 110; Lady Beauvale to Lady Holland, 11 Sept. 1843.
85. Mrs G. Lamb to Lady Carlisle, n.d.; Castle Howard MSS, J18/44/143.
86. Lady Holland to H. Fox, 28 Aug. 1845; Lord Ilchester, *Elizabeth, Lady Holland to Her Son*, 230.
87. W. Leigh to Lord Hatherton, 1 March 1842; Staffs. RO, Hatherton MSS, D260/M/F/5/27/fo. 3.
88. Greville, vi. 123, 22 Jan. 1848.
89. Cecil, 373.
90. Diary of Lord W. Russell, 24 Feb. 1844; Blakiston, *Lord William Russell and his Wife*, 488.
91. Greville, v. 238–9, 25 Feb. 1844.
92. Ibid. 298, 28 Aug. 1845.
93. Ibid. 295, 21 Aug. 1845.

94. G. Anson to Lord J. Russell, 3 July 1846; Gooch, *The Later Correspondence of Lord John Russell*, i. 109.

95. Lord J. Russell to Melbourne, 3 July 1846; Melbourne MSS, Box 15/84. See also QVJ, 11 Dec. 1845.

96. Melbourne to Lord J. Russell, 3 July 1846; Melbourne MSS, Box 15/85.

97. Mrs G. Lamb to Lady Carlisle, 24 Dec. [1845]; Castle Howard MSS, J18/44/145.

98. Greville, v. 218–19, 13 Dec. 1843.

99. Melbourne to Victoria, 3 April 1844; Lord Esher, *The Letters of Queen Victoria*, ii. 8.

100. Ibid. 21 July 1846; ibid. ii. 92.

101. Diary of E. Lamb, 15 June 1843; Hatfield House MSS.

102. BL Add. MSS 45552, fos. 169–70; F. Lamb to E. Lamb, 1843.

103. Mrs Hardcastle, *Life of John, Lord Campbell*, ii. 173.

104. Melbourne to Lord J. Russell, 7 Oct. 1841; Melbourne MSS, Box 15/54. See also Lord J. Russell to Melbourne, 2 Oct. 1841; ibid. 53.

105. Palmerston to Lord J. Russell, 14 Jan. 1842; Gooch, *The Later Correspondence of Lord John Russell*, i. 53. Lord Duncannon to Melbourne, 3 May 1842; Melbourne MSS, Box 3/114. *Parl. Hist.* lxiv. 57, 17 June 1842.

106. *Parl. Hist.* lx 19, 3 Feb. 1842; and lxix 1096, 4 Oct. 1841.

107. Mrs G. Lamb to Lady Carlisle, n.d.; Castle Howard MSS, J18/44/145.

108. Melbourne to Lord J. Russell, 13 May 1847; Melbourne MSS, Box 15/88.

109. Sydney Smith to Melbourne and vice versa, 26 and 27 May 1842; Melbourne MSS, Box 36/56 and 57.

110. *Parl. Hist.* lx. 21, 3 Feb. 1842.

111. Melbourne to Victoria, 19 July 1842; Windsor, Royal Archives, A4 fo. 74.

112. Cecil, 372.

113. Melbourne to Lord J. Russell, 13 Oct. 1841; Melbourne MSS, Box 15/56.

114. Melbourne to Lord Hatherton, 29 Dec. 1841; Staffs. RO, Hatherton MSS, D260/M/F/5/27/14, fo. 120.

115. *Parl. Hist.* lxii. 723, 19 April 1842.

116. Ibid. 724.

117. Melbourne to Lord J. Russell, 18 Jan. 1844; Melbourne MSS, Box 15/79. Lord Campbell to Sir G. Campbell, 31 Jan. 1844; Mrs Hardcastle, *Life of John, Lord Campbell*, ii. 184.

118. C. Wood to J. Stansfeld, [April 1842]; Hickleton MSS, 50A.

119. Mrs G. Lamb to Lady Carlisle, n.d.; Castle Howard MSS, J18/44/145.

120. Melbourne to Victoria, 2 Dec. 1845; Windsor, Royal Archives, A4 fo. 141.

121. Melbourne to Lord J. Russell, 13 Dec. 1845; Gooch, *The Later Correspondence of Lord John Russell*, i. 88.

122. Greville, v. 359, 13 Jan. 1846.

123. Mrs G. Lamb to Lady Carlisle, n.d.; Castle Howard MSS, J18/44/145.

124. Greville, vi. 125, 26 Jan. 1848.

125. Lord Ashburton to J. Croker, 26 May 1846; Jennings, *The Diaries and Correspondence of J. W. Croker*, ii. 71.

126. *Parl. Hist.* lxxxvi. 1407; 28 May 1846.
127. E. Lamb to Mrs Huskisson, 19 March 1846; Lever, *The Letters of Lady Palmerston*, 274.
128. Lord Ashburton to J. Croker, 26 May 1846; Jennings, *The Diaries and Correspondence of J. W. Croker*, ii. 71.
129. Lord J. Russell, 6 Nov. 1841; Melbourne MSS, Box 15/58.
130. Melbourne to Lord J. Russell, 6 Aug. 1842; ibid. 61.
131. Lord J. Russell to Melbourne, 9 Aug. 1842; Southampton Univ. Lib., Melbourne MSS, MEL/RU/131.
132. Melbourne to Palmerston, 7 Dec. 1845; ibid. Palmerston MSS, GC/ME/496.
133. Lord J. Russell to Melbourne, [22 May 1846]; Melbourne MSS, Box 15/82.
134. Mrs G. Lamb to Lady Carlisle, [19 Nov. 1842]; Castle Howard MSS, J18/44/143.
135. Ibid. [11 June 1845]; ibid. J18/44/145.
136. Ibid. Dec. 1844; ibid.
137. Ibid. n.d.; ibid. J18/44/141.
138. BL Add. MSS 45552, fo. 155; F. Lamb to E. Lamb, [*c*.1842].
139. Lady Holland to H. Fox, May [1843]; Lord Ilchester, *Elizabeth, Lady Holland, to Her Son*, 205–6.
140. Lord Campbell to Lady Stratheden, 24 Oct. 1847; Mrs Hardcastle, *Life of John, Lord Campbell*, ii. 226.
141. BL Add. MSS 51602, fo. 215; E. Lamb to Lady Holland, [15 Nov. 1842].
142. QVJ, 4 Jan. 1845.
143. BL Add. MSS 51613, fo. 94; Lady Beauvale to Lady Holland, [14 Nov. 1842].
144. Ibid. fo. 85; ibid. 31 Oct. 1842.
145. Mrs G. Lamb to Lady Morpeth, [June 1837]; Castle Howard MSS, J18/44/140.
146. Palmerston to Lord Hatherton, 4 Dec. 1842; Staffs. RO, Hatherton MSS, D260/M/F/5/27, fo. 50.
147. Lord Campbell to Lady Stratheden, 24 Oct. 1847; Mrs Hardcastle, *Life of John, Lord Campbell*, ii. 226.
148. BL Add. MSS 51602, fo. 210; Lady Palmerston to Lady Holland, [13 Nov. 1842].
149. Ibid. fo. 230; ibid. [27 Nov. 1842].
150. Mrs G. Lamb to Lady Carlisle, n.d.; Castle Howard MSS, J18/44/143.
151. Melbourne to W. Cowper, 24 May 1837, 7 Nov. 1838; 'January'; 19 April 1839; Southampton Univ. Lib., Melbourne MSS, MEL/CO/12, 16, 18, 21.
152. Cecil, 370.
153. BL Add. MSS 51559, fo. 143; W. Cowper to Lady Holland, 22 Nov. 1842.
154. Ibid. 51613, fo. 94; Lady Beauvale to Lady Holland, [14 Nov. 1842].
155. Mrs G. Lamb to Lady Carlisle, n.d.; Castle Howard MSS, J18/44/145.
156. Diary of Lady Palmerston, 7 July 1845; Hatfield House MSS.
157. Mrs Norton to Lady Dacre, [1848]; Lyster, *A Family Chronicle*, 248.
158. BL Add. MSS 39949, fo. 232; Lady Palmerston to Mrs Huskisson, n.d.
159. Ibid. fo. 242; ibid. [1848].

160. Ibid. 45553, fo. 192; Lady Palmerston to Palmerston, [18 Oct. 1848].
161. Ibid. fo. 211; ibid. 25 Oct. 1848.
162. Diary of Lady Palmerston, 11 Nov. 1848; Hatfield House MSS.
163. Ibid. 13 Nov. 1848; ibid.
164. BL Add. MSS 45553, fo. 226; Lady Palmerston to Palmerston, 20 Nov. 1848.
165. Diary of Lady Palmerston, 24 Nov. 1848; Hatfield House MSS.
166. BL Add. MSS 39949, fo. 251; Lady Palmerston to Mrs Huskisson, 26 Nov. 1848.
167. *Morning Chronicle*, 4 Dec. 1848.
168. Melbourne MSS, Box 106/141 seq.
169. BL Berg MSS, micro. 593; Mrs Norton to W. Cowper, 29 Nov. [1848].
170. Diary of Lady Morgan, 25 Nov. 1848; Lady Morgan, *Memoirs*, ii. 498–9.
171. F. Lamb to Lord J. Russell, 30 Jan. 1851; PRO, Russell MSS, 30/22/9A xc11506, fo. 284.
172. Duke of Somerset to Duchess of Somerset, 29 Nov. 1848; Anon., *Letters and Memoirs of Edward Twelfth Duke of Somerset* (London 1893), 276–7.
173. Lord Dacre to Mrs Grey, 24 Nov. 1848; Lyster, *A Family Chronicle*, 35–6.
174. De Fonblanque, *The Life and Letters of Albany Fonblanque*, 86–7.
175. Jenkins, *Lady Caroline Lamb*, 242.
176. E. B. Lytton, *St. Stephen's* (London 1860).

Select Bibliography

1. Manuscript Sources

ANN ARBOR, MICHIGAN
Correspondence of Lord John Russell.

BIBLIOTHEQUE NATIONALE, PARIS
n.a.f. 20606–15 Papers and Correspondence of A. Thiers.
n.a.f. 12219–20 Papers and Correspondence of F. Sébastiani.

BODLEIAN LIBRARY, OXFORD
Bruce MSS. Papers and correspondence of Michael Bruce.
Lovelace–Byron MSS. Papers and correspondence of the Byron, Noel, and Milbanke families.
Clarendon MSS. Papers and correspondence of the Fourth Earl of Clarendon.
Melbourne MSS. Papers of the Second Viscount Melbourne held at Windsor Castle (microfilm).
J. C. Clark, 'From Business to Politics, The Ellice Family 1760–1860' (Oxford D.Phil.).
V. H. Crossman, 'A Study of the Official Reaction to Rural Unrest in Ireland, 1821–1841' (Oxford D.Phil.).
R. D. H. Custance, 'The Political Career of William Lamb, Second Viscount Melbourne, to 1841' (Oxford D.Phil.).

BRITISH LIBRARY
Frampton MSS, Add. MSS 41567. Correspondence of J. Frampton.
Gordon MSS, Add. MSS 49479. Correspondence of Sir J. Gordon.
Hobhouse MSS, Add. MSS 56555–64. Diaries of J. C. Hobhouse.
Holland House MSS, Add. MSS 51558–60. Correspondence of the Lamb family with the Third Lord and Lady Holland.
51570. Correspondence between the Third Lord and Lady Holland.
51600–02. Correspondence between Lady Palmerston and Lady Holland.
51613. Correspondence between Lady Beauvale and Lady Holland.
51723. Correspondence between Lady Holland and Lady Bessborough.
51725. Correspondence between the Third Earl of Egremont and Lady Holland.
51754, 51757. Correspondence between the Third and Fourth Lords Holland.
51870. Political Journal of the Third Lord Holland.
Huskisson MSS, Add. MSS 38753–8, 39949. Papers and correspondence of Mr and Mrs William Huskisson.
Lamb MSS, Add. MSS 45546–56. Correspondence of members of the Lamb family.
45911, 50142, 54088. Papers and correspondence of Lady Caroline Lamb.
60463–73, 60482. Papers and correspondence of Frederick Lamb, First Baron Beauvale.
Norton MSS, Add. MSS 42767 and Microfilm 593. Correspondence of Caroline Norton.

Peel MSS, Add. MSS 40310. Correspondence of Sir R. Peel.
Place MSS, Add. MSS 35149–51. Papers and correspondence of F. Place.
Russell MSS, Add. MSS 38080. Correspondence of Lord J. Russell.
Spencer MSS (unfol). Correspondence between Lady C. Lamb and the First Lady
    Spencer.
Wellesley MSS, Add. MSS 37305–12. Papers and correspondence of the First
    Marquess Wellesley.

BROOKES'S CLUB, LONDON
    The Brookes's Club Betting Book.

BURY ST EDMUNDS; WEST SUFFOLK RECORD OFFICE
    Grafton MSS. Papers of the Fourth Duke of Grafton.

CASTLE HOWARD, YORKSHIRE
    Carlisle MSS. Correspondence of the Sixth Earl and Countess of Carlisle with the
        Lamb family.

CHATSWORTH, DERBYSHIRE
    Chatsworth MSS. Correspondence of William, Sixth Duke of Devonshire and his
        sisters Caroline and Harriet.

DEVON RECORD OFFICE
    Fortescue MSS. Correspondence of the Second Earl Fortescue.

DURHAM UNIVERSITY LIBRARY
    Grey MSS. Papers and correspondence of the Second and Third Earls Grey.
    Correspondence of the Second Countess Grey and Emily Eden.

HATFIELD HOUSE, HERTFORDSHIRE
    Salisbury MSS. Diary of Emily, Lady Palmerston.
    Correspondence of First Viscountess Melbourne.

HERTFORDSHIRE RECORD OFFICE, HERTFORD
    Lytton MSS. Correspondence of Bulwer Lytton.
    Panshanger MSS. Papers and correspondence of the Lamb family.

HICKLETON, YORKSHIRE
    Hickleton MSS. Papers and correspondence of Sir C. Wood.

INDIA OFFICE, LONDON
    Broughton MSS. Papers and correspondence of J. C. Hobhouse.

LEEDS CITY RECORD OFFICE
    Canning MSS. Papers and correspondence of G. Canning.

LEICESTERSHIRE RECORD OFFICE, LEICESTER
    Halford MSS. Papers and correspondence of Sir H. Halford.

LIVERPOOL RECORD OFFICE
    Derby MSS. Papers and correspondence of the Fourteenth Earl of Derby.

MAIDSTONE, CENTRE FOR KENTISH STUDIES
    Stanhope MSS. Correspondence of the Fifth Earl and Countess Stanhope.

MELBOURNE HALL, DERBYSHIRE
  Melbourne MSS. Papers and correspondence of William, Second Viscount Melbourne.

NATIONAL LIBRARY OF SCOTLAND, EDINBURGH
  Abercromby MSS. Correspondence of J. Abercromby.
  Ellice MSS. Correspondence of E. Ellice.
  Minto MSS. Correspondence of the Second Earl of Minto.

NATIONAL REGISTRY OF ARCHIVES, LONDON
  Anglesey MSS. Transcript of the Correspondence of the First Marquess of Anglesey.

NORFOLK RECORD OFFICE, NORWICH
  Wodehouse MSS. Correspondence of Sir J. Wodehouse.

NOTTINGHAMSHIRE RECORD OFFICE, NOTTINGHAM
  Barber MSS. Correspondence of T. F. Barber.

NOTTINGHAM UNIVERSITY LIBRARY
  Denison MSS. Correspondence of E. Denison.
  Newcastle MSS. Correspondence of the Fourth Duke of Newcastle.

ORIEL COLLEGE, OXFORD
  Hampden MSS. Correspondence of R. D. Hampden.

PUBLIC RECORD OFFICE, LONDON
  Home Office MSS.
  Russell MSS. Correspondence and Papers of Lord John Russell.

SCOTTISH RECORD OFFICE, EDINBURGH
  Clerk of Penicuik MSS. Papers of Sir G. Clerk.
  Loch MSS. Papers of James Loch.

SHEFFIELD CITY LIBRARY
  Wentworth Woodhouse MSS. Correspondence of the Second Earl Fitzwilliam.

SOUTHAMPTON UNIVERSITY LIBRARY
  Broadlands MSS. Papers and correspondence of the Second Viscount Palmerston.
  Melbourne MSS. Papers and correspondence of the Second Viscount Melbourne.
  Wellington MSS. Papers and correspondence of the First Duke of Wellington.

STAFFORDSHIRE RECORD OFFICE
  Hatherton MSS. Diaries and correspondence of the First Baron Hatherton.

UNIVERSITY COLLEGE, LONDON
  Brougham MSS. Correspondence of H. Brougham.
  Parkes MSS. Correspondence of J. Parkes.

VICTORIA AND ALBERT MUSEUM, LONDON
  Forster MSS. Correspondence of H. Colbourne.

WEST SUSSEX RECORD OFFICE, CHICHESTER
  Bessborough MSS. Papers and correspondence of the Third and Fourth Earls Bessborough and their families.

Egremont MSS. Papers of the Third Earl of Egremont.
Goodwood MSS. Correspondence of the Fifth Duke of Richmond.

WINDSOR CASTLE

Royal Archives. Journals and correspondence of Queen Victoria.

WOBURN ABBEY, BEDFORDSHIRE

Bedford MSS. Correspondence of the Seventh Duke of Bedford.

2. Printed Sources

ARTICLES

CONDON, M., 'The Irish Church and Reform', *Journal of British Studies*, 3 (1964).
KRIEGEL, A., 'The Politics of the Whigs in Opposition, 1834–5', *Journal of British Studies*, 7 (1968).
NEWBOULD, I. D. C., 'Whiggery and the Dilemma of Reform', *Bulletin of the Institute of Historical Research*, 53 (1980).
OLNEY, C., 'Caroline Norton and Lord Melbourne', *Victorian Studies*, 8 (1965).

NEWSPAPERS AND MAGAZINES

Blackwood's Magazine
Edinburgh Review
Fortnightly Magazine
Fraser's Magazine
Gentleman's Magazine
Morning Chronicle
The Nation
Quarterly Review
Temple Bar
Westminster Review

BOOKS

AIRLIE   Lady Airlie, *In Whig Society* (London 1921).
ALTHORP   D. Le Marchant, *Memoir of Viscount Althorp* (London 1876).
ANGLESEY   Lord Anglesey, *One Leg: The Life and Letters of the First Marquess of Anglesey* (London 1961).
ANON.   Anon., *A Heavy Blow and Great Discouragement of Protestantism* (London 1838).
ARBUTHNOT   F. Bamford, *The Journal of Mrs. Arbuthnot* (London 1950).
ASPINALL   A. Aspinall, *Three Early Nineteenth Century Diaries* (London 1952).
BADDELEY   E. Steele, *The Memoirs of Sophia Baddeley* (London 1787).
BARNES   D. Barnes, *Thomas Barnes of The Times* (Cambridge 1944).
BERKELEY   G. Berkeley, *My Life and Recollections* (London 1866).
BERRY   Lady T. Lewis, *Extracts from the Journals and Correspondence of Miss Berry* (London 1865).

BESSBOROUGH   Lord Bessborough, *Lady Bessborough and Her Family Circle* (London 1940).

BRENT   R. Brent, *Liberal Anglican Politics* (Oxford 1987).

BROCK   M. Brock, *The Great Reform Act* (London 1973).

BROUGHAM   A. Aspinall, *Lord Brougham and the Whig Party* (London 1972).

BROUGHTON   Lord Broughton, *Recollections of a Long Life* (London 1909).

BROWNLOW   Lady Brownlow, *The Eve of Victorianism* (London 1940).

BRUMMELL   L. Melville, *Beau Brummell* (London 1924).

BUCKINGHAM   Lord Buckingham and Chandos, *Memoirs of the Courts and Cabinets of William IV and Victoria* (London 1861).

BYRON   L. Marchand, *Byron's Letters and Journals* (London 1973–81).

CAMPBELL   Mrs Hardcastle, *Life of John, Lord Campbell* (London 1881).

CAVENDISH   Sir G. Leveson Gower, *Hary-O, The Letters of Lady Harriet Cavendish* ((London 1940).

CLARENDON   Sir H. Maxwell, *The Life and Letters of the 4th Earl of Clarendon* (London 1913).

CREEVEY   Sir H. Maxwell, *The Creevey Papers* (London 1904).

CROKER   L. J. Jennings, *The Correspondence and Diaries of J. W. Croker* (London 1885).

DISRAELI   B. Disraeli, *The Runnymede Letters* (London n.d.).
W. Monypenny and G. Buckle, *The Life of Benjamin Disraeli* (London 1920).
H. and M. Swartz, *Disraeli's Reminiscences* (London 1975).

DUDLEY   Anon., *Letters of the Earl of Dudley* (London 1840).

DURHAM   S. J. Reid, *Life and Letters of the First Earl of Durham* (London 1906).

EDEN   E. Eden, *Letters From India* (London 1872).
V. Dickinson, *Miss Eden's Letters* (London 1919).

FONBLANQUE   E. B. de Fonblanque, *The Life and Labours of Albany Fonblanque* (London 1874).

GASCOYNE   C. Oman, *The Gascoyne Heiress* (London 1968).

GEORGE IV   A. Aspinall, *The Letters of George IV* (Cambridge 1938).
—— *The Letters of George, Prince of Wales* (London 1963–71).

GLADSTONE   J. Morley, *Life of Gladstone* (London 1903).

GOWER   F. Leveson Gower, *Letters of Harriet, Lady Granville* (London 1894).
—— *Bygone Years* (London 1905).
Lady Granville, *Lord Granville Leveson Gower* (London 1916).

GRAHAM   J. T. Ward, *Sir James Graham* (London 1967).

GREVILLE   H. Reeve, *A Journal of the Reigns of King George IV, King William IV and Queen Victoria by the late Charles Greville* (London 1888).

GREY   E. A. Smith, *Lord Grey 1764–1845* (Oxford 1990).

GUEST   Lord Bessborough, *The Diary of Lady Charlotte Guest* (London 1950).

GUIZOT   F. Guizot, *An Embassy to the Court of St. James in 1840* (London 1862).

HATHERTON   Lord Hatherton, *Political Occurrences in June and July 1834* (London 1872).

HAYDON	F. W. Haydon, *Correspondence and Table Talk of Benjamin Haydon* (London 1876).
	T. Taylor, *Life of Benjamin Robert Haydon* (London 1853).
HAYWARD	A. Hayward, *Eminent Statesmen and Writers* (London 1880).
HERON	Sir R. Heron, *Notes* (Grantham 1850).
HOLLAND	Lord Ilchester, *The Journal of Elizabeth, Lady Holland* (London 1908).
	—— *The Journal of Henry Edward Fox* (London 1923).
	—— *Chronicles of Holland House* (London 1937).
	—— *Elizabeth, Lady Holland to Her Son, 1821–45* (London 1946).
	S. Keppel, *Sovereign Lady* (London 1974).
	A. D. Kriegel, *The Holland House Diaries* (London 1977).
HOWARD	Lady Leconfield and J. Gore, *Three Howard Sisters* (London 1955).
JORDEN	W. Jorden, *Autobiography* (London 1852).
LAMB	H. Blyth, *Caro: The Fatal Passion* (London 1972).
	Lord D. Cecil, *Melbourne* (London 1955).
	H. Dunckley, *Lord Melbourne* (London 1890).
	D. Howell-Thomas, *Lord Melbourne's Susan* (Woking 1928).
	E. Jenkins, *Lady Caroline Lamb* (London 1932).
	Lady C. Lamb, *Glenarvon* (London 1816).
	—— *Graham Hamilton* (London 1822).
	—— *Ada Reis* (London 1823).
	G. Lamb, *Whistle For It* (London 1807).
	—— *The Poems of Caius Valerius Catullus* (London 1821).
	W. Lamb, *Epilogue to the Comedy of the Fashionable Friends* (London 1801).
	—— *Essay on the Progressive Improvement of Mankind* (London 1860).
	D. Marshall, *Lord Melbourne* (London 1975).
	B. Newman, *Lord Melbourne* (London 1930).
	L. C. Sanders, *Lord Melbourne's Papers* (London 1889).
	W. Torrens, *Memoirs of Lord Melbourne* (London 1890).
	P. Ziegler, *Melbourne* (London 1976).
LEE	Anon., *Extracts from the Diary of the late Dr. Robert Lee* (London 1897).
LENNOX	Lady Ilchester and Lord Stavordale, *The Letters of Lady Sarah Lennox* (London 1901).
LEWIS	L. Peck, *A Life of Matthew G. Lewis* (Harvard 1961).
LIEVEN	P. Quennell, *The Private Letters of Princess Lieven to Prince Metternich* (London 1937).
	L. G. Robinson, *Letters of Dorothea, Princess Lieven* (London 1902).
	Lord Sudley, *The Lieven–Palmerston Correspondence* (London 1943).
LYNDHURST	Sir T. Martin, *A Life of Lord Lyndhurst* (London 1883).
LYSTER	G. Lyster, *A Family Chronicle* (London 1908).
LYTTELTON	H. Wyndham, *The Correspondence of Sarah Spencer, Lady Lyttelton* (London 1912).

LYTTON   E. B. Lytton, *St. Stephen's* (London 1860).

Lord Lytton, *Edward Bulwer, Lord Lytton* (London 1883).

MACKINTOSH   P. O'Leary, *Sir James Mackintosh* (Aberdeen 1989).

MALMESBURY   Lord Malmesbury, *Memoirs of an Ex-Minister* (London 1884).

MOORE   W. S. Dowden, *The Letters of Thomas Moore* (Oxford 1964).

MORGAN   Lady Morgan, *Memoirs* (London 1862).

NEWBOULD   I. D. C. Newbould, *Whiggery and Reform 1830–41* (London 1990).

NORTON   A. Acland, *Caroline Norton* (London 1948).

J. Hoge and C. Olney, *The Letters of Caroline Norton to Lord Melbourne* (Ohio 1974).

J. G. Perkins, *The Life of Mrs. Norton* (London 1909).

O'CONNELL   A. D. Macintyre, *The Liberator: Daniel O'Connell and the Irish Party, 1830–1867* (London 1965).

M. O'Connell, *The Correspondence of Daniel O'Connell* (Dublin 1972–80).

PALMERSTON   Lady Airlie, *Lady Palmerston and Her Times* (London 1922).

K. Bourne, *Palmerston* (London 1982).

T. Lever, *The Letters of Lady Palmerston* (London 1957).

PEEL   Lord Mahon, *Memoirs of the Rt. Hon. Sir Robert Peel* (London 1856).

ROEBUCK   R. Leader, *Life and Letters of John Arthur Roebuck* (London 1897).

RUSSELL   G. Blakiston, *Lord William Russell and His Wife* (London 1972).

G. Gooch, *The Later Correspondence of Lord John Russell* (London 1925).

Lord G. W. E. Russell, *Collections and Recollections* (London 1903).

R. Russell, *The Early Correspondence of Lord John Russell* (London 1913).

SHELLEY   R. Edgcumbe, *The Diary of Frances, Lady Shelley* (London 1913).

SMILES   S. Smiles, *A Publisher and His Friends* (London 1891).

SMITH   Mrs Austin, *Memoir and Letters of the Rev. Sydney Smith* (London 1855).

E. A. Smith, *Whig Principles and Party Politics* (Manchester 1975).

SOMERSET   Anon., *Letters and Memoirs of Edward Twelfth Duke of Somerset* (London 1893).

STEUART   A. F. Steuart, *The Diary of a Lady-in-Waiting* (London 1908).

STOCKMAR   E. von Stockmar, *Memoirs of Baron Stockmar* (London 1873).

STUART   D. M. Stuart, *Dearest Bess* (London 1914).

VICTORIA   Lord Esher, *The Letters of Queen Victoria* (London 1908).

WALLACE   Lord Wallace, *Three Letters addressed to the Rt. Hon. Lord Viscount Melbourne* (London 1835).

—— *A Letter to Lord Viscount Melbourne* (London 1836).

WELLESLEY   Anon., *The Wellesley Papers* (London 1914).

WHARNCLIFFE   C. Grosvenor, *The First Lady Wharncliffe and Her Family* (London 1927).

WHATELY   E. J. Whately, *The Life and Correspondence of Richard Whately* (London 1875).

WILSON   Anon., *The Memoirs of Harriette Wilson* (London 1825).

Index